DEATH BY A THOUSAND CUTS

Timothy Brook

Jérôme Bourgon

Gregory Blue

Death by a Thousand Cuts

HARVARD UNIVERSITY PRESS

Cambridge, Massachusetts, and London, England   2008

Library of Congress Cataloging-in-Publication Data

Brook, Timothy, 1951–
    Death by a thousand cuts / Timothy Brook, Jérôme Bourgon, and Gregory Blue.
        p.   cm.
    Includes bibliographical references and index.
    ISBN-13: 978-0-674-02773-2 (alk. paper)
    ISBN-10: 0-674-02773-6 (alk. paper)
    1. Capital punishment—China.   I. Bourgon, Jérôme.   II. Blue, Gregory.   III. Title.
    HV8699.C6B76   2008
    364.660951—dc22   2007031346

What does it mean to protest suffering, as distinct from acknowledging it?

Susan Sontag, *Regarding the Pain of Others*

Contents

Illustrations

Acknowledgments

This collaborative enterprise got under way at a symposium on the comparative history of torture held at the University of Toronto in March 2001. Over the many years of working our way to this book, we have received encouragement and advice from many friends and colleagues. At the risk of offending those who are missing from this list, we especially wish to acknowledge Alison Bailey, Maria Pia Di Bella, Jim Elkins, Yvonne Hsieh, Richard King, Claire Margat, Nancy Park, Haun Saussy, Enrico Sturani, and Bin Wong.

Some of the ideas in this book were presented to the Modern China Seminar at Columbia University, the China Studies Group at the University of British Columbia, and the conference on the representation of pain that Jim Elkins and Maria Pia Di Bella convened at University College Cork in 2005. We are grateful for the feedback and encouragement that these symposia provided.

The Social Sciences and Humanities Research Council of Canada and the Action Concertée Initiative of the Ministère de la Recherche of France generously funded some of the research that supported this project. We also wish to acknowledge the editorial assistance that Kevin Lu and Neil Burton provided as we moved unsteadily from manuscript to book.

DEATH BY A THOUSAND CUTS

CHAPTER 1

The Execution of
Wang Weiqin

The procession taking Wang Weiqin to his death in the autumn of 1904 emerged from Beijing's Inner City through the Gate of the Dark Military Lord and headed south to the big market intersection known as Caishikou, Vegetable Market Entrance. The prisoner, a middle-aged man, arrived barricaded in a cart and accompanied by a squad of soldiers belonging to a detachment of the Northern Army. With this procession came a contingent of officials from the Board of Punishments. Their task this chilly morning was to supervise the execution from under an awning that had been set up before dawn at the side of the intersection. From there, one of them read out the crime for which the convict was to be executed, using the categories and language of the official law book of the dynasty, the Qing Code.[1]

The execution of Wang Weiqin unfolded in the middle of a crowd of soldiers and onlookers who had gathered to watch the most severe legal penalty the Qing state could impose. Two soldiers brought forward the basket holding the knives that the procedure required. Others stripped the victim and bound him by his queue to a tripod in such a way that the front of his body was fully exposed to the state executioner and his assistant. The executioner began by slicing off pieces of flesh from the convict's breasts, his biceps, and his upper thighs. Before the slicing went any further, the executioner punctured Wang's heart with a swift stab, putting the man to death. Thereafter he proceeded to methodically sever the limbs, first at the wrists and ankles, then at the elbows and knees, lastly at the shoulders and hips. His final cut severed the head from the body. A practiced executioner made roughly three dozen cuts to reduce his victim to an incoherent scattering of body parts, though this number could vary. His work completed, he turned toward the officials and called out, *"Sha ren le!* The person has been killed!"

As the executioner's assistant gathered up the swords and returned them carefully to their carrying basket, waiting undertakers robed in white came forward to collect the body parts and take them to the public cemetery southwest of Vegetable Market for burial in an unmarked grave. The order for execution could include the supplementary penalty of exposing the severed head for public ridicule in the marketplace, but Wang's sentence spared him that final indignity, so the undertakers took his head as well. All that remained was his blood on the ground, and soon enough that would be lost in the dust. The entourage of officials formed up in ranks and returned to the Inner City with the executioners and their military escort.

This form of the death penalty is known in Chinese as *lingchi chusi*, "to put to death by lingchi." Western observers have variously translated this as "death by a thousand cuts," "death by slicing," and "the lingering death"— all graphic phrases, and none of them an accurate description of the procedure. The executioner did not leave Wang to linger long at death's door while cutting away his body slice by slice. Nor did it take him a thousand cuts to get from his first slicing to his last. And as painful as the punishment of lingchi must have looked to those who watched, Wang was in all likelihood under heavy opium sedation before it started.

The procedure that Wang Weiqin underwent at Vegetable Market was not exceptional within the context of late imperial Chinese criminal law. A limited number of statutes of the Qing Code, which we examine in Chapter 2, mandated this particular punishment for what the state considered the very worst crimes. In Wang's case, the provision of the Code that required him to be executed in this fashion was Article 287, dealing with the crime of "killing three or more persons in the same family." To kill three members of one family, in Chinese judicial logic, was more than multiple murder. It implied a vendetta and threatened to extinguish a family line and cut ancestors off from the possibility of receiving sacrifice. This was a deed far more terrible than the killing of any one person. Wang in fact had gone well beyond the minimum three. Deep in the night of April 26, 1901, he and his henchmen in the militia of Funing, an obscure county almost two hundred miles (three hundred kilometers) east of Beijing, descended on the home of Li Jichang. Wang and Li had been embroiled for years in lawsuits over property, and Wang saw his chance to end the struggle. He and his militia gang killed twelve members of Li Jichang's family. The youngest was a child of three.

Many circumstances could have intervened to save Wang Weiqin from the penalty of lingchi. First of all, Wang was a minor official, a person with powerful friends at many levels of the state bureaucracy. Such men had access to people in power who could protect them from criminal proceedings if they knew how to work the system. Wang certainly did. His friends included the magistrate of Funing county who was in office when the crime was committed, who did what he could to let procedure drag the legal process to a standstill. A second factor that should have worked in Wang's favor was timing. The attack on the Lis took place in 1901, at a time when the capital was under foreign military occupation. The Boxer Rebellion of the previous summer had failed, a joint foreign army had landed on the coast and driven out the rebels, and the regular administration of justice was in some disarray. Cases as serious as Wang's had to go through careful and lengthy steps, which meant they moved forward slowly even under normal circumstances. Once the death penalty was mandated, the sentence had to be reviewed by several government agencies before going to the throne for final ratification. Much could happen as a case made its way upward to the imperial court that might derail the process. Even if it did not, the emperor could decide for any number of reasons to lighten the penalty. Wang could not expect this escape, as Emperor Guangxu had been forced into internal exile in 1900 and was out of the capital when the crime was committed. Instead, Wang believed that the chaos in Beijing would work in his favor. As the final judgment put it, Wang Weiqin knowingly "took advantage of the confusion" when he massacred the Lis.

An unexpected countervailing force worked against Wang's hope of hiding his crime. Following the restoration of Qing rule in 1902, a reform faction within the central government introduced a wide range of administrative innovations to refashion Chinese government along the lines of modernizing regimes elsewhere in East Asia, notably Japan. The Board of Punishments was one of the beneficiaries of the "New Policies." One of its new administrative arms was the Bureau of Public Works and Inspection (Gongxun ju), was a police agency through which the justice ministry could investigate cases that reached Beijing on more than procedural grounds. The bureau was not yet co-opted into the usual networks of authority through which powerful officials connived to interfere in legal cases in which they had an interest, and it managed to get to the bottom of the Wang Weiqin affair.

The case might not have reached the Bureau of Public Works and Inspection had it not been for two determined women. The first was Li Jichang's wife, Madam Ma. So frustrated did she become over the property war between the Li and Wang families that, when Wang Weiqin managed to get her husband thrown in jail several years earlier, she had cut her own throat in front of his home. The state could not ignore this time-honored weapon of the weak. Her suicide was enough to win Li Jichang's release and prompt an investigation into Wang's doings. That investigation may also have led to Wang's night raid on the Li family. It was then a second Madam Ma— probably a younger relative of Li's wife, who also married into the Li family—who pursued Wang through the courts. Wang's protectors had to abandon him and let the law run its course. That course came to its conclusion three years later, when Wang was sliced and dismembered at Vegetable Market (Figure 1).

Figure 1. The first phase of the execution of Wang Weiqin, Beijing, 1904. © Ville de Chalon sur Saône, France, Musée Nicéphore Niépce.

A Turning Point

If this gruesome conclusion was the one Madam Ma wanted, she was lucky to get it when she did. In April 1905, a few months after Wang's execution, the penalty of lingchi was forever removed from the imperial law books. Even as the executioner was cutting up Wang's corpse, officials back at the Board were drafting the very legislation that would put an end to this form of the death penalty. The first memorial advocating the abolition of harsh penalties reached the throne in 1903, signaling that the regime was prepared to accept the idea that China's punishments should be brought into line with the new international standards. The new laws governing such punishments had not been promulgated by the time Wang was taken out for execution, however. Had the delays and appeals on his behalf dragged on for another six months, it would have been illegal for the judicial authorities to impose this penalty. Wang was put to death in the last season of lingchi executions, though his lingchi was not the last. That distinction fell to a Manchu servant, Fuzhuli, whose execution on April 9, 1905, was the last. On that date, China's legal history turned a corner. Thousands had been put to death by lingchi over the two and a half centuries of Qing rule, but no longer.

That we know anything about Wang Weiqin's execution is also thanks to its timing, as it took place before the abolition of lingchi but after the arrival of foreigners in Beijing. With the suppression of the Boxer Rebellion, foreign governments were granted the right to station soldiers in their legations. This is why soldiers attached to the French legation were at Vegetable Market that day. They must have learned about the execution ahead of time, for they arrived prepared to record the event with a camera. This circumstance too was a matter of timing. A decade earlier, the only people who owned cameras were professional photographers who could manage the technicalities of producing pictures. Thanks to the improvement and mass production of portable cameras, after 1900 ordinary people could own and operate them. By our count, amateur photographers stationed themselves at three lingchi executions in the final season of their legality. Wang Weiqin's had the sad distinction of being one of these three.

There is no chance that the Frenchmen were simply out for a stroll and happened on the execution, given the care with which the man holding the camera took the sequence of pictures showing the process from beginning to end. They knew what was on offer and went with the intention not just to watch but to photograph. As no penalty this severe remained in European capital statutes, the soldiers must have gone out of curiosity. Were they shocked, revolted, or even amused at the sight of an execution conducted in this way? We have no way of knowing, as no notes survive alongside the photographs. But we should be careful about attributing to them reactions that we think would have been ours, for we cannot share their perspective. The executioner's methodical butchery may have been no worse than the extrajudicial executions European soldiers had themselves performed on the Boxer rebels they had seized and put to death in their own retributive orgy of "law and order" four years earlier.[2] And however powerful their disgust, if such they felt, their emotions were not so disturbing as to inhibit them from taking the pictures.

What the law chose to banish, the new technology of portable photography enabled foreigners to keep alive as a cultural memory. By preserving images of cruel punishments from the last execution season of the old penal regime, European photographers preserved the gap between Chinese and European penal practices that the Qing state was about to close, making these shocking deaths a permanent memorial of cultural difference. Had the French soldier not been there with his camera that morning, Wang would still have been cut apart. Without these photographs, though, the chasm between East and West that these pictures have subsequently been used to demonstrate might have closed the following spring. Without the photographs, far less potent traces of this form of execution, such as written accounts, might have survived, but they would have been less likely to find their way into public consciousness. "Death by a thousand cuts," "to suffer a thousand cuts"—these phrases would not have crept, as they have, into an expressive vocabulary that makes China the heterotopia where such unpardonable acts were practiced as though they were normal.[3]

Our task in this book is to reconstruct the history of lingchi on both sides of this strange relationship between what imperial Chinese law once allowed and what global memory has preserved. That makes our project doubly difficult. On the Chinese side, we face the challenge of entering the severely underdocumented history of the death penalty to make sense of this particular form, which today seems only a meaningless butchery. On the global side, we face the rather different challenge of understanding why the image of lingchi burst into the Western iconosphere so dramatically at the turn of the twentieth century and lingered on as an ancien régime memory that has haunted the Western imagination to the present, and that now haunts the Chinese imagination as well.

These challenges coincide in the photographs themselves, which mark the moment when the history of the procedure ended and the story of its cultural representation took new life. The photographs are as much points of masking as they are points of access, however, for they tempt us to begin not within the context in which lingchi made some kind of sense, but within our own context, where it does not. Our minds naturally revolt at the idea of Wang's execution, just as our eyes look away from the photographs when they are put before us. As historians of the China–Europe relationship, however, we cannot simply set the photographs aside. They reveal a plethora of details for exploring the Chinese end of that relationship, though they are equally capable of misleading viewers into false observations, as we shall show.

The photographs are equally significant for exploring the European side of the relationship, being the main foundation on which it now rests. So we need to study the acts that the photographs record, but we also need to study how the photographs were produced, how they circulated, and how they were received and used in the West. These photographs have proved not to be transparent records of an act that was straightforward in either performance or meaning; neither are they innocent of the circumstances surrounding their production and circulation. Certainly they show what transpired in front of the camera, but at the same time they allude to much that is not visible. Among these hidden elements are the man behind the camera, the circumstances that made it possible for him to be there, and the powerlessness or indifference of those present to object to his taking pictures. The photographs also imply that this sort of image circulated among an audience, whether it was an audience of friends or a larger popular audience that was reached via commercial means. They point to the fact that there was a demand in the West to see such "Chinese" sights, a demand organized in relation to the popular belief that there existed an irreducible difference between East and West, and that this was what the Eastern half of that dichotomy looked like.

The history of lingchi might well have been written differently had these photographs never existed, but as they do, our working assumption has had to be that this history cannot be approached without taking them into account. The photographs do not change the history of Chinese penal practices, which unfolded without them; but they do change our relationship to that past by situating us within other histories: the history of European ideas about what is just and what is cruel, for instance, as well as the history of aesthetic representations of justice and punishment in European culture. These are extraneous to Chinese practice, but they are not incidental to our capacity to go back to the past and understand what went on prior to our present imaginings. As much as the photographs reveal, they also obfuscate and confuse, cloaking this penal practice in a sensationalism that burdens the topic with anxieties and agendas we cannot pretend are not there. Rather than accept the notion that lingchi is quintessentially "culturally" Chinese, our goal is to situate Chinese practices of penal torment within longer judicial traditions, both within China and without. The outcome we hope for is that such practices no longer appear "quaint and original," as they did to nineteenth- and early twentieth-century European observers, or, for that matter, blankly barbaric, as they do to us today.[4] We desire to see such practices located within a larger, global history of punishments that declines to isolate depravity at one end of the spectrum of civilization and compassion at the other, but rather is able to see both at many points between.

The circulation of sensational images of the punished body has tended more to interfere with than to inform the study of judicial torment in imperial China. While earlier scholars have not left these subjects entirely unaddressed, they have usually cited punishments to buttress arguments about something else—the harshness of state administration under the emperors, the depravity of corrupt officials, failure to accede to international standards—rather than to address the role of bodily torment in judicial processes, penal administration, and the negotiation of power relationships in daily life. What has been written on the history of Chinese torture and execution has not much considered how practices of torment came into being, what they were devised to accomplish, or what larger meanings they bore within the semiotics of state rule and social hierarchy. Mostly these practices are cited as testimony to the failure of the Chinese state to measure up to standards elsewhere.[5] Rather than treat tormented execution as an occasion to explain something else, our goal is to go back before the turning point and examine what this form of punishment involved and where it came from, and then, equipped with this knowledge, to explore some of the effects it produced both within and beyond China.

Lingchi as One Form of the Death Penalty

A common reaction to the photographs of lingchi is to see them as scenes of torture. Torture may not be the most useful category for understanding what is going on, however, if we understand "torture" as the use of pain to elicit information, confession, or compliance.[6] Lingchi demanded no such response from its victim. It did not invite the victim to do anything that could bring his suffering to a close. So we will here invoke a distinction, well known to legal historians, between torment and torture. Torture seeks to produce an outcome, whereas torment applies pain solely for the purpose of making the victim suffer. The use of torment as a form of punishment is a practice that has become displaced from Western judicial culture. The performance of tormented execution has slipped even further from anything that Western law acknowledges as legitimate. Yet this is exactly what lingchi involved: putting a person to death while, at least by intention, inflicting the greatest possible torment. To make sense of lingchi in its own context we have to regard it not as an exceptional punishment, but as a form of the death penalty that happens to be no longer in use.

Offering the argument that lingchi is simply one form of the death penalty rather than a peculiar cultural aberration may seem at first to be a perverse move to normalize dismemberment. In fact, our goal in carrying out this research is not only to shed new light on Chinese legal culture, but also to make the findings available for a fuller understanding of the all too human practice of executing criminals. From this point of view, lingchi is an extreme form of a penalty that always possesses a capacity for going to extremes. Taking life pushes a society to the edge of its assumptions about law and social order. As legal historian Douglas Hay has recently observed, "Capital punishment raises important questions for historians of law because of the centrality of the death penalty and its cultural history in our societies. No history of criminal law can avoid it. It is always there, either as the ultimate sanction, or (after repeal) in the threat of its return. What the rule of law means, as inspiration or practice, seems particularly salient when we summon up the will to look at what happens on the gallows, or in the electric chair, or at that travesty of medical procedure lately favoured in the United States, execution by the injection of drugs."[7] If we allow ourselves to think of penal dismemberment as one point along this continuum, then it becomes very much a part of a history of capital punishment that extends to what we in our legal regimes do today.

Where lingchi and the forms of capital punishment conventionally regarded as acceptable appear to diverge is over the question of pain. Most states in which the death penalty is still practiced today require executions to be carried out in a way that produces the minimum amount of pain and degradation for the victim. Our executions are supposed to be clean and painless, and indeed, to be performed with a medical doctor in attendance. All possible torment has been banished from our procedures. Not so in earlier times. An execution performed almost anywhere in the world as late as the eighteenth century was carried out with the understanding that someone who had committed the most horrifying of crimes should be punished in the most horrible of ways. The perpetrator should not simply be killed; he should be made to suffer—physically, psychically, or spiritually—with as much extravagance as was deemed appropriate. To people in earlier ages, to execute someone while refraining from imposing pain or degradation was absurd. A crime had been committed for which killing could not be vengeance enough nor death alone a sufficient atonement. This logic began to shift in European states in the eighteenth century, as the death penalty came under increasing restriction, and in states elsewhere over the following two centuries, China included.[8] The death penalty was restricted to ever fewer crimes, and executions were carried out as quickly and painlessly as possible. The guillotine, the electric chair, and lethal injection were all developed for the explicit purpose of achieving painless death. With the decline of tormented execution came also the withdrawal of executions from public space. The death penalty became a closed event in which the victim was no longer exposed to the humiliation of being viewed while dying. The United Nations has aligned these developments to the eventual goal of abolishing the death penalty, mandating that, in the interim, "where capital punishment occurs, it should be carried out so as to inflict the minimum possible suffering and shall not be carried out in public or in any other degrading manner."[9]

Standing as we do on the far side of the divide opened by the abolitionist ideal, it is difficult to regard tormented executions with anything but baffled horror.[10] With the death penalty coming under an ever wider moratorium, the idea that tormenting a capital criminal could be legal, or even that it could make any sense whatsoever, lies well beyond what most of us wish to accept or perhaps even imagine. Pursuing the body of the condemned "beyond all possible pain," in Michel Foucault's resonant phrase, seems to us a pointless extravagance, pure excess, utterly irrational and perverse.[11] To unlock this conundrum, we need to look beyond our current understandings of what bodies mean and consider instead what embodiment meant to those who lived within a culture that accepted that the body could be extravagantly punished. This reorientation demands that we consider not just the symbolic values that the body carried within that culture but also the metaphysics within which the culture framed its understanding of the body.

Suffering was not extraneous to the logic of lingchi, but it may not have been the entire purpose of the punishment. The earliest lingchi executions in the Liao and Song dynasties in the tenth and eleventh centuries appear to have been performed to produce the greatest possible pain and degradation. And certainly maximizing suffering was the goal of some Ming emperors who imposed lengthy lingchi executions on officials they particularly loathed. As we will note in Chapter 4, the longest lingchi on record, that of the hated eunuch Liu Jin, lasted for two days (it was originally planned to last three days, but Liu succumbed sooner). But there is more to lingchi than this sort of exemplary spectacle. Filtered through Chinese cultural understandings of death and the worship of ancestors, the penalty came to assume a meaning the most salient feature of which may not have been pain.

To approach this idea, consider lingchi in relation to the other harsh penalties that Chinese law mandated. From a legal point of view, lingchi was regarded as the most extreme form of the death penalty. It was worse than decapitation, which in turn was worse than strangulation. This upward gradient from strangulation to decapitation to dismemberment suggests that pain may not have been the key feature organizing the scale of severity among these penalties. Strangulation, legally the mildest of these penalties, was surely a more prolonged and painful experience for its victim than decapitation, yet it was much preferred as a death sentence. What organized the scale of severity was not the pain the victim suffered, it seems, but the consequences for the body that had been separated into parts: into two parts in the case of decapitation, and into many in the case of lingchi.[12] The more the penalty reduced its victim to a form that could no longer be assimilated to the human, the more severe it was considered. More than any other penalty, lingchi violated what one historian of Chinese law has termed "somatic integrity"—the capacity of the body to remain whole, in death as well as in life.[13] The loss of somatic integrity was the outcome most feared and the threat most potent in the system of imperial punishments.

Lingchi in the Popular Imagination

If lingchi was the ultimate penalty in Chinese imperial law, it was also the ultimate penalty in the popular imagination. Ordinary Chinese understood that the state could hand down no worse punishment than this, and on this point they were in complete agreement with judicial officials. But what was popularly imagined about lingchi went well beyond judicial reasoning, just as it did in the West, as we shall see. Confronted with this exercise of exemplary violence to the body, ordinary Chinese produced understandings of lingchi that went well beyond the official concerns of judicial officers or the context of codified law. Unlike judicial officials, ordinary Chinese could not retreat to legal reasoning to make sense of this most atrocious penalty, nor could they probe the annals of the distant past to justify the penalty or challenge its legitimacy, as legal scholars throughout the imperial era did. Instead, they had to imagine why it should be considered the very worst form of execution, and to do that their minds turned to religious imagery and discourse.

The Jade Register (Yuli), a nineteenth-century morality book discussed in detail in Chapter 5, provides a point of entry into the popular imagination of the great issues of life and death. This book supplied the reader with prose and pictures detailing the consequences that wrongdoing in this life brings in the afterlife. After dying, a person had to proceed through a series of ten courts, in each of which a high official examined the person's conduct and then handed down a sentence of corporal punishment, which demonic minions then administered to the bodies that the dead were deemed still to inhabit in the afterlife. The moral consciousness pervading this handbook of purgatorial suffering is the belief that all deeds that have gone unpunished or unrewarded in this life will be duly redressed in the afterlife as well as in the reincarnation to follow. Those who have harmed other sentient beings will "receive suffering" *(shou ku)*, and those who have aided others will not. "Suffering" was the very currency of punishment: only by undergoing physical pain could a person's moral debt be cleared. The more terrible the evil, the more extravagant the torment; and the writers and illustrators of *The Jade Register* had no difficulty in coming up with unimaginably gruesome punishments that they considered as retribution appropriate for the moral crimes of their peers.

The popular imagination understood posthumous suffering in ways that linked it to penal suffering in the real world. Thus the 1892 edition of *The*

Jade Register includes an appendix entitled "The Sixteen Punishments of the World of Light" (Yanglü shiliutiao) listing all forms of real-world corporal punishment. The author explains to the reader that witnessing the suffering of real-world punishments is what inclined him to believe in the even greater terrors of this book's vision of purgatory. So he lists everything that could happen in a real magistrate's court, hoping to stimulate the same reaction in his reader. At the head of the list of sixteen punishments are four forms of the death penalty, listed in order from greater to lesser severity:

1. Smash up the body and grind the bones to dust, such that not a hair remains—this is the most extreme punishment for the very worst of crimes that neither heaven nor earth can tolerate;
2. Lingchi, disembowelment, dismemberment, chopping of the body into small pieces;
3. Death by decapitation such that the head is separated—the usual form of the death penalty;
4. Death by strangulation, meaning the tightening of a cord around the neck in order to cause death—although the body remains whole, death always occurs.

The foregoing four punishments for capital crimes, though they all end in death, are different in terms of the pain *(tongchu)* each causes. How can these [bare] descriptions convey [the actual experience]?[14]

What might this account of the death penalty and its gradations tell us about the popular imagination of lingchi? Note first that lingchi comes second in order of severity. The highest form of the death penalty on this list—the complete eradication of the victim's bodily form—goes well beyond anything the Qing Code permitted magistrates to impose. Its inclusion here as the most extreme punishment that could be imagined is significant because it signals that what people feared most was total somatic annihilation. "Neither heaven nor earth can tolerate" the crimes for which this is the fitting penalty; so too, translating the phrase *tiandi burong* in a different way, "neither heaven nor earth has room" for such a criminal. He must be thoroughly negated, transformed into permanent nonexistence. Moving to the third form of the death penalty, we see that decapitation is defined as separating the head from the body. This description of decapitation is not simply a tautological definition: it pinpoints the source of the dread that ordinary Chinese felt at its prospect. As noted in regard to the fourth form of the death penalty, strangulation, the mildest form of the death penalty is the one that leaves the body intact. The criterion organizing these four levels of the death penalty, at least in the view of this pious writer, is the degree to which the penalty preserves or disturbs somatic integrity. The less the body is permitted to remain intact, the more terrible the punishment, thus rendering lingchi a punishment more dreaded than decapitation. Although the writer insists that the distinguishing factor is pain, as long as strangulation is placed below decapitation, another consequence besides pain was clearly at work, and another principle was informing the popular understanding of lingchi.

The writer does not specify that other principle, perhaps because it was too self-evident to his readers to need spelling out. We catch a glimpse of this principle in another section of the book, "The Six Discriminations of the *Jade Register*" (*Yuli* bian liutiao). This section deals with some of the trickier aspects of purgatorial inquisition. The fifth discrimination, entitled "Sacrificing Life," explains how the system would apply to someone who loses his somatic integrity through no fault of his own. The case has to do with the posthumous fate of a soldier who, having volunteered for military service against bandits or rebels, "dies in such a way that his body and head are in different places or his skeletal remains are scattered." According to the fifth discrimination, as long as the soldier has not raped, looted, or otherwise caused harm to people during his military service, the purgatorial officials will make his original body whole again and then expedite his passage through the afterlife so that he can be "despatched into his next life in a fortunate place as a man or a woman, to live a peaceful life and to end his days in goodness."[15] This dispensation revolves around the dread of having one's body cut into pieces, a dread greater than the prospect of death itself. The fifth discrimination implies that a dead person could not enter purgatory and go through the process of paying off his karmic debt that would allow his rebirth if his body were in pieces.

We get another glimpse of the calculus around somatic disintegration in a story in *The Jade Register* telling of a man sentenced to decapitation. The story begins: "A warder named Yang was on very good terms with a prisoner named Mo, who was sentenced to decapitation. A short time before the execution, Mo gave Yang thirty ounces of silver to sew his head onto his body and to bury him entire" after the execution. The story that follows this deal centers on the predictable fraud of Yang taking the money and neglecting to do as he promised. As a result, Mo's ghost curses Yang until his dying day.[16] The author of the story does not deign to lay out a theory of decapitation, but he clearly assumes that Mo suffers as a hungry ghost—the posthumous form in which the dead haunt the living—as a consequence of not having been sewn together.

The religious implications of annihilation, as these stories suggest, come in two forms, Buddhist and Confucian. In popular Buddhism, existence is conceived as a cycle of birth, death, and rebirth. Popular Confucianism imagines the afterlife as a realm in which ancestors receive offerings from their descendants. The one theology has the dead return, the other leaves them where they are, yet these two contradictory ways of imagining death coexisted in the popular mind. The consequences of the loss of somatic integrity differ in form: the Buddhist is robbed of a chance to be reborn, and the Confucian is deprived of the power to receive the balm of sacrificial offerings. Given that dismemberment was rated as worse than decapitation, the consequences of undergoing lingchi might be even worse. This is a matter about which hard assertions are difficult to make, as we have found no Chinese source from the imperial era that explicitly spells out the afterlife consequences of lingchi. This reticence may reflect the inclination of most educated authors to follow Confucius's dictum about spirits: "keep aloof from them."[17]

We do have another literature to which we can turn, for European visitors to China in the decades after the Opium Wars were fascinated with public executions and curious to note how people reacted to them. Typical in this regard is the observation of A. H. Rasmussen, a Norwegian who worked for the China Customs Service in Zhenjiang in the last decade of the Qing empire, that "decapitation is a horrible thing to the Chinese, for they firmly believe that they go into their next world headless and remain so."[18] There are good reasons to discount much of the testimony of European visitors when reconstructing the history of lingchi, as we will argue in Chapters 3 and 7. Even so, the notion that Chinese feared the disarticulation of the body because of its posthumous implications is too consistently reported to be dismissed as a Western fantasy. This notion has become conventional wisdom in Chinese legal histories by Western scholars and will have to stand until we have an alternative understanding of the religious logic behind popular conceptions of lingchi that is better grounded in the logic and language of indigenous texts.[19]

Popular lore about executions imagined more than just the fate of the victim in the next life; it also imagined a great force of power being released at the moment of violent death. Rasmussen recounts coming unexpectedly upon an execution in Zhenjiang. The victim was kneeling in the open space at the center of a tightly packed crowd. The Norwegian was on horseback and thus able to watch the proceedings over the heads of the onlookers: "Another man was pulling his queue and stretching his neck, and then I suddenly saw the executioner with his sword lifted high above his head. The whole thing happened so quickly that I did not realize what I was looking at before the head was severed with a single stroke. Then came a loud chorus of *"Hao!"* (Good!), as applause for the executioner, and a mad rush of women and children were throwing strings of Chinese coins into the pool of blood. I was sick with horror, and the scene haunted me for days." Later that day, when the Norwegian asked his Chinese language tutor why the women and children were throwing cash into the blood, "my teacher explained that amulets were made of them for children who hung them round their necks. Fresh blood from a decapitated man was a very powerful means of frightening away evil spirits, and the gall of an executed criminal, especially a bandit, made you very strong and brave after you had eaten it. Selling it was one of the executioner's perquisites."[20]

The notion that Chinese were superstitious about the blood of executed convicts is not merely an artifact of Western accounts. The same sort of account, tinged with the same disgust, can be found in Chinese writings of the period, most famously in Lu Xun's short story "Medicine." The story begins as Old Chuan walks out early one morning with a mission to buy medicine to save his tubercular son:

> The next second, with a trampling of feet, a crowd rushed past. Thereupon the small groups which had arrived earlier suddenly converged and surged forward. Just before the cross-road, they came to a sudden stop and grouped themselves in a semi-circle.
>
> Old Chuan looked in that direction too, but could only see people's backs. Craning their necks as far as they would go, they looked like so many ducks held and lifted by some invisible hand. For a moment all was still; then a sound was heard, and a stir swept through the on-lookers. There was a rumble as they pushed back, sweeping past Old Chuan and nearly knocking him down.
>
> "Hey! Give me the cash, and I'll give you the goods!" A man clad entirely in black stood before him, his eyes like daggers, making Old Chuan shrink to half his normal size. This man thrust one huge extended hand towards him, while in the other he held a roll of steamed bread, from which crimson drops were dripping to the ground.[21]

Old Chuan shared the common belief that a dumpling soaked in the blood of a freshly executed corpse had medicinal powers beyond those of ordinary medicines.[22]

Between this passage and Rasmussen's account lies a difference of genres. Lu Xun was writing fiction, whereas Rasmussen claimed to be describing the events of his life. Yet both present executions in the closing years of the empire in much the same way, as atavistic barbarism still capable of gripping the popular mind. Neither the Qing state nor its jurists had anything to do with this trade in the blood of those whom the state executed, just as neither the state nor its officials engaged in speculation about the theology of the somatic disruption that bloody executions caused. In the popular mind, however, the legal power to execute was too great, and the passage from this world into the next too terrifying, for this punishment not to inspire enormous fears.

Lingchi in Comparative Perspective

In the global history of punishment as much as in the popular mind in China, lingchi stands apart as a penalty worse than any other. On the strength of this practice, many European observers, and even some Chinese, have allowed themselves the judgment that Chinese culture has a unique capacity and taste for bodily cruelty unacceptable elsewhere; indeed, not found anywhere else. From a global comparative perspective, however, the penalty is not quite as unique as many have assumed. Seen within the repertoire of extreme cruelties that have been documented for societies around the world, lingchi might better be approached as one among many extreme procedures by which executioners have legally tormented others to death.

Penalties of analogous ferocity throng the historical annals of many cultures, including those in the West. In the seventeenth century, the English dispatched traitors by hanging them, then having their bodies "drawn" (disemboweled) and "quartered" (chopped into portions with an ax).[23] And in the pan-European practice of breaking on the wheel, an executioner tied the victim to the spokes of a large cart wheel and then pounded his body with a sledgehammer until the limbs and body were completely intertwined with the spokes. It is hard to see much distinction in degrees of cruelty between these elaborate public executions and the methods used to put Wang Weiqin to death. Objections on the grounds of cruelty or inhumanity were rarely raised before the seventeenth century, as the suffering visited on the victim served important ends that transcended his own person, such as "re-inforcing the basic myth of the state."[24]

By the eighteenth century, however, such practices were disappearing in Europe and the Americas. No student of torture can forget Michel Fou-cault's vivid reconstruction in the opening chapter of his masterful *Discipline and Punish* of the tormented execution of François Damiens for a minor as-sault on the person of Louis XV in 1753, yet this sort of execution was an anachronism by this time. Confidence that punishing the body of the crim-inal could reveal the truth of his crimes had been weakening in Europe for some time, the iron logic of retribution giving way to more redemptive pat-terns of sentencing.[25] This did not mean an end to the use of violence in punishments. As John Beattie has argued for eighteenth-century England, "few questioned the rightness of the massive physical terror deployed by the State to punish convicted criminals and to discourage others."[26] Only in exceptional cases, such as the drawing and quartering of Damiens, was the old logic allowed to prevail.

Popular opinion in the eighteenth century not only turned against the performance of elaborate executions on the bodies of criminals but even came to resist the idea that criminals forfeited their right to control the dis-position of their bodies after death. This opinion appeared in the context of the rising use of anatomy in medical education and experimentation. Dis-memberments were taking place elsewhere than on the scaffold, more par-ticularly at the hands of surgeons, and ordinary people were alarmed by such practices. The philosophers scoffed at what they regarded as backward-looking thinking, as we can see from the entry on "Anatomy" in Denis Diderot's *Encyclopédie*, the great French Enlightenment project of the eigh-teenth century. Recalling the etymology of "anatomy" as "to cut up," Diderot celebrates the heroic debut of the new science and the audacity of its inno-vators in terms that link directly back to the history of penal suffering: "One cannot but praise the courage of Herophilus and Erasistratus, who received the wrongdoers and dissected them all alive; and the wisdom of the Princes, who delivered the latter to the former, and thus sacrificed a small number of wicked people to the conservation of a great multitude of innocents of all conditions, of all ages, and for the centuries to come."[27] The Swedish scien-tist Anders Celsius had proposed earlier in the century that it would be more humane to cut open ("anatomize") corpses than to sacrifice living people, though even then people rioted against the use of executed bodies for surgical experimentation, considering "anatomization" worse than death itself.[28] Diderot scoffed at such squeamishness. If humanity is endowed with "an habitual disposition by heart to employ our faculties to the advantage of human kind," then, he asks, "what is inhumane in the dissection of a wicked fellow?" Diderot even proposed that criminals on death row be offered the option of undergoing a risky operation after which, should they survive, the penalty would be annulled, opining that "however one might consider the death of a wicked fellow, it would be at least as useful in an operating theater as on the scaffold."[29] The scopic privileges of the new humanism pushed aside the old spectacle of Christian execution, but then the demands of the new science trumped the new humanism's sensitivities. The irony that dismemberment should reemerge as a medical practice after it had been displaced as a judicial practice was not lost on contemporaries. Alert to the ironies of his age, the English illustrator William Hogarth catches the irrepressible link between execution and vivisection in his famous engraving of 1751, *The Reward of Cruelty* (Figure 2). A bad person could now receive his due punishment not on the executioner's scaffold but on the surgeon's table.[30]

We refer to this history not to cast doubt on the reality of the shift in the European penal system away from practices that brutalized the body, but to remind ourselves that in historical terms such shifts have been recent within Western culture and that they were not accomplished in straight-line fashion leading unwaveringly from depravity to enlightenment, but rather came about as piecemeal adaptations to changing social conditions. If the European public by the nineteenth century could accept the appropriateness of cutting up bodies so long as the context was medical and not penal, that does not say anything about the tolerance of the Chinese public for dismemberment so long as the context was penal and not medical. (Unlike their European counterparts, nineteenth-century Chinese were appalled by the European practice of dissection.) What it does bring to notice is that Chinese judicial institutions disposed of the very worst criminals in a way not dissimilar to how European medical institutions made use of corpses that came into their possession.

The separation between Chinese and Western sensibilities at the turn of the twentieth century, when Europeans showed up in China to photograph the public slicing and dismemberment of criminals, has as much to do with cultural expectations as it does with social institutions or even timing. European executions were imbued with a different symbolic logic. In Christian Europe, a tormented execution was known as a *supplice*, from

Figure 2. William Hogarth, *The Reward of Cruelty* (1751). This verse appeared at the bottom of the engraving: "Behold the Villain's dire disgrace! / Not Death itself can end. / He finds no peaceful Burial Place; / His breathless corpse, no friend. / Torn from the Root, that wicked Tongue, / which daily swore and curst! / Those Eyeballs from their Sockets wrung, / That glow'd with lawless Lust! / His Heart exposed to prying Eyes, / To Pity has no Claim: / But 'dreadful' from his Bones shall rise, / His Monument of Shame."

the Latin *supplicium*. The word is virtually extinct in English, having disappeared from use in the Germanic languages several centuries ago along with the practice of tormented execution. William Blackstone uses the word in the 1760s in his *Commentaries on the Laws of England,* but only in Latin and only to designate capital punishment in general.[31] "Supplice" survives in the Latin languages, as *supplizio* in Italian and *supplice* in French. In current French usage, though, the word is used most consistently in the expression *supplice chinois,* "the Chinese torment": lingchi, that most "Chinese" of punishments.

A supplice was originally much more than a harsh penalty. In the European Catholic tradition, where the crucified body of Jesus symbolized the core mystery of Christian faith, it constituted a sacrifice. Not just lethal, it was ceremonial in performance and transcendent in meaning.[32] The complex representational power of supplice in European culture—in which punishment was tightly connected to redemption, martyrdom to beatitude, and suffering to joy—meant that a tormented execution in a Christian context had symbolic and expressive functions unknown to lingchi. True, both involved submitting the body to carefully performed gestures of violence, but the gestures on each side operated within very different symbolic systems, as we show in Chapter 7. This difference works both ways, of course. When a Chinese official was inspecting the luggage of a Jesuit missionary early in the seventeenth century and discovered a vividly carved crucifix, he could only assume that it was an instrument of black magic.[33] Why else would anyone desire to possess the carving of a suppliced male body? He had no way of assimilating the image of a tormented body to any other register of meaning.

Because visual similarities masked symbolic differences, notions of crucifixion furnished the philosophical and aesthetic context into which Europeans inserted what they saw in China in the nineteenth century.[34] They were able to do so in part because gruesome executions of that sort could no longer be seen in the West, and Westerners had forgotten their own history of such practices. As we have noted, punishments in the West had shifted from the ritual excess of bodily exposure to the impersonal discipline of the prison regimen, following Cesare Beccaria's injunction that punishments should work on minds, not bodies.[35] These changes in Europe were what made Wang Weiqin's execution incoherent to European visitors. By 1904, no European could believe that such a penalty was performing what it was supposed to achieve—and to be fair, legal specialists inside the Qing Board of Punishments were doubtful as well and were drawing up new legislation to get rid of it.

Once European visitors in China were able to take photographs of lingchi executions and circulate them as curiosities (especially in the form of post-cards) back in Europe, tormented execution became a distinctive cultural icon of Chinese inhumanity and barbarity not just in law but in all things. When we today look at these photographs of near-naked prisoners brought to the execution ground and sliced beyond life and recognition, it is very difficult to get past our natural revulsion and actually think about the event we are supposed to be viewing. If we want to really understand what is going on in them, it is essential to distance ourselves from the emotive power of these scenes—not by investing them with iconic status, as earlier generations of viewers did, but by resituating them in their legal and cul-tural context and asking, as we do in this book, what is going on, how did it come about, and why did these photographs assume a life of their own out-side China?

What interferes with such untrammeled looking is not simply the natural reaction of disgust at these sights. It has to do as well with the lens through which our own cultural formation has trained us to see such scenes, and be-yond that, to recognize the act of comparison by which we inevitably frame what we are seeing. An implied comparison is at work within the photo-graphs. They assert a claim of singularity: that what was done in this place and time is not done elsewhere. The challenge of comparison is to establish a baseline from which the exercise is viewed not simply as a reaffirmation of the inherent superiority of one side to the other, but as an opportunity to use each side to throw new light on the other.[36] What is needed in the com-parative history of tormented execution, as Talal Asad has argued, are de-tailed ethnographies of pain and cruelty for the cultures outside Europe to which Europe is invariably favorably compared; only then will we be in a position to do the work of comparison.[37] Until such ethnographies are avail-able, we must do what we can to interpret the evidence that lies to hand without granting Europe's historical experience with crime and punishment the status of the norm from which all other cultures must fall short.[38]

Oriental Torments and the Western Imagination

What makes the implicit contrast between Chinese and European justice so powerful is the charged presence of the human body in the lingchi photographs. The body is the most emotionally compelling site of cultural difference. Europeans already had a long history of using tormented bodies to highlight difference and excite cross-cultural loathing even within Europe. When the Catholic polemicist Richard Verstegan in 1587 desired to stimulate popular hatred for the enemies of France in the immediate wake of the English execution of Mary Stuart and the defeat of the Spanish Armada, he had only to print extravagant scenes of devout Catholics being tormented by their religious others—English schismatics, French Huguenots, and Dutch Calvinists most conspicuously.[39] Verstegan's *Le Théâtre des cruautés* struck a chord because of its political-religious message, not because it was doing anything especially novel aesthetically. He was working within a long tradition of theatrical visuality that was accustomed to representing tormented bodies to produce an emotional effect.

The Chinese archive of visual representations of bodily torment cannot compete with the vast repertoire of torments recorded in European sources before and after Verstegan. Indeed, from a Chinese perspective, the plethora of European images of suffering is overabundant. Take the eleventh-century *Sachsenspiegel* (The Saxon Mirror). This legal handbook furnishes us with more images of judicial acts in general, and of physical punishments in particular, than the entire Chinese corpus of visual materials portraying bodily punishment.[40] Europeans regarded such images of official cruelty as acceptable means to stimulate lawful behavior and religious piety and to mobilize public loathing for society's enemies. Chinese writers and illustrators were equally keen to vilify evil, and used visual means to do so, yet they did not pursue the same work of gruesome representation. Extreme bodily suffering was not something to celebrate visually, nor was its depiction a sight to contemplate on a regular basis. The infrequency of Chinese images of cruel punishments has influenced the scholarly literature on Chinese punishments, which has tended to use the same few images over and over again, often with complete disregard for their historical provenance or the period they are supposed to depict, thereby reinforcing the decontextualization that dogs the study of Chinese torture.[41]

In addition to scale, what sets the repertoire of punishment images in the European iconosphere apart from those in other iconospheres is the extent of its capacity for iconic reference. Viewed in the European context, the tormented human body unavoidably reminds the viewer of Christ's mutilated body, which since the High Middle Ages has sat "at the centre of a constellation of religious doctrines, beliefs and devotional practices" animating representational practice in the West down to the present.[42] The visual reference to Christ crucified not only governs how images of naked, mutilated bodies are interpreted in that iconosphere, it also regiments responses to such images outside it. Many Europeans who view pictures of a body undergoing lingchi cannot help but recall the body of Christ—and see it where Chinese see nothing of the sort. The habit of iconically referencing Christ has not been entirely innocent in its effects. It has induced Western viewers to look for traces of sacrificial communication with God in the suffering body of the lingchi victim, and to judge it missing. Dismayed by the apparent absence of such traces, they have imagined a spiritual void at the heart of Chinese culture, an empty space of degradation and cruelty—just as Catholic viewers of Verstegan's engravings could only regard the schismatics who tormented the bodies of their coreligionists as embodying nothing but the purest cruelty.

Tunneling through this aesthetic misalignment is the divergent penal practice and judicial reform in the two culture areas. *Le Théâtre des cruautés* was published in the context of a tradition of public executions—which provided spectators with a "theater" of penal cruelties—that was in the process of coming under restriction. European soldiers would go on committing spectacular atrocities on soldiers and civilians for centuries after Verstegan's publication, and public punishments continued to be performed through the eighteenth century, but European jurists even in Verstegan's time were doubting the moral logic or deterrence value of cruel punishments. Illustrations such as his might continue to circulate in the European iconosphere, but reality and visuality thenceforth diverged, as the acts depicted became increasingly rare as acts seen.

As the sight of judicial torment was withdrawn from the public realm in Europe, an ongoing visual appetite for the sight of mutilated bodies migrated to other sources, and did so at the same time as images of the world beyond Europe began to circulate within Europe. Europeans wanted to see what the world far from them looked like: how people in other places looked, where they lived, what they believed, what they did—and how they managed bodies. The images that gave them this information were of two sorts: native-produced images that Europeans who went abroad acquired and brought back to Europe, and images that Europeans themselves produced of the places where they traveled. The two did not necessarily coincide, however, for native images did not always capture the scenes that Europeans wanted to see, or capture them in the ways they expected to see them. Out of this mismatch emerged a hybrid form: images that native watercolor artists produced on commission according to the buyers' aesthetic.

This hybridity dominated the production of Victorian-era images of China. Chinese artists set up business in Guangzhou (Canton) and produced pictures of the scenes and subjects their European customers wanted. The demand for these images induced engravers back in Europe to acquire and re-render them according to a more familiar visual vocabulary. The commercial engravings of China that circulated in Europe thus tended to be hybrid concoctions derived from Chinese originals. But a feedback mechanism also kicked in, for buyers in turn passed these pictures back to Chinese artists as samples of the work they wanted them to produce. Chinese watercolor artists quickly learned what would sell and happily allowed European aesthetic and moral tastes to determine what "China" should look like— indeed, to determine what aspects of Chinese life should be judged visually appropriate or desirable.[43]

European publishers were eager to acquire and reproduce these images, though they were careful to sanitize the images and remove all traces of blood or evisceration so as not to offend public taste. However much they were doctored, Chinese punishment scenes—which were safely ethnographic and therefore tolerable as a legitimate category of viewing— retained the capacity to shock, which was exactly why publishers wanted to publish them. This process of sensationalism and self-censorship was at work in George Mason's *The Punishments of China*, published in 1801, which included some of the first European adaptations of Chinese watercolors. Figure 3 exemplifies the decorous aesthetic governing the representations in his book. Mason advised the reader that he had been careful not to include pictures that could be thought of as "committing an indecorous violence on the feelings."[44] Yet George Staunton, the first translator of the Qing Code into English, still thought Mason's illustrations too sensational. They had more to do with "the fancy of the painter," he insisted, than with what actually had "a place in the ordinary course of justice."[45]

A Trick of Timing

Mason and Staunton were caught in a moment of transition in the history of European representations of China, before which China was seen as a paragon of civil order and after which it became the great exemplar of barbarity. Both men looked back to the eighteenth century, when Westerners did not associate China with tyranny or intemperance as strongly as they would in later decades. Staunton, who had extensive commercial experience in Asia, wanted to uphold China's reputation against the incriminating visual materials that circulated in the nineteenth century. Popular opinion was against him, which is why, when Thomas de Quincey in 1818 described the "unimaginable horror" and "utter abhorrence" he felt when experiencing "dreams of oriental imagery and mythological tortures" during an opium nightmare, he could expect his readers to agree that his illusions expressed what nearly everyone believed to be Chinese reality.[46] The circulation of commercial images made this association possible; indeed, inescapable.

China was available for such denigration only through what might be called a trick of timing, in two ways. First, China opened its doors more widely to Western visitors in 1860 after the second Opium War, at a time when its government was making widespread use of public executions to suppress several major midcentury rebellions, including the vast Taiping Rebellion that almost toppled the regime. The state's punishment of bodies

Figure 3. *The Capital Punishment of the Cord,* an early European adaptation of a Chinese watercolor showing strangulation. From George Mason (ed.), *The Punishments of China* (1801), Plate 21. Courtesy of the University of British Columbia Library.

during these years was unusually harsh and visible, calculated to communicate the official resolve to destroy the rebels as a warning to others. At the same time, European sensitivities to public mutilation had recently changed. Judicial torment was increasingly being delegitimized, and any memory of the role it had played in Europe's "civilizing process" rapidly suppressed. Judicial torment, recently banished from Europe, survived as an object of contemplation in the exotic realm of the "Orient." As the tormented body vanished from the West, it reappeared in that now quintessentially Oriental place, China.

During the decades when this voyeur's window was open, Western visitors were only too happy to peek in. They went to courts and execution grounds, then reported to readers at home that Chinese "jailors and magistrates frequently resort to modes of punishment and torture."[47] In so doing, they were not just filing information on Chinese penal conditions so much as producing evidence that China was a place where practices Westerners no longer tolerated—at least toward each other—were still in vogue. Cruelties that were judged "unheard of" and "unimaginable" now that Western states had reformed their own penal practices were readily interpreted as signs of China's failure to be civilized. This was grounds for disdaining the "inhumanity and injustice" of the Chinese legal system and confirming the cultural superiority of the West. China's backwardness could then be pushed back by millennia, not just decades. Chinese treatment of prisoners of war resembled the conduct of "ancient Egyptians," insisted an English observer in Canton in 1854.[48] Six years later a French officer in China declared the gruesome executions of two French captives during the 1859–1860 Anglo-French campaign "crimes of another age."[49] From where they stood, China had been left behind in Europe's steady ascent from barbarism to civilization, from irrationality to rationality, from a benighted past to an enlightened present.

But wasn't this the age when European soldiers were policing colonies all over the globe by means of the most frightening corporal methods? The moral condescension that flowed from Europe's belief that it had liberated itself from "crimes of another age" is bluntly compromised by the fact that Europeans continued to subjugate and torture the natives in their colonies. Even after slavery's abolition, beating, judicial torture, and so-called "exemplary" physical punishments were systematically employed against colonized populations. Where "traditional" local practices had involved corporal beating, colonial masters cited native customs to justify continuing their use as part of the colonial disciplinary regime, long after such practices were regarded as unacceptable in Europe. Where such a tradition could not so readily be tapped, imperial agents argued nonetheless that primitive peoples were unable to understand any language but that of force.[50] Torture and exemplary execution remained means of colonial discipline right up until decolonization, on the one hand inspiring a wave of anticolonial resistance that helped strip imperialism of some of its legitimacy within Europe as well as beyond it,[51] and on the other hand enabling precedents for cruel treatment to reemerge back in Europe, notably in the Nazi use of colonial techniques for the eradication of unwanted peoples.[52]

During the nineteenth century, the historiography that equated cruel punishments with historical backwardness was sufficiently resilient as a state ideology, and sufficiently insulated from critique, to turn China into a museum of all that Europe had left behind, a Pandora's box of leftover images blending moral denunciations with realistic reports, fictive fantasies with picturesque imaginings. Out of these fancies and fears, Western observers produced an image of a torturing China that, among other consequences, gave the imperialist West the justification it sought to prove that it had to act in China, carving it up just as the executioner cut up his victims (Figure 4).

The Chinese government hoped to disrupt this historiography with the abolition of cruel penalties on April 24, 1905. The abolition was one component of a larger reform program designed to align Chinese practices with emerging international standards of state administration. The venerable system of appointing officials on the basis of competitive examinations also disappeared in 1905 as part of the same revision of government operations known as the New Policies. As Alexander Woodside has observed, reformers were keen to implement these radical changes in order to deal with what they had come to regard as "deficits" in the Chinese tradition. This was not simply a matter of substituting Western practices for Chinese. These were deficits "about which sensitive scholar officials had been worrying for many centuries."[53] The New Policies gave them the opportunity to resolve issues that had troubled them, such as the dubious legitimacy of lingchi, in the process of bringing China into the ranks of those nations considered truly civilized. China's many Western critics were not so easily persuaded. Chinese reformers may have closed the account on cruel punishments, but a deficit stayed on its books well after 1905. China remained caught in "another age" in which the brutalization of bodies was part of the symmetry of justice, even if such sights were no longer visible in the flesh.

Text within the image: *Encore, une vigoureuse poussée et le colosse sera en morceaux.*

1900 - 27 - 1bre

Figure 4. A postcard dated 1900 representing the carving up of Chinese territory—by implication, a just retribution for a country that dismembered its criminals. Kunzli frères éditeurs; compliments of Ernico Sturani collection, Rome.

Photography and Rhetoric

China remained at the center of this theater of depravity longer than it might have thanks in considerable part to the rise of portable photography. This new technology fueled a popular pornography of tormented bodies in which China featured long after Chinese legal culture prohibited such violence. The portability and affordability of the new cameras enabled amateurs to create visual images for their own pleasure as well as for consumption back home. Sensualized images of the tortured foreign body thus came to circulate within a market in which the local mutilated body had disappeared, or at least gone underground as sadomasochism.

The amateur photographers were anything but naive or random in selecting scenes to shoot. When it came to photographing executions, the photographers seem to have been particularly alert to the visual trope of "Chinese cruelty." This trope reduced the complex questions that the body in pain raised in legal systems to the assumption that the Chinese had perfected and refined the art of inflicting the utmost suffering. The photographer was thus challenged either to capture or to satirize that alleged perfection and refinement. "Chinese cruelty" became a fictive déjà vu that shaped both the taking of photographs and their reception in Europe. Even undertakings with the legitimate ethnological aim of inquiring into the practices of others contributed instead to received ideas. Photography's new visual archive overwhelmed Chinese pictorial resources, just as the perspective from which they were taken overwhelmed any Chinese point of view (including the consciously self-critical) on the subject of torment.

With the new portable cameras, amateur photographers could snap scenes that had been technically impossible in the nineteenth century—at the very time when the foreign military occupation of Beijing following the Boxer Rebellion allowed European camera owners to wander more or less at will through the streets of Chinese cities. For both technical and political reasons, photographers could roam wherever they wished and impose their presence and perspective as they maneuvered to get the best shot, even getting the executioners to pose with their victims. Western witnesses expressed extreme distress at the sight of these executions. After describing the execution he witnessed from horseback, the Norwegian Rasmussen could declare that he "was sick with horror" and assure his readers that "the scene haunted me for days." Even so, this was just the sort of scene that China hands made a point of including in their memoirs and that readers of such memoirs expected to find. They staged what Rasmussen deplored as "misrule, tyranny and corruption."[54] If he had had a camera, he would have taken a picture, so much the better to excite reactions of horror and disgust in his readers when it came time to write his memoirs—as others did.[55]

The temporal window for photographing lingchi was open only briefly. The three sets of lingchi photographs that survive today were all taken during the final execution season between the autumn of 1904 and the spring of 1905. A palpable mix of technical, diplomatic, and military domination seeps from these photographs, revealing much about why the photographers were there and how they were able to get their pictures. Once possessed and archived by the West, however, the circumstances of their having been taken were completely forgotten. Images of lingchi were absorbed into what Susan Sontag has called a "species of rhetoric," a way of talking about suffering that could be manipulated for political and commercial purposes.[56] In the case of these photographs, the political purpose of this rhetoric was to reveal to ordinary Western viewers a depravity so apparently self-evident that judgment could be passed without further consideration. From the repugnance they excited flowed an explicit political message: Asia needed Western colonialism to put a stop to this sort of violence. Only colonialism could save Asians, whether executioners or victims, from themselves. The photographs further implied that only Western civilization could rid China of such practices; they asserted that the Chinese legal system was inadequate to secure life and limb, especially of foreigners.

Given this political context, these images have to be seen as documents of colonialism as well as evidence of Chinese penal practice. They do show penal practice, to be sure, but they show it within a rhetorical frame that, by foregrounding the violence of the colonized, obscures the violence of colonialism. They also willfully neglect the history of earlier penal violence in Europe. Qing China may have deserved the censure it received for the punishments it used, yet just imagine how the history of Europe would be written had there been amateur photographers at the last eviscerations in Cato Street in London, or had someone with a handheld Verascope recorded the execution of François Damiens.

These images fed an "Oriental" aesthetics of horror that became popular after the turn of the century, particularly, it seems, in France. Postcards, paintings, scientific treatises, and illustrated newspapers picked up the images; the gory theater of the Grand-Guignol as well as operas and movies acted them out; literary novels and popular detective stories wove them into their plots. Consumers seemed to crave images of the body in pain, just as they craved images of the body in pleasure. Pictures of Chinese judicial punishments were valued because they still had the power to deliver an "aesthetic shock" within an iconosphere that had grown numb to the cliché of Christ's tormented body.[57]

Among those who contemplated these images is the French theorist of excess, Georges Bataille. Bataille declared that he was moved by the profound power of lingchi photographs to awaken within him a mystic sympathy with the man under torment; in effect, to place him in contact with the sacred. Bataille incorporated images of tormented execution in his "transgressive" meditations on the sacred in his effort to think about bodily suffering in a way that "is not flustered before horror."[58] This is not the first reaction of viewers today, and it has inspired much speculation as to what led Bataille to want to view bodies in torment. "Bataille is not saying that he takes pleasure at the sight of this excruciation," Susan Sontag has suggested. "But he is saying that he can imagine extreme suffering as something more than just suffering, as a kind of transfiguration. It is a view of suffering, of the pain of others, that is rooted in religious thinking, which links pain to sacrifice, sacrifice to exaltation—a view that could not be more alien to a modern sensibility, which regards suffering as something that is a mistake or an accident or a crime."[59] Bataille's recirculation of images of Chinese lingchi victims is most instructive for understanding an aspect of twentieth-century European culture, not that of late imperial China. How he read the photographs has nothing to do with how Chinese in the imperial era reacted to lingchi. Both readings—Bataille's and the conventional Western one—in fact interfere with our capacity to make sense of what was actually going on when the pictures were taken, which is the task we take up in the following chapters. We circle back to Bataille in Chapter 8, however, to propose that he may have perceived the vulnerability of these photographs to misreading and may not have intended them to be published as they were in his much discussed final opus, *The Tears of Eros (Les Larmes d'Éros)*.

Regardless of the academic caveats that may be placed in the way of intentional misreadings, images and descriptions of lingchi and other forms of Chinese execution continue to find aesthetic niches in Western culture today. In every case that we have unearthed, the culture these images construct is based on a profound ignorance of the context within which such punishments were performed.[60] It is not our purpose to censure aesthetic experimentation, yet we cannot help but regard such appropriation as prejudicial to genuine cross-cultural understanding. A less deficient historiography might encourage philosophers and artists to pause before playing with, consuming, and marketing Chinese images of torment as though they were free-floating cultural elements, without regard to the political work such images do. When facing horror, it is all too easy to forget Foucault's sensible reminder that a public execution is not an abstract ritual performance but "a political operation."[61] Removing lingchi from its judicial context and inserting it into the realm of pure imagination reduces the political to the purely cultural, neglecting what it was that tormented execution was enacted to do. These images have enabled Western viewers to assume an excessive authority in declaring what legal and moral development consists of, and in judging "timeless China" to be in permanent exile from that development.[62] So too they are even now shaping Chinese interpretations of their own past among artists and novelists, who resurrect evidence of legal cruelty in the past as a vehicle for condemning aspects of their own tradition.[63]

This book takes on the dual challenge of both looking at and looking past the evidence of legal cruelty in the Chinese tradition, first by reconstructing the practice of lingchi within the Chinese legal and cultural context (Chapters 2–5) and then by analyzing appropriations of lingchi in Western culture (Chapters 6–8). Chapter 2 surveys imperial penal law; Chapters 3 and 4 reconstruct the practice of lingchi from the Liao to the Qing dynasties; and Chapter 5 explores the popular reception of the idea of bodily torment in the Chinese religious imagination. In the book's last three chapters, we turn to our second task, plumbing the history of Western interpretations of Chinese punishments of the body and assessing the impact of those interpretations on the contemporary understanding of lingchi. Both halves of the book are needed if our understanding is to have more substance than the worst nightmare the West can imagine. Once historicized, the subject of lingchi may be allowed to take its place among the more deplorable forms of the death penalty found in global history, rather than continue to stand out as a unique and bizarre exception to civilized norms. Our purpose is not to trade on the shock of violence but to encourage a recognition of what East and West share and how they differ in real rather than fantastical ways, so that we can then begin the work of comparative history.[64]

We also hope this study will have an effect in the field of China studies. The flip side of the sensationalism surrounding ideas of Chinese penal suffering in the West is the occulting of penal suffering, both by traditional Chinese sources and by modern scholarship, which sometimes gives the impression that state-making in imperial China was more noble, rational, and "clean" than state-making in Europe. A more reflexive account of the role of torment in China should serve to question the image of late imperial China as an empire purely of rules and officials. It should also help us to see China as an empire of persons and bodies that the state's law and criminal administration subjected to harsh penalties, employing torturers and executioners just as it employed Confucian teachers and wise administrators. An analysis of China that leaves out the beatings and executions—just as much as one built entirely from grotesque pictures of tortured bodies—can give an image of the culture that says more about those who view than about those who are viewed.

Violence and the provision of public goods were coactive in the creation of social order in imperial China, as indeed they have been in every state system. Reconstructing the history of this punishment may thus help to release China from a habit of mind that continues implicitly to take Confucian ideals of good government and responsible statecraft as adequate descriptors of social reality.[65] China's imperial government could at times be as good as its moral model proclaimed, and its officials as responsible as the Confucian commitments they espoused would have them appear. Yet the virtual image of the Confucian past that the sinological tradition has tended to sustain expresses only part of what the late imperial state did to reproduce itself and sustain its legitimacy. Punishments imposed in the course of protecting the state and maintaining social order were too real for us to dismiss as the collateral damage of Confucian paternalism. Bodily suffering shaped the Chinese world as much as it did any other, and it is too much a part of state control for us not to alter the picture by drawing a fuller one.

CHAPTER 2

The Laws of Punishment
in Late Imperial China

In dynastic China as in every other historical polity, each person was present in society as a body upon which the imperial state imposed the expectations and burdens of being a subject. The body could be conscripted for labor service, regulated through rites, mobilized for war, or punished by any number of means from restraint, imprisonment, and exposure, to branding, beating, and exile, to death, mutilation, and dismemberment. Imperial China was not alone in the methods it developed for punishing its subjects' bodies, nor is China unique in sustaining its own repertoire today, despite the global trend toward convergence in the use of penal methods. The Chinese tradition may appear distinctive, but it is neither utterly unique nor so continuous as to be unchanging. Penal practices have changed over time, and judicial standards have varied from one period to the next, coming into use at one time and later being abolished as political norms and moral tolerances shifted. While the history of corporal punishments in China can be approached purely on its own terms, that history also belongs to a global history of corporal punishments, at least until the point of transition to the "modern" regime of punishment when, as Foucault put it, "the body as the major target of penal repression disappeared."[1]

The body was not, however, the only part of the person with which the Chinese tradition of law and punishment concerned itself, nor was the disciplining of the body the only or even the primary concern of the Chinese state. Beyond the body, guiding its actions, lay the mind, or what in the Chinese legal context might better be called intent. Chinese law from its earliest foundational texts has made it clear that what is punishable is the intent to commit a crime, not merely its commission. Unintentional misdeeds should be pardoned, and cases in which criminal intent cannot be clearly established dismissed.[2] This concern with intent imposed an informal procedural restraint on judges, who had to evaluate a crime in relation to the intent behind it and weigh the punishment accordingly. These restraints were not always built into institutional procedures as securely as they might have been, and judgments—particularly when the crime was violent—were not always handed down with the circumspection that the tradition might prefer to claim. Nonetheless, law and punishment were not only technologies of bodily discipline; they were, in their ideal form, methods by which minds were transformed so as to conduce the people to virtuous conduct.

This chapter focuses not on minds but on bodies. The punishment of bodies, at least in theory, was carefully regulated according to the principle that it should correspond precisely to the severity of the crime it punished. Much of what this chapter describes will strike the reader as excessively severe, but that is a judgment we make from outside the penal and moral context of late imperial justice. Those who lived within that context had their own very clear standards regarding excess and arbitrariness in punishments. Their thoughts on these matters emerge most sharply in their commentaries on foreign cultures, when they were quick to notice such faults. For example, a sailor with the Zheng He voyages early in the fifteenth century was dismayed to discover that Javanese did not flog, which meant that they resorted to capital punishment for far too many crimes. He regarded this lack of discrimination as "terrible" because it reduced all crimes to the same crime and failed to distinguish between milder and worse.[3] Excess in punishment is likewise a common theme in Qing Chinese writings about Tibet. A typical mid-eighteenth-century commentary on Tibetan justice notes that "their laws are extremely cruel, and include such penalties as shooting a criminal full of arrows, putting him in a scorpions' lair and letting the scorpions eat him alive, or gouging out eyes and cutting off hands." After listing several more, the writer is moved to observe that "given that the people are treated like animals in this way, it is hardly surprising that they kill and steal from each other."[4] From his perspective, the consequence of cruel punishments is that justice does not civilize but only punishes. To be fair, Tibetans made the same judgments of the Qing penal practices. When two ringleaders of a revolt against Qing rule in 1728 were executed in Lhasa by lingchi, even those who did not support the rebellion were appalled by this atrocious penalty. It was a punishment beyond anything they could tolerate.[5] The contrast in perspectives reminds us that judgments of cruelty are made within specific cultural contexts.

From the Chinese perspective, a punishment of this type was carefully graded in relation to the severity of the crime, as well as in anticipation of the moral consequences it might produce in society. Accordingly, late imperial justice did not randomly determine punishments nor casually execute them. It is true that all manner of circumstances—pardons, amnesties, legal redemptions of penalties in cash or grain—could intervene to make the course of imperial justice less predictable than the model laid out in this chapter might suggest. Despite such variations, however, imperial Chinese criminal administration operated on the basis of precise and complex regulations that provided strict guidelines to determine how judicial officials addressed crime and to ensure that they produced consistent judgments and handed down predictable sentences. We will now survey the full range of corporal methods available to a Chinese magistrate to investigate and punish crimes so as to situate lingchi as the crowning penalty within the larger penal system.

Corporal Punishments

Each dynasty, on its founding, promulgated a Code *(lü)*, a body of core criminal laws and the punishments that should follow for every infraction. The earliest complete text in this tradition is the seventh-century Tang Code, though earlier codes have been partially reconstructed from textual and archaeological sources. Although the court regularly produced regulations and ordinances covering a wide range of administrative matters, the Code remained the sole basis for judicial decisions and the gate governing punishment. At the head of each edition of the Code may be found an account of the punishments a judicial official could impose on the bodies of those found guilty of contravening the laws listed in the Code. This set of official sanctions, known collectively as the Five Punishments *(wuxing)*, remained basically unchanged between the promulgation of the Sui Code in the early 580s and the introduction of a new scale of punishments in 1905.[6] They are listed as the first five articles of the Tang Code of 653, in order from lighter to heavier; in the Ming and Qing codes they are combined as a single introductory article. This set of Five Punishments has also prevailed in other states in East Asia. Even Meiji Japan, which had been using these penalties since the eighth century, reaffirmed their legitimacy in the new Code of 1871.[7]

The two lightest of the Five Punishments, which appear as the first two articles of the Tang Code, are floggings. The sentence of being beaten by the *chi* or light flogging stick entailed ten to fifty strokes, and the *zhang* or heavy flogging stick, sixty to one hundred strokes. In practice, these two corporal punishments were regularly discounted to a percentage of the number of strokes stipulated in the Code. Floggings were reduced to 70 percent of the official rate in the Yuan dynasty and 60 percent in the Ming and Qing. The discount may have been introduced to bring the performance of sentences into line with their pronouncement, or it may have been an attempt to produce a more carefully graded system of punishments than the letter of the Code allowed. Flogging sentences could also be redeemed by cash payments, the values of which are listed in the Code.[8] A beating with a flogging stick, referred to in English as "the bamboo" or the "bastinado" (in French, *bastinado* was for the beating itself, not the stick), was the commonest penalty in imperial law (Figure 5).

The next two articles in the Tang Code provide the penalties of deportation. The lighter was the sentence of *tu* or penal servitude away from one's native place, in five durations between one and three years. The heavier was *liu* or exile, at three distances between 2,000 and 3,000 *li* (roughly 650 to 1,000 miles), depending on the severity of the crime being punished. To these penalties, the Ming Code of 1368 adds an additional penalty of flogging with the heavy stick, lest simple servitude or exile seem too gentle. Sentences of exile thenceforth included a beating of a hundred strokes, and the five degrees of penal servitude a variable number of strokes from sixty to one hundred.[9]

The death penalty appears in the fifth article of the Tang Code. The Code recognized two degrees of this "fifth punishment." The lighter degree was strangulation and the heavier, decapitation.[10] We will return to the death penalty in the second half of this chapter.

Despite formal continuity from the Tang Code to the Qing Code, actual penal practice changed over time, in several ways. The most significant innovation increased the gradations in penalties, providing judges with finer sentencing distinctions. For instance, the Ming doubled the number of deportation sentences by adding distinctions based on the severity of conditions in the regions to which criminals were deported. The Qing supplemented and topped these grades with the penalty of Great Deportation, which entailed enslavement in a Tartar garrison. In addition, posthumous penalties were added for crimes for which death alone was considered too mild: exposure of the head after decapitation *(xiaoshou)*, for example, or the dispersal of the corpse after execution *(lushi)*, though some of these practices

Figure 5. A court minion administering a beating with a long flogging stick. Illustration from a 1630s edition of *Sanguo shuihu guanzhuan yingxiong pu* (Album of the heroes in the complete editions of *Three Kingdoms* and *Water Margin*).

go back to the Song dynasty. Minor changes were also made to the guidelines governing the implements for administering corporal punishments, most importantly the size of the sticks that could be used for floggings. These sticks, thinner at the holding end and thicker at the beating end, got longer from dynasty to dynasty. Flogging sticks in the Tang and Song were thirty-two inches (2.5 *chi*) long. The Mongols accepted this at the beginning of the Yuan dynasty, but later added another foot to the length of the stick. The Ming dynasty followed the Mongol precedent. The Manchus, however, added twenty-five inches (two *chi*), so that the heavy stick reached its final length of seventy inches (5.5 *chi*) in the Qing dynasty.[11] More length meant more leverage for the flogger and greater suffering for the victim.

The flogging stick was not the Chinese state's only tool for punishing lesser crimes. Also in common use, and subject to the same size inflation, was the large wooden neck board known as a cangue. Although in universal use, the cangue rested at the edge of legality by virtue of not appearing among the Five Punishments. The cangue was regarded more as a device of restraint than a tool of punishment and so was viewed as a different category of penal instrument. Still, wearing a cangue could be harsh enough to cause death, and quite intentionally.[12] While the Code did not recognize the cangue among the Five Punishments, it regulated its size and weight. The Ming Code set its dimensions at seventy inches (5.5 *chi*) long and eighteen inches (1.5 *chi*) wide; the Qing shortened the cangue by almost half but widened it, changing its shape from a wide plank to almost a square.[13] The Ming device varied in weight from twenty to thirty-three pounds, depending on the seriousness of the offense, while the Qing version was set uniformly at thirty-three pounds. The weight meant that the cangue was not just a tool of restraint but a means of inflicting pain, though the Code forbade its use on prisoners whose crimes merited only a light beating. Quite aside from the physical suffering a cangue could cause, the humiliation of being forced to wear one could be great. In his widely read 1699 handbook for prospective magistrates, Huang Liuhong notes that putting a cangue on someone of good repute could mean "humiliation worse than death. One day's humiliation produces shame that lasts a lifetime."[14] Wang Huizu, the eighteenth-century author of another widely read guidebook for magistrates, retells a case in which the penalty drove the victim's new bride to suicide, an act he imitated once the cangue was removed. Wang includes the case in this book to caution overly zealous officials against applying the penalty too cavalierly.[15]

Despite the specifications laid down in the Code—or more accurately, perhaps, because of the temptation to evade them—actual penal practice exhibited great variation. One could expect to find variation at the bottom of the system, but it was there at the top as well. To offer one example at the top, the third Ming emperor, Yongle (r. 1403–1422), declared in the first year of his reign that should a witness to armed robbery not attempt to stop the crime while it was in progress, the magistrate trying the case should "take a great cangue weighing one hundred catties and cangue him with it."[16] A hundred catties is roughly 130 pounds—four times the legal weight limit for cangues in the Ming Code. The heavy cangue (Figure 6) was never written into the Code, but an emperor had declared it could be used. And it was. Huang Liuhong's handbook records that some magistrates owned cangues weighing over 150 pounds, though to display, it seems, rather than actually to use.[17]

The sight of a criminal wearing this wooden frame around his neck was particularly intriguing to European visitors. These "portable stocks" or "portable pillories" as the English called them (*piloris portatifs* or *carcans* in French) should not have surprised them, given that criminals in Europe before the nineteenth century were regularly pilloried. Those guilty of transgressing public morals could be made to wear "collar boards," which differed from Chinese cangues only in shape and weight. During his visit to Amsterdam in 1641, for example, the English royalist exile John Evelyn described one such penal device that he saw on display in the Senate House: "a certaine weighty vessel of Wood (not much unlike to a butter-Churne) which the adventurous Woman that hath two husbands at one time is to weare for a time about the Towne, her head comming out at the hole, and the rest hanging on her shoulders, as a penance for incontinency."[18] Evelyn would have been familiar with the English practice of putting in stocks persons "not fit to be trusted, but to be shunned and avoided by all creditable and honest men," in the language of a London magistrate of the early eighteenth century. The use of the pillory was restricted in England only in 1816 and abolished altogether in 1837.[19] Europeans visiting China after the first Opium War in 1840 may be excused for being fascinated by cangues, these objects being no longer available for viewing at home.

Judicial Torture

Punishment following sentencing was not the only condition under which the Chinese state could order the beating of subjects' bodies or the locking

Figure 6. A prisoner in a heavy cangue. Illustration from a 1614 edition of Shi Naian's novel *Shuihu zhuan* (Water margin), engraved by Liu Qixian and Huang Cheng.

of cangues on their necks. Corporal suffering was regularly imposed before sentencing, and a variety of sticks, presses, and chains were available to interrogators to prompt suspects and witnesses to provide the information necessary for passing a judgment of guilt. With the beating of the body we move swiftly from penal torment to judicial torture, from sanctions imposed to punish the guilty to methods employed to terrorize and intimidate those whose guilt had not yet been determined. This is not purely a modern distinction. Chinese law distinguished the flogging stick *(zhang)* from the "interrogation baton" *(xunzhang)*, the latter being 1.5 inches thicker than the former.[20] These minor differences reflect an awareness within the judicial system that beating someone to extract a confession was a different task, and involved different methods, than beating someone to impose a penalty.

Torture has had a large role to play in Chinese judicial practice, as the legal process, both imperial and modern, hinges on the production of a confession. Confession is the final proof. With it, a conviction can be handed down and a case closed.[21] As in early modern continental Europe, the importance of confession encouraged aggressive interrogation as standard judicial practice. That said, in China the choice of whether or not to use torture was left to the individual magistrate. He did not have to impose judicial torture in the course of an interrogation; nor did he have to be consistent in applying torture across cases. Where he did have to be consistent was in using only the implements that published law made available to him, and only in ways that imperial direction allowed. Only certain implements of torture were legal, and their legality depended on their being used only in the way and to the extent that the regulations permitted.

The interrogation baton was regularly used to prod suspects and witnesses during judicial proceedings. An inquisitorial magistrate could avail himself of more gruesome tools than the baton, however. Two that the law permitted interrogators to use in "serious cases of homicides or robbery when there is a false confession" were the ankle press and the finger press. The ankle press consisted of three wooden boards roughly a yard in length and eight inches across, through which ran cords that the interrogator could tighten to crush a suspect's ankles. Women were spared this treatment, but could be tortured instead with a finger press consisting of five wooden rods.[22] The illustrator of a Ming novel shows some of these implements in a courtroom context in Figure 7. Figure 8, an illustration taken from a late Ming encyclopedia, shows a fuller selection. With the exception of the

Figure 7. A prisoner under interrogation, showing wooden manacles, restraining board, and ankle press. From a 1630s edition of Luo Guanzhong, *Sanguo zhi yanyi* (Romance of the Three Kingdoms).

"box-bed," to which we will return, all these instruments were accepted as tools in the arsenal of judicial inquisition.

A Ming reader would not have been surprised to turn the page of the encyclopedia and find this illustration there for his scrutiny. There was nothing occult about these items or their uses. Their display was part of their use, after all. When a Korean visitor to Ming China in 1487 noted in his diary that he saw flogging sticks and finger presses—"the usual punishment instruments of the public offices," as he put it—hanging on the wall of a magistrate's court, he expressed neither surprise nor dissatisfaction at the sight.[23] He was simply observing that the things he expected to find in a place of judicial investigation were there for all to see. Indeed, their absence would have elicited more

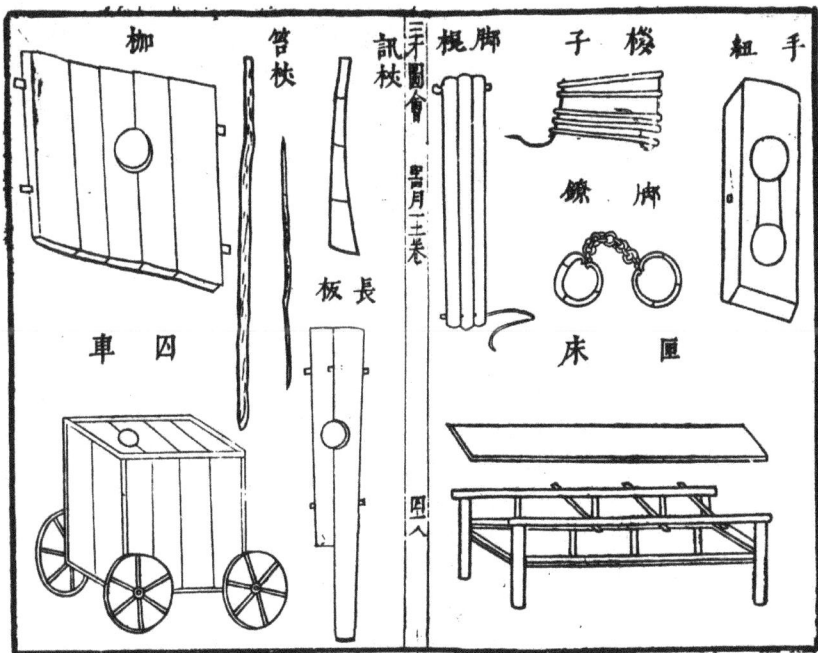

枷　笞杖　訊杖　三才圖會　脚梖　杻子 楎　手杻

卷二十一　脚镣

板長

車囚　　床 匣

Figure 8. Selected implements of torture in the Ming dynasty, from Wang Qi (ed.), *Sancai tuhui* (Illustrated compendium of heaven, earth, and human), 11.48a–b. Right leaf, counterclockwise from upper right: wooden manacles, finger press, ankle press, fetters, and "box-bed." Left leaf: interrogation baton, light and heavy flogging sticks, cangue, prisoner's cart, and restraining board.

comment than their presence, as the process of judicial investigation was not something to be obscured from general view. The contrast with the European practice of holding torture sessions behind closed doors is striking.[24] The language of torture was similarly unocculted. Europeans tended to speak of torture euphemistically, using phrases such as "putting the question."[25] Chinese expressions were more forthright: *xingxun*, "employing corporal beating to interrogate," or *kaowen*, "interrogating by beating."[26]

The European and Chinese legal systems both required confessions, but they used them in different ways. A continental European magistrate was not allowed to rely for evidence solely on what he might learn from a confession extracted by torture. European justice since the time of the ancient Greeks has relied mainly on oral declaration. That confession had to be repeated "spontaneously" in open court for it to have legal validity. In China, by contrast, evidence extracted under torture and written down was admissible in court and allowed to carry more weight than was a confession in Europe, which had to be freely repeated in court to have legal value. When no confession could be obtained, a European magistrate could still convict on a capital charge, provided that he obtained oral testimony from two credible eyewitnesses. A Chinese magistrate was under less pressure to find independent evidence, should a confession prove impossible to obtain, and under none to force the confessor to reproduce it orally in court.[27] This difference does not mean that he did not have to proceed with care, for an ill-founded judgment based on coerced testimony that ended up being exposed at a higher level (all serious cases were reviewed) could ruin his career. Indeed, it may have forced the conscientious Chinese magistrate to proceed more cautiously than his European counterpart.

Despite their differences, Chinese and European courts shared a concern to limit the use of judicial torture. Common sense suggests that a victim will say anything under torture, and that the more it is applied, the further it can divert the victim from the truth. Critics of the excessive use of torture in both East and West endorsed this common sense. Magistrates' handbooks in China repeatedly warned that evidence given under torture was unreliable. As the handbook author Wang Huizu observed in 1793, "When confession is obtained by torture, how can one's mind be at ease?"[28] Published regulations imposed strict limits to forestall this kind of error. The magistrate had to follow precise rules regarding how, when, and on whom torture could be used. There had to be evidence already before him that strongly indicated the guilt of the suspect before he could apply torture. The law did not tolerate "fishing" for evidence. The kinds of torture an interrogating magistrate could apply were also restricted. The ankle press could be used only on a male adult suspected of a crime, such as armed robbery or homicide, for which the penalty was exile or death. Males younger than fifteen or older than seventy were immune from torture, as were notables. The duration and frequency of the application of torture were also strictly limited. The ankle press, for instance, could not be employed on the same suspect more than twice without special authorization from the Ministry of Justice (Board of Punishments).[29]

Some scholars have expressed suspicion regarding the careful quantification of penalties in Chinese penal law. Étienne Balazs, who translated a famous debate on torture that took place during the Sui dynasty in the sixth century, was struck by its "cold objectivity," "detached tone," and "inhumanity," as well as by its almost exclusive focus on technical issues like "the duration and the efficacy of torture" and its tacit acceptance of torture as "an absolutely legal method."[30] This attitude resonates with a trope in nineteenth-century Western writing on Chinese penal law, which declared Chinese judicial cruelties to be "refined" and therefore, puzzlingly, "perfectly according with the placid selfishness which marks every feature of their character."[31] Traces of this attitude survive in the first modern classic of Chinese legal history, *Law in Imperial China*, where Derk Bodde and Clarence Morris suggest that the Chinese legal system was "complex, over-refined," and "perhaps unduly ritualized." The fact that Chinese law provided what they reported as "a kind of 'due process' which, different as it is from our own, certainly deserves admiration and respect" was not enough to outweigh these flaws.[32] But it should not be surprising that the regularity, accuracy, and accountability that are seen as defining features of Chinese bureaucratic rule also characterize the Chinese judicial system. The administration of justice was as closely regulated as any other branch of the bureaucracy, and as sensitive to the need for making fine distinctions in relation to particular circumstances rather than using one blunt instrument for all occasions—even if that was occasionally what a lazy official might end up doing.

Even in cultures that regard torture as legitimate, practice invariably diverges from the rules regulating its use, as the overzealous press for results that regular procedures may not be able to guarantee. First was the gap between what a magistrate ordered and what the lackey administering the sentence actually did. Huang Liuhong reminds the reader of his handbook,

The Complete Book concerning Happiness and Benevolence, that the choice of which torture to use may be "entirely in the hands of the magistrate, but whether it is applied severely or lightly, whether it allows the culprit to live or kills him, is up to the corrupt lictors."[33] There could be a second gap between what procedures proposed and practice required. By its very logic, torture resists regimentation. Compliance with rules deprives torture of some of the terror that enables it to get results. Confession cannot be as readily extorted when the victim knows exactly how long he may suffer, that he is guaranteed recovery, and that all these limits must be respected in court. Lictors and magistrates alike were tempted to ignore the regulations in order more effectively to intimidate their victims. Moreover, the implements of torture and restraint actually used in a yamen (magistrate's court) might well diverge from those listed in the Code. When the operations of the Beijing military governor were investigated following the collapse of the eunuch faction with which he was allied in 1627, for example, it was found that his jailers were using five implements of torture not specified in the regulations, and using them in ways that the regulations did not allow. This evidence weighed against the governor in his impeachment.[34]

Ambitious magistrates were not always sticklers for the rules, given the career benefits of case completion and lack of motivation at most levels of the system to interfere. Occasionally, however, emperors saw the value of reining in their officials when they suspected that interrogation techniques were going beyond what was set down in law. In 1679, Emperor Kangxi learned that suspected bandits were being subjected to all sorts of illegal devices, naming "box-beds" *(xiachuang)* and "head squeezers" *(naogu)* among them. He reminded his magistrates that "those who indulge in such cruelties and thereby cause the deaths of human beings will receive the severest sentence provided by law." Nineteen years later, in 1698, he complained that the box-bed was still in use and that some interrogators were shortening their ankle presses to a third of their regulation length to increase the damage they caused. He also noted that some cangues weighed over 120 pounds, well in excess of what Qing law permitted. "These are all cruel punishments," Kangxi sternly reminded his officials, "and each of them is severely proscribed."[35]

For a magistrate whose career depended on completing cases, the emperor's official pronouncements against the use of illegal techniques might count for very little. Huang Liuhong acknowledged the abuse of torture and warned the magistrate-to-be not to forward a forced confession that might be retracted at a higher level. He also doubted the wisdom of imposing suffering on the innocent. "Alas, aren't the skin and flesh of the common people being subjected to such vicious cruelty merely to compensate for the stupidity of the interrogating official? It goes against the harmony of nature and it burdens the people with a passionate sense of injustice," he argued. "I can't imagine what someone who has studied and taken public office thinks he is doing by showing this sort of behavior!"[36] In other words, allow the lictors to perform their theater of intimidation, but do everything to avoid actually applying torture.[37]

The Confucian ideal preferred that officials use punishments sparingly, and only after the calculus of crime and punishment had been clearly publicized.[38] Best of all was the official who could bend the people to lawful conduct without resorting to physical intimidation and drawing them into false testimony. An examplar of this ideal was the seventeenth-century legal scholar Lu Longqi, of whom it was said that while serving as a county magistrate outside Shanghai in the mid-1670s, he "left the implements of torture hanging [on the wall] and did not use them."[39] This was the sign of the skillful magistrate. Officials who regularly resorted to torture were generally regarded as lazy, incompetent, or looking for bribes. Torture might close a case, but it might also lead a tribunal away from the truth. It was a basic principle of Confucian justice that the innocent should not be harmed. Gratuitous suffering itself was not an issue; the issue was that indiscriminate torture could create more injustice than it stemmed, and in doing so undermine the legitimacy of the dynasty on whose behalf it was inflicted.

Lurking behind the idea of restraint in the use of torture was the concern that the judicial process should not cause any deaths prior to sentencing. As the late Ming philosopher Liu Zongzhou expressed the Confucian ideal of punishment in a memorial to the Wanli emperor, "punishment gains its authority by not killing."[40] A magistrate who caused the death of a suspect, even in a capital case, before having determined guilt faced an inquest that could lead to a conviction for homicide and a sentence of execution. The judgment against him depended greatly on whether the instruments employed under his order had conformed to the law, and whether the guilt of the victim had been sufficiently established before the confession was extracted. If the victim was a notorious criminal, the magistrate was unlikely to be prosecuted for causing an outcome that would have occurred anyway. When the hapless victim of excessive torture was found to be innocent, the magistrate was placed under close examination. If his treatment of a suspect involved mere "inobservance" *(buru fa)*, such as substituting one legal instrument for another (using the heavy instead of the light flogging stick, for example) or exceeding the legal number of blows, he might be excused from wrongdoing. If he had made "vicious use" *(feifa)* of a legal instrument, such as using the heavy stick to beat forbidden zones of the body such as ankles or genitalia, or used a "vicious instrument" *(feixing)*, such as the box-bed or the shortened ankle press, he faced more serious consequences. A second criterion of judgment had to do with his intent. If the magistrate was merely overzealous in fulfilling his duty, his infraction was considered "public misconduct" *(gongzui)* and netted him only moderate administrative sanctions. But if he used abusive torture to cover up his own injustice, illegal exactions, or other corruption, the case fell under the rubric of "private misconduct" *(sizui)*, for which he was stripped of his status as a degree holder and prosecuted as a commoner. The punishment for "submitting an innocent to torture and causing him to die" was delayed execution, which in practice was often lightened to exile or banishment.[41] The pronouncement of death was nonetheless intended to warn magistrates not to abuse their power of life and death over the people.

The Death Penalty

As the worst punishment the state could inflict, the death penalty had to be reserved for those whom the state had carefully and correctly determined should die for crimes they had actually committed. It should not fall on those who were innocent or who had committed crimes for which lesser penalties were mandated. This concern did not derive from a reluctance about putting people to death when the authorities thought there was cause to do so, however. As one of the Five Punishments, the death penalty enjoyed all the legitimacy that judicial tradition and legal codification could give.

The lighter form of the death penalty, strangulation, permitted the victim "to preserve his corpse whole," according to the Code, implying the importance of retaining somatic integrity even after death. The next heavier form, decapitation, in contrast, meant that "the head and the body should be separated."[42] The Code further acknowledged the anxiety about somatic integrity by noting that, in a case in which official provisions called for a sentence to be increased to match the severity of a crime, it was not permissible to increase a sentence of strangulation to decapitation, unless the Code specifically allowed for this escalation.[43] The gulf between strangulation and decapitation was too great to be jumped by a technicality.

From a cosmological perspective, the death penalty disrupted the natural order of life and death. It also carried a political sense of disruption, for it exposed the failure of the ruler to provide the people with the good order needed to live a moral life, which it was his responsibility to ensure. The goal of law was to bring into being a realm of harmony in which the people would no longer commit capital crimes: "a time," as a subcommentary on the Tang Code phrases it, "when killing would cease."[44] Executions were the baldest evidence that such a time had not come. Some emperors were accordingly sympathetic to proposals to reduce the crimes for which the death penalty was mandated. Thus the founding Tang emperor in 617 decided to eliminate the death penalty for all crimes except murder, robbery, military desertion, and high treason; in the same vein, his successor reduced the sentences on ninety-two capital crimes.[45] Such lenience was taken to demonstrate the success of an emperor's rule.

When the death penalty had to be used, it was understood that every effort must be made to ensure that the innocent were not executed and that only those who deserved to die were killed. To declare of one's dynasty that "not once has someone been executed who committed no crimes," as the philosopher Shao Yong (1011–1077) declared of the Song, was high praise.[46] Similarly, a good emperor should not let people imprisoned for noncapital crimes die in jail. As the third Ming emperor, Yongle, declared in June 1404, approving the standard summer request that prisoners in capital jails dying of heat and sickness be released, "It is not permissible that everyone should be put to death regardless of whether his crime is big or small."[47]

Caution regarding the taking of life also encouraged delays in the judicial system to allow for a full and careful review of capital cases at court. Yuan law required that sentences of exile or death be centrally reviewed by the Board of Punishments; Khubilai Khan personally reviewed many capital sentences at the end of the agricultural year and looked for ways to mitigate the penalty.[48] In the Ming, this review was regularized into an annual practice known as the Autumn Assizes. In general, autumn was the season when executions could begin, this being the time of decay and death, while spring was the season when they should cease, though actual practice did not stick to this model.[49] While the very worst crimes could proceed to immediate execution regardless of the season, the greater number of capital cases were delayed for review at the Autumn Assizes. The delay gave the convict on death row the chance to have his case reviewed and possibly reduced on compassionate or other grounds before the final confirmation of his sentence.

In addition to being excused on procedural or compassionate grounds, the convict might also gain release from execution through a general amnesty issued by the court. Amnesties did not constitute a procedural control on executions, nor did they provide any sort of constitutional check on judicial decisions, but they came often enough that convicts under noncapital sentences could entertain some hope of escaping their punishments.[50] There were many reasons why an emperor might offer an amnesty: to strengthen loyalty to the regime,[51] to diffuse popular anger or distress, or to curry heaven's favor in the face of disturbances in the natural world. Plunging winter temperatures or a summer heat wave also became occasions for emptying the jails, lest those who were not guilty of capital crimes die from cold or heat while in custody.[52] When Beijing reached record temperatures in June 1504, for instance, Emperor Hongzhi declared that he wished to spare prisoners death by heat prostration so that heaven might witness his benevolence and intervene to end the drought. After reviewing the cases, he decreed that sixty prisoners on death row should have their sentences commuted to penal servitude and another two be released after a beating. He also ordered cangues removed from the forty-eight prisoners condemned to wear them and freed all prisoners against whom no evidence had been found—these numbered a remarkable 575.[53]

Aside from these occasional or seasonal amnesties, emperors could also intervene on a case-by-case basis to lighten sentences. For instance, the Hongzhi emperor in 1498 commuted a death sentence passed on a Tibetan nobleman to penal servitude in a border garrison on the grounds that "foreigners were not worth disciplining too severely."[54] Presumably diplomatic concerns also shaped this intervention. The first Manchu emperor, Shunzhi (r. 1644–1661), chose to lighten the sentencing recommendations presented to him in the spring of 1658 by the president of the Board of Punishments. Twenty-five examination officials had been found guilty of taking bribes. The president recommended that the eight worst culprits be immediately decapitated, their property confiscated, and their parents, brothers, wives, and children exiled to the border. For the next eleven he suggested the same penalties minus the exile of family members; for the next five, immediate strangulation. The remaining official's sentence of strangulation could be delayed until after the mandatory review of capital sentences at the Autumn Assizes. Shunzhi had no doubt as to the guilt of the officials, and he agreed that official bribery and embezzlement should be treated according to Article 344 of the Qing Code on officials who accept bribes— although the maximum sentence in Article 344 is strangulation, not decapitation; perhaps the board president was trying to impress Shunzhi with his toughness. Still, the emperor decided to lighten all the sentences, declaring that "human life is extremely precious." The eight worst offenders were given forty blows with the heavy stick and banished to the border with no penalty on their families, a lighter sentence allowed by the article. The rest he let off with a severe warning. Politics may well have played a role here. Shunzhi was concerned not to alienate his ethnic Chinese officials, given the humiliation many Chinese felt serving a foreign ruler. He might also have worried, on a more practical level, that reliable examiners were in short supply. Aware that he was going against the Code, Shunzhi warned his judicial officials not to take this judgment as a sentencing precedent for similar cases. This was not a case of reducing the penalty for official corruption; it was to serve his regime-building needs.[55]

Murder, robbery, official malfeasance, and failure of military duty account for most of the death sentences in the Code: these were the crimes for which the judicial system put people to death in the late imperial period. However, a somewhat different profile of capital crimes emerges from a formal article entitled "The Ten Abominations" *(shi'e)* that appears near the beginning of every Code. These Ten Abominations, which like the Five Punishments did not vary from dynasty to dynasty, spelled out what the state considered the worst types of crime; perpetrators were not eligible for amnesty. The first three are crimes that threaten the dynasty, the emperor, and the state. The fourth, seventh, and eighth abominations list various crimes that go against the authority of parents, elders, and husbands. The fifth covers two crimes: murdering three members of the same family—the deed for which Wang Weiqin was dismembered—and dismembering a living person. The sixth is failing to protect the person of the emperor; the ninth, attacking or otherwise disrespecting officials, teachers, and deceased husbands; and the last, committing incest. Not all of these crimes, distasteful as they were to Chinese sensibilities, carried the sentence of death. Failure to observe mourning for a close relative, which comes up in both the seventh and ninth abominations, was not a capital crime.[56] Nonetheless, the Ten Abominations cover most of what Chinese law considered the worst offenses: not just the taking of life, which is punishable by death in most historical cultures, but also attacking the authority of the dynasty or the family, the survival of the male line, and the hierarchies of age and gender that threaded Chinese society together.

In 1497, the Ministry of Justice presented the Hongzhi emperor (r. 1488–1505) with a comprehensive list of capital crimes in the dynasty's law books. The Ministry included both crimes directly referenced in the Ming Code and crimes for which the death penalty could be imposed by analogy with those listed in the Code. The list enumerates 241 offenses, marginally more than the 233 capital offenses in the Tang Code but significantly less than the 293 crimes listed in the Song Code of 963 and the 282 in the 1397 Ming Code.[57] It is worth noting that the Mongols had reduced the number of capital crimes to 135. By way of comparison, English law in 1819 had 223 capital crimes on the books, up from the 160 that William Blackstone listed half a century earlier.[58]

The laws in the 1497 list are arranged in three sections: "execution without delay" (60 crimes), "execution after the Autumn Assizes" (170), and "capital crimes of lesser infraction" *(zafan sizui)* that were almost automatically commuted to exile or penal servitude (11). In each section, the crimes are grouped according to the three forms of the death penalty. Tormented execution is mandated for twelve crimes, the first of which are rebellion and Great Sedition. These are followed by 134 cases requiring decapitation and 99 calling for strangulation. The second-to-last crime on the 1497 list, one of the "capital crimes of minimized infraction," is opening a grave and exposing a corpse—which, as we will see, migrated into the Code as a lingchi penalty under the Qing if the corpse exposed was that of the exhumer's parents or grandparents. The last on the list is none other than the crime of receiving bribes, which nearly cost twenty-five examiners their lives in 1658.[59]

The continuing elaboration of codified law in the Qing dynasty seems to have encouraged the ongoing enlargement of the death penalty. The *Huidian shili* or *Collected Administrative Precedents and Substatutes* of the Qing dynasty lists a total of 3,987 offenses that were punishable under the Qing Code, of which 813 were capital offenses: 272 slated for strangulation after the Autumn Assizes, 218 for decapitation after the Assizes, 71 for immediate strangulation, 222 for immediate decapitation, and 30 for lingchi.[60]

Tormented Execution

Lingchi was the most extreme form of bodily punishment a Chinese tribunal could impose. It involved the methodical slitting and cutting apart of the body of the condemned in a stipulated number of cuts performed in a prescribed sequence.[61] The cutting began before the convict was dead, proceeded according to prescribed numbers, and continued well beyond the point of death until the body was fully dismembered. Lingchi commands most of our attention in this book in part because it is the extreme case in the Chinese culture of execution, and in part because of the notoriety it has achieved in the West. As we discuss in Chapter 3, the term *lingchi* and the particular practices associated with it came into the Chinese judicial system during the Liao and Song dynasties, probably from an Inner Asian origin, which is why there is no mention of it in the Tang Code. An anomaly when it was first adopted, in time the penalty found its way into what were called the "flesh penalties" *(rouxing)*. Lingchi was formally acknowledged in the Code for the first time in the Yuan dynasty, which appears to have reserved it for political offenses.[62] In the Ming, lingchi was regarded as standard punishment for the very worst political and moral offenses. It continued in force during the Qing, becoming for outside viewers in the nineteenth century the quintessential "Chinese torture."

Lingchi was put on the same legal footing as the Five Punishments briefly in the Yuan dynasty, when it replaced strangulation, but it was removed from all later codes. Because the Code is organized according to category of offense rather than type of punishment, it has no lingchi section. Rather, the lingchi statutes are scattered across the Code to punish particular crimes that could not readily be reduced to a single type. The nine articles in the Ming Code mandating lingchi as punishment are as follows (the translation is adapted from that of Jiang Yonglin; the numbers in square brackets are the article numbers in William Jones's translation of the Qing Code):[63]

Article 277 [254]. Plotting Rebellion or Great Sedition
In all cases of plotting rebellion or great sedition, those who jointly plot shall be sentenced to death by lingchi, without distinction of principals and accessories. Their paternal grandfathers, fathers, sons, sons' sons, brothers, those living in the same household whether or not their surnames differ, paternal uncles and brothers' sons whether or not they are in different family registers, and [male] relatives of sixteen years of age or older,

including those who are incapacitated or disabled, shall all be punished by decapitation.

Article 307 [284]. Plotting to Kill a Paternal Grandparent or Parent
In all cases of plotting to kill a paternal grandparent, parent, senior or older relative to whom one year's mourning is due, maternal grandparent, husband, or husband's paternal grandparent or parent, if action has already been taken, the offender shall in every case be punished by decapitation. If the killing has already been done, he shall in every case be sentenced to death by lingchi.

Article 308 [285]. Killing a Husband while Plotting with an Adulterous Lover
. . . If a wife or concubine, because of adultery, plots [with her adulterous lover] and kills her husband, she shall be sentenced to death by lingchi. The adulterous lover shall be punished by decapitation. If the adulterous lover himself kills the husband, the adulterous wife shall be punished by strangulation even if she is unaware of the circumstances.

Article 310 [287]. Killing Three Persons from One Household
In all cases of killing three persons from one household who have not committed capital crimes, or of dismembering others, the offender shall be sentenced to death by lingchi. His property shall be confiscated and given to the family of the decedents, and his wives and children shall be exiled to a distance of 1,000 kilometers. Accessories shall be punished by decapitation.

Article 311 [288]. Extracting Vitality by Dismembering a Living Person
In all cases of extracting vitality by dismembering a living person, the offender shall be sentenced to death by lingchi. His property shall be confiscated and given to the family of the decedent, and his wife, children, and those living in the same household shall all be punished by life exile to a distance of 1,000 kilometers. Accessories shall be punished by decapitation.

Article 337 [314]. A Slave Striking a Household Head
In all cases in which a slave strikes his household head, he shall be punished by decapitation. If he kills him, he shall be sentenced to death by lingchi. If he accidentally kills him, he shall be punished by strangulation.

Article 338 [315]. A Wife or Concubine Striking Her Husband
In all cases in which a wife strikes her husband, she shall be punished by 100 strokes of the heavy stick. . . . If she causes his death, she shall be punished by decapitation. If she deliberately kills her husband, she shall be sentenced to death by lingchi.

Article 341 [318]. Striking a Superior or Elder Relative of the Second Degree of Mourning

If a younger brother or sister strikes an elder brother or sister, that person shall be punished by 90 strokes of the heavy stick and penal servitude for two and a half years. . . . If someone strikes his father's brothers or their wives, his father's sisters or his maternal grandparents, the penalty shall be increased by one degree. If the assailant kills or injures accidentally, in each case the penalty shall be reduced two degrees from that for killing or injuring. If deliberately, then in every case he shall be sentenced to death by lingchi.

Article 342 [319]. Striking a Paternal Grandparent or Parent

In all cases in which a son or son's son strikes his paternal grandparent or parent, or in which a wife or concubine strikes her husband's paternal grandparent or parent, he or she shall be punished by decapitation. If he or she causes their death, that person shall in every case be sentenced to death by lingchi. If the death is accidental, that person shall in every case be punished by 100 strokes of the heavy stick and exiled for life to a distance of 1,500 kilometers.

These are the only articles in the Ming Code that stipulate the use of lingchi. Perusing this list, it is difficult to see what the crimes punishable by lingchi have in common. One (Article 277) protects the dynasty against sedition, another (Article 311) underscores a deep-seated cultural horror at the idea of using human corpses for magical or medicinal purposes, and a third (Article 310) targets feuding between families. The rest have to do with extreme domestic violence, more particularly the murder of elders or male spouses within families. None is new to the Ming, in the sense that all appear, directly or by analogy, among the Ten Abominations. Three of the articles police the first, second, and fifth abominations. The other six (four directly and two indirectly) protect superiors against their kin inferiors as laid out in the fourth abomination; the two indirectly related articles are Article 308, which extends the protection to husbands against their adulterous wives, and Article 337, which protects masters against their slaves.[64]

The list of capital crimes the Ministry of Justice submitted to the Hongzhi emperor in 1497 goes a step further by adding hired laborers to the group of those whose crimes deserve the severest punishment for being committed within the household. Reasoning that the duty a hired laborer owes his master is analogous to the duty a son owes his father or a grandson his grandfather, the 1497 list mandates tormented execution for the hired laborer who intentionally kills his employer, his employer's parents or grandparents, or his employer's wife's parents or grandparents.[65] In 1585, a similar enlargement of criminal liability extended these laws to include adopted sons and their wives.[66] In fact, as discussed in Chapter 4, the actual use of lingchi in early Ming reign-periods went well beyond these crimes into the political realm, but the theme of offense against the authorities to whom one owes allegiance, whether the head of the household or the head of the state, runs through all its uses.

The Qing dynasty increased the number of lingchi statutes, mostly between the mid-eighteenth century and the early nineteenth, largely in response to memorials from gubernatorial officials regarding difficult cases. The new provisions for lingchi penalties follow, according to their numbering in the Qing Code (the numbers in square brackets are the corresponding article numbers in the Ming Code, though in some cases the Ming article did not mandate the penalty of lingchi):[67]

Article 26 [25]. Sentencing on the Basis of the Punishment for the More Serious Crime When Two Crimes Are Discovered Together
Substatute 3. A criminal who commits two crimes both of which are liable for death by lingchi will be inflicted with additional cuts during the execution.[68]

Article 267 [290]. Rescuing Prisoners by Force
Substatute 1. If people in the course of banding together to rescue jailed criminals resist and kill officials or officers, the principals and the accessories in the killing will all be put to death by lingchi on the basis of Plotting Rebellion or Great Sedition (Article 254) and their relatives prosecuted accordingly. Accomplices who cause injuries will all be liable to decapitation with exposure of the head; the rest of the accompanying offenders will all be sentenced to immediate decapitation. . . . If no one is injured, the chief perpetrator who devised the scheme to raid the prison will be sentenced to immediate decapitation and the accomplices to decapitation after the Assizes, their case to be included in the category "circumstances deserving of capital punishment."[69]

Article 276 [299]. Uncovering Graves
Substatute 2. Anyone who starts digging to uncover a grandparent's or parent's grave but without exposing the coffin will be liable to immediate

strangulation, without distinction of principal and accessory. Should he open the coffin and uncover the corpse and scatter the remains, he will in every case be punished by lingchi. If coffins have been opened and corpses uncovered in three different graves, in addition to the sentence of lingchi for the chief perpetrator, his sons will be deported to Yili and put to labor service.[70]

Article 282 [305]. Plotting to Kill Others
Substatute 9. Anyone who for reasons of greed commits premeditated murder against a direct or indirect relative to whom he owes respect and obedience will be sentenced to lingchi or immediate decapitation on the basis of his degree of mourning. In all cases the head will be exposed.[71]

Article 284 [307]. Plotting to Kill a Paternal Grandparent or Parent
Substatute 6. The sentence provided by law for committing the crime of plotting to kill an elder relative within the fifth degree of mourning is death by lingchi for the principals. Accessories who actively take part will be sentenced to deferred strangulation [pending review at the next Autumn Assizes], for which an imperial rescript to execute the sentence must be asked for; those who do not take part will be sentenced according to the [main] statute.[72]

Article 285 [308]. Killing a Husband in Conspiracy with an Adulterous Lover
Substatute 14. An adulterous concubine who agrees with her lover to plot to kill [her master's] wife will be put to death by lingchi in accordance with the section [of Article 284] on plotting to kill the head of the household. If the plot results in injuries but not death, or even if it is initiated without causing injuries, the sentence is immediate decapitation by analogy with a slave who plots to kill the head of his household.[73]

Substatute 16. When close relatives have illicit intercourse, the sentence is limited to penal servitude plus beating with the heavy stick. The Code provides the deferred death penalty [pending the next Assizes]. If the lover kills the husband or agrees with the wife [to kill the husband], the wife will be sentenced according to this article [which mandates death by lingchi] and the lover to immediate decapitation.[74]

Article 286 [309]. Plotting to Kill the Parent of a Deceased Husband
A remarried wife or concubine who plots to kill a paternal grandparent or parent of her deceased husband shall be punished according to the sentence for plotting to kill her current parents-in-law [Article 284, which mandates death by lingchi].[75]

Article 287 [310]. Killing Three Persons from One Household
Paragraph 1. In all cases of killing three persons from one household who have not committed capital crimes, or of dismembering others, should the principal die in prison, his property shall be confiscated and given to the family of the decedents, his body lacerated and cut into pieces, and his head exposed to the public.[76]

Article 299 [322]. Using Coercion to Cause Others to Die
Substatute 19. Anyone who attempts to rape a senior family member within a mourning relationship closer than the fifth degree, or the concubine of such a member, and who, even though they do not succeed, drives the woman to die [by suicide] will be sentenced to lingchi or immediate decapitation depending on the mourning relationship, with exposure of the head. Attempted rape of an affinal family member will be spared exposure of the head.[77]

Article 311 [334]. Striking a Teacher from Whom One Receives an Education
Substatute 1. In all cases when someone plots to beat to death or injure the master from whom he has received his education, if he is a disciple of a Confucian teacher, he will be sentenced by analogy to Article 284 in the case of a relative to whom he owes one year of mourning [lingchi if the killing is deliberate]; if of a Buddhist monk, Daoist priest, Tibetan lama, nun, or craft master, he will be sentenced by analogy to the same article in the case of a relative within the fifth degree of mourning [death by strangulation or decapitation] . . . [78]

Article 319 [342]. Striking a Paternal Grandparent or Parent
Substatute 7. When a grandson or son strikes a grandparent or parent, once an investigation has determined the severity of the injury, a memorial must be submitted asking for immediate decapitation. If the injury to the grandparent or parent causes death, the offender will have his corpse broken and exposed to the public.[79]

These additions to the lingchi laws cannot be regarded as a major shift in the use of this penalty, yet they do suggest change within Qing law. The changes to Articles 26 and 287 are merely procedural adjustments to deal with unforeseen eventualities. Article 26, which holds that a person convicted of two crimes shall bear the punishment for the heavier, provides a solution for the difficulty that arises in a case in which someone is convicted of two crimes that both deserve lingchi: administer more cuts. To undergo one lingchi sentence for two lingchi crimes seems to have been regarded as tantamount to letting the criminal off for one of them.

The other procedural clarification, inserted into Article 287, explains what to do should a lingchi criminal die in prison before execution. Should his corpse simply be disposed of? Cutting the surface of the body would seem to have lost its purpose when the victim was dead and could not feel the punishment, but that was not the entire purpose of lingchi, as we will argue in later chapters. His corpse could still be hacked up and put on public display, and this is exactly what the newly inserted clause directed. The substatutes attached to Articles 282, 284, 285, and 319 in the Qing Code simply plugged loopholes in already existing lingchi laws having to do with murders within families and between marriage partners when the offense was against the superior party.

Setting these six changes aside, there are four substatutes that extend death by lingchi to crimes that had previously entailed only decapitation: killing officials in the course of attempting to spring prisoners from jail (Article 267), exposing the buried corpses of parents or grandparents (Article 276), causing a female relative to commit suicide by attempting rape (Article 299), and murdering one's teacher or craft master (Article 311). The rape-suicide clause can plausibly be regarded as another extension of lingchi into the intrafamily realm. That leaves jailbreaking, exhumation, and the killing of one's teacher as the three significant additions the Qing made to the capital statutes imposing lingchi. Of these, the injunction against exposing the corpse of a parent or grandparent comes closest to the original literal import of lingchi, a matter we return to Chapter 3.

The Execution of Capital Statutes

Written laws are an essential source for reconstructing punishment practices in the past, but they cannot reveal all aspects of how punishments were actually administered. Other types of sources are needed to allow us to get past the formal judicial legislation and begin to assess the place and social impact of execution in history. Compared to the literary and pictorial sources available for the study of punishment in Europe, Chinese sources are formulaic and few, particularly in the case of lingchi. Vignettes of executions occasionally appear in the official dynastic histories, but the reports there of extreme punishments carried out on, or by, infamously evil figures are given in the service of biography and moral edification, not of legal understanding.[80]

Even more surprising is the virtual silence surrounding cruel punishments in the copious writings on judicial administration in the imperial period.[81] Privately produced handbooks to guide magistrates in their conduct in office were published in the hundreds during the Ming and Qing dynasties, yet this greater corpus of information on the operation of justice reveals almost nothing of how executions were actually conducted. Huang Liuhong in his widely popular 1699 handbook for magistrates, *The Complete Book concerning Happiness and Benevolence,* provides detailed notes on the steps a magistrate was to follow in running a judicial proceeding, from the capture of a suspect through his investigation and the taking of evidence against him to the final stages of sentencing, jailing, and transferral to the execution ground. Huang even includes a long section explaining what implements of torture penal officers can employ, how they differ, and how they should be used. Yet he says nothing as to how an execution should be carried out. He gives no advice to the prospective magistrate about how to conduct himself when overseeing one; he does not even mention lingchi as one of the sentences that the magistrate could pronounce.[82] Scholars using this sort of source to research the history of local administration are obliged to be similarly prescriptive rather than descriptive when writing about executions.[83] Studies done on this basis provide a general idea of the penal web in which criminals were captured and condemned and the procedures that should be followed to get the correct result, yet they give little sense of actual practice.[84] Punishments are treated variously as generic, collective, or equivalent to the crimes committed, with little attention paid to how they were carried out.[85]

As a general rule, fictional sources hardly compensate the historian for the gaps in the administrative handbooks. In this case, one might have thought they could, given that the plot of many a Ming novel turns on an interrogation, during which a magistrate forces out a hidden truth and then concludes the story by punishing the evildoers. The problem is not the fictionality of these narratives but their lack of close description: they simply do not give the torturers and executioners substantial roles. They occasionally appear in the woodblock illustrations of popular Ming novels. If illustrators show them, it is only in scenes in which the execution is about to take place, not during or after the event (Figure 9). A rare exception is a

Figure 9. Two executioners about to perform a decapitation. From a 1630s edition of Luo Guanzhong, *Sanguo zhi yanyi* (Romance of the Three Kingdoms).

Figure 10. A lingchi execution as depicted in late Ming fiction. From a 1630s edition of the novel *Zhongyi shuihu quanzhuan* (Complete account of the loyal and the righteous of the water margin).

lingchi execution that appears in an illustrated Ming edition of the popular novel *Water Margin* (Figure 10). The event in the novel that the woodblock illustrates—the execution of the bandit leader Wang Qing—makes no reference to his dying by lingchi, though his rebellion against the Song imperial house would have justified it. It seems that the artist, Liu Junyu, a prominent illustrator from the Nanjing region, decided to insert this image into the story without worrying about the fact that the novel makes no mention of Wang being subjected to lingchi.[86] Given the absence of a genre of such representations, plus the unlikelihood that any other illustrated edition of this novel would have shown Wang Qing's execution in this fashion, we have to assume that Liu produced the image from real life. We might also propose that Liu chose to engrave this image in order to catch the attention of bookstore browsers.

Marketplaces were traditionally used as temporary execution grounds; indeed, the standard term for "public execution" is "abandoned in the marketplace" (*qi shi* or *qi yu shi*).[87] Because of the rarity of reports of executions in local sources,[88] most urban historians of imperial China are unable to identify the marketplace in which executions were carried out in the cities they study or are even unaware that this might be a fact worth discovering.[89] In the case of Beijing, we know that executions were performed at Vegetable Market intersection (Caishikou) in the Chinese city, but little else: not how frequently executions were conducted there, nor what role these events played in urban life.[90] As for the executioners, we do not know the name of a single one.[91] One might suppose that the routine of bureaucratic administration would have generated detailed personnel and financial records relating to executioners, yet we have turned up only the sketchiest fragments in two county sources. A published budget that a county magistrate in Beijing compiled in 1590 contains a list of twelve penal instruments, including finger and ankle presses, whose purchase he authorized.[92] The other passing reference, this time to execution rather than torture, appears in a nineteenth-century inventory of yamen purchases in an archive of a county on Taiwan: four red and green suits of clothes for the county executioners plus four decapitation swords.[93] That we have been able to find only these two records seems incommensurate with the known incidence of a penal function that occupied many people and concerned many more in every county in the realm.

This occlusion in Chinese sources is glaring when set against what is recorded of executions and executioners in Europe. The early tales of Jack

Ketch, the name by which the London hangman was popularly known, may be difficult to credit, but we have considerable information about his nineteenth-century successors.[94] In France, the Sanson dynasty of Parisian executioners, which lasted from the reign of Louis XIV in the seventeenth century down to the mid-nineteenth, has received more attention than Chinese penal practices of all periods in all languages. European executions were minutely described, illustrated, and discussed by contemporaries in relation to moral, philosophical, aesthetic, and political issues. Historians of Europe have collected volumes of primary source materials, enabling them to argue that the appearance of professional executioners and the display of public executions in reserved areas were landmarks in the making of the nation-state in early modern Europe. Chinese studies are impoverished by comparison.[95] Faced with a nearly blank record, China historians have cast about for analogies elsewhere in Asia. For instance, one result of using Asian analogies has been to posit infamy as a feature of the executioner's profession. While it is intuitively plausible that the Chinese executioner was a despised figure, no actual Chinese evidence has been brought forward to prove the point.[96]

Given this absence, China historians must turn to the only substantial records of executions that survive, those in the writings of European visitors. A. B. Freeman-Mitford, a British official in Beijing in the 1860s, attended an execution at Vegetable Market with two other members of the British legation in mid-December 1865. He first describes a small altar that the soldiers attending the executioner and his assistant set up to one side of the booth temporarily erected for officials from the Board of Punishments who attended the event: "In front of the altar a small brick stove had been built, over which was a caldron of boiling water, like a huge barber's pot, to warm the swords." There are five swords: Great Lord, Second Lord, Third Lord, Fourth Lord, and Fifth Lord. These are kept in the executioner's house in a tower on the Beijing city wall. According to Freeman-Mitford's Chinese teacher, these swords "are often heard at night to sing gruesome songs of their past feats. When they are wanted their Lordships are 'requested' to come out." The chief executioner, who is treated with deference by the soldiers guarding the execution, Freeman-Mitford describes as "a short, thick-set, but not ill-looking man, with that curious, anxious, *waiting* expression on his face that a man wears with serious work before him." He appears in a fur coat, which he then takes off and replaces with a yellow leather apron stained in blood. The executioner does not address his victim before putting him to death, unless he is a ranking official, in which case he says, "I pray that your Excellency may fly to Heaven." His work completed, he shouts, "The person has been killed."

Freeman-Mitford does not register huge distress at the experience. In fact he is able to conclude: "I was glad to see that the execution was conducted far more mercifully than one is led to suppose by certain writers," especially those who have made much of the "disgraceful slow death" of lingchi. To support his contention that tormented execution was not administered as atrociously as foreign fantasy claimed, he mentions hearing from an Englishman who witnessed a lingchi execution "that the criminal he saw so executed was put out of his misery at once, and that the mutilation took place *after* death and not before."[97] This is a slim bit of evidence, but from such reports it is possible to reconstruct at least the last years of the history of tormented execution.

Having outlined some of the interpretive problems entailed by studying Chinese punishments in the preceding chapter, and having surveyed the statutes governing punishment and the curious reticence in reporting about the performance of executions in this chapter, we turn in the next three to the challenge of placing lingchi within the criminal administration of imperial China, within the political imagination that employed the penalty as a bulwark of state control, and within the religious imagination of the people whom the state chose to discipline and punish in this way.

CHAPTER 3

The Origins of Lingchi
and Problems of
Its Legitimacy

By the end of the nineteenth century, the Chinese form of execution known as lingchi had become for Europeans the *supplice chinois,* the archetype of a supposed Chinese penchant for "refined cruelty." This notion was the product of a process of intercultural communication that arose from actual penal practices in China and dead-ended in the European fin de siècle taste for sensation, entertainment, and shock. European travel writers in China obliged this taste by reporting on scenes of "Chinese horrors" they claimed to have witnessed. Lingchi, the most revolting horror of all, became an icon of the real China.

"Nobody can claim to have an adequate and accurate appreciation of the Chinese character who has not witnessed a Chinese execution," asserts Henry Norman in *The Peoples and Politics of the Far East* (1895).[1] He then thrills his shocked audience: "I have looked upon men being cruelly tortured." "I have stood in the shambles where human beings are slaughtered like pigs; my boots have dripped with the blood of my fellow-creatures;—repulsive as all this is, it is one of the most significant and instructive aspects of the real China, as opposed to the China of native professions and foreign imagination, and therefore it must be frankly described." As though words were not enough, Norman includes a photograph of a truncated body lying in a street, with the caption "China: 'Death by the Thousand Cuts'" (Figure 11). He boasts that "the photograph here produced is no doubt the only one ever taken." Caught in the grip of such sensationalism, China lost any reality as a legal culture. The scene that Norman described was real, as was the scene that an acquaintance photographed, and yet his China was as much a place in the European imagination as a nation in Asia.

Norman's may well have been the only photograph of a lingchi at the time he published, but more would be taken in the following decade. Their appearance in books and on postcards—journalistic fact blending with sadistic fantasy and political rhetoric—would haunt the Western iconosphere for the next century. The visual abruptness of such photographs has blocked viewers ever since from seeing that China—even under the Qing, when lingchi was still performed—had a coherent, rational legal culture and history in which the practice of dismemberment was recurringly matched by an intellectual tradition that challenged its legitimacy.

Chinese jurists of the imperial era debated whether lingchi was even of Chinese origin, which was an oblique way of casting doubt on the place it assumed in Chinese penal practice. They doubted the process through which what had been an exceptional penalty came to be regularized and codified. They also questioned the morality of punishing people with a penalty that, were it conducted privately, would entail the very same punishment for the perpetrator. The history of lingchi we reconstruct in this chapter is thus simultaneously the history of challenges to its legitimacy.

How ancient was the practice of lingchi? Did it date to a remote past, or was it a more recent penal innovation introduced by the "barbarian" dynasties that from time to time occupied China? Both readings are plausible, but the answer depends on whether we argue from actual practice or codified law. If, as some scholars have done, we reduce lingchi to quartering, slicing, or hacking a body to pieces—gruesome acts that are widely attested in the official histories of early reigns—then it is a punishment whose roots go deep into China's past.[2] But is "punishment" the best way to characterize what was going on when Sovereign X had Minister Y hacked to pieces and pickled in a jar, or King A ordered his disloyal Minister B's sons sliced and served to B at a banquet? However many sensational incidents of human butchery can be fished out of early Chinese records, these do not add up to a conclusive demonstration that such penalties were characteristic of Chinese government or that dismemberment was a fully legal punishment. Perhaps the best argument against such hasty conclusions is the fact that Chinese historiography honored regimes that avoided using cruel punishments as "good" dynasties and condemned rulers who committed exorbitant cruelties as "bad"—and not because clemency was a virtue in itself, but because good government led the people away from crime. Bursts of cruelty, such as the extensive use of lingchi in the first reign of the Ming dynasty, which is our focus in the next chapter, may better be regarded as exceptional episodes than as evidence of a timeless, inherent cultural tolerance for cruelty, especially in ancient times before the penalty subsequently

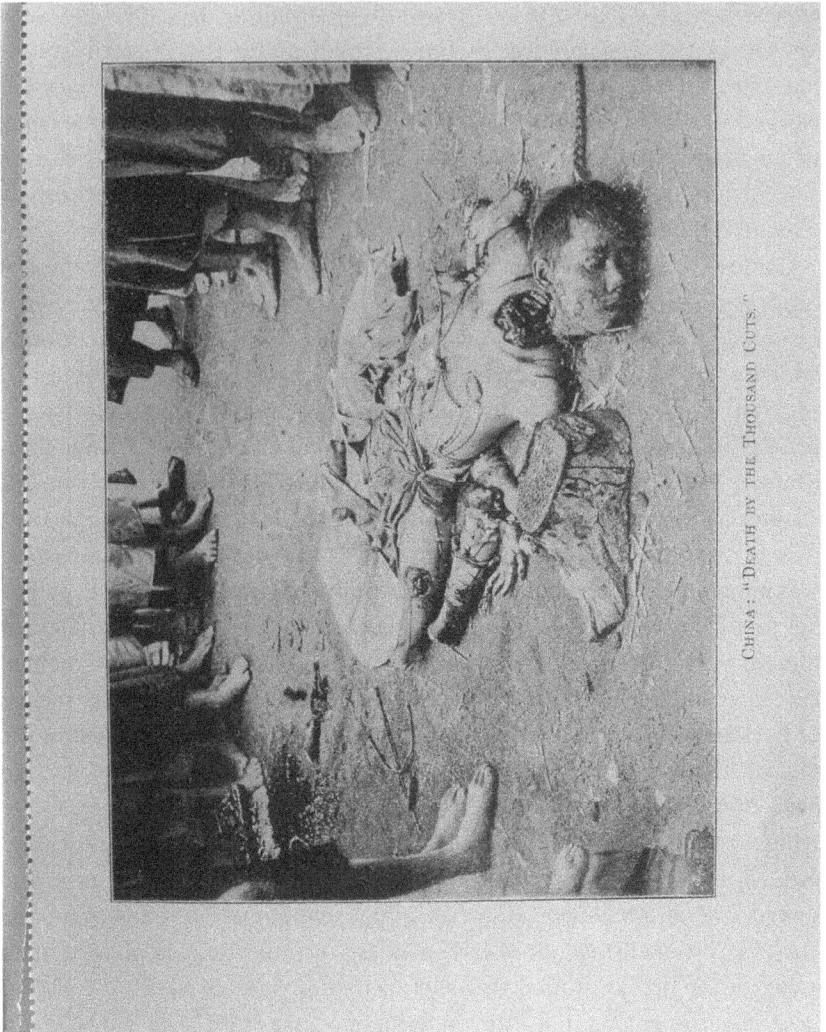

CHINA: "DEATH BY THE THOUSAND CUTS."

Figure 11. *China: "Death by the Thousand Cuts,"* as reproduced in Henry Norman, *The Peoples and Politics of the Far East* (1895). A message at the bottom of Norman's page ran: "This page is perforated in order that it may be detached, without mutilating the volume, by any reader who prefers not to retain permanently so unpleasant an illustration of the condition of contemporary China."

known as lingchi was codified.[3] The extreme cases were incidental to the development of Chinese law.

More illuminating are the brief allusions to the use of punishments to deter rebels. The dismembering or quartering of a rebel chief was a special measure, restricted in time and space and not permitted to stand as a precedent beyond the emergency during which it was invoked. Such practices were marked by particular terms, such as *zhe, luan,* or *gua,* or combinations of these, most frequently *luangua.* These episodes form a kind of continuum that persists beyond the insertion of lingchi as a penalty into the Chinese legal code. Accordingly, in our view the term *lingchi* should be treated as a separate case and made to represent only those instances of quartering that were executed under this legal label. The issue is not whether Chinese generals were unique in quartering their enemies; European armies treated their enemies in just the same fashion, as Goya reminds us with his gloomy scenes of lingchi–like executions committed by Napoleonic troops against Spanish patriots. The problem we want to address is how special measures adopted in emergency situations found their way into the legislation of ordinary times, apart from any individual despot's whim or general's excess. The reasons must be sought within the dynamics of the legal system. Rather than bring to light a litany of bizarre practices, a proper history of this particular "cruel punishment" needs to be pursued in terms of its place within the history of Chinese law.

Lingchi as a Semantic Enigma

Late Qing legal scholars regarded the term *lingchi* as obscure in both meaning and origin. The brilliant scholar Qian Daxin (1728–1804), an outstanding representative of the evidential research *(kaozheng)* movement, opens his influential essay entitled "Lingchi" with the statement: "Recently, [codified] laws have included the penalty of dismemberment. This is an innovation of the Yuan and Ming dynasties, but the origin of the term is unknown."[4] Shen Jiaben, who spearheaded China's legal reform at the end of the Qing dynasty, understood China's traditional legal system as based on the principle, intrinsic to benevolent government, that punishments had to be clearly named, precisely applied, and uniformly valid throughout the system.[5] Obscurity in origin and uncertainty in meaning, which Qian Daxin ascribed to lingchi, bespoke the illegitimacy of a punishment. Such shortcomings were sufficient grounds for him to advocate the abolition of "cruel punishments" such as lingchi and their substitution by the penalties used by European states.

In modern Chinese, the characters that make up the term *lingchi* have no self-evident meaning. The first character, *ling*, means "ice" when written with radical no. 15, which is common to characters with meanings connected to ice. The second character, *chi*, means "delay" or "lateness." From these elements comes the transferred notion of lingchi as "lingering death," or death that comes on as slowly as ice forms. However, this common idea of lingchi as the delaying of death, conveyed and enriched by countless Western and some recent Chinese authors, is not adequately sustained by the dubious etymological claims put forward to support it.[6] We need to examine the etymology of the term more carefully.

In its classical form, the first character, *ling*, was written with a different radical, not "ice" but "hillock" or "mound."[7] Written this way, *ling* can mean "tumulus" or "burial mound." The second character, *chi*, in this case is not "lateness" but has to do with sudden "leveling" or progressive "erosion."[8] The etymological meaning of the phrase is thus "the leveling or erosion of a hillock." In its earliest usage, this phrase was a metaphor for the gradual decay of an institution. The locus classicus of this figured sense appears in the writings of the fourth-century B.C. philosopher Xun Kuang (Xunzi): "A sheer obstacle only three feet high cannot be surmounted even by an empty carriage, whereas a hill a hundred rods high can be surmounted even by a heavily loaded one. Why is that? It is because of the slow ascent [*lingchi*]. People cannot climb a wall several rods high, but a mountain a hundred rods high small boys will play on as though it were flat, and the reason for this is its gentle ascent [*lingchi*]." Xun Kuang then gives the moral of this parable: "Now the slow erosion [*lingchi*] in the present generation has certainly been going on a long time, and yet is it enough to cause the people to be unable to surmount it?"[9]

How does this idea of "slow ascent" link to the "slow death" by dismemberment by which lingchi became known? No less an authority in Chinese law than Shen Jiaben, who helped to legislate its abolition, interprets this passage thus: "The meaning of *lingchi* is that the hill rises gradually, just as, when killing a man, the wish is that his death be slow and gradual. This is how the language of 'step by step' or 'gradual' was transferred" to the term for gradual execution.[10] A careful reading of Xun's passage, however, indicates that the term carries a more precise meaning than "gradual." The sentences preceding the quoted passage are a reflection on institutions and penal policies, in which Xun recalls the ideal of Confucian government that should education prevail over punishments, and then recalls that when educations falls into abeyance, punishments are insufficient to keep the people on the straight and narrow. "Now in the present generation," Xun continues, "this is no longer so. So chaotic is the instruction and so abundant are the punishments, that the people are led astray and bewildered and they fall into error for which they are then to be punished. On account of this, although punishments are frequently and abundantly applied, evil is not overcome." From here the text proceeds to the passage above ("A sheer obstacle only three feet high . . ."). The sequence of ideas that leads to Xun's comment about lingchi shows that, for him, the concern with "slow erosion" is connected to a broader field of meaning than mere gradualness. The contrast between the "slow ascent" and the "sheer obstacle" highlights the failure of rulers to use institutions that control people principally through education and only secondarily through moderate punishments—hence the process of gradual decay leading to the present calamitous situation. The word *lingchi* thus expresses this whole process of institutional failure that has compromised the dialectic link between morality and punishments. But this explanation remains at the level of discourse. In Xun's time the term had no direct connection with any specific punishment, and certainly none with dismemberment. Even so, a certain spirit of moral decay is present in early occurrences of the term.

"Tumulus erosion" continued to mean "institutional decay" until the tenth century, when two significant changes occurred. First, the "tumulus" radical in the character *ling* was replaced by the "ice" radical.[11] The second change was the emergence of a penal meaning. The two meanings—the figurative erosion of a tumulus and the penal notion of dismemberment—can be attested simultaneously in the official histories of the Liao and Song dynasties. By the Yuan period, the first meaning falls into abeyance and the second stands alone, both in the dynastic histories and in codified law. Thus, during a relatively brief time span of a century (roughly, the eleventh), the meaning of the word shifted dramatically, producing the new penal expression, *lingchi chusi,* "to put to death by cutting / dismemberment."

How could this transformation have happened? Consider first what happened during the preceding century, the tenth. This is when the decisive shift from the old meaning to the new took place, during the Liao dynasty (907–1125). The Liao was a Khitan dynasty, which coexisted for almost two centuries with the Song and attained recognition as a legitimate dynasty after defeating the Song in the north. The appearance of the newly framed term *lingchi* using Chinese characters of ambiguous meaning strongly suggests that the term was used to approximate the pronunciation of a Khitan expression meaning something like "dismemberment."[12] Our knowledge of ancient steppe languages is so sketchy, and the Chinese equivalents so uniformly unfaithful, that this explication may never find definitive linguistic evidence to support it, but it is not an unreasonable hypothesis.[13]

As the first of a series of non-Han dynasties that dominated first North China and then all of China through the second millennium of imperial rule, the Khitans mark the beginning of a powerful tradition of Inner Asian rule in China (the Liao was followed by the Jin dynasty of the Jurchens, the Yuan dynasty of the Mongols, and the Qing dynasty of the Manchus). The growing steppe influence on China is understood as having extended to Chinese law, which became harsher under their tutelage.[14] As one Song politician declared in 1062, "The laws of the barbarians are extremely harsh. If a crime is punishable by death, they will certainly slaughter and brutally massacre [the offender]. Their ruler has once stated, 'The Khitans are wild animals. They cannot be ruled with written laws like the Chinese.'"[15] The likelihood that lingchi was of Khitan origin was picked up on by late Qing legal reformers, who argued that only a non-Han Chinese dynasty could devise such an inhumane way to execute someone.[16] Given that the Mongols codified lingchi into law during the Yuan dynasty, late imperial legal scholars were even more inclined to see the penalty as an intrusion of steppe methods into Chinese civilization.[17] Despite the prejudicial bias against "barbarians" inherent in such a view, it appears that Khitan rulers did punish heavily and that the penal meaning of the term *lingchi* did emerge during this period.

No complete version of the Liao Code of 1036 has survived to help us fully analyze the Liao legal system, but surviving excerpts, as well as the "Treatise on Punishments" in the official dynastic history, provide some insights.[18] Dismemberment makes its first appearance as a legally codified punishment in the Liao Code. It is listed in an early passage in the "Treatise on Punishments" along with the two standard death penalties, beheading and strangulation, as the three "forms of execution" under the Liao dynasty.[19] The same treatise includes an account of the evolution of punishment in the early Liao from steppe practices to a codified law. Before 913, during the early years of the founder's reign, capital punishment came in many forms:

Imperial princes who joined the rebels were not strangled by the huntsmen, but were killed by being thrown from a cliff. Those who committed incest and treason were pulled to pieces by five chariots. Those who turned against their parents were punished in the same way. Those who offended against superiors by slander and vilification were killed by having a hot iron awl thrust into their mouths. Accomplices were punished by beatings in accordance with the seriousness of the crime. Beatings were of two degrees: the heaviest was of five hundred lashes and the lightest of three hundred lashes. There were also the punishments of exposure of the head after decapitation *(xiao)*, hacking into pieces *(zhe)*, burial alive *(shengyi)*, shooting by devil arrows *(she guijian)*, being hurled from catapults *(paozhi)*, and dismemberment *(zhijie)*. These belonged to the most severe punishments. They were a precaution against rebellion by the people.[20]

The punishment of lingchi, or at least a punishment bearing that name, is not attested at this stage. Dismemberment is included, but it is named using a more technical term (*zhijie* "the severing of the limbs") and not in conjunction with the knife cutting that came to characterize lingchi, which is in any case referred to in Liao sources as *luangua*, not *lingchi*.[21] The implication of the treatise is that the mature Liao abandoned these steppe practices for the provisions of Chinese-style law, though most of these dramatic forms of execution continued in use after this early period, to judge from the stories of rebellion preserved elsewhere in the dynastic history.[22] Curiously, lingchi is not named in such stories. Lingchi is named as the penalty for treason by members of the imperial clan, but the application of the punishment, its performance, and even its judicial or political nature are unclear.[23]

Where lingchi is mentioned in Liao sources, it is consistently recorded within a fuller phrase, "to lingchi to death" *(lingchi er si)*, a formula that was later changed to "to put to death by lingchi" *(lingchi chusi)*.[24] This remained the standard phrasing for lingchi until the penalty was abolished in 1905. The inertia peculiar to codification might explain the retention of the formula "to put to death" long after *lingchi* had become the unambiguous term for dismemberment, but we can ask why this precision was originally thought necessary. Was death a less obvious consequence of dismemberment than of, say, decapitation or strangulation? Or might we turn this question another way and consider the proposal that under the Liao, and maybe even under the Song, lingchi was not necessarily a death penalty in itself, but rather signified a general conception of penalty. Perhaps it was closer to a term like *qishi*, "to be abandoned in the marketplace." Although *qishi* could mean a particular punishment—namely, to be torn apart by a crowd[25]—it became a general appellation for "public execution," especially when combined with other penal terms, such as "dismembered in the marketplace" *(zhe yu shi)*[26] or "pulled apart by carts in the marketplace" *(huanlie yu shi)*.[27] Could *lingchi er si* have meant something like "to put to death under lingchi conditions," that is, under circumstances permeated by a particular spirit of execution?

If so, what might that spirit be? One possibility is that the term *lingchi* was chosen consciously to link back to the classical meaning of "institutional decay"; that is, that this was a punishment invoked in the face of the decay of fundamental norms and institutions. There is also a linguistic connection with an ancient penalty famously imposed to collectively incriminate and execute a culprit's entire family, known as Extermination of the Three Clans *(yi sanzu)*. The meaning of the term "three clans" has changed over time, at times referring to the "three generations" of father, son, and grandson, at other times the "three relatives": agnatic (through the father), collateral (through the mother), and affinal (through the wife).[28] The penalty was intermittently invoked to execute a criminal's relatives, though it could also take the form of castrating male relatives and enslaving female. Only under the Qin dynasty, which unified China in 221 B.C., did it enter codified law.[29] In practice, however, the law was not always applied: deportation was regularly substituted for the death penalty, and the number of people drawn into a conviction could be far fewer than the rule prescribed.[30] When lingchi entered the penal realm a dozen centuries after the Qin, these preexisting rules of collective incrimination may have been amalgamated with the new penalty, for the language of the two terms preserves the trace of a connection between them. The character *yi*, meaning "extermination," can be found in the expression *lingyi*, an exact synonym of *lingchi* (in which *yi* has the same meaning as *chi*), which was also used to refer to institutional decay.[31] This usage implies a linguistic equivalence between "leveling the tumulus" and "exterminating the three clans," reinforcing the idea of lingchi as a penalty that takes aim not just at the culprit but also at his family's ritual community of deceased ancestors ("tumulus") or at the corporate body of living family members ("three clans").

References in the early dynastic histories appear to link *lingchi* when the term still expressed the spirit of institutional decay to problems of legal standards, though not to penal consequences. Consider, for instance, this memorial by Wang Jia, a prominent scholar-official of the Han dynasty:

> Revolt against hierarchy [in family or state] is just like the cosmic disorder of *yin* and *yang* and lèse-majesté, a major danger for the empire. If officials are biased instead of being straightforward, if the populace falls into error without being corrected, if evil reaches the sovereign while the sovereign does not rely on legal standards *(fadu)*, the order of subordination between upper and lower [ranks] collapses. King Wu personally engaged in the Way, and his benevolence entailed prosperity. But thereafter, arbitrariness and whim ran free and legal standards collapsed *(fadu lingchi)*, to the extent that ministers killed their sovereigns and sons their fathers. There is no tighter relationship than that between father and son, yet the breaking of ritual respect can result in attempts on [the father's] life; how much more so between subjects [and sovereign] who do not bear the same surname.[32]

This invocation of revolt, patricide, and regicide in the context of *lingchi* as the collapse of legal institutions may point to the link that was later formed, in reverse, between these symptoms of institutional collapse and the punishment that came to be used to cure them. The replacement of the metaphorical meaning of "tumulus erosion" as "institutional decay" with the new spirit of punishing the greatest crimes with the greatest brutality during the Liao dynasty may thus have been constructed across a conceptual bridge that was already in formation as early as the Han dynasty.

Questioning the Legitimacy of Lingchi

By the Northern Song, *lingchi* was unambiguously defined as dismemberment. This is when we first encounter detailed discussions of the punishment. Some of the Song commentators who discuss lingchi concern themselves with aligning it with specific categories of crime, but others, more importantly, contest its introduction in the legal system. Indeed, instead of demonstrating a regular and steady process toward legalization of the practice, the evidence of Song history shows great resistance and opposition to its introduction. The legitimacy of the new penalty was challenged so radically that the history of lingchi, as we have noted, is as much the history of opposition to it as it is the history of its use.

Several Song emperors firmly resisted proposals to legalize slicing practices. When, for example, an appointee to the censorate named Wang Sui proposed that murderous bandits he had just seized be dismembered *(luangua),* the imperial response was to refuse the request. "The Five Punishments are by essence a regular system," the emperor noted in reply. "How could they involve [such] cruelty?"[33] During the Zhenzong era (997–1022), Yang Shouzhen, a eunuch in charge of quelling bandits in Shaanxi, asked to be allowed to dismember those he had just captured as punishment. The emperor replied: "Bandits must be transferred to their jurisdiction to have their cases adjudicated according to law, which includes no provision for dismemberment." Here is the first occurrence of *lingchi* that can be safely translated as dismemberment: "first cut the limbs, then cut the throat." A magistrate in central China who similarly requested that six bandits be executed by lingchi received the same answer. Even though bandits were regarded as the worst category of criminals, a magistrate without special powers had no authority to inflict dismemberment.[34]

These references suggest that this penalty could be imposed only in extraordinary circumstances. Indeed, the first authorized use of lingchi in the Song dynastic history shows this to be the case. The penalty is connected with the repression of sects practicing human sacrifice. The relevant edict, dated 1028, reads: "We have learned that in Jinghu human beings have been killed to offer sacrifices to the spirits. Those who have organized and taken the lead [in this action] as those who participated in it will be condemned to lingchi or beheading."[35] This sacrifice may well have involved the ingestion of human flesh. Cannibalism was common during rebellions, rebels being known to slice and then ritually eat magistrates or agents of the state, but this is not our concern here.[36] We focus instead on the ritual degradation of the body, which when performed by any but the state was considered an offence of great enormity, hence the logic of imposing the mirror punishment of lingchi. The specificity of the lingchi sentence in the Song is confirmed in the *Qingming ji* (The enlightened judgments), the great Song compendium of judicial cases published in the thirteenth century. Lingchi occurs only once in this book, and again it is in the context of curbing human sacrifice. This is also the only case in the collection requiring the emperor's express authorization.[37]

According to the great Song historian Ma Duanlin, the big move toward a more frequent and uninhibited use of lingchi occurred in 1075, when a plot to rebel was discovered. The alleged head of this plot, the commandant of a military prefecture, was a descendant of the founding Song emperor. The real instigator, however, was an official linked to Wang Anshi

(1021–1086), who had supposedly enticed the imperial descendant to take power by magic. Other officials were condemned as accomplices, some of them merely because they refused to prosecute people they deemed victims of slanderous denunciations. The emperor personally initiated the procedure, and the trial resulted in a volley of unusually harsh punishments: two of the condemned were sentenced to dismemberment *(lingchi)*, and two to chopping in half at the waist *(yaozhan*, a penalty of ancient pedigree little used in later times). In fact, biographical notes in individual diaries cast doubt on whether the convicts actually suffered these outrageous punishments.[38] Fictive or not, the important point is that these verdicts were epoch-making in the eyes of Ma Duanlin and most legal historians after him:

> Before Renzong's reign [1022–1063], devices like *lingchi* and *yaozhan* were never employed. [But in this trial] the defendants who suffered these extreme penalties merely uttered words of rebellion. Incrimination by imperial decree increased in the Xining and Yuanfeng eras [1078–1086], initiated by ministers in power in order to terrorize officials. Had there not been strong animosity between opposing factions, private resentments could not have run amok: in the absence of such extreme ways, rivalry between factions could not have become so intense. This is how the harshest punishments came to be so easily meted out.[39]

It was not for mere erudition or moral edification that Ma Duanlin selected this passage in the Song historical records. The case was meant to highlight institutional dynamics, particularly the rationale that set it into motion. Factious ministers intent on seizing power resorted to terror, including special imperially decreed procedures and cruel punishments revived from a remote past or imported from nomadic peoples. Though the plot was a case of rebellion, and Emperor Renzong is clearly presented as pressing his officials for forced confessions, the punishment did not arise simply from an autocrat's whim, but rather emerged from a decay of the balance of power within the bureaucracy. Ma's account highlights the moment when extreme means used during a military expedition to subdue local populations of peripheral regions came back to haunt portions of the ruling elite. Emperors and ministers who had long been reluctant to resort to cruel punishments, or at least were cautious toward their application by their subordinates, here invoked state security to employ them as legitimate means to deter rebellion by their underlings.

The new penalty was never again backed by a Song imperial edict; however, opposition to it did not disappear after this episode. The most influential opponent of lingchi was certainly the famous poet and official Lu You (1125–1210), whose arguments, transmitted across the centuries, would inform the memorial calling for abolition in 1905. The relevant text was one item among many controversial legal points Lu included in his lengthy "Memorial of Itemized Answers" (Tiaodui zhuang):

> Reading the [Song] Code shows that, however serious a crime was taken to be, the sentence could not exceed decapitation. This consists of severing the head from the body. This extreme penalty is the ultimate means to curb evil: how could it be increased? The Five Dynasties [907–960] experienced so many troubles that the then current laws were deemed inadequate. For the first time, a special article on dismemberment was issued outside codified law. Flesh was stripped off before breathing ceased, and liver and heart were laid bare while sight and hearing still persisted. Wounding the harmonious interaction [of heaven and earth] and jeopardizing the benevolence of government in this way is not something a sagely era praises as worthy!
>
> Now some argue [firstly] that [cruel punishments] habitually seen and heard over a long time come to be deemed normal. [Secondly] they say that in the absence of a penalty such as lingchi, those who commit mutilation will find no just retribution for their crime. Your servant declares that this is not so! If those who commit mutilation must be dismembered by way of retribution, then must ruffians who exterminate a clan or open their tumulus be treated in the same way again as retribution? Should the law of the empire equal ruffians in its ferocity? As for those who say that decapitation is not [severe] enough to forestall crime, they too must reconsider. The Three Dynasties of antiquity used "flesh punishments," whereas the Sui and the Tang [abolished them and replaced them with] bamboo blows on the back. At that moment there must also have been some who claimed that without flesh punishments the bamboo blows would not be enough to curb evil. And yet, from the time when emperors Wen of the Han and Taizong of the Tang abolished [flesh punishments], offenders against the law decreased in number.
>
> Any penal system must include benevolence to work efficiently. This is so obvious! In the hope of restoring the compassion of the ancient sages, a special order [should go out] to all magistrates prohibiting the punishment of dismemberment, so as to highlight Your Majesty's benevolence and

increase the happiness of the empire's Great Peace. Your servant has no greater wish.[40]

This important text, which provides the thread for the rest of this chapter, belongs to a genre the rules of which become apparent as one sifts through similar memorials. An earlier text in this genre is a memorial first issued in 928, which is quoted in a subsequent memorial of 946 by the remonstrating official Dou Yan:[41]

> On the day when extreme penalties are meted out, it is proper to not play music and to observe fasting. A [previous] memorial from the Ministry of Justice also says: "The verdict of being beaten to death on the spot with bamboo is the severest penalty." This was the way of compassion worthy of gentlemen. I think that the Yellow Emperor imposed on Chi You [and the Miao rebels whom this mythical figure commanded] his own cruel penalties, which involved whips and rods. Emperor Gaozu of the Han dynasty [Liu Bang] proclaimed the Three Articles to restrict capital punishment to strangulation, which keeps the body intact, and decapitation, which severs the head from the trunk. Every capital crime has to be punished by one of these two penalties. Nonetheless, there have been reports of shameful punishments *(yinxing)* being inflicted with growing frequency in recent times. This is done by magistrates who do not abide by general rules and arbitrarily arrange the facts and the circumstances [of the cases]: here they use big nails to pierce through people's hands and feet, there they carve their skin and flesh with short knives, leaving their victims to linger half dead, half alive for many days. Consequently, the clamor over injustice converges on the central judicial authorities, attesting that the harmonious interaction [between rulers and ruled] has been seriously breached. All those who serve a public function must return to benevolence and the strict observation of the law. I hope for a decree severely forbidding such practices.[42]

This memorial, which precedes Lu's memorial by three centuries, addresses one particular punishment abuse, the practice of cutting a criminal with short knives. The author takes a similar approach of weaving historical precedents with legal considerations. He thereby shows that practices involving the slicing of the body were unlawful and that *lingchi* was not yet the official denomination for such practices. The emperor's rescript to this memorial agreed with Dou Yan: "When civilization flourishes, the punishments must [decrease] in accordance; if crimes still occur, they must be prosecuted in strict observance of the law, in order to eradicate evil and gradually revive the old ways. Dou Yan's recommendations in his memorial are reasonable. This edict orders their application according to the laws and ordinances."

The internal referencing of earlier memorials in later ones gradually produced a chain of texts that led to the formation of a genre in which the writer was expected to invoke general principles of legality and morality in order to call for the suppression of punishments in accordance with a model established during the Han dynasty.[43] Even though cruel punishments were not eradicated, and even proliferated, one cannot dismiss these remonstrations as mere dead letters or rhetoric. What we face here is an ideological construction that sheds important light on the spirit of Chinese legal institutions, a significant feature of which was to make a clear-cut delineation between legitimate and illegitimate punishments. From our perspective, what falls within or outside this framework of legitimacy is somewhat surprising: in both memorials, beating to death with bamboo sticks is deemed "legitimate," while slicing with short knives is included among "shameful punishments." Nonetheless, we need to excavate the historical and ethical reasons for such distinctions if we are to reconstruct the conceptual background of this debate.

The foregoing memorials repeatedly rely on key historical precedents to construct their standard narrative of penal mitigation. This narrative is never completely realized, but it postulates a gradual humanization of law paralleling the gradual inculcation of mores through Confucian persuasion in a kind of progressive scheme that runs throughout the history of the empire. During the originary Three Dynasties, the narrative says, the Five Punishments were excessively cruel. They included the "flesh punishments" *(rouxing)* such as the cutting off of feet, hands, or genitals, as well as the "ink punishments" *(moxing)* or penal branding. Such cruel punishments, the narrative goes on, reached a peak under the notorious Qin dynasty, prompting the revolt that toppled it. The founding Han emperor, while still a contender for the throne, promulgated to his followers the Three Articles *(san zhang)* promising a general suppression of flesh punishments. This promise was breached as soon as the new dynasty was stabilized, as legal cruelties were abundantly applied to strengthen its power.[44] The initial promise was not completely nullified, however, as a movement for reform started during Emperor Wu's reign (141–87 B.C.). The abolition of mutilating punishments was regularly ordered. The fact of their repetition, however, casts serious doubt on the efficacy of the abolition orders.[45]

This narrative always finds its happy ending with the reformed scale of penalties included in the Tang Code, which largely followed the Sui Code. The new Five Punishments were beating with the light bamboo rod; beating with a heavy bamboo rod; penal servitude for one to three years; life exile to distant places; and execution, by either strangulation or decapitation. This scale, according to the Chinese conception, included no "flesh punishments." Although some were "corporal," as convicts were still hit on their skin, new punishments were not intended to leave indelible effects on their flesh. The Sui-Tang penal scale thereafter served as the legal model for assessing the legitimacy of all punishments. The ideal was so eagerly pursued, at least in the elevated world of memorials and edicts, that in 747 the Tang decreed the abolition of the death penalty, just over a millennium before Cesare di Beccaria famously put the idea forward in Europe.[46] The Tang decree explains why Ma Duanlin and his followers, looking back, held that the 1075 event was a regression to pre-Tang punishments.

From Rules to Law

Looking forward in time, however, we can identify 1075 as the starting point of a new trend, and the story hereafter is that of a long march toward the legalization of bloody punishments. Under the Song, lingchi was sufficiently common to prompt Lu You to seek its abolition. But it is not mentioned at all in the Song penal code, the *Xinglü tonglei* (Classified compendium on punishments and law), nor is it referred to in the Jin dynasty's Taihe Code of 1202.[47] The Yuan was the first dynasty to include the term in its penal regulations. The *Xingfa zhi* (Monograph on punishments and law) in the dynastic history lists *lingchi chusi* (to put to death by dismemberment) in its opening section on the Five Punishments, specifying that it was one of two forms of capital punishment used by the Yuan, replacing strangulation.[48] This is why subsequent commentators, such as the great policy analyst Qiu Jun (1420–1495), felt justified in castigating the Mongols for the insertion of lingchi into Chinese law. As Qiu complained, "since the Sui and the Tang abolished cruel punishments, the death penalty was limited to strangulation and decapitation. This lasted till the Yuan added the death by lingchi. What is called *lingchi* is what the previous dynasties called *gua* [dismemberment]. Though previous dynasties might use this device 'outside the law' *(fawai)*, they never introduced it in the penal code. This was a Yuan innovation."[49] The Mongols thus ended the distinction between the privileged

Five Punishments and the "flesh punishments" they were supposed to have superseded, thereby strengthening the Han Chinese prejudice that Inner Asians were the authors of the worst penal practices in their tradition.[50]

The Mongol rulers indeed appear to have made free use of dismemberment when quelling rebellions.[51] Their record would, however, be surpassed by their successors. The anti-Mongol founder of the Ming dynasty as well as his son resorted almost routinely to dismemberment as a device to deter officials from engaging in corruption (see Chapter 4). The comforting narrative of a gradual mitigation in the severity of punishments from the Han to the Tang was thus reversed from the Song through the Ming. Once codified under the Yuan, dismemberment crept into many articles of the Code for crimes less exceptional than the negative example in the dynastic histories. What started as an ad hoc, exceptional measure, and came to be employed more regularly under the Song dynasty, had by Ming times been formally recognized as a legal penalty that judges could impose on those convicted of the four worst crimes of treason, parricide, vendettas, and the cutting off of parts of a living person's body for purposes of cruelty or magic.

The link between high treason and familial crimes followed from the ancient belief in a direct correspondence between the macrocosm of the polity and the microcosm of the family. Penal laws consistently analogized the killing of a family head by his inferiors to high treason against the state, as we see in the Tang Code. While most cultures have linked parricide to regicide, that the two crimes should be punished to the same degree was a peculiarity of the Chinese legal system, starting in the Yuan dynasty.[52] The Tang had highlighted crimes against emperors and parents as particularly evil, but the punishments were basically of the same nature as for other crimes. Admittedly, the Code provided immediate beheading for the main culprit and his sons, but the other relatives were not put to death, meaning that the "three-clan" rule was suspended. Moreover, there were many cases of mitigation, such as for those who had only schemed or conspired, uttered words of rebellion, or merely listened to them.[53] At any rate, the punishments were restricted to the regular forms of capital punishment, beheading and strangulation. It was in the Yuan that a special realm of extraordinary law emerged that departed from common rules and procedures. Culpability could be extended from the criminal himself to three degrees of kinship, that is, to include all the direct relatives of the criminal's grandparents. So too, any association with great rebellion or Great Sedition, even the mere awareness that it was being plotted, became punishable in this way. Lingchi became the seal of the extraordinary law that was put in place to protect imperial and familial authority. Extraordinary law went beyond harsh penalties protecting special powers (particularly those of the emperor and family head) to special rules that turned upside down basic principles of ordinary law. Extraordinary law imposed collective incrimination and punishment, with almost no consideration of intent.

During the mid-Qing, a long peace led to a relative moderation in the treatment of political crimes. Although lingchi was formally imposed in the famous literary inquisition under Qianlong, sentences were frequently commuted to milder penalties.[54] Yet while collective punishment for Great Rebellion receded, lingchi gradually intruded into individual "private" cases. Thus, while the numbers affected by extraordinary punishment shrank, the punishment itself permeated a broader range of ordinary cases. A compendium of penal cases published in the mid-nineteenth century shows that a penalty once reserved for military campaigns against armed rebellion had become a sanction for familial crimes as well.[55] Moreover, extenuating circumstances were downplayed in favor of all-out measures in adjudications of familial crimes among commoners.

Although lingchi became a common penalty, Ming and Qing scholars regularly revived Lu You's arguments against its legitimacy. Wang Mingde, an outstanding jurist of the early Qing, follows Lu's lead in contesting the codification of what he called "irregular punishments" *(runxing):*

We would remark that the regular list of the Five Punishments as it was fixed after the Han includes only the light bamboo, the heavy bamboo, penal servitude, exile, and the death penalty, and this is all. This is why the [first part of the Code entitled] "Names and General Rules" has this list [of legal punishments] at its head, so that each punishment is seen to be correct vis-à-vis the law. However, [the Code] reads, "Apart from the Five Punishments, there is also dismemberment *(lingchi),* exposure of the head *(xiaoshou),* and dispersal of remains *(lushi).* Basically these were not regular punishments [promulgated by] the state. All resulted from the necessities of a certain period, or from a unique application, which meant that they could not be named among the Five Punishments. Thus they remained scattered among particular statutes and substatutes, or were placed [in the appended commentaries] outside of the statutes and substatutes. They must definitely not be included within the regular list of the Five Punishments, the general purpose of which is to clarify the penalties. Originally, what did not conform to the will of the sage-rulers was categorically excluded from the itemized matters published and transmitted to later generations. All the more reason why these remnants of chaotic periods should not be confused with the clear teachings in the Codes promulgated by the sages of the past, in which their dispositions were so lucidly organized![56]

What is striking in this passage is that a Qing jurist is continuing to refuse to extend to lingchi the legitimacy that was exclusive to the Five Punishments, despite the growing codification that had occurred under the Yuan and Ming. The Ming founder claimed he was returning Chinese law to its Tang model by reinstating the traditional Five Punishments, which allowed only strangulation and beheading as forms of the death penalty, and yet he encouraged the incorporation of lingchi both in the Code and in judicial practice. Excluding it from the Five Punishments was purely nominal. Principled jurists such as Wang Mingde felt they were the keepers of a semantic Great Wall that they hoped would prevent extreme but temporary measures adopted during "episodes of chaos" from becoming codified rules, but that is what happened. Song jurists lost the battle at the boundaries, when a brutal expedient used in extreme situations intruded into the body of the Code under specific laws. Lingchi was then entered into the Five Punishments in the Yuan, but it remained there only briefly, as the Ming founder's restoration of Tang law meant that lingchi and other cruel punishments had to be removed from the penalty list at the head of the Code.

This exclusion may have been of some consolation to jurists who rejected lingchi as a legitimate punishment, yet these penalties survived elsewhere in the Code. In fact, they rested at the threshold of legality as *runxing* (irregular or interstitial penalties) rather than as *zhengxing* (regular penalties). This distinction was analogous to the irregular *(run)* status imputed to the alien conquest dynasties of the Khitans and Jurchens which, some argued, should have excluded them from being entered within the *zhengtong*, the legitimate continuity of dynasties that constituted regular Chinese history.[57] The standard historical narrative thus allowed critics of cruel punishments to deem lingchi illegitimate and outside the authentic Chinese legal tradition, even though it was regularly imposed in accordance with certain laws laid down in the Code.

The exclusion of "irregular punishments" from the Five Punishments created a gray area of practice. Shen Jiaben, the legal reformer who spearheaded the campaign within the bureaucracy to abolish lingchi, summarized the weakness of the penalty's authority this way:

> How could something like this [lingchi] be deliberately instituted? The [ancient] codes include not a word to clarify this point, so it is impossible to answer accurately. Nor does our current Code devote a word to this [question]. This method [of execution] has been transmitted under the common appellation of "the eight knives": first the face, then the arms and legs, then the belly, and finally the head is [cut and] exposed. This [procedure] has been orally handed down among executioners from masters to disciples and other people do not know of them. [Also,] there are slight differences [in the local performance of lingchi] between Beijing and Baoding. Such a heavy penalty, yet the state neither clearly made it part of a unified system nor explained its raison d'être! Fortunately, our benevolent dynasty has just decreed its abolition.[58]

The reluctance of Chinese jurists to include the bloodiest torments in the official list of punishments encouraged them to resist its standardization as a regular penal practice. It also resulted in weaker control from the center. Because the uniform application of standardized laws was evidence that imperial rule was equally present in all corners of the empire, local variation in the performance of lingchi was regarded by these jurists as jeopardizing the very spirit of imperial law and indeed could be considered a breach in the legitimacy of the dynasty itself—though no jurist was willing to explicitly go quite that far. All they could do was point to the irregularities and hope to initiate a bureaucratic logic that might lead to their suspension.

Ethical Challenges to Cruel Punishments

In late imperial Chinese culture, historical and legal reasoning were secondary to ethical reasoning, by which the fundamental legitimacy of the state was confirmed. Lu You's memorial raised ethics in two forms—the ethical standards that the state is charged with diffusing, and the ethical relationship that should exist between ends and means—and used both to imply the illegitimacy of the state's use of lingchi. The idea that lingchi was unethical found expression most consistently in arguments revolving around the "harmonious interaction between heaven and earth," to use Lu You's language. The gambit is a common one going back to the Han dynasty, since which time "cosmic" principles have been invoked not to justify bloody sacrifices but to support calls for moderation in punishment. Although such references appear to invoke metaphysical constraints on human action, the more salient consideration in the memorial of 928 cited above was a concern over the "clamors of injustice converging on the central authorities." The memorialist understood, just as he thought his ruler should, that the state had to limit the suffering of the people to a level they could tolerate, just as it should limit how far it pressed them with taxation and corvée. This was a matter of practical administration rather than cosmic harmony. In this sense, appeals to "cosmic order" can be read either metaphysically or in a more utilitarian fashion, since both senses argue against forcing people to conform to unjust laws or subjecting them to inhumane punishments. In the language of Confucian statecraft, "cosmic order" meant moderation.[59]

Did Chinese traditional ethics broadly conceived articulate a reason for opposing cruel punishments based on an ethical understanding of cruelty? As we have seen, Chinese law allowed "flesh punishments," though Lu You and others argued that these were illegitimate and should have been eliminated during the process of mitigation between the Han and the Tang. The irreparability of the damage the flesh punishments inflicted on the body was what marked them as illegitimate. Indeed, the first and oft-repeated argument against mutilating punishments that we find in Chinese historical records is that "once cut off, life (or limbs) cannot grow again."[60] This sensible observation points to a meaningful distinction between the Chinese and Western cultures of punishment. Chinese law and popular perception considered prolonged strangulation, despite the pain it caused, a punishment less severe than the instantaneous death of beheading. The crucial issue was not bodily sensation but, as we suggested in Chapter 1, somatic integrity: the preservation of the body whole and entire.

To what extent was physical pain a consideration in the decisions that Chinese jurists made regarding the legitimacy of a punishment? It is clear from descriptive sources that it was understood that punishments were "administered to cause pain," in the words of a Liao imperial edict of 1032.[61] Yet it is not obvious that this was the primary factor in weighing a punishment's gravity. Chinese officials were certainly not indifferent to the agony a convict suffered. Lu You's short but moving description of the tormented body is frequently quoted in this regard: "The flesh was stripped off before breathing ceased, and liver and heart were laid bare, while sight and hearing still persisted. Wounding the harmonious interaction [of heaven and earth] and jeopardizing the benevolence of government in this way is not something a sagely era praises as worthy!" Lu regarded the degradation of the body as offensive, yet he does not explicitly address the issue of pain. Instead, his overt concern is that the desecration of the body of the condemned breaches the proper harmony of the cosmic order, an offense that could in turn point to the illegitimacy of the regime using such penalties. From Lu's point of view, the victim's experience of pain is not relevant to the ethical argument he is making.

Lu You was not alone in this view. In the early Qing, jurist Wang Mingde follows suit in his account of what he deemed an "irregular penalty":

> Lingchi is the most extreme of the extreme punishments. Not only is it not included within the Five Punishments as listed in the "Names and General Rules" [the opening section of the Qing Code]; it cannot be found among the Five Punishments of antiquity. The process is nothing less than dismemberment *(zhe)*. All parts of the body are sliced, and then the reproductive organs are cut off. In the case of women, the belly is cut open and the entrails removed. In order to end life, the joints are severed and the bones cut, at which point all is over. In the old days, rulers of the Shang dynasty eviscerated pregnant women and chopped up scholars. Slicing Bo Yikao was the beginning of this mode of punishment.[62] In the time of the Warring States, the rulers of the state of Han employed Shen Buhai, and the Qin hired Shang Yang [legalists who imposed harsh punishments]. This was when the drilling of the skull *(zuodian)*, the pulling out of the ribs *(chouxie)*, death by scalding, and Extermination of the Three Clans started, all of which are of the same kind as lingchi. When the Han dynasty came to power, despite the promise of the Three Articles, Extermination of the Three Clans was retained among the punishments. The old methods were not abolished and eventually came back.[63]

Like Lu You, Wang Mingde is not ethically disturbed at the pain someone would experience being punished in this way. His focus is on the violent opening up of the body and the exposing of parts of the body, such as the bowels, ribs, and skull, which should not be exposed. He also links this exposure directly to the issue of regime legitimacy. The slicing of Bo Yikao by the last Shang ruler precipitated the collapse of his dynasty and its replacement by the Zhou. This coup was legitimated after the fact by the theory of the mandate of heaven, which held that heaven looked down on the atrocities the Shang ruler had committed and removed his mandate to rule for that reason. The first lingchi in history was thus associated with the first change of heaven's mandate. For Wang Mingde as for Lu You, lingchi is out of bounds because its desecration of the human body not only insults the natural order but also makes a mockery of the benevolence that should guide good government. It commits the very crime it professes to punish.

The first nineteenth-century Western observers of lingchi were overwhelmed by the horrified anxiety they felt watching the powerless victims of this penalty in agony. For them, the penalty was barbaric because it was about nothing but pure suffering and the prolongation of that suffering—hence the literary hyperbole about "lingering death." Eyewitnesses who closely watched what went on were surprised, however, by the swiftness with which lingchi was performed and by the apparent passivity, even "callousness," of the victim, as well as of the executioners and public onlookers, during the torment.[64] George Morrison, the London *Times* correspondent in Beijing, was struck by the swiftness of the operation. Sword in hand, the executioner "makes two quick incisions above the eyebrows, and draws down the portion of skin over each eye, then he makes two more quick incisions across the breast, and in the next moment he pierces the heart, and death is instantaneous." These steps performed, he then "cuts the body in pieces." Morrison goes on to explain that "the mutilation is ghastly and excites our horror as an example of barbarian cruelty; but it is not cruel, and need not excite our horror, since the mutilation is done, not before death, but after."[65] At least as it was performed in the late Qing, lingchi was not a slow death, nor did it leave its victim "lingering" at death's door, nor did it involve a thousand cuts. It was a methodical and relatively swift technique for putting someone to death.

Struck by the contrast to the logic that prevailed at executions elsewhere, Western observers had trouble explaining exactly why "no punishment is more dreaded by the Chinese than the Ling chi," as Morrison put it. For an answer he appealed to the afterlife consequences of the loss of somatic integrity. Lingchi "is dreaded not because of any torture associated with its performance, but because of the dismemberment practised upon the body which was received whole from its parents." Morrison explains that "the degradation consists in the fragmentary shape in which the prisoner has to appear in heaven."[66]

Ernest Alabaster, a British barrister who in 1899 published a classic study of Chinese penal law, similarly noted the swiftness of execution and attributed the terror of the penalty not to the victim's sensation of pain but to the later consequences of being cut into pieces: "This punishment, known to foreigners as 'lingering death,' is not inflicted so much as a torture, but to destroy the future as well as the present life of the offender—he is unworthy to exist longer either as a man or a recognizable spirit, and, as spirits to appear must assume their previous corporal forms, he can only appear as a collection of little bits. It is not a lingering death, for it is all over in a few seconds, and the *coup de grâce* is generally given on the third cut; but it is very horrid, and the belief that the spirit will be in need of sewing up in a land where needles are not, must make the unfortunate victim's last moments most unhappy."[67] Puzzled by this quaint logic, Alabaster ends his account with an ironic comment about the dismembered corpse needing to be sewn together in a land without needles. Curiously, Morrison makes the same retreat to irony: "As a missionary said to me: 'He can't lie that he got there properly when he carries with him such damning evidence to the contrary.'" The two authors therefore agree that the intense pain the body of the convict suffered did not explain the power of lingchi. They intuit instead that the punishment's deterrent effect has to do with a concern about the body's prospects in the afterlife.

This hypothesis does have some basis in the Chinese religious worldview, as we suggested in Chapter 1—but not quite in the way Morrison and Alabaster thought. The comments of both men are shaped by a Christian misinterpretation of the Chinese notion of the afterlife common among Western observers in the nineteenth century. This misinterpretation may have originated with the erudite Dutch sinologist, J. J. M. de Groot, whose *Religious System of China*, first published in 1892, stood for many decades as the best authority on Chinese religion in English and is still consulted. De Groot devoted himself to the study of funeral rites as a point of entry into Chinese religion. Though he was not a missionary, his Christian understanding of the subject crept into his analysis of Chinese views of the afterlife, which he too quickly interpreted as a belief in the resurrection of the body. This interpretation led him to treat lingchi as a corroboration of these beliefs: "The belief in the resurrection of the dead having obtained such a firm hold upon the Chinese of ancient times as to prompt the creation of numerous practices for the purpose of preserving corpses from decay, it is but natural to find them also cherishing a conviction that mutilation renders a body unfit to receive the soul again. . . . The idea that mangling a person after death constitutes a punishment of the severest kind still plays an important part in the criminal legislation of modern China."[68]

De Groot was correct in noting that popular religion fixated on what happens to a person after death, but he analogized the Chinese sense of the afterlife with the Christian, and in so doing assumed that the concern of Chinese was with resurrection of the body after death, not with its status as a corpse. At a later point in his study, he cites a text by the brilliant scholar Huang Zongxi (1610–1695), in which Huang comments critically on the widespread practice in his home province of Zhejiang of exhuming and reburying deceased parents in a more geomantically favorable location in order to improve one's family's fortunes. Huang Zongxi categorically condemns this practice, in the course of which he makes what is, for us, an instructive comparison: "To be dismembered alive is awful *(can)*, as everyone knows. Once the corpse has been buried, the coffin rots and the bones scatter. To collect them together and place them in a little coffin is just as awful *(can)* as being dismembered alive." His implication is that the awfulness consists in having what lies within the body in life—and analogously after death, within the earth where the body is buried—exposed to the outside. The bones of the deceased, having already been covered before the corpse rots, are exposed to view in the course of being exhumed, just as the internal body parts of the condemned are exposed to view in the course of his dismemberment. The awful thing is revealing what should remain in the earth, or in the case of lingchi, under the skin.

De Groot translates the passage thus: "Everybody knows how *horrid a torment* it is to be quartered alive;—if the bones of an interred corpse be picked up when the coffin is decaying and the bones lie apart from each other, and are then deposited in a small coffin, this causes *little less torment* than such quartering."[69] He seems to be saying that Huang believed that the bones "suffered" just as a person does when being dismembered. His translation hinges on treating *can*, rendered above as "awful," as though it means "torment," such as what, to a Christian mind, Christ suffered at his crucifixion. In Chinese, however, the word contains an ethical objection, alluding to the term *canxing* or "cruel punishments," that is, penalties regarded as repugnant for exceeding what is appropriate under a wise ruler. De Groot substitutes the pain of torment for the metaphysics of somatic degradation and cosmic reversal, apparently without any idea that he is doing so or that his interpretation has nothing to do with Huang's ethical concern about exposing that which should not be exposed. De Groot's interpretation has continued to color treatments of the topic.[70]

Huang Zongxi did not believe that a corpse had the capacity to suffer pain as a living person did. To think so places us in the unfortunate Orientalist position of ascribing to Chinese bizarre primitive beliefs about suffering corpses and trivializing the ideas of one of China's greatest thinkers. De Groot chose to read his observation in this way because "cruelty" *(can)* as he perceives it can only be the cruelty of physical pain; there is no posthumous experience in the Christian framework to which the notion of cruelty or suffering can be ascribed. Only by dissociating "cruelty" from physical pain can we appreciate what Huang Zongxi is saying. Huang was not indifferent to the suffering of the lingchi victim; he just did not attach significance to it from an ethical point of view. It was the exposure of buried remains that offended him; the offense went against the proper working of nature and, in effect, threatened the somatic integrity of the culprit's family—just as the Extermination of the Three Clans did in a more literal fashion. As noted in Chapter 2, the exhumation of buried relatives was so loathed, at least by the state, that a special statute was inserted into the Qing Code condemning sons who exposed their parents' or grandparents' bodies—the penalty being the matching penalty of lingchi. The state thus rendered the public atrocity of dismemberment literally equivalent to the private atrocity of disrupting the "tumulus" of the deceased. Lingchi was designed to suppress, practically and symbolically, the body of the criminal, the body of his kin, and the continuant aspects of the body in the next life, just as the Extermination of the Three Clans aimed to do in an earlier era. Thus the etymological meaning of *lingchi* as "leveling the tumulus" is not entirely extraneous to what the word *lingchi* came eventually to name.

This account of lingchi offers an "ideal type" (an unfortunate expression for this sort of practice) that was almost never carried out fully in reality, particularly the draconian execution of all one's relatives to the third degree of kinship. The ideal type reveals what the penalty meant; it also suggests that it conferred no significance on the suffering of pain. The meaningful moment did not come with the slices of the knife that made Western observers shudder, nor at the moment the victim died. It occurred at the last moment of the operation, well after the victim's death, when his physical remains lay in the dirt of the execution ground, utterly exposed and formless. This was the moment when the "tumulus" was "leveled," the moment beyond which the body could not reassume its integrity or its dignity. With the tumulus "leveled," the ritual continuity of the family came to an end. The desecration of the body of the individual thus stood for the loss of the integrity of the family. Through the lingchi of one member, the family was ritually destroyed. This "leveling" was also a political act. The law allowed the ruling family to pursue a lethal vendetta against a clan whose members challenged its hegemony, exempting the dynasty from being held to account for a form of behavior the Code judged atrocious when performed on the order of anyone but the emperor. The prerogative of the dynasty to survive overrode any question regarding the legitimacy of lingchi.

The equivalence between the penalty and the crime is what disturbed Lu You. His argument against "retribution" rejects the legitimacy of the punishment because it was the same as the crime it was used to punish. "Mirror penalties" are commonly found in ancient legal systems, according to which the sinner was punished "in the same manner he sinned," so that, for example, a blasphemer or a slanderer would have his tongue cut or pierced.[71] Unlike *lex talionis* (an eye for an eye), which imposes a penalty of merely arithmetical equivalence, a mirror penalty acts out a much more complex and meaningful system of equivalence at the symbolic level. It constitutes a legal discourse in which acts, instead of words, are employed to illustrate the nature of the crime and teach the meaning of the punishment. For Lu You, however, this parallelism exposes an error of the state in performing a deed it stigmatized and punished. Punishing the mutilation of the body by lingchi meant subjecting the offender to the same process he had himself committed, albeit publicly at the hands of an official executioner as opposed to privately at the hands of an amateur. Lingchi in this instance was the quintessential mirror penalty. The same notion of equivalence commended the use of lingchi to punish someone found guilty of murdering three people in the same family. If one clan sought to annihilate another by vendetta, then it deserved the same annihilation, which lingchi provided.

The Outcome

"How could something like this [lingchi] be deliberately instituted?" Shen Jiaben's perplexity, expressed while he was preparing the edict for lingchi's abolition, expresses a strong thread of shared opinion among Chinese scholars ever since the appearance of lingchi in the arsenal of state penalties in the Song. Far from being the epitome of Chinese law that Western observers liked to think it was, lingchi was resented in Chinese intellectual circles as the law's most paradoxical and deleterious element. It was, from its first appearance to its abolition, an "irregular" penalty, alien to the penal system codified under the Tang, which subsequent dynasties officially claimed as their model. So strong was the conviction that lingchi did not belong in Chinese law that we so far have found in the writings of Chinese jurists only opinions against it, and none in favor.[72]

It is striking to realize that the critics of lingchi consistently enjoyed a moral authority for their arguments, even though they were opposing a penalty that was legally pronounced in the name of the emperor. The scholars quoted in this chapter—Lu You, Ma Duanlin, Wang Mingde, Qiu Jun, and Qian Daxin—were not clandestine dissenters but active officials in good standing. They were eminent writers whose works, including their writings against lingchi, were published and widely circulated. Admittedly, their arguments for centuries had no effect on the imperial legal system, which turned a deterrent initially employed in emergency situations into a common punishment for domestic crimes, until prompts from outside finally led the imperial regime to alter its penal practices. But they pressed their views nonetheless.

This gap between jurists' opinions and the punishments they had to enforce reached a climax in the last decade of the Qing. Despite their full awareness of the anti-lingchi position of their superior officials, such as Xue Yunsheng and Shen Jiaben, legal officials in the Board of Punishments were still obliged by law to pronounce sentences of lingchi right up until the moment of its abolition. Many were troubled by this disjunction, not only because of the gap between law and attitude, but also from Buddhist anxiety that meting out excessive punishments could entail evil consequences in the next life.[73] As scholars of the Chinese legal tradition, they were free to criticize lingchi as a departure from the "true meaning" of the law as it stood at the time the Tang dynasty abolished "flesh punishments." Yet they had no choice but to follow the existing statutes until these were changed in April 1905.[74]

"The spur came from abroad," wrote Martinus Meijer by way of explaining the abolition of cruel punishments as part of the introduction of Western law into China.[75] This contingency did indeed force the change, but we believe that it would be a mistake to discount the strong tradition of opposition to lingchi and presume that it played no part in bringing about this fundamental shift. The unfortunate irony here is that a civilization that early on regarded the use of humane penalties as a marker of state legitimacy was one of the last to abolish cruel punishments, for which it earned global notoriety. This unfortunate record could lead us to dismiss the opinions of Chinese jurists as so much trifling chatter in an age that was anything but a time when sages and statesmen ruled China, and to concentrate our attention instead simply on the reception of Western legal concepts and moral standards. Yet the success of the reformation of Chinese law according to Western standards rested in no small part on indigenous legal traditions that shaped how Western law was received and interpreted. The declaration of the abolition of lingchi issued on April 24, 1905, opens by expressing the need for China to adapt to the legal concepts and moral values of the contemporary world, but its arguments revert to the indigenous discourse presented in this chapter, with Lu You's thought taking pride of place. The first part of the edict was written by Wu Tingfang, a Hong Kong barrister-at-law and former ambassador to the United States. The second part was written by none other than Shen Jiaben and reproduces arguments that jurists within the Board of Punishments had been voicing for decades before the introduction of Western law.[76]

Moreover, if the spur for the legal reforms came from abroad, the success of the reform still depended on the capacity of indigenous arguments to win over the bureaucratic elite. The Chinese push toward abolition might have been unable to succeed purely on the strength of its own arguments, yet even if we accept that abolition required pressure from outside the system, opposition to harsh punishments ran deeply enough within the bureaucracy to ensure the quick and effective application of the legal reforms once they were promulgated. (This disruption in China's penal regime did not mark the end of extreme punishments. Torture and execution continued to be used, albeit in a different legal context and in different forms, complicated by the modern state's obsession with secrecy as a condition of its legitimacy.) The writings of the Chinese jurists who opposed the use of harsh penalties as illegitimate intrusions into the Chinese tradition provide the historian with valuable glimpses into the legal context within which they worked and the processes by which they thought about the administration of justice and punishment. They also show that behind the orderly regulatory facade of laws and decrees published in the official regulations lay sharp conflicts over the legality and morality of what foreigners took to be something quintessentially Chinese. This is where we hear echoes of "the rumble of battle" with which Foucault ends *Discipline and Punish*—the conflicts that lie at the heart of the law, and that cannot be understood simply by molding them to the European narrative of judicial reform that Foucault himself has made so familiar. It is the Chinese story that we need to hear.

CHAPTER 4

Lingchi in the Ming Dynasty

In Chapter 3 we identified the Liao dynasty as the regime when lingchi execution entered China's repertoire of penal practices, the Northern Song as the regime under which it was accepted as the form of the death penalty to be used to punish the most extreme crimes, and the Yuan as the dynasty that entered lingchi into codified law. Records of the penalty's actual use, however, suggest that it was not until the early decades of the Ming dynasty (1368–1644), toward the end of the fourteenth century, that lingchi became a common, even mundane punishment and so much a part of the Chinese criminal administration as to go unremarked. This chapter takes us back to this time, which is also a time when the surviving sources are good enough to allow us to examine in close detail the legal framework within which one Chinese emperor made use of this penalty.

Sources for the history of lingchi are unevenly distributed over the imperial period. The end of the Qing dynasty was the richest period for the production of sources, particularly visual sources, on the practice of lingchi execution. We can also find abundant and reasonably consistent sources for the study of lingchi in the opening reign of the Ming dynasty (1368–1398), particularly the mid- to late 1380s. Lingchi looms large in this period in part because this is when the founding emperor published an extraordinary series of documents on administrative crimes, for many of which he prescribed lingchi as the punishment. Whether lingchi was more heavily used in the 1380s than it had been before or would be after, and whether it surged under the grim justice of the founder or was simply better archived during the 1380s, are questions the surviving documents do not allow us to answer. We do know that later commentators singled out the 1380s as a violent decade in the history of imperial autocracy, though that may be in part an effect of the records that the emperor himself compiled and circulated to his officials as testimonies to the righteousness of his rule.

If lingchi was the most extreme punishment that an emperor could impose on the body of a subject, its extremity was matched by its relative exceptionality within Chinese law. As noted in Chapter 2, the Ming Code does not list the penalty among the standard punishments at the beginning of the book. It appears within the Code, where nine statutes mandate its use. When it came to his own sentencing, however, the founding Ming emperor did not regard himself as bound by the limits of his Code. He applied the penalty liberally in the 1380s as a punishment for a far wider range of crimes. This chapter examines his record of lingchi sentences to explore when and why he invoked this penalty, and more to the point why he made a public record of his use of lingchi. What we can learn of the emperor's deliberations is limited largely by his own records, yet even this knowledge is an important component in our understanding of the significance of lingchi in China's political and legal context, as well as in coming to terms with the image of imperial China, and particularly the Ming dynasty, as a barbarous era in Chinese history.

Driving Water Uphill

Zhu Yuanzhang ruled as the dynastic founder for thirty years. Midway through his career, in the 1380s, he was consumed by a problem he struggled with and failed to solve: how to make evil people good. Hongwu ascended the throne in 1368 after a decade of war that shook off China's Mongol rulers, the descendants of Khubilai Khan (r. 1264–1294), though most of that decade was spent in civil war against other Chinese pretenders to the throne. Zhu believed that his reign, known as the Hongwu era, was ushering China into a new age of great tranquility *(da'an)* or ultimate peace *(taiping)*, as he variously called it (1.47; 3.20).[1] He put into place new laws, new rites, and new systems of fiscal administration that were expressly designed to achieve this. His goal was to cleanse China of the Mongol influences he believed it had acquired during the Yuan dynasty and return to the tradition of the sages associated with China's ancient past. This meant easing the penal system. "Controlling the people is like controlling water," he declared to his officials. "You have to follow their nature. By nature all people cherish life and loathe death, so the way to nurture them is to reduce punishments and suspend warfare. . . . Pressuring them with authority and using force to compel them to do what they do not wish to do, and then asking for their submission, is like driving water uphill. It goes against their nature."[2]

Despite these aspirations to a Daoist virtue of less government rather than more, Hongwu's imagination of judicial administration was entirely shaped by the experience of growing up poor under Mongol rule. Indeed, nothing communicates the reality of the Mongol legacy more strongly than the Ming Code, the compilation of core laws that Emperor Hongwu personally oversaw, for the Code perpetuates Mongol legal practices more than it revises them. And none of the Mongol innovations in legal codification stand out more starkly than the insertion of the form of execution known as lingchi.[3] This penalty was absent in the Tang and Song law codes, yet Hongwu would not go so far in restoring the glories of the Tang and Song dynasties as to abandon its use.

The project of imperial rule went well initially, but after a dozen years the emperor began to believe that reality was falling too far short of his ideals. When in 1380 he thought he discovered his chancellor Hu Weiyong concocting a plot against the financial well-being of his empire and even against his life, he not only executed Hu but carried out a purge that raged on for at least the next four years. Thirty thousand people alleged to be in on the alleged plot to overthrow the regime and seize the throne were executed. The administration was paralyzed. The discovery of the plot—was there one?—shattered Zhu's confidence in the wisdom of delegating authority to professional bureaucrats. The grand ship of state he had been guiding had turned out to be a rotten hull with tattered sails and a mutinous crew. The reign of the monarch of wisdom and compassion was over in 1380; the reign of the tough autocrat had begun. Anyone who had ever been linked to Hu Weiyong was interrogated and executed. However wide and deep the purge went, it was difficult to discover and exterminate every tendril of Hu's influence. The emperor was sure Hu's faction had extended its reach into every corner of the bureaucracy, even when he could find no proof that it had. He not only thought that he had to execute any who might have joined the plot against him; he also believed that the people had to be made aware of his willingness to do so. The emperor had to teach his officials to fear him, to know that those with evil intentions would eventually be found out and treated to the cruelest punishments he could devise. And he had to communicate to the people that this was what he was doing.

Five years later, Hongwu uncovered an embezzlement scheme that led back to his vice-minister of revenue, Guo Huan. There followed a second vast purge, as extensive as the first. The realization that the punishments he had handed out during the Hu Weiyong purge had not been sufficient to make his officials walk the straight and narrow meant he had to go further. He decided to recruit his subjects as allies in his war on official corruption. He had to tell them what was going on and alert them that he expected their support for his campaign against such malfeasance. And so toward the end of that year, he turned to the task of compiling and publishing a book that would publicize his battle against corrupt officials and highlight his personal role in seeing that the best interests of the people were protected.

The Grand Pronouncements

The Imperially Authored Grand Pronouncements (Yuzhi dagao) is a collection of short summaries of legal cases about officials who fell afoul of Hongwu's rules and were later exposed and punished for their misdeeds. The 1385 compilation was the first of four such collections of case summaries he would issue (the longest covers eighty-seven cases, the shortest thirty-two).[4] No emperor had ever compiled such a catalogue denouncing his own officials, which meant that Hongwu had no precedents for what he was writing. Each edition has a preface in which he explains his motivations and expectations for producing something this novel and arresting. The preface to the first edition of 1385 announces clearly that the *Grand Pronouncements* are for admonishing his officials: "Today, should there be any harm to the affairs of the people, let it be announced to the officials of the realm that if there is anyone not devoting himself to the public good but instead devoting himself to private interest, or going about soliciting bribes and causing suffering to Our people, We will get to the bottom of it and investigate and charge them for their crimes. This order having been issued, let every generation respect it and carry it out." The expression "Our people" was a favorite one with the emperor: he was their master and they were his charge, and any official or imposter who dared come between him and them, as he believed Hu Weiyong had done, would be dealt with in the harshest possible manner.

   There is no indication in the first edition of the *Grand Pronouncements* that Hongwu intended a second collection to follow it, let alone a third or fourth. Yet he got right to work on a second compilation of case summaries as soon as the first was done, publishing it barely five months later. The speed with which the second compilation appeared suggests that the emperor felt his officials were not taking him seriously. In the preface to the 1386 edition, he reflects on the difficulty of bringing the present in line with the ideals of antiquity and worries again about the suffering of "Our people." This time, though, he does not single out his officials for special condemnation. He presents criminality as a more general problem. This new posture does not last, however. In the very first line of the preface to the third compilation of 1387, he returns to the problem of corrupt officials: "We note that among the officials and people there are evil ones who are always deeply mired in crime." Thereafter he drops the distinction and speaks only in moral rather than status terms, yet it was his fundamental assumption that his subjects were basically good, and that the real threats to the security of his dynasty were his officials. This posture is confirmed in the text. In every case summary, if the evildoer is not an official, then he is a local bully who either holds a local service post or relies on his connections to the local magistrate to perform his evil deeds.

Unique in the history of imperial publications, the *Grand Pronouncements* can nonetheless be set within a textual genre known as "case" literature, which recorded legal, medical, and religious lore.[5] The genre narrates a process of discovery. The subject of the case encounters a problem, finds a way to analyze it, and then achieves a solution. It is unidirectional, unfolding its facts from a beginning through a middle and on to an end. Hongwu's choice of the case genre to describe the faults of the age and his measures to correct them does not just enable him to demonstrate the working of justice. It also gives him the opportunity to tell good stories. Hongwu wrote plot as well as the best of writers.[6] He presents the reader with one or more evil characters, shows how their evildoing came to light, sometimes reconstructs the verbal give-and-take of the trial, then crowns the tale of their misdeeds with a carefully chosen and well-deserved penalty.

The most important part of each case summary comes at the end, when the judgment is handed down and its logic demonstrated by an appropriate sentence. The sentence serves to confirm the severity of the crime, but it is the judgment that shows the legitimacy of the retribution. Modern readers may well find Hongwu's stories "horrific accounts of punishment of officials and functionaries,"[7] but it is not clear that this is how the emperor intended his public to read them or how they were indeed read. After all, Hongwu chooses this genre, rather than another, precisely because it allows him to write himself into the stories as the voice and hand of justice. Sometimes he is the judge who hands down the sentence; sometimes he is the investigator who brilliantly exposes the suspect's nefarious activities and perfidious evasions. At the very least, he is the narrator who gets to tell the story from his point of view. These are not stories of a hapless ruler duped for long by his subordinates; they portray the benevolent ruler stepping in to make tough decisions to protect his people from financial corruption and obstruction of justice. His posture is not that of the crazed tyrant blindly thirsting for revenge; rather, he pictures himself as the righteous sage who sympathizes with the sufferings of his people. If the book has a hero, it is he. To fail to see his use of lingchi in this light is to misunderstand what this book, and indeed imperial justice itself, was all about.

The Constant Inadequacy of Punishments

The first article of the Ming Code sets out the Five Punishments, the standard sentencing options in the imperial judicial system that range from execution to banishment, penal servitude, and beating. The emperor acknowledges the general authority of the Five Punishments in the Code in his preface to the third collection of *Grand Pronouncements*, observing that the work of developing the laws and penalties in the Code was not a simple task to be accomplished in a year. Yet the modes of "putting to death" specified in the case summaries show that he was willing to go beyond the Five Punishments specified in his own Code, in both type and severity of punishment. Hongwu quite understood that he was imposing "measures beyond the law,"[8] but he justifies his actions on the grounds that he was living at the end of a century of abuse, immorality, and evil customs sown by the Mongols, whose dynasty, the Yuan, his coming to power had brought to an end. Desperate times called for desperate measures.

Many times in his writings, in fact, Hongwu regrets that the Five Punishments have proved inadequate to achieve the respect for law they were intended to produce. Always this complaint sits within a narrative of decline. In an appeal he circulated to his officials soliciting their opinions on how to adjust punishments and rewards, Hongwu looked back to the mythic rule of the Three Sovereigns and Five Emperors as an era when "their use of punishments was extremely simple and their conduct also extremely strict." As a result, the people were content. All subsequent history has been a falling away from this state of perfection, greater crimes producing greater penalties. And yet previous emperors usually were stymied by the conundrum that the more ferocious the punishments, the less stable the government that legislated them. Greater penalties only seemed to produce greater crimes. Hongwu accepts the standard notion that the Qin dynasty (221–206 B.C.) was quickly overthrown because of the harshness of its penalties, and he expresses admiration for Emperor Wen of the Han (r. 179–157 B.C.), whose abolition of corporal punishments was celebrated for bringing great relief to the people.[9]

Torn between compassionate moderation and judicial severity, Hongwu began his reign aspiring to practice the former. In the 1380s, however, he switched sides.[10] "The Five Punishments are used to punish crimes, yet who is bothered enough to fear them?" he asks rhetorically in the preface to the second edition of the *Grand Pronouncements*. The virtuous ancients had been able to get away without using even the Five Punishments, but the crimes in the present age were so terrible that Hongwu had to inflict awful punishments, even after the first *Grand Pronouncements* had been circulated. "Unable to bear this, we issued the second collection to warn the ignorant and recalcitrant not to continue on this course," he recalls in his preface to the third. The good, when they saw the second edition, "were filled with respect, like water flowing downward," but "evil, obstinate fellows" unfazed by the threat of punishment "were still unwilling to change their hearts and embrace the good," hence the need for a third collection. Hongwu never repudiates the honorable Five Punishments, but he does expect the reader to take his officials' reluctance to obey his laws as reasonable grounds for punishing them more harshly. He wants to "alert them" that they will be treated as harshly as the criminals in the third compilation are treated. The gruesome penalties in the *Grand Pronouncements* were now to be taken as standard rather than exceptional.

In 1397, a year before his death, Hongwu looked back on his effort to create a comprehensive legal order and insisted that he had done what was necessary. He stated that he had hoped initially that the Code would be sufficient, and yet the number of criminals only grew. "Accordingly, in the time We had to spare from the work of administering state affairs, We wrote the *Grand Pronouncements* to show the people the way to tend to good fortune and avoid disaster."[11] There is no sign of internal tension in this declaration of intent, and yet it avoids addressing the problem that dogs every judicial regime that escalates penalties, namely, that harsher punishment does not usually have the effect of reducing crime. The closing passage of the preface to the third collection hints at this intractability: "Alas! The hearts of loyal subjects and cultivated persons are such that, without using many words, they turn to the good. As for evil and obstinate types, you can go on for many tens of thousands of words and in the end they show neither vigilance nor self-reflection. They bring misfortune on themselves. Is it not wonderful that loyal subjects and cultivated persons, who pass the *Grand Pronouncements* down through their families and recite them aloud, will regard this third edition as a precious treasure of fortune and longevity?"[12]

Hongwu declares himself certain that a third collection of admonitions is all that is needed to overcome the failure of the first two. Yet this assertion seems to be contradicted by the observation that only the good can be expected to respond to the wisdom of the *Grand Pronouncements*, and that even given a knowledge of this wisdom, the corruptible will sink further into corruption. The third compilation would be the last of his compilations for civilians. Did he realize that neither the penalties he imposed between 1385 and 1387, nor the texts he circulated to publicize them, were deterring those who were willing to gamble their lives to gain wealth and power? Or did he feel that the legal and ritual frameworks of the new order were now complete, and that only time was needed for the people to absorb what they had been given and be led into the era of ultimate peace?

The Emperor's Use of Lingchi in the First and Second Collections

In the history of the Chinese legal system, the *Grand Pronouncements* stands out not just because the emperor consistently exceeded his own Code when sentencing, but also because he made extensive use of lingchi. The cases in which Hongwu specifies lingchi as the penalty constitute the single largest trove of information about the judicial use of lingchi in the printed imperial archive.[13]

Hongwu's first compilation includes only one clear case specifically reporting an execution performed by lingchi. The case appears late in the collection under the title "Concealing Files" *(Chenni juanzong)*. Here it is in full:

> Jin Qian, magistrate of Jinwu Rear Guard [a county-level military district], started out as a minor functionary who got sent to serve in the capital. Noticed for his vitality and intelligence, he was entrusted with the magistracy of Jinwu Rear Guard, where he handled documents and controlled the Guard troops. When We first noticed his intelligence, We thought that he could be completely trusted and relied on him implicitly. Even when there was secret business to transact, We did not hesitate to order him to

deal with it. After a few years, official matters were being handled without respect for the law. All who deviated from the law were charged with crimes. Qian was alone in being excused. Qian did not recognize the kindness he had received, and after getting away with several infractions assumed that this [way of doing things] was normal. Only then did We realize that he was not a gentleman of the sort who cherishes the kindnesses done to him. We appointed an assessor to examine the Guard files and ordered Qian personally to bring the files to the assessor for inspection.

The reference to Jin Qian's not being punished indicates that he was in office in 1380 during the Hu Weiyong purge and that this story postdates that event. The emperor does not indicate why he suspected Jin was embezzling funds. The story continues:

When he got to the office, not even a tenth of all the files for the Guard were there. When the official tried to get clear as to what had happened, Qian prevaricated from morning till night, offering his body as surety against the charge and ordering his wife and concubine to strike the drum [outside the court] to file suit [against the assessor]. After careful examination revealed he was not telling the truth, the assessor made his report to the throne. When We personally interrogated him, Qian did not explain what happened to the files, but argued that the assessor was slandering the court. When We called in the assessor Zhou Shiming and asked him to answer his questions, he distorted the truth and slandered him. So We then told Qian, "Never mind the faults of the assessor. Where are all the files for the Guard?" Qian did not answer. We asked again whether the files existed or not, and still he did not answer. Again We asked him whether he had or had not brought the files. Qian replied, "I haven't brought them." So he was put to death by lingchi.

Alas, before Qian was appointed, Jinwu Rear Guard had over seven thousand troops. After Qian was appointed, they expanded to over eight thousand. The amount [of cash] to pay rewards and monthly salaries for all of them was vast. Qian illegally sold off granary stocks in substantial volumes, and he reduced salaries and rewards in equally vast amounts, which is why he kept no records. He made excuses, but his intention was entirely to escape with his life. How could he be excused? (1.60)

Jin Qian was found guilty of embezzling state funds earmarked for military expenses and illegally selling military grain stocks for his own profit.

For such financial misconduct on the part of an official, the Ming Code prescribes strangulation. Jin was executed, according to the story, because he failed to maintain accurate financial records, for which the normal penalty in the Code is eighty strokes of the heavy bamboo, not execution.[14] The emperor does not explain what induced him to exceed the Code and impose the sentence of execution by lingchi. The only hint may be one detail woven into the plot, for the penalty follows directly after Jin admits to the only thing he ever does admit to: not bringing the files. The meaning of the penalty depends on how we read that admission. Was he being punished as a consequence of implicitly admitting to embezzlement? Or was he refusing to admit to anything more serious than having failed to bring the files, in the hope that the emperor would have nothing on him and might continue to favor him? If so, was that expectation what drove Hongwu to lingchi? Since Hongwu tells the story in such a way that the actual crimes come out only after the sentence, the punishment seems to have been for Jin Qian's presumption that he could rely on the emperor's patronage to get away with his crime. So Jin was being punished only partly for his corruption. His real crime lay in taking advantage of the trust Hongwu had shown him. This was not Great Sedition in the usual sense of conspiring to overthrow the dynasty. Indeed, overthrowing the emperor was the furthest thing from Jin's mind. He wanted things to remain "normal," normalcy being the condition he needed to enrich himself. The crux of the matter was that the emperor felt personally betrayed.

The "Concealing Files" case may not be the sole lingchi judgment in the first collection of *Grand Pronouncements*. Many cases simply give the phrase "capital crime" without specifying the form of execution. In two of these, the condemned persons received what Hongwu calls the "extreme punishment" (*jixing*). This term, today the standard word in Chinese for capital punishment, conventionally meant the most extreme of the standard Five Punishments, decapitation, during most of the Ming, yet in one passage in the third collection, Hongwu equates *jixing* with lingchi. If lingchi is what he meant every time he called for the "extreme punishment," then the first collection includes two other lingchi cases.[15]

One of these two cases tells of a local yamen underling who refused to be reined in by his county magistrate and struck a garrison soldier (1.17). Hongwu's account implies that the soldier was demanding a bribe from the magistrate, an act to which his subordinate took offense. Striking an official was not a capital crime. It normally entailed at most a hundred blows of the heavy bamboo and three years' penal servitude. Hongwu does not explain why "his crime was of a degree deserving the extreme punishment," but the soldier's status appears to have been the determining factor—this soldier served under the imperial banner. The authority of imperial bodyguards could not be challenged.[16]

The other "extreme punishment" case, entitled "Paying with Beans Soaked in Water" *(Nadou rushui)*, is more revealing. When it came to the emperor's attention that some taxpayers were soaking their beans before handing them over as fodder for government horses, thereby increasing their volume and lessening the number of beans they had to submit (1.53), Hongwu declared lingchi to be the appropriate punishment. It was not just for handing in fewer beans than the taxpayers were supposed to give: underpaying taxes was not a capital crime. The penalty was for the more narrowly defined infraction of "trying to coerce the official assistants" assigned to receive tax payments into accepting wet beans. Paying off a minor functionary was also not a capital crime, however. The capital crime in this case was knowingly doing something that would have the effect of causing an entire storehouse of beans to spoil, which in turn could mean having to demolish the infected warehouse. Hongwu declared that those who coerced tax collectors into accepting wet beans "will be treated with the extreme punishment." We shall return to the significance of this case later in this chapter.

When the *Further Collection of Grand Pronouncements* appeared five months after the first in 1386, it added one more lingchi story to the public record, though in this case, the sentence fell on not just the guilty ringleader but four of his accomplices as well (2.62). The case, "Not Checking Precautionary Tallies" *(Bu dui guanfang kanhe)*, is preceded by a short section entitled "Idle People Conspiring to Commit Evil" *(Xianmin tong'e):* "Hereafter, should any person not in government employ dare, with the active support of an official, to privately impose a corvée that this court did not specifically impose as a form of official service, and should he be aided and abetted in this evil practice by stupid officials or functionaries and so do harm to my people, the penalty shall be extermination of his patriline. Should anyone who has been harmed report this, the family property of the condemned will be given to the first person to file a report. The official is to be put to death by lingchi." The formal tone of this declaration suggests that Hongwu intended it to be taken not as a warning but as a new law. Private corvée was now tantamount to Great Sedition.

The case that follows this declaration, "Not Checking Precautionary Tal-lies," tells a complex story. It takes place in Suzhou, a place where, Hongwu says, officials had been lax in upholding the laws for some time. He was pre-disposed to be suspicious of Suzhou in any case, as it had been the base of his chief rival for imperial founder prior to the man's defeat in 1367. Lesser officials in Suzhou had been caught forging officially stamped documents to permit them to corvée the people's labor for private purposes. Several offi-cials had been punished to warn others not to do the same thing, and yet the abuse continued. In Hongwu's words, "the fraud and extortion troubled and harmed Our people." More executions followed, without effect. The so-lution was to set up a registration system requiring every government office in Suzhou to keep a register in which each corvée order was recorded. When an order was authorized, the tally confirming the order had to be stamped with the office's seal, half on the tally and half on a sheet in the record book. Anyone requisitioning labor without a tally, or with a tally that had not been properly stamped, was to be bound and sent to the capital for punishment. After this system was instituted, a man named Shen Yi, claiming to be a chiliarch (the commander of a unit of a thousand soldiers), showed up at the prefectural office with a forged imperial labor requisition. Prefect Zhang Heng approved the order without checking to see whether the requisition tallied with the books of the issuing department, then passed it down to county magistrate Yao Xu, who also accepted its authority. A censor and a centurion (the commander of a unit of a hundred soldiers) ex-posed the fraud. As a result, Zhang and Yao were decapitated and their heads exposed.[17] Shen Yi and four of his associates were executed by lingchi. The emperor judged that Shen had dared engage in just the sort of corrupt practice he had specifically outlawed, and so needed to be severely punished. The first set of abuses had produced a new procedure; the second produced a new precedent for punishment.

Six centuries later, Shen Jiaben, the jurist and legal historian, singled out the judgments in "Not Checking Precautionary Tallies" for particular criti-cism. He noted that lingchi far exceeded the Tang Code precedent for this sort of crime, which was decapitation. What disturbed him more, though, was Hongwu's failure to distinguish leader and followers. It was a core prin-ciple of Chinese penal practice that penalties exactly mirror degrees of cul-pability. Shen Jiaben doubted that Shen Yi should have suffered lingchi, but he was certain that the penalty should not have been imposed on the asso-ciates.[18]

The Emperor's Use of Lingchi in the Third Collection

Lingchi is uncommon in the first two collections of the *Grand Pronounce-ments*, as we have seen. If there had been restraint in Hongwu's use of lingchi, it was gone when the third appeared twenty-one months later.[19] The 1387 collection records thirteen men put to death by lingchi: three magistrates, two vice-magistrates, six censors, and two civilians. The first five appear in "Officials and Commoners Using the Law to Engage in Cor-ruption" *(Chenmin yifa weijian),* a compendium of eighteen cases that Hongwu ran together in the long opening section of the collection to underscore his intolerance of corruption (section 3.1).

In the first of these cases, Magistrate Xu Yi was embezzling tax funds and interfering with justice, and was amazingly persistent in refusing to respond to the emperor's demand for an accounting of his mismanagement. "Twenty times, forty times, thirty times, seventeen or eighteen times he did not re-spond," is how Hongwu expresses his frustration with this man. Any official who tried as many tricks as Xu did had to "be executed by lingchi to alert the masses." The people should be made to know about this punishment, both to caution them and to show them that he, their emperor, could be counted on to take their side against rapacious officials.

Just across the river from the capital city of Nanjing, magistrate Yang Li was eating and drinking at the expense of the ward captains of the *lijia* (hundred-and-tithing) system for registering and taxing local households. Yang's attempt to get away with embezzling government salt might not have invited Hongwu's particular ire but for two factors. First, he tried to link up with a capital official in the hope of striking some sort of deal that would allow him to keep some of the salt. Second, and more saliently, none of this would have come to light were it not that the missing salt was part of an investigation into the theft of government property by associates of the demonized Chancellor Hu Weiyong. Anyone caught with his fingers in what Hongwu believed (rightly or wrongly, though his beliefs probably ex-ceeded what was possible) to be Hu's vast corruption schemes could expect no leniency. Yang's audacity in lording it over his ward officers within sight of the capital must not have helped his case in Hongwu's eyes. Although the penalty in the Code was decapitation, Hongwu ordered him to be "executed by lingchi to alert the masses."[20]

Hongwu provides less detail about the three other lingchi sentences in "Officials and Commoners Using the Law to Engage in Corruption." The vice-magistrates Chen Youcong and Xu Tan did not just rebuff requests from their prefectures to audit their fraudulent accounts (Chen refused twenty-seven such requests, Xu eleven) but also seized the officials sent against them and turned the tables by packing them off to the capital in cangues under the charge of interfering with justice. *Lijia* captain Li Fuyi did the same thing when his county magistrate sent tithing head Wang Xinsan to order Li to stop his construction of seawall defenses against Japanese pirates because of the burden the corvée was imposing on the people. Li got Wang drunk, tied him up, and sent him to the capital on the charge that Wang was trying to bribe him with liquor.

These three lingchi stories share a theme with the first two. They are not just about corruption, which was fairly modest in each case, but about interference with the judicial procedures Hongwu had put in place to control corruption. It was for perverting the course of justice and confusing right and wrong that they were all "executed by lingchi to alert the masses." Shen Jiaben judged the first of the three sentences as "too harsh" and the second as "not terribly explicable."[21]

The next criminal Hongwu declares deserving of lingchi in the third compilation is Wu Qingfu of She county, an emerging commercial area in the hills south of Nanjing (3.20). The case is called "Patrolman Harming the People" *(Xunlan haimin)*. Wu's family was notorious for being local bullies, and when Wu obtained a patrolman's post from the county magistrate, he felt he had the protection he needed to run tax rackets. Hongwu must have had the man's case file on his desk when he wrote this summary, for he mentions a long litany of specific instances of fraudulent taxation. Wu levied twenty-six strings of cash on farmer Cheng Bao who had just bought new oxen from a livestock dealer and had even filed the sales contract (and presumably paid the contract tax) at the magistrate's office. He levied another eighty strings of cash on the wood in the man's house, which had been cut from public land. He demanded payment of thirty catties of fish from an itinerant dried fish merchant (a tax rate of close to 40 percent, based on Hongwu's own estimate that a person of moderate strength could pack eighty catties). Wu also forced homeowners to pay a shop tax, even those who didn't run shops out of their houses. "With this kind of high-handed oppression," Hongwu asked, "how can the people survive? So We ordered Our judicial officials to arrest Wu Qingfu and take him back to his original place of residence to be put to lingchi. His brothers and sons shared in his evil of harming people, so they were all beheaded and had their heads

displayed on poles." From this case follows a new rule: "Hereafter, any patrolman who relies on the authority of an official to exploit the people's
wealth is to be punished in the same way. The tax rate is fixed at one-
thirtieth. How can anyone levy more than that? If anyone hereafter dares to
try, then even should there be an amnesty he will not be excused."

The next lingchi story, concerning magistrate Pan Xing, "Allying with the
Corrupt and Forming Hidden Factions" *(Pengjian nidang)* (3.37), is so involved that it rivals the most extravagant fantasies of corruption and political skulduggery to be found in Cultural Revolution denunciations. Rather
than following the complicated ins and outs of the story, we will focus on
the main conflict. This developed between Chen Tianyong, a commoner
who tried to blow the whistle on another alleged associate of Hu Weiyong,
and magistrate Pan, who was duped and bribed by his friends into blocking
Chen's plaint. Pan may have earned his sentence of lingchi because Chen
and a dozen friends, whom Pan falsely arrested, overpowered their guards,
broke their cangues, and ended up in Nanjing waving a copy of the *Grand
Pronouncements* (which Hongwu promised would get any commoner a fair
hearing from his court) to expose the whole thing, though probably the Hu
Weiyong connection was decisive. Hongwu explains the penalty as follows:

> Pan Xing thinks nothing of the grace with which the court educates him
> and does not understand the way of bringing glory and a good name to
> himself. He is unable to create good fortune for the people but can only
> provide cover for the private aims of his friends. Dazzled by the bribes he
> receives, he dares hide the facts of the plaint against him and has tried sev-
> eral times to do harm to the plaintiff. This sharing in evil and peddling in
> greed, befriending the bad and going against his superior, are crimes
> heinous enough to anger gods and men. The law cannot bear to be gen-
> erous. Although we wish to grant him life, his way is not one that others
> should follow. Therefore let him be executed by lingchi to alert the masses.

Pan's case of regrettable connivance with powerful interests and the acceptance of bribes should have been a relatively minor infraction, but it became
serious in Hongwu's estimation for making a mockery of justice.

Mocking justice is also the offense that animates Hongwu's decision to
sentence the six censors who are singled out for lingchi sentences in two
cases toward the end of the book. In "Censor Liu Zhiren and Others Acting
Stupidly" *(Yushi Liu Zhiren deng bucai)*, two officials are punished for trying
to bribe the chiliarch sent to investigate an extortion racket they had set up

using the files of two military guards (3.39). In "Slandering a High Official" *(Paixian dachen),* four censors involved in a massive conspiracy in Beijing in early 1387 are executed for perverting the course of justice to their financial advantage (3.40). The officials in the first case were "executed by lingchi to alert the masses, so as to lighten the hearts of Our good people whom they harmed"; those in the second case received the same sentence because "they muddled right and wrong and in so doing threw administration into chaos."

One case in the third collection, "Subofficials and Jailers Selling Prisoners" *(Guanli changya mai qiu)* (3.19), refers to the "extreme punishment," which probably denotes lingchi. Hongwu does not provide a story to illustrate this case. He simply decrees that prisoners were not to be sold either by the jailers who had them in custody or by the soldiers charged with transporting them to the capital. Anyone who sells prisoners will "suffer the extreme punishment," his household will forfeit its registration status and property, and his family members will be exiled not just *to* the border but *beyond* it—a symbolic acting out of the old penalty known as the Extermination of the Three Clans (see Chapter 2). Punishments of this severity seem far out of line with the crime. Could it have been because prison labor was in desperately short supply in the capital? Unfortunately, no actual case is given to exemplify the crime or justify the judgment.

The Significance of Lingchi in Hongwu's Judgments

The lingchi case summaries in the *Grand Pronouncements* have more than corruption in common. They involve actions taken to prevent corruption from being discovered and to subvert attempts to bring it to justice should it be discovered. The perversion of justice seemed to distress Hongwu even more than corruption itself, for he compounded the penalties that would have been appropriate to state economic crimes had there been no conspiracy to prevent their being reported from below or investigated from above. Hongwu went very hard on officials who tried to subvert the laws as well as break them. The punishments issued were harsh, as he says in each case, "to alert the masses," but he expected his officials to pay equal attention. He declares at the end of "Allying with the Corrupt and Forming Hidden Factions": "All academy students and metropolitan graduates in office, look upon this and take it as a great warning. Only by committing yourselves to remaining proper men throughout your career will fortune be yours!" He makes the point even more bluntly at the end of the case of the two censors who tried to bribe the chiliarch: "all ye officials who are morally superior men, look on this [or, look on them] and avoid acting thus [or, as they did]" (3.39).

None of the lingchi cases in the *Grand Pronouncements* was for Great Sedition in the usual sense—which means that the punishment in every case exceeded the penalty the Code prescribed.[22] If the condemned were aware of the penalties stipulated in the Code for their actions, they must have been surprised at their sentences. Hongwu was not simply raising penalties by one grade, from decapitation to lingchi, for example, for only a few were decapitation cases. True, Shen Yi's forgery of an imperial document to levy Suzhou labor was a clear decapitation offense, as was Yang Li's connivance with a capital official to keep his purloined salt. But most lingchi verdicts involved crimes subject to lesser punishments. The serious bribery and embezzlement cases should have resulted in strangulation, the next grade of execution down from decapitation. Some of the cases did not even involve capital crimes. Imposing illegal corvée was weighted in the Ming Code at a hundred blows of the heavy bamboo and three years' banishment to the border, not execution. Altering or destroying administrative account books, as Jin Qian did, was punishable by eighty blows of the heavy bamboo. Li Fuyi's trick of getting a tithing head drunk to prevent him from stopping his forced labor levy was certainly not a capital crime; nor were Wu Qingfu's numerous high-handed exactions on the people of She county, however much his tactics may have enraged a poor peasant such as the emperor once was.

What was it about the particular cases that ended in lingchi that caused Hongwu to apply that penalty? Three elements run through the cases, though not equally in every case. The first is a feeling of personal betrayal. Whether moral outrage was really a salient element in shaping sentencing is difficult to determine, given that it is part of the storytelling pose that the emperor adopts in this text. Still, the sense of betrayal is there, though it is perhaps more ardent in the earlier cases than in the later. In 1385 Hongwu was still angry about the betrayal he felt Guo Huan and Hu Weiyong had perpetrated against him, and he could still be hurt and dismayed that an official would directly flout his laws. Perhaps by 1387 he could no longer affect surprise that his officials would act this way, but only express amazement that his harsh handling of earlier cases had failed to convince them to stay within the law. But other matters came into play in each case. Even with his ungrateful favorite Jin Qian, something more fundamental was at stake than the emperor's feelings: the perpetration of massive fraud, and more generally the indifference of highly privileged officials to the abuse of power.

Second, the lingchi cases have in common a concern that the course of justice had been perverted. Often this involved making a false accusation to cover up one's own guilt. From the emperor's point of view, however, the perversion of justice was not itself the main issue; it was the accountability of the system, and therefore the legitimacy of the dynasty. Hongwu had put an administrative system into operation, but that system worked only if those who disobeyed the rules were caught and punished. The legitimacy of the system depended on the public's seeing that this was done. If justice were not seen to be done, then the Ming system was little better than the Yuan system it replaced, and the founder could not claim to have merited the mandate of heaven. This meant Hongwu had to view the integrity and effectiveness of administrative justice in such stark terms. His claim to have legitimately founded a new dynasty depended on punishing not just those who broke the laws, but those who mocked them by short-circuiting the judicial process.

A third common element in the lingchi cases is the economic nature of the crimes being punished. The case that best illustrates Hongwu's sensitivity to economic crime is the one about soaked tax beans. Hongwu felt amply justified in calling for lingchi for a crime with such serious economic consequences. The person who submitted soaked beans may not have intended to cause an entire storehouse of beans to rot, but he should have understood the consequences of his minor fraud. Accordingly, the act was not the judicially trivial one of underpaying tax. The soaker had to bear responsibility for causing such a large loss for the state.[23]

In short, the lingchi sentences in the *Grand Pronouncements* communicate Hongwu's sense of personal betrayal, his dismay at the perversion of justice, and his abhorrence of economic crime. The one thing they do not communicate is lack of reflection or blind fury. The task of judgment, according to traditional judicial thinking, is to use penalties to distinguish the degree of the moral offense of the crimes they punish. Harsh penalties frame mild ones, and vice versa, thereby communicating the structure of the moral order they are intended to uphold.[24] Hongwu was extreme in the punishments he handed down, but he felt that extremity was justified because it served to distinguish the most serious crimes from the lesser ones.[25] Lingchi was not a blanket sentence he used every time he lost his temper. The

Grand Pronouncements includes well over two hundred other cases in which he did not impose lingchi. He used this sentence only when, in his judgment, it was fully deserved. If the hectoring narrative voice suggests the emperor was taking his officials' misconduct personally, he probably was. But that does not mean that he had gone mad. He was simply using the penalties the Chinese penal repertoire made available to him, albeit applying them rather more freely than had been previous practice. "Punishment is the way of castigating the evil," he once declared. The ancients had relied on the Five Punishments to bring the people to a state of benevolence; he was simply following their example.[26] Even though lingchi was outside the Five Punishments, the penalty conformed to the principle of the Five Punishments, which was to punish so as to achieve ultimate peace.

Hongwu was not unaware that contemporaries regarded his punishments as excessive. "Those who do not know the troubles of the court will say the punishment is cruel," he acknowledges defensively in the first compilation, but harsh penalties are unavoidable in the degraded times in which he has the misfortune to rule. "To be able to set one's mind in this way," as he himself had done by being so tough on crime, "shows the understanding of the morally superior man" (1.53). His responsibility, he states in his preface to the first compilation, is to strive toward the ancient ideal of "creating good fortune for the people";[27] it is not to create a system that allows his officials to oppress the people and feather their nests. Only when he has succeeded in putting in place a proper social hierarchy in which each can survive and be protected according to his station will the realm enter a time of ultimate peace. Lingchi was a tool toward that will. Hongwu was sure that good people would approve of his willingness to exceed the sentences in the Ming Code. They would understand he was doing it for their sake.

Hongwu's willingness to exceed the sentencing guidelines of his own Code created a legal problem for his judicial officials: how to adjust the provisions in the emperor's sentences with the judgments enshrined in imperial case law. The emperor was untroubled by the inconsistency and made several moves over the following decade to confirm the authority of both. In 1391 he ordered the Ministry of Rites to direct all students registered at county schools throughout the realm "together to read the Pronouncements and the Code."[28] The questions on the annual tribute student examination that year were supposed to be drawn from the *Grand Pronouncements,* and students were expected to discuss contemporary policy issues in their answers. The next year he reconfirmed the primacy of the *Grand*

Pronouncements by informing officials and people that they should recite all three compilations within their families to ensure that the wisdom they expressed was passed down to the next generation. He also promised that any student who came to the capital and recited one of the three by heart would get a reward.[29]

In the latter years of his reign, Hongwu's officials tried to follow what they saw as his example by calling for heavier punishments to be written into the Code. On April 19, 1397, Minister of Justice Xia Shu asked permission to upgrade the punishment for great sedition in the Code to Extermination of the Three Clans, a sentence that would be carried out by hacking apart all male relations of the culprit and enslaving all his female relations. Extermination of the Three Clans was a penalty that Hongwu himself imposed in a few cases; it appears six times in the second compilation of the *Grand Pronouncements* and once in the third.[30] Minister Xia must have thought that he was simply suggesting something that his emperor wanted. To justify the move, Xia pointed out that this would restore the practices of the Han dynasty. He must have been surprised when his emperor roundly declined the suggestion. Hongwu pointed out that Han law was nothing but a copy of its predecessor, Qin law. He had no wish to revive the excessive practices of that most evil of dynasties. Nor did he wish to burden his successors with severe sentences that, once entered into the Code, could not be changed. Minister Xia dared to press his case further, insisting that heavy penalties were better deterrents than light ones. Hongwu disagreed and ordered the minister to continue using the punishments in the Code.[31]

Hongwu's Legacy

A month and a half after rejecting Minister Xia's proposal for revision, on May 29, 1397, Hongwu issued his final edition of the Ming Code. This edition included an appendix presenting a digest of the main points in the *Grand Pronouncements*. In the preface, the emperor tells his officials that they should use both the Code and the Pronouncements when deciding legal cases.[32] Unfortunately, no book bearing the title that Hongwu gave it—*Da Ming lügao* (The Code and Pronouncements of the Ming dynasty)—has survived, so we have no way of assessing the weight he gave to his own sentencing in this new recension of Ming law. The new law book was certainly published, for the dynastic history makes a point of noting its influence.[33] Huang Zhangjian, the historian who has worked on the puzzle of this lost text, believes that it circulated under the title *Qinding lügao tiaoli* (Imperially authorized regulations from the *Code and Pronouncements*), and has found fragments copied into other texts.

Of more direct value for studying the history of punishments in the Ming are two lists from the Imperially Authorized Regulations that have survived: a list of twelve capital crimes in the Code and the *Grand Pronouncements* that are strictly ineligible for redemption by cash payment, and a list of twenty-four that are eligible.[34] Whereas it has become conventional to suppose that the authority of the *Grand Pronouncements* in Ming law declined after Hongwu's time,[35] these redemption lists suggest a more ambiguous history. Two lingchi cases are on the list of the two dozen cases eligible for redemption: "Idle People Conspiring to Commit Evil" (2.62), which forbade the use of state corvée to force people to labor for the benefit of private individuals, and "Subofficials and Jailers Selling Prisoners" (3.19). That these two cases were reduced to cash-redemption penalties could be taken as a sign that later practice desired to mitigate the more extreme lingchi judgments. On the other hand, the number of judgments not on the eligible list suggests that most of Hongwu's precedents stood.

Of the dozen crimes declared ineligible for redemption, only one comes from the *Grand Pronouncements:* "Officials and Commoners Using the Law to Engage in Corruption" (3.1). This is the long section at the beginning of the third compilation, in which Hongwu runs together eighteen cases of official corruption, five of which end in lingchi sentences. The decision to keep this penalty on the books indicates that the Ming state did not back away from Hongwu's conviction that officials should be held to a higher standard because of the responsibilities and privileges they enjoyed and the personal loyalty to the emperor their appointment implied.

Hongwu did not stop issuing lingchi sentences after the third edition of the *Grand Pronouncements* was published. A stream of similar proclamations *(bang)* summarizing judicial decisions, excoriating corruption and naming villainous officials and the penalties he made them suffer, continued to flow from the court. Although Hongwu did not produce another edition of the *Grand Pronouncements*, the Nanjing Ministry of Justice circulated a set of forty-four proclamations from the last decade of his life, between 1389 and 1398, plus another twenty-five issued during the first decade of the Yongle era between 1402 and 1411.[36] They indicate that Hongwu continued to regard lingchi as an appropriate punishment for those he considered the worst offenders. Eleven of Hongwu's proclamations involve a lingchi sentence, if we include three cases for which "extreme punishment" was designated as the penalty. Half the cases deal with crimes with which we are already familiar, such as bribing officials and destroying fiscal records, though the emperor does depart from *Grand Pronouncements* precedents by having military officers, not just civilian officials, dismembered. Even more striking, however, are the sentences handed down for matters having nothing to do with the security or financial viability of his regime. In 1389, he legislated lingchi as the punishment for showing up in Nanjing to file a false legal suit; in 1393, for impersonating an official to secure favors; and in 1394, for buying a young man who had been forced into slavery, for entering into improper adoption and marriage relations, and for failing to observe mourning for a parent.[37] These cases suggest that the elder Hongwu was willing to extend the use of dismemberment as a punishment in two new ways. Lingchi could now fall on ordinary people as well as officials, and it could be used to punish not just corruption and the breach of imperial trust but also violations of morality. In other words, lingchi was now showing up freely across the entire penal system, punishing anyone for anything the emperor found offensive.

Hongwu's successor, Emperor Jianwen (r. 1399–1402), was not keen on his grandfather's use of cruel punishments, but he was not on the throne long enough to reverse the legislation.[38] When his uncle usurped the throne in 1402 and took the title of Emperor Yongle, he reconfirmed his father's use of punishments.[39] Yongle did mitigate certain harsh penalties of the Hongwu era, such as removing the sentence of execution on private silver trading in 1404 in tacit acceptance that his father's system of paper currency was a dead letter.[40] But Yongle made use of extreme penalties when moved to do so, especially in the first year of his reign when dealing with anyone who challenged his usurpation. Huang Zicheng and Fang Xiaoru, prominent officials under Emperor Jianwen who refused to transfer their loyalty to Yongle, were condemned to die by what their biographers in the dynastic history refer to as *zhe*, "butchering," rather than as lingchi (Fang's biography specifies that he was "put to *zhe* in the marketplace"). It is said that their ordeals lasted for three days. Yang Ren, a prefect who tried to hide Huang Zicheng, was also condemned to *zhe*.[41] Yongle's Ministry of Justice in Nanjing also made heavy use of lingchi at the beginning of his reign.[42]

Yongle went beyond his father's precedents by legislating lingchi for new offenses: in 1403 for corruption committed by officials overseeing imperial textile production, and for bringing a false legal suit against ten or more people; in 1404 for making unauthorized state levies of labor and supplies; and in 1419 for failure of military officials to post copies of Hongwu's final hortatory text, the *Proclamation to the People (Jiaomin bangwen)*, for their soldiers to read.[43] If these new cases suggest a common concern, it is with officials who fail in their duties—which is in keeping with Hongwu's use of lingchi. It is difficult to say whether these penalties were ordered in extraordinary moments or were consistent with regular practice. What we can conclude is that Yongle was willing to continue his father's penal regime. In so doing he accomplished just what his father would have wanted, the extension of Hongwu's legacy beyond the Hongwu era.

Countervailing forces nonetheless arose as soon as Yongle died in 1424. His successor, Emperor Hongxi, issued a general instruction as soon as he ascended the throne ordering his judicial officials to return to the Code and not to exceed the sentences therein. Hongxi mentions lingchi in this instruction, declaring that it could be applied only for the crimes to which it was attached in the Code.[44] Hongxi did not live beyond the year of his enthronement, as it turned out, yet he set an example that his successors followed, which was to issue an inaugural statement confirming the correctness of the Ming Code and warning officials against exceeding its stipulations.

The aura of the *Grand Pronouncements* continued to influence judicial proceedings, nonetheless, and it is important to note that not everyone objected, especially as the Hongwu reign receded further into the past. When the retired official Lu Rong (1436–1494) at the end of the fifteenth century looked back to praise Hongwu, he singled out the *Grand Pronouncements* as one of three initiatives that enabled the founder to "renovate the realm." He reports that the text continued to serve as a reference for judicial officials ever after, though the people, he notes, no longer recited the text and in fact lacked any knowledge of its contents.[45] An activist county magistrate in Fujian in 1570 continued in this reverential vein by urging the local people to gather for group recitation of the *Grand Pronouncements* and the Code—though there is no evidence that anyone followed his advice.[46] A jurist writing half a century later similarly saw fit to praise both the Code and the Pronouncements as the core of Ming law around which the gathered substatutes and precedents produced a complete legal system for ruling the realm.[47]

There is no consistent evidence after the Yongle era regarding the use of lingchi during the rest of the Ming dynasty, but fragmentary evidence indicates that it continued in use. The most famous such execution was of the hated eunuch Liu Jin, whose treasonous plotting so enraged the Zhengde emperor (r. 1506–1522) that he ordered him to undergo a three-day lingchi in 1510. In fact, Liu expired on the morning of the second day.[48] Zhengde also handed down sentences of lingchi for men who led a rebellion in the Beijing region in 1512, and for a foreign envoy who murdered a fellow envoy.[49]

While such evidence suggests that lingchi continued to be used as a punishment for the worst crimes beyond Zhengde, it is impossible to say how frequently the penalty was imposed.[50] On the one hand, one seventeenth-century scholar observed that the Jiajing emperor (r. 1522–1566), although willing to punish censors who spoke out against him, nevertheless declined to execute them—with only one exception, which ended in lingchi.[51] On the other hand, we get a different impression from a magistrate's report on the penal affairs of a prosperous county in Zhejiang in 1566. When the eminent scholar Gui Youguang (1507–1571) arrived at Changxing county on the south shore of Lake Tai that year to take up his magistracy, he had to file a report to his superiors on the state of judicial matters in the county, and this report has survived in his collected works. According to the report, seventy-nine people were in the Changxing county jail awaiting execution: twenty-five by strangulation, fifty-one by decapitation, and three by lingchi. If this figure is in any way representative, it suggests that 4 percent of capital cases may have ended in lingchi. Even more striking is the sense this statistic gives that the penalty had expanded well beyond the court and was being applied to more than high officials suspected of treason. Gui does not say whether he thought the sentence of lingchi appropriate, legitimate, or even severe, suggesting that the penalty was too thoroughly embedded in judicial culture to excite comment at this time. He regrets that so many people have been sentenced to execution, but he does not single out lingchi for comment.[52] It was simply one form of the death penalty among several that the law required him to use.

Was there something unique about Gui's time and place? We get a very different picture from the legal records of Yan Junyan, who served as a provincial judge in Canton at the end of the 1620s when piracy was a serious problem, and later compiled his judgments into a vast compendium of some thirteen hundred case summaries. Not one of the thirteen hundred ended with a sentence of lingchi. The worst penalty Yan handed down was *xiao*, exposing the head of a criminal in a public place after decapitation. Yan reserved this treatment for half a dozen of the worst cases of armed robbery resulting in homicide.[53] Exposure of the head had been a device favored by the Hongwu emperor, but it was not dignified with a place among the Five Punishments. In a practical sense it was superfluous to the sentence of decapitation, but in a legal sense it communicated a higher degree of disapproval of the crime in question. The absence of lingchi sentences in Yan's collection may simply demonstrate that most Ming judges, who anyhow had little occasion to try treason cases, remained within the Code when sentencing. Yan's casebook should caution us not to take the occasional reference to the use of lingchi as evidence of a judicial system in which dismemberment was consistently a typical way of dispatching detested criminals, as visitors to China in the nineteenth century were wont to think.

What we can conclude is that the Hongwu emperor, in this as in so many other matters, powerfully shaped the realm he ruled and set patterns for institutions and practices that lasted long into the future. Extending the use of lingchi beyond the crimes for which it was listed in the Ming Code may have only temporarily altered the judicial landscape of China during his dynasty. Nonetheless, the penalty remained in use through the remainder of the late imperial period, and so was there for Europeans to witness when they began to visit China in significant numbers during the nineteenth century. Coming as they did from penal regimes where tormented execution was no longer practiced or tolerated, they were naturally shocked by what they saw. Lingchi then served to confirm their worst prejudices about the barbarity of China and its inferiority to the West. This judgment was understandable, but it also failed to recognize the complexity of the penal legacies of both China and Europe. But how were nineteenth-century Europeans to know that the use of lingchi derived in part from the Ming founder's desire to bring an end to official corruption so that he could lead his people into the realm of ultimate peace?

CHAPTER 5

Tormenting the Dead

The history of tormented execution in China is more than a history of laws and actions. It is also a history of representations and visualities, including what could be imagined as well as what could be seen. In this chapter we shift our attention from the doings of emperors and magistrates to the responses ordinary people had to the reality of living in a polity in which tormenting others was a regular practice. Although there is almost no direct record of such responses, we can trace the shadows of popular thoughts and fears by examining representations of a part of Chinese society no one could really visit—purgatory. Purgatory was a place of the popular Buddhist imagination between death and life through which all people had to pass when they died. This was where good deeds were rewarded and bad deeds punished, where the dead were forced to pay for the unfinished moral business of their past lives before they could be cleared to return to the wheel of existence and be reborn. If that moral business had left a deficit, as it did for most people arriving in purgatory, payment on that debt was exacted in the most basic currency of all, bodily suffering.

To judge from the rich pictorial evidence that survives from the nineteenth century, there was almost no limit to the extravagant torments of posthumous punishments that the zealous could imagine and the pious were invited to fear. Chinese called the place where these punishments were administered "the underground prison" (*diyu*). The earliest Europeans to hear about this underground prison called it "hell," following their own Christian understanding of the suffering that the evil could expect after death. Christian hell was a permanent sentence of everlasting torment, however, whereas Chinese hell was a transitional phase that everyone passed through between departing the life just lived and entering the life to which one was to be reborn. Given the transitory character of the suffering that the sinful experienced in the underground prison, we have chosen to translate *diyu* using a different Christian term, "purgatory." As Jacques Le Goff has shown in the case of mediaeval Europe, purgatory—"an intermediary other world in which some of the dead were subjected to a trial that could be shortened by the prayers, by the spiritual aid, of the living"—has not always been present in the Christian imagination. It was a fairly late addition, achieving its full theological form only in the twelfth century.[1] Keeping in mind that the analogy between *diyu* and purgatory is a rough one and that the Chinese drew no strong distinction between purgatory and hell, then we can note Chinese culture invented this intermediate period of posthumous suffering much earlier than did European. The Chinese were perhaps slower in imagining purgatory in all its lurid details than were their mediaeval European counterparts, though.[2] Also, the Chinese version was tied to a different eschatology. Postmortem suffering was not designed to achieve perfection prior to eternal communion with God. It was not a place to which sinners went to "purge" their sins once and for all.[3] The underground prison was instead the place to which everyone went immediately after death: the good were quickly excused once their cases had been examined, while those who had moral accounts to settle from their previous life received the punishments that paid off those debts before going on to the next.

This purgatory was vividly embedded in the religious imagination of the era and it was made familiar by its surreal similarity to the real world of everyday life, including real-world mechanisms of retribution. In this chapter, we shift from the torments real people suffered at the hands of the judicial system to the torments that they could imagine suffering after their death. This exploration allows us to open a window on the psychic burden of living under a penal regime that battered bodies, decapitated heads, and cut its very worst criminals to pieces.[4]

The connection between the real and the imagined is never straightforward, we realize. We nevertheless resort at points to reading from the imaginary back to the real hypothetically, because of the dearth of material from the late imperial era that would allow us to approach directly the experience of living under the severe penal regime of that time. Allowing that connection commits one to accepting, at least provisionally, that at some level the imaginary relies on the real to be intelligible, and that the worst the imagination can envision reflects what people most feared. For heuristic purposes, we posit that the torments that filled purgatory related, at least indirectly, to real-world practices, if not real-world experiences. Yet we do not want to allow ourselves to glide too far on this assumption, given that the imagination is capable of giving form to and investing meaning in things that could never happen in the here and now. The next world is never a pure reflection of this one; we have to bear in mind that their relationship is much more complicated.

Many cultures have imagined a postdeath purgatorial transition during which bad people are made to suffer for their sins; so too, many cultures have used images of real-world suffering to portray the purgatorial experience. Our main concern in this chapter is not with identifying precise correlations between real and imaginary punishments, however, but with understanding how the afterlife was depicted in China as a place of postmortem torment, why that torment was administered as it was and to whom, and what effects the idea of purgatorial torment might have produced on those who were shown pictures of this torment. If we could assume that these pictures had real-world correlatives, we might try to read back to those correlatives from the pictures. As Le Goff observed in passing regarding Christian images, European torments in purgatory were "all too obviously copied from practices that unfortunately had not yet vanished from this world."[5] But were they? Was the relationship between what was represented as happening in the afterlife and what could be seen taking place in this life always so close? We find that Chinese pictures of the afterlife that appear in nineteenth-century morality books often reveal a great deal more about stereotypes of judicial torment than they do about actual practices, that they are more fantasies than sketches from life. We must beware of reading them naively as depictions of what went on in Chinese courts, despite the overt invocation of the yamen (magistrate's court) setting. We can, however, take these pictures as evidence of how people felt about tormented execution—not the highly educated jurists we encountered in Chapter 3 who could expound upon classical references to the desecration of the body, but rather the ordinary folk who may have quailed at the sight of lingchi executions, and who lived in near-constant fear of becoming bodies in pain and dissolution. The images of purgatory that circulated among them bear telltale signs in particular of the motivations of the people who produced them. We take these to be suggestive of the sociopolitical elements that pervaded the Chinese religious imagination in the nineteenth century (and possibly beyond) and made the experience of the afterlife believable as a realm of unrelieved torment and endlessly repeated executions.

The Homology of Imagined Worlds

Nineteenth-century Chinese imagined the afterlife as the *yinshi*, "the world of shadow," in perfect counterpoint to the *yangshi*, "the world of light." The world of shadow was the realm where divine justice caught up with every unrewarded goodness and unpunished evil.[6] This conceptual structure assumed that the worlds of shadow and light, of the dead and the living, were homologous, in the sense that what went on in one also went on in the other, but in a different mode or key. The *yinshi* reiterated the contours of the *yangshi* and enhanced them by rendering visible the deities and demons that remained potential and invisible in the world of light. But it is not enough simply to accept that the world of shadow is a replica of the real world, for we need to understand the precondition that makes imagining things possible in the first place. To imagine a realm we cannot know, we can only begin from the realm we experience as real: we can only mime it. But this process of imagining does not simply render the imaginary as the real is; it filters and simplifies the real world into something more bounded, more regular, more under our control. Only within those bounds, where the experienced slides into the representable, is it possible to imagine the world of the dead. The *yangshi*, the "world of light," must first be defined before the *yinshi* can assume definition. The relationship between the two worlds is never mechanistic, since the imagination has the power to depart from reality at any point; even so, the designer of the afterlife cannot imagine what is to be experienced there except by distilling or stylizing what can happen in this life.

Netherworlds seem to require this sort of structured idealization. In no religion is the world of the dead a place of random chaos; it is a place where certain things can be expected to occur, and in certain ways. Without this predictability, the world of the dead would not be regarded as the appropriate, if regrettably delayed, realm in which the morally unfit could be forced to complete the moral tasks left over from the world of the living. The homology between them may allow the religious imagination to project the certainties of the *yinshi* back onto the *yangshi*, but this idealization of the world of the living had to precede the construction of the world of the dead. The world of shadow is where the failure of righteousness to prevail in the world of light can be compensated for by being imagined as a realm in which things are always put right and righteousness never fails. The fact that it never fails in just the ways in which it always fails in this life is what creates the sense of homology between their punishment systems. There is no reason why punishments in the afterlife should have the same functions and be performed in precisely the same ways as in this life, but they can be imagined only through such parallelism. The world of the dead does not so much recapitulate the world of the living as propose what the world of the living could be if it had the rationality, order, and systematic moral logic that are imagined to govern the world of the dead.

The homology in the structures of this-worldly and netherworldly punishments should not incline us toward that most widespread, but highly reductive of essentialisms about China, that the religious imagination of the late imperial era was trapped within the cultural parameters of a bureaucratic polity. Looking at pictures of underworld judges in government offices handing down sentences of corporal punishment and tormented executions even worse than lingchi, as we will do, could lead us to suppose that the world of the dead has been made to look that way because this is how nineteenth-century Chinese experienced the world of the living: as a realm where moral discipline emanated from the state, and where the state imposed hideous mutilations on those who failed to observe that discipline.[7] A parallel is implied, yet can we accept this logic of representation? Did most Chinese in this period have an opportunity to see in the *yangshi* any of the sights shown in these pictures of the *yinshi?*

Consider, by contrast, the basis of representations of religious torment in late medieval Europe. When thirteenth-century Florentine painters had to depict scenes from the Last Judgment, they had only to go out to the local sites of public chastisement to see punished bodies in pain.[8] Far less of such visible physical torment was available to Chinese illustrators. They were more likely to make copies of pictures, not copies from real life. Niida Noboru has proposed, with only slight caution, that the pictures of whippings and canguings in tenth-century illustrations of *The Scripture of the Ten Kings* (see below) can be taken as reasonably faithful accounts of actual practice in the Tang dynasty.[9] The beguiling simplicity of the pictures may have induced him to think this, as only the most uncomplicated punishments are illustrated there, but can we assume the same with the more violent pictures we examine here? Ordinary Chinese under the Qing did not get to see most of the torments shown in these pictures, for the simple reason that no magistrate would dare let his underlings commit such atrocities, which vastly exceed what Qing law permitted. The illustrators who drew these images of netherworldly torment intended to make them *look like* the acts of torture that went on inside state judicial institutions, but they projected an image that was not real, except perhaps during the reigns of exemplary tyrants such as the Khitan founder of the Liao dynasty.[10] The pictures show how the illustrator imagined the dead could be tormented, not how the living were. By the same token, they gave viewers an opportunity to imagine the intensity with which state torment could be applied rather than to see firsthand what the state actually did, the better to fear that prospect.

Reflecting on how little Chinese readers would have actually known about the torments shown in these pictures is important if we wish to approach the social and political effects of viewing them—an approach that the pictures invite, as they were published with the intention of producing social and political effects through mimesis. Anthropologist Michael Taussig describes mimetic representation as "the magical power of replication, the image affecting what it is an image of, wherein the representation shares in or takes power from the represented." Mimetic representation, as he puts it, "sutures the real to the really made up."[11] Every society depends on this work of fantasy in order to give those living in the society a sense of coherence between their experiences and the political and moral demands placed on them. How far the coherence of the "really made up" can be sustained in displacement from "the real" varies culturally, though it is never at such a distance that "the real" entirely disappears. The value of such representational work to any political regime is that it operates on subjectivities rather than just on bodies: it is economical in cost, subtle in its oppressions, and pervasive in its effects. The state does not have to mutilate bodies in order for its subjects to fear such mutilation or believe that it will fall on them; it has only to encourage its representation. If we think of the purgatory pictures we are about to examine as mimetic representations rather than as transcriptions of reality, then we can better understand the intended effects of these pictures on their consumers and, more to the point, understand why depictions of tormented bodies were judged to be appropriate for suturing the political realm (where torments were occasional and exemplary) to the religious (where torments remained ubiquitous and endless).

However purely imaginary the religious realm was, the political realm was not a fiction: this was where the mutilation took place and where real people had to think about the threat it posed to their own somatic integrity. This was after all the foundation from which the imagination of purgatory was launched. As one commentator insisted, real-world torments being as horrible as they are, the torments of the afterlife could only be that much worse. Recall real judicial suffering, he tells the reader, and you will be persuaded of the truly dreadful suffering that awaits the sinful on their return to the world of shadow.[12]

The Jade Register

The images of bodily torment examined in this chapter are taken from nineteenth-century woodblock prints of purgatory depicting the Ten Kings in their ten courts before whom all must appear after death. The Ten Kings examine the records of what the dead did in life, reward those who have done good, and punish those who have done evil. These images circulated as illustrations of a popular religious text known as the *Jade Register (Yuli)*.[13] Of the nine versions of this text published between 1863 and 1898 that we have examined, we have chosen *Yuli chaozhuan zhujie jingshi baofa* (Precious account of the Jade Register annotated and explicated, as a precious raft to warn the age) as the main text source for the observations and illustrations in this chapter.[14] The title page of this edition identifies Chengdu, Sichuan, as the place of publication, Wang Chengwen's Studio as the publisher, 1890 as the year the blocks were reengraved, and 100 bronze cash as the price.[15] A colophon by a minor literatus from nearby Guan county dates the actual printing of this copy to 1892. It was one of a print run of a hundred that he sponsored to assure the auspicious reburial of his parents.[16]

The history of the text is difficult to decipher.[17] Legend dates the original *Jade Register* to a Daoist priest of the Liao dynasty, Danchi, who received it from the Jade Emperor and later transmitted it in 1068 to his disciple Wumi, who wrote it down thirty years after that. This history suggests that the *Jade Register* was first printed in 1135. A now lost text entitled *Yuli qinfa* (Latch for opening the Jade Register), which surfaced in a campaign to destroy heterodox texts in 1390, may have belonged to this tradition. The man who identifies himself as the compiler of the edition on which we mainly rely in this chapter takes the pseudonym Zhenjizi, the Pure Master of Good Omen. He claims that the book, long lost, was rediscovered in Jiangxi province in 1761. His preface is dated 1837, though his edition may not have been published until Master Huang added a preface five years later.[18]

The origin of the illustrations is likewise obscure. Zhenjizi says he engaged "a skilled draftsman" to draw the pictures while he was working on his annotations, but are the pictures in the 1890 edition the work of the illustrator Zhenjizi hired? Liu Pinghai, editor of an 1871 edition, claims that it was he who had the illustrations made and inserted them into the book so that readers could "roam the world of shadow and examine things there." The close attention that both Zhenjizi and Master Huang pay to the illustrations in their prefaces (1837 and 1842, respectively), combined with the fact that a later editor's preface (1867) neglects to mention them, suggests that the illustrations go back at least to the 1830s. Stylistic features indicate that the illustrators were working within a genre that goes back at least to the Ming, if not before, but the sources have not yet been found that would allow us to trace their past in any detail.[19]

The pictures are framed by a text in which the Jade Emperor warns that goodness will be rewarded in the afterlife and immoral conduct will bring terrible consequences. The logic combines the ancient Chinese belief in the afterlife with the Buddhist mechanism of reincarnation, filtered through the Pure Land doctrine of accumulating merit through devotional practices. A 1572 inscription from a Buddhist monastery outside Shanghai outlines this doctrine: "Call the Buddha once to mind and you produce one item of goodness; produce one item of goodness and you get rid of one item of evil; get rid of one item of evil and you extinguish one punishment."[20] The "one punishment" was something the sinner would otherwise have had to suffer in purgatory; in other words, merely reciting the Buddha's name was all one had to do in this life to extinguish suffering in the next. The *Jade Register* takes this logic and dramatizes it by fully imagining what purgatory looks like and how every sin, great or minor, will be tallied and punished. It also, however, revises the confessional context. In the system of rewards and punishments the Jade Emperor oversees, Buddhist devotion has no role to play, nor do Buddhist values top the list of right conduct. The controlling cult is the cult of the Stove God, and the dominant virtues are almost exclusively the secular Confucian values of deference, filial piety, sexual continence, fair commerce, and refraining from slandering or making false accusations. The book's fixation on Confucian order is further enhanced by staging the punishment of sin within a series of what look like ten yamens, or magistrate's offices, the judicial environment of state Confucianism. The book indicates that the deceased should not think that they can trust their fate to a merciful Buddha. They should expect, rather, to find themselves thrown into a scarily familiar imperial cosmocracy in which members of a judicial hierarchy and their fearsome assistants process their cases according to strictly observed bureaucratic procedures.[21]

The idea that the deceased should expect to appear before ten kings belongs to a theology of purgatory that may have taken form before the Han dynasty, well before the introduction of Buddhism into China two millennia ago, and that was broadly accepted by the Tang. The earliest fully illustrated version of the story that survives today, however, is *The Scripture of the Ten Kings*, a manuscript preserved at Dunhuang and dated to the tenth century.[22] The motif of ten courts was much recycled and circulated subsequently in popular culture, particularly in the genre of vernacular literature known as "transformation texts" *(bianwen)* that emerged in the late Tang, which crossed freely between story-telling and sutra-lecturing.[23] Not surprisingly, between the time of the original *Scripture of the Ten Kings* in the tenth century and the *Jade Register* in the nineteenth, elements in the story changed. The *Jade Register* preserves the basic narrative of the deceased's passage through the ten courts, but it switches the order of some of the courts, alters the names of some of the kings, and attaches an elaborate prison bureaucracy overseeing a bewildering warren of 128 "minor earth prisons," which serve as permanent hells, each specialized in tormenting those guilty of a certain category of offense. Purgatory has become far more elaborate, and the dangers it poses for the timorous living far more explicit and threatening, in this "baroque cult of death," as Richard von Glahn nicely labels this new complex.[24]

While the details have grown more vivid in the later cult of the Ten Kings, its moral theology has gone through even greater changes. The *Jade Register* has discarded the original scriptural text, substituting entirely different explanations for what is going on. The greatest alteration between these versions of the text is the religious iconography that frames the story. The *Jade Register* encases the courts in a cosmos that subordinates the Buddhism of the original to a Confucian ideology favoring family and state. It imposes this reorientation at the start by inserting alongside Dizang and Guanyin, who were the presiding Buddhist deities of the tenth-century scripture, three non-Buddhist deities as arbiters of the moral judgments dispensed by the Ten Kings: the City God (Chenghuang) and the Emperor of the Eastern Peak (Dongyue dadi), popular worship of whom the state authorized in its ritual pantheon, and at the head of the queue of divine overseers, the supreme progenitor, the Jade Emperor. The Ten Kings then follow, more as officials appointed by these higher powers than as lords in their own right.[25]

The nine late imperial editions of the *Jade Register* we have seen all date from the nineteenth century. The earliest was originally published in 1863 in Chaozhou, Guangdong, and then enlarged and printed in Hubei province.[26] The others were all produced either in Sichuan or in Beijing, both centers of the cult of the Ten Kings in the late Qing. Sichuan appears to be the cult's place of origin from at least as far back as the Tang dynasty.[27] The *Scripture of the Ten Kings* comes from that region, and the elaborate Buddhist complex of purgatory statuary at Baodingshan, a thirteenth-century Buddhist site in central Sichuan, is today its most striking representation.[28] Beijing emerged later as a second center for the cult. A temple depicting the courts of the Ten Kings, attached to the complex of the Temple of the Eastern Peak (Dongyue miao) on the eastern side of the city, was a favorite tourist site, for foreigners as much as for Chinese. Postcards of the temple that tourists could buy and send home, bearing the title "Temple des Supplices," helped to put these images into circulation abroad and insinuate them into the aesthetic of Chinese horror that was infecting the European imagination early in the twentieth century. Temples of the Eastern Peak were common throughout North China, and at least some of them, such as the temple just outside Taiyuan, housed representations of purgatorial inquisition.[29] This incomplete evidence indicates that the purgatory cult was widely distributed across at least northern and western China in the late imperial era.

The *Jade Register*'s illustrations betray no visual debt to the Dunhuang versions of *The Scripture of the Ten Kings*. They draw instead from a richer and more sensational iconography of purgatory that proliferated subsequently throughout Chinese culture. In the tenth-century scripture, the dead passing through purgatory are forced to wear cangues and are threatened with sticks; none is shown suffering the vicious torments awaiting the nineteenth-century reader of the *Jade Register*. The text of the tenth-century scripture refers to these acts as "annoyances" *(xihuang)* rather than as soul-crippling torments.[30] The iconosphere of the *Jade Register* is far harsher and of a piece with the grisly pictorial representations of hell that Ming Buddhist monasteries posted when conducting the popular *shuilu* (water-and-land) masses for the dead, or that publishers inserted into popular tales about descending into hell.[31] These illustrations position the viewer at a later point in the history of Chinese pictorial representation, and possibly at a later point in the history of the Chinese religious imagination.

Representing Purgatory

The 1890 Chengdu edition of the *Jade Register* depicts each of the courts of the Ten Kings in a set of three panels extending over one and a half folios. The first panel shows the court of the presiding deity. He is dressed in full judge's regalia and seated behind a desk littered with documents. Attended by a host of minor civil and military aides, he has turned his stern attention onto the kneeling figures before him. The next two panels, spread over two facing pages, reveal a tableau of about half a dozen torments: the deity's execution ground. Each little scene stands as a demonstration of what can happen to the sinful in purgatory. In this judicial context, there is no need to extract truth or prompt confession, since the Ten Kings are omniscient. The penalties they dole out are nothing but just retribution on the wicked who escaped punishment before they died.

The pseudojudicial setting for these torments establishes a series of expectations on the part of the reader: that the good will be recognized, and the evil will be found out; that exact procedures will be followed to the letter to ensure that justice or retribution will be faithfully administered; that those who should suffer will; and that the sufferings inflicted will be commensurate with the evil done. These expectations are built on the idealization of how justice should be dispensed in the world of the living. Whereas the framing deities appear lenient, the Kings are shown to be remorseless in punishing the guilty to the letter. Only after the sentences have been completed are the tormented released from their particular hells and forwarded to the King Who Turns the Wheel of Rebirth (Zhuanlun wang) in the tenth court, for rebirth in their next incarnation. Torment is inescapable, but it is only imaginable in this system as finite.

Lest the inescapability of the torments doled out in purgatory provoke moral paralysis in the reader, the last piece of commentary closing the section for each court explains that a solemn vow never to repeat a punishable offense made to the Stove God on a designated day of the year will release the reader from afterlife punishment. (The Stove God, believed to inhabit the stove of every house, was the most familiar figure in the late imperial Chinese pantheon and the first to whom appeal was made to manage the small tribulations of daily life.[32]) The reader thus receives contrary instructions: the slightest slip from good conduct will result in torment, yet moral lapses can be canceled once a year by affirming the Stove God's power of redemption.

In this purgatory, each punishment must fit the crime. Sometimes the equivalence is literal: the person who has done harm is forced to have the same done to him through what we described in Chapter 3 as a mirror punishment. Sometimes the equivalence is literal in a different sense, through applying torment to the part of the anatomy that caused the offense.[33] There is otherwise no obvious underlying principle organizing the torments depicted in the *Jade Register*. They seem to unfold in random fashion one after the other as the viewer turns the pages. Certain crimes and torments appear clustered in certain courts, as we shall see, but there seems to be no consistent principle of grouping across the various regions of purgatory. All we can do is follow the illustrator by addressing the torments in the order in which he has arranged them in the book.

The pictures follow the text, which provides both more and less than the pictures. Where the text provides more is in the long roster of punishments that appears at the end of each court illustration. This is the list of the sixteen unique "minor hells" *(xiao diyu)* that are attached to each court. Although our usage departs from common Western conceptions, we shall refer to these minor hells as regions of purgatory. Each such region is specially prepared to receive those who have committed either of the two sins assigned to that hell, some of which are referred to explicitly in the illustrations. Where the text provides less than the illustrations is in the page or two that follow, where from eight to twenty-five sins punishable in this court are briefly described. The text makes no effort to align crimes to punishments. The illustrator makes the connections he chooses. Lest the precise consequences of a sin be lost on the viewer, the illustrator has inserted captions stating which punishment he is illustrating and what the victim did to deserve it. Even with the captions, the illustrations are not as informative as the text, but they are more dramatic. As Zhenjizi explains in his preface, the illustrations are there "to frighten and shock the viewer" so that "the ignorant" will "genuinely not dare not to reform themselves."[34] Master Huang in his preface initially gives equal weight to both the text, which one "reads" *(du)*, and the illustrations, which one "examines" *(an)*. Both are means intended to force the reader-viewer to reflect on the terrible consequences of sin. Thereafter, he tends to leave the text behind and dwell on the illustrations to provoke the heartfelt response from the reader that he is looking for. As he himself observes, "the illustrations have been drawn to perform many functions."

Master Huang is the reader's guide on his "return to the world of shadow" *(gui yin)*, as death is referred to. He closes his preface by inserting himself into the story and telling his reader, "I am happy to precede you into hell, where I will wait for you to follow me to the Ghost Gate and see for yourself."[35] The pure of word and deed pass a preliminary hearing before the Emperor of the Eastern Peak (Dongyue dadi) and are then permitted to bypass the Ghost Gate and go straight to the tenth court, where they are assigned their next incarnations. Everyone else must pass through the Ghost Gate and proceed to the first court, where they meet King Guang of Qin

玉歷鈔註
活大地獄
銅釜獄
在生奸謀圖利惧人終身誘引少年男女入空門者又入受此刑
又生前枉言殺害人並罵天地罰此小獄又殺小獄
三十一

玉歷鈔註
鐵碓獄
凡明瞞賠騙及含糊不以實告誤人終身者罰受此刑
劍葉獄
凡男不忠主女不忠夫者受此刑
凡男女乱淫者罰抱火銅柱
此犯点唱淫戲造淫詩淫畫受此刑
此女奸淫乱
此婦人乱淫
此人謀人妻女

楚江王
不忠不恥貪淫者罰銅掛刃山
此男女褻習字紙交十殿投生貴人子孫科甲報
悔後遲

(Qin guang wang). King Guang puts the dead through a first round of questioning, then stands them before the Mirror of Sin (Niejing), where they must review their evil deeds and thoughts from the world of light. Those who skipped words while reciting the sutras are sent off to a special lodge where they have to make up for the gaps. Suicides are singled out for confinement in the Yard of Starvation and Thirst (Jike chang). The rest are moved on to the next eight courts, where the magistrate-deities wait to judge their sins and mete out fierce punishments. We will limit ourselves to examining the torments in the first four, as the illustrator tends to repeat himself through the second half of purgatory.

The Punishments of the Underworld

The illustration of the execution ground of the Chu River King (Chujiang wang)[36] (Figure 12) depicts seven forms of tormented execution. In the upper right corner of the right-hand panel, demon attendants cast people off a cliff to be impaled on a mound of knives. The victims are identified as men who were disloyal to their masters and women who were disloyal to their husbands. This is the Minor Hell of Sword Blades (no. 14 in the numbered series of minor hells reserved for this king's use). To the left of this scene, two demons insert a person headfirst into an iron grindstone; blood drips between the stones and into a pan below, where a dog laps it up. This is the Minor Hell of the Iron Grindstone (no. 9) for those who deceive or bear false witness. In the bottom half of the panel, four people appear naked and bound front-first to heated bronze pillars: two women who engaged in indiscriminate sex, a woman who seduced a younger man, and a man who had sexual intercourse with another's wife. The curling of their arms and legs around the pillars alludes to fornication.[37] To the right, a fifth prisoner, charged with singing lewd songs, composing erotic verse, and drawing erotic pictures, is pinned down by a fan- and scissor-wielding demon who keeps the fires burning, while awaiting the same treatment.

In the left-hand panel, several people are being cooked in a copper pot for scheming to profit from other people's misfortunes or for corrupting youth;

Figure 12. *(Opposite Page)* The court of the Chu River King; this and the next two sets of illustrations are taken from the 1892 reprint of *Yuli chaozhuan zhujie jingshi baofa* (The precious account of the Jade Register, annotated and explicated, as a precious raft to warn the age).

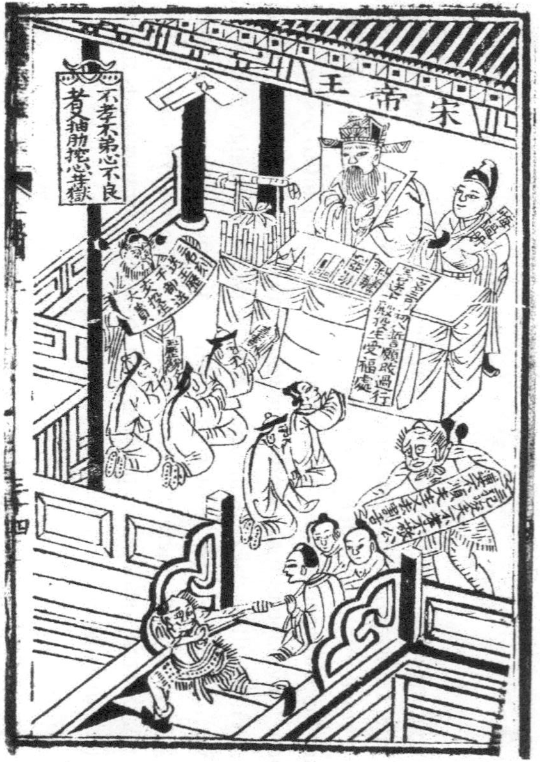
宋帝王
不孝不弟心不良
者入抽肋挖心獄

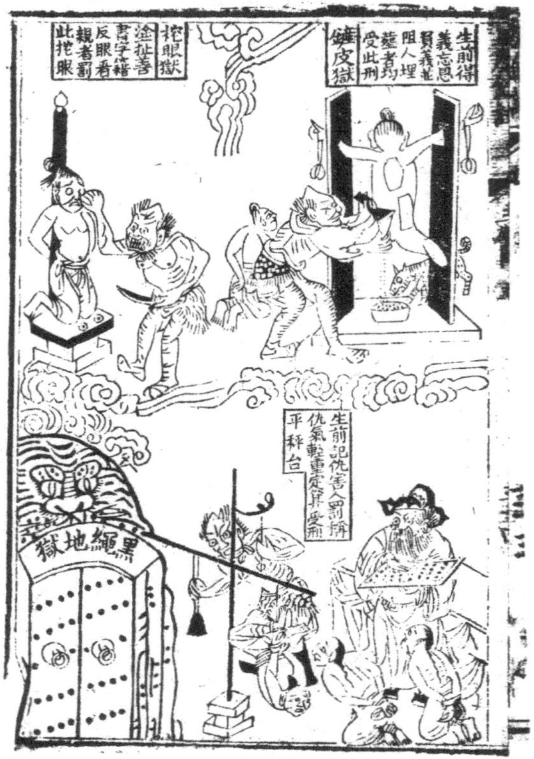
鏟皮獄
挖眼獄
黑繩地獄
平秤台

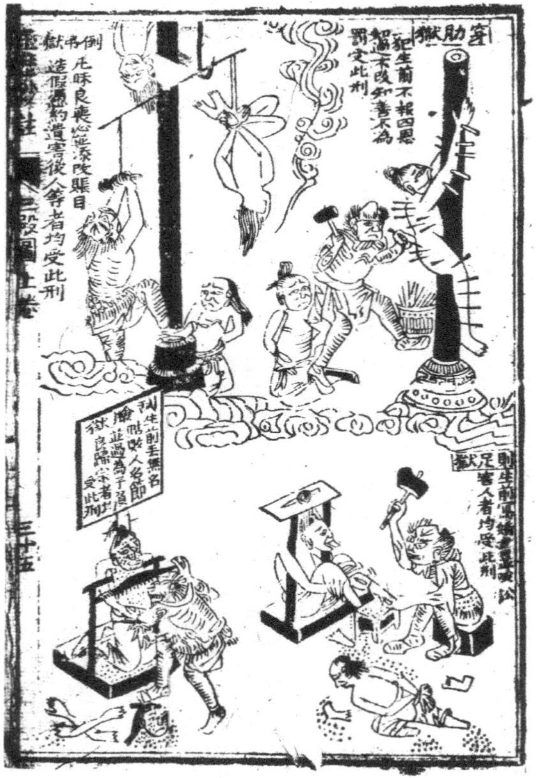
穿肋獄
倒吊獄

this is the Minor Hell of the Copper Pot (no. 7). At the bottom right, a man with an iron chain around his neck sits facing a demon about to pierce him from above with an iron rod. The image represents the Minor Hell of the Five Forks (no. 5), where those who spread rumors harming others are skewered. The bottom left-hand corner shows demons casting men and women into a pit of ice for contaminating the world or cursing their parents; this is the Minor Hell of Cold and Ice (no. 16). Finally, at the far left another demon has decapitated one person and is about to do the same to another. No caption explains what sin these people committed, but the image probably represents the Minor Hell of Cutting in Two (no. 13).[38]

These are only some of the harsh punishments one could expect to suffer on the order of the Chu River King, but it is immediately clear that all are quite beyond what a Qing magistrate could legally impose. They are imaginary torments that no viewer could see or experience in the real-world Chinese judicial system. These illustrations do not show people undergoing torment; they mime what imagined torments might look like, not how real torments appeared. And yet they are offered to the viewer as visual transcriptions of something real, in the expectation that literal readers will be shocked and scared by what they see. The logic of this representation runs counter to the logic of secrecy by which real-world penal systems operated. Tribunals in the late imperial judicial system were public, yet what happened while a prisoner was incarcerated was kept out of sight as a deterrent. In the *Grand Pronouncements* (see Chapter 4), the founding Ming emperor writes about the value of keeping the details of penal operations out of public view in what might be called the mystery of imprisonment. What goes on inside the penal system, he states, should not be allowed to become too widely known so that people will be doubly anxious about doing anything that might get them thrown in jail. Prisons should be places of mystery into which the innocent may not see so that their innocence might be preserved.[39] The strategy by which the *Jade Register* aims to excite fear is the exact opposite: put everything on display and in as much detail as the engraver can muster so that the sinful are intimidated into stopping their crimes.

In the next court, that of the Emperor King of Song (Songdi wang) (Figure 13), the torments seem less extravagantly fanciful. There are no mounds of knives or pits of ice here. Yet an attentive individuality to the sufferings that are depicted heightens the intensity of the violence. In the

---

Figure 13. *(Opposite Page)* The court of the Emperor King of Song.

upper right of the right-hand panel, a demon uses what looks like a hide scraper to take patches of skin from a man suspended on a rack by his wrists and ankles while another victim looks on. This is the Minor Hell of Skinning by Scraper (no. 8) for those who fail to repay kindnesses or who interfere with a burial. To the left, another demon has pulled out the eyes of a man bound to a stake on a platform; this is the Minor Hell of Eye Gouging (no. 7), reserved for those who blot or tear a morality book such as the *Jade Register*, or treat their relatives with contempt. The artist intensifies the image's effect by placing the victim's eyeballs on the platform in front of his knees. Below these scenes a man is being suspended upside down from a steelyard (used for commercial weighing) by a rope tying his wrists behind his back. Two others await this punishment for taking revenge on others or altering financial calculations.

Four punishments are shown in the left-hand panel (35a). In the upper right, a man is tied front-first to a pole and pierced along his sides with nails for failing to repay a kindness or for doing what he knows is evil; this is the Minor Hell of Side Piercing (no. 3). To the left, two figures with their ankles and wrists tied together are being suspended upside down on a mobile in the Minor Hell of Inverted Suspension (no. 12), for those who alter receipts or forge documents. Both these scenes have onlookers. In the lower right, the feet of a man tied to a restraining frame are being cut off. Another man who has already suffered this punishment lies facedown nearby with his hands bound behind his back. They represent the Minor Hell of Foot Amputation (no. 9) for those who draw up betrothal contracts with the intention of launching a lawsuit. Finally, at the lower left is a scene labeled as the Minor Hell of Face Gouging (no. 4), to which are consigned those who harm the reputations of others or oblige their sons to make good their errors. The artist has gone beyond the description in the text, for he shows a demon raking a long-toothed instrument down the face and the bloodied torso of a man who is locked in a restraining frame. A head and amputated arms lie on the ground nearby, suggesting the lethal extent to which this gouging could be carried.

The crimes that the Emperor King of Song punishes seem less extreme than those dealt with in the court of the Chu River King. In the preceding court, fornication, disloyalty, and the destruction of people's reputations were at the fore; here the acts have more to do with breaches of social, commercial, and familial reciprocity. The torments too are different. Instead of displaying the theatricality of knife mounds and ice pits where numerous bodies are thrown together, they tend to focus on individual bodies undergoing more precisely applied torments. The body is not overwhelmed from the outside, except for the minor hell in which the evil are immersed in brine (the Chu River King's minor hells included five immersions), but invaded. Metal instruments are applied to body parts that, other than fingernails and toenails, are all internal. The parasites in two of the minor hells also target the body's interior: scorpions inject venom into the body and leeches burrow into the body to drink the victim's blood from the inside. Instead of invoking the generalized mass anxiety of the Chu River King's execution ground, the illustrator here invites a more individual panic.

The torments on display in the next court, that of the King of the Five Offices (Wuguan wang), largely repeat those in the two preceding courts. Here the illustrator combines the extravagance of the River King's torments with the corporally invasive techniques of the Emperor King. The captions reveal that many of the sins being punished here fall into the category of economic crimes. For faking silver, one is confined to the Minor Hell of Burning the Hands with Boiling Water (no. 3). Sellers of fake medicines are condemned to climb Sisyphus-like up oiled rocks in the Minor Hell of Slipping on Oil Seeds (no. 14). Those who use inaccurate measures suffer in the Minor Hell of Pouring Bitter Medicine into the Mouth (no. 13). Damaging property or refusing to pay rent brings stoning in the Minor Hell of Broken Rocks Burying the Body (no. 16). The King of the Five Offices thus seems to oversee the punishment of tradesmen who, because their work cannot be readily verified, are suspected of defrauding their clients in real life.

The sixteen hells of Son-of-Heaven Yama (Yanluo tianzi) (Figure 14) are for punishing evil thoughts more than evil deeds. In the lower part of the right panel, five people are tied to pillars awaiting the execution depicted in the left panel, which is to have their abdomens cut open and their evil hearts removed. These are the first eviscerations we have seen in purgatory. Three others are shown in the third panel, and more appear in three of the later courts. In the last panel, dogs and birds feed on the entrails spilling from abdomens in two separate scenes. Horrible though this punishment is, it is not lingchi, which did not involve slitting the belly. As for the other two legal forms of the death penalty, the *Jade Register* shows many decapitations but not a single strangulation. If we are correct in regarding strangulation as the mildest death penalty because it leaves the body intact, then perhaps it lacked the visual ferocity of more visceral brutalities. There was nothing spiritually terrifying about this way of dying when there were so many more horrible ways to die.

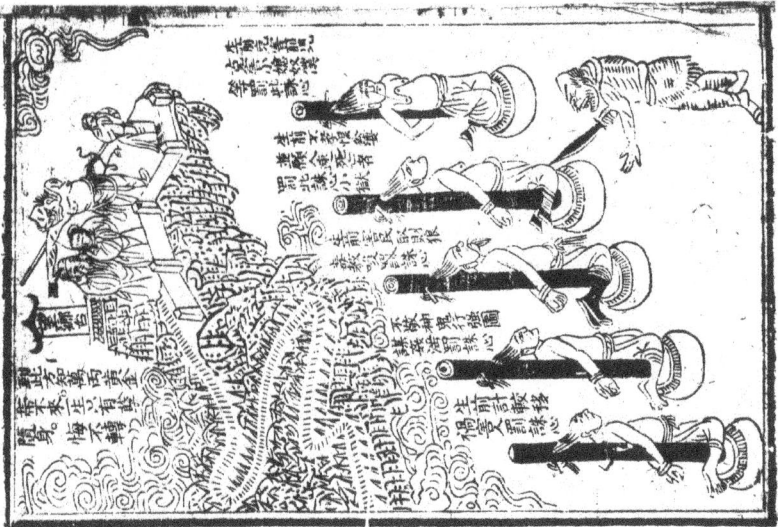

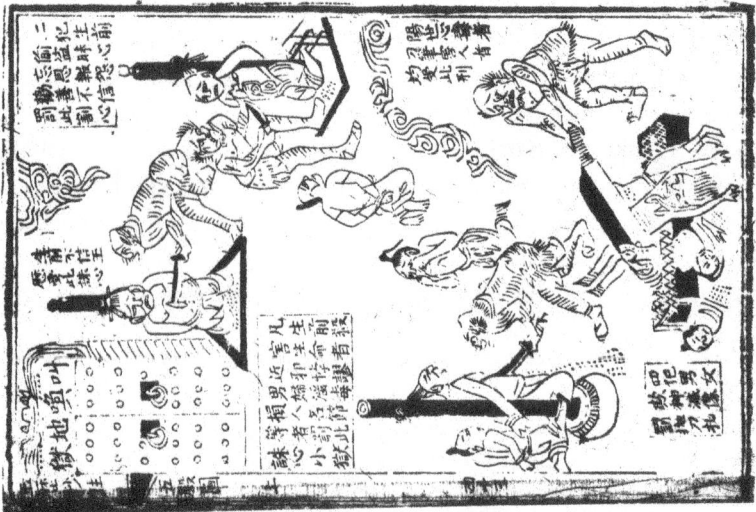

The Visibility of Mutilation

Through the pictures of the courts of the Ten Kings runs a consciousness of the experience of vision and a fear of seeing. In the very first court, the new arrival in purgatory is made to watch himself in the Mirror of Sin, the archetype of self-visibility in which one is permitted to glimpse not the surface of things but the reality beneath that surface. The horror of seeing—which is precisely the experiential mode through which the reader engages with the scenes of purgatory—is also highlighted in the first panel of the court of Son-of-Heaven Yama. A demon has led a wealthy family up a picturesque mountain path, which is lined with knives, and forces them to look down on the home to which they cannot return. A stele behind the family names the place as the Terrace for Gazing Homeward. A caption on the left reads: "When they reach this place, they realize that they can't bring their mounds of gold with them: all that accompanies them from their life is their sins. They want to turn away [from the sight] but cannot" (42b). The reader is reminded that the capacity to see brings with it the possibility of suffering.

For the figures caught in the illustrator's purgatory, seeing is one of the sources of suffering. Almost every punishment scene shows not just the person undergoing the punishment, but others in line for the same punishment who must wait and watch what is happening, knowing that this is what will happen to them. Those who are undergoing the experience are also depicted as seeing what is happening to them, and are horrified as much by the sight as by the experience. Torment victims are generally depicted with their eyes open, forced to suffer by seeing. The most intense objects of their vision seem to be their own bodies, blood, and discarded body parts. The tortured are thus not simply made to suffer physical torment, but to witness what is being done to their bodies. Even in the three scenes in the court of the Emperor King of Song for which the artist has not drawn an onlooker, the victim is made to see his body parts scattered about below him. Viewing the degradation of their bodies thus becomes part of the suffering, for it ensures that the victims know that their bodies are being taken apart. They are made to look at what is happening to them—something that Western writers alleged that lingchi victims experienced as they were being cut up.

The illustrator's concern with seeing is of course natural, for his task is to render visible the world of shadow, and through his work to provoke a

Figure 14. *(Opposite Page)* The court of Son-of-Heaven Yama.

response of horror in his viewer.[40] Master Huang certainly believed that the images he commissioned would go straight to the viewer's heart as soon as he laid eyes on them. So too Zhenjizi writes that he expects the scenes of physical torment to frighten and shock the reader. The pictures should first awaken belief, then stimulate fear, then inspire courage, then prompt goodness, and finally encourage steadfastness.[41] Even though Zhenjizi tells his literate readers how they are expected to react, we have little to go on to determine how ordinary readers saw these pictures. Passing comments in local sources from the late imperial era suggest that devout belief was not universal. For example, the 1488 gazetteer of Wujiang county, directly south of the city of Suzhou, notes that only in one township do most people "believe that heaven and hell really exist," and that this belief is fading among the "great families."[42] Some of the stories included in the second half of the *Jade Register* suggest that true believers, at least among the mildly educated of the nineteenth century, were in a minority, though even they display skepticism. Typical in this regard is Qiu Fuchu, a Nanjing merchant who picked up a copy of the book while on business in Suzhou in 1792. Though he was a filial person, the story relates, "Fuchu did not believe that ghosts existed or that there was a hell." Fuchu had a natural goodness, but it did not derive from the fundamental belief in the workings of fate and retribution and rested instead on nothing other than his good will. His first viewing of the book did not alter his views: "When Fuchu and his son looked at it, Fuchu declared it nonsense." He resisted its claims almost to the end. Only a vision of hell on his deathbed—persuasion often takes place through a vision, especially right before death—induced him to change his mind.[43]

Apart from the testimonials the book itself provides, there is little material revealing how people might have reacted to the *Jade Register*. Interestingly, some of the most earnest testimonials vouching for a literal viewing of the purgatory pictures come from converts to Christianity—another religion in which the pious were encouraged to imagine the suffering awaiting them beyond death. A Fujian schoolteacher who recalled seeing such pictures when he was a child in the late 1840s credited the fear of retribution they implanted in him with predisposing him to turn to Christianity later in life.[44] Another would-be convert from Fujian encountered purgatory pictures as an adult. "I was so affected by what these books said," he attested in a newspaper article in 1878, "that I felt my very hair and bones grow stiff with fear."[45] Converts may have had a particular interest in reacting just as the book invited them to, for a literal viewing of these pictures opened a conduit between the two traditions that may have enabled converts and missionaries to persuade Chinese of the "correctness" of the Christian version of purgatory. The similarity in how the purgatory was imagined in both cultures was perhaps the reason missionaries liked to collect copies of the *Jade Register* and why it was one of the first texts of Chinese popular religion to be published in English.[46]

The problem with accepting either a Christian or a deathbed convert such as Qiu Fuchu as our authority on how the average viewer responded to the pictures is inherent in the structure of the stories they usually tell. To be effective, the story has to allow that the subject at first did *not* read the pictures literally and was not emotionally affected by them, as was the case with Fuchu. This then allows for a conversion moment when the meaning of the images shifts and the viewer comes to accept the reality to which they point. A shift from an ironic, or at least skeptical, viewing to a literal one is what plots the movement in these stories from indifference and contempt to fear and belief. Not only that, but the convention of the genre assumes that most readers never made the jump, and that the subject who did was a person of exceptional moral or spiritual insight.

This quiet admission that most people were not persuaded by the images suggests that we have to entertain a different logic of viewing. Rather than assume that nineteenth-century Chinese were more literal in their viewing than we are, less canny and less alert to manipulation than we take ourselves to be, we should consider the possibility that these pictures of penal torments were about something else, and that nineteenth-century Chinese who viewed them did so not literally, as visions of purgatory, but vicariously, as mimetic representations of the real world around them.

Regimes of Fear

If we accept that the purpose of the *Jade Register* was to frighten viewers into realizing that sinful deeds had punishing consequences that would come in the afterlife if not in this life, then we have to ask in whose interest it was that people should fear. Referring to the very different context of European culture, Jean Baudrillard has argued that "the management of the imaginary sphere of death" was a significant basis for the power that priests and religious activists were able to claim for themselves, and in turn to use for the enlargement of state control. Catholicism institutionalized death by making it the point before which the individual, burdened with a lifetime's accumulation of merits and sins, was able to clear accounts through penances and indulgences. This "political economy of individual salvation" confirmed the logic of accumulation; it also brought death within the range of manipulation of elites working on behalf of the state's project of social control.[47]

A similar political rationality would seem to be at work in the *Jade Register*. The agents of this rationality are not the same as in Europe, for the *Jade Register* was not a state production, nor was it distributed by orthodox religious institutions, nor was it standard fare among the Confucian elite. Those who produced and sponsored the text occupied a lower rung on the social ladder. Who they were is not easy to detect because of the veil of pseudonymity that enshrouds the extant copies, yet there are clues in the testimonials to the book's impact on its patrons' social status that suggest how that status may have directed the ideological work the book was intended to do. These testimonials, which tell of good fortune coming to pious individuals who sponsor or distribute the book, are problematic as evidence, as the compiler's urge was to enhance the social status of those he associated with the book.

The occasional merchant appears, such as Qiu Fuchu. Far more consistently represented, however, are men who struggled as candidates at the lower rungs of the state examination system. Pan Yangzhi was a "Confucian student" in Guidong county, Hunan. Fan worked in a prefectural school. Li Shuyu was the son of a county school instructor. The only case that reports actual examination success is the story of Li Hengfa, whose "sons and grandsons" were said to have passed the exams because Li gave away copies of the *Jade Register*. There is no indication, however, that Li's offspring themselves took this ideology of redemption on board.[48] The testimonials in *Yuli chaozhuan jingshi*, an 1883 edition printed in Wanxian, Sichuan, include similar stories of men who were outside the charmed circle of the gentry elite but whose progeny later succeeded in the examination system, though in the cases of a philanthropist from Suzhou and a wealthy man from Changshu, the effect did not show itself for three generations.[49] These stories and references suggest that the social stratum that sustained the *Jade Register* was the lower end of the educated elite, the most eminent of whom ascended only as far as the bottommost rung of the educational bureaucracy. The state existed for them as the ultimate point of status reference, but they were excluded from sharing in its legitimacy and authority: none was ever in the position of the magistrate whose inquisitorial actions the fearsome Ten Kings appear to mime.

The visual references to magistrates and their potent means of coercion in the world of the living suggest that the regime of fear in the *Jade Register* depended on a mimetic relationship with the state. This is clearly the context that the pictures themselves advocate. The text tells readers that they are viewing purgatory, but the pictures portray all the signs of a magistrate's yamen. The judge appears framed by the pillars and roof surrounding a magistrate holding court. He is in full official regalia, seated behind a desk piled with the documents and reports that a magistrate was obliged to consult in order to pronounce a verdict. Attendants stand at the ready to do his bidding, and when they act, comport themselves according to everyone's most nightmarish version of yamen underlings. The setting is perhaps grander than a yamen in a poor county could boast, and the interrogations in progress before the judge more grisly than what usually transpired in a yamen courtyard. But all signs suggest that what went on in purgatory was an analogue of judicial procedure.

Something more than analogy is at work in this transition from the *yangshi*, the world of light, to the *yinshi*, the world of shadow. Their relationship is mimetic, but it is a distorting mimesis. The world of shadow does not simply reflect the world of light; it refashions the mundane world—arranged according to the logic of government offices, bureaucratic pomp, and state torture—into a more fantastic one. Every act in the world of light is transposed to the world of shadow according to a political economy of good and evil in which the values of both are enhanced so that accounts can be drawn up and debts cleared. This mimetic relationship makes everything in the world of shadow more intense than what it was in the world of light. In the process of turning judicial torment into purgatorial torment, the mimesis intensifies the violence of what the victim is imagined to suffer as well as the possibility of suffering—which in the world of shadow is no longer a possibility, as it is in the real world, but a certainty.

Not everyone was convinced of the alleged mimesis between the world of shadow and the world of light. This relationship caught the attention of the great seventeenth-century Confucian historian Huang Zongxi. In a short essay entitled "Diyu" (Purgatory / Hell), Huang works over their relationship to voice his doubts about the very idea of this "underground prison." He opens the essay with the declaration that "the doctrine of purgatory / hell is something on which Confucians do not speak." He then proposes two arguments that expose the logical impossibility of such a place. The first has to do with the common notion that purgatory is full of cruel figures who torment sinners. In the world of light, such tormenters, being more numerous and more powerful in times of chaos, are agents of evil. If there are such figures in the world of shadow, and they are under the orders of the supreme deity Shangdi, how can they be regarded as agents of evil, since Shangdi himself is not evil? His second argument against the homology of the world of shadow to the world of light is based on the torments popularly associated with purgatory. Sinners in the world of shadow are subject to a bewildering array of torments—grindstones, awls, bronze pillars, mountains of knives, pits of ordure, to mention only a few he lists—that are entirely illegal in the world of light. Those who believe in tales of purgatory are thus willing to assert a degree of chaos so unbridled that it entirely denies the standards and judgments that prevail in the real world, the world of light.

To those who might try to defend the vision of torment in the world of shadow by declaring it to be a last resort imposed by Shangdi to terrify into repentance those on whom Confucian teaching has no effect, Huang responds that punishments do not intimidate the very worst people. The doctrine of purgatory has been handed down for a long time, he observes, and yet there has been no break in the parade of evil people across the ages. Having demonstrated the ineffectiveness of the doctrine, he turns to a logical problem of cosmology inherent in the nature of *yin* (the "shadow" of the world of shadow). Evil deeds are *yin;* but so too are the implements of punishment. As *yin* cannot be countered by *yin,* punishments cannot ultimately triumph over evil, nor can a world of shadow. The notion of purgatory, Huang argues, is nothing but "the sectarian teaching of the Buddhists"; it has no role within Confucianism. To control those who commit evil, "it is enough that everyone wishes to put the blade to their necks and humiliate them as animals"[50]—as good a description as any of the lingchi procedure. So imperial law is sufficient to punish evil: no need to imagine a realm of punishment into the afterlife. Purgatory is nothing but a Buddhist mimetic fantasy of retribution. Yet Huang's deconstruction of purgatory, however satisfying to his intellectual circle, must have had little purchase outside it—precisely where we could expect to find the sponsors and supporters of the *Jade Register.*

Michael Taussig has invoked the concept of mimesis to analyze the use of violence to control native labor in late nineteenth-century Colombia. Plantation labor overseers justified the use of extreme punishments by alleging that their Indian laborers were prone to extreme violence. The only way to counter their violence was to install a reign of terror. Such violent practices constituted "the colonial mirror that reflects back onto the colonists the barbarity of their own social relations, but as imputed to the savage or evil figures they wish to colonize." This was not the Mirror of Sin in the court of King Guang, which showed the sinful the deeds for which they must be punished. Like that mirror, however, it magnified the violence of punishment into a force greater than those who administered it. In both cases, violence could appear as necessary, even curative—"inseparable," as Taussig puts it, "from paradise, utopia, and the good."[51]

In Taussig's example, the mimesis was produced in the context of the white settler need for Indian labor on their rubber plantations, within a political economy in which labor had not yet been fully commoditized and therefore, four centuries after Columbus, had to be coerced to keep investments productive. The story the settlers told to themselves gave them the role of agents of civilizational improvement and portrayed those they tormented as inferiors who had yet to climb the evolutionary ladder leading upward to white culture. In the *Jade Register*, the position of privilege is occupied by the Ten Kings, who direct the operation of retribution on which the moral economy of purgatory is based. By tormenting the sinful dead, the Kings confirm the moral depravity of their victims while at the same time asserting their own moral untouchability. The use of mirror penalties restates the correctness of the moral order against which the dead have sinned. Torment in this political economy is not an aberration but the device by which aberration is overcome, proof of purgatory's necessity.

Who controls this vision? In Putumayo, the agents of mimesis are the settlers in need of Indian labor; not the high bourgeoisie back in Europe, but their agents, less privileged individuals who aspired to wealth and social advancement. This is where the analogy to the *Jade Register* is instructive. In purgatorial Sichuan, the agents of mimesis are the people the book identifies as its subjects and patrons: not the high gentry who could place themselves above the social realm in which ordinary people did bad things and who could expect in the course of a career as a magistrate to put suspects to torture and convicts to torment, but the petty gentry and lesser mercantile elite whose struggle to improve their status was entwined with a need to exercise control over the social conduct of their own underlings. Consider the comments of the county school instructor who wrote an 1873 preface to *Yuli zhibao bian* (The most precious edition of the Jade Register).[52] He speaks of "we Confucians" and puts himself among that privileged group, yet he also defects from those ranks to complain that "we Confucians" often fail to match ordinary people in doing good in the world. In so doing, he speaks on behalf not of the elite gentry, of which he would like to be a part and is not, but of lesser elites that included people such as himself who felt the need to compensate for their lesser status by asserting claims of higher morality against those who could afford to live morally better lives.

The agents of mimesis—the school instructors in the *Jade Register* and the plantation managers in Taussig's Colombia—have in common the use of fear to bring the intransigent into line. The economies of repressive action were no doubt quite different in the two cases, as were the power relations in which the actors were involved. The rubber plantation overseers managed actual bodies and were employing mimesis to justify the violence of that management, whereas the book's patrons were powerless outside their households. The fact that no one was physically hurt by the pictures does not rule out the possibility that the promoters of the *Jade Register* intended it to have tangible political effects, however. In presenting the world of shadow as a mirror image of the world of light, the book upholds the legitimacy of violence in the real world, even invites it. The displacement from the real to the representational was only possible, after all, because in the real county yamens to which the pictures allude, torment was actually taking place. The representation of torment reminded the viewer that he was living under a judicial system in which torment was freely used. The pictures of the torments of purgatory could not but be part of the regime of fear through which the late imperial Chinese state operated. The religious framing of these torments only enhanced their role in sustaining a culture of terror. As the Bolivian context suggests to Taussig, "cultures of terror are based on and nourished by silence and myth in which the fanatical stress on the mysterious side of the mysterious flourishes by means of rumor and fantasy woven in a dense web of magic realism."[53] Magic and myth romp together in the Ten Kings pictures to project a purgatorial realm where the asserted realism of courts and magistrates veers off into the hallucinatory magic of demons and unimaginable bodily torments.

A Utopia of the Dead

The problem of homology raised at the beginning of this chapter is not solved just by appealing to the practice of judicial torment in the real world. It is true that the controlling referent in the *Jade Register* is the magistrate at his bench, even if the Ten Kings do not look like any real-world magistrate.

Buddhas may hover around the apparatus, but what is being imagined in operation is the power of the imperial state. Yet there is difficulty in claiming that the world the *Jade Register* depicts is a simple rendition of the world of Qing judicial practice. Look again at the victims in the execution grounds. These are not pictures of what real bodies have experienced; they are pictures of representations of bodies. A resident of Chengdu would have had several opportunities to attend public floggings and executions, as the provincial capital served as the seat of three administrative jurisdictions, all of which carried out judicial functions. But most people did not gain access to these events, which occurred within yamen precincts and generally excluded those they did not directly concern. The likeliest places an ordinary person would have seen what is on display in the pictures were Buddhist monasteries, which often were decorated with murals or figurines depicting purgatorial torment. As we have noted, Sichuanese monasteries were known for housing vivid images of torment, arranged in lifelike fashion in grottoes dedicated to the local cult of the Ten Kings.[54] In this context, the *Jade Register* looks more like a portable version of the statuary in such a grotto than like pictures of people under judicial torture. The book was a way of disseminating the cult and its fearful lessons among those who needed to be reminded of purgatory on a daily basis, not a transcript of what happened when criminals were executed.

Now look again at the magisterial trappings of the Kings. They dispose us to think that Chinese fashioned hell in imitation of the feared state bureaucracy, that the viewer was being invited to recall the real world of the yamen when imagining the courts of the Ten Kings. This assumption involves an oversimplification. It neglects the fact that most people never got inside a yamen, and if they did, rarely had the chance to glimpse a magistrate at work. And so the problem of homology outlined at the start of this chapter remains. If the illustrator has positioned the judges within yamen architecture in order to create verisimilitude, what is being made similar to what? If this is mimesis, what is miming what?

The images in these pictures are not reproductions of scenes illustrators or those who bought illustrations actually saw in places of state execution. They are mediated by another, different type of cultural performance. If ordinary Chinese ever saw the costumes and gestures of magistrates consulting documents, deliberating on cases, and ordering suspects beaten, it was not in a government yamen, but on stage. Drama, not law, is the reality to which the illustrator gestures.

This contention finds its most eloquent demonstration in the detailed images of the ten courts of purgatory that dramaturge Zheng Zhizhen inserted into the 1582 edition of his masterwork, *Mulian jiumu quanshan xiwen* (Mulian rescues his mother: an opera to exhort goodness).[55] The Mulian story tells of a boy who must go to the underworld to redeem his mother, who in the earliest version of the story is being punished for the sin of giving birth to him. In Zheng's version, he finds her in the sixth court but has no power to release her, and must wait for her rebirth as a dog in a neighboring village. Zheng's libretto confirms that images of torment circulated between religious and literary texts (though in an explicitly religious drama such as the Mulian opera, the distinction is moot). This circulation must have taken place as well between the engraved images of purgatorial torment that appear on the pages of these books and their representation by actors on stage. This may help explain why the Kings in their elaborate hats and absurd beards look less like magistrates than like opera actors. The pictures show us grisly sights that an opera could stage but no official could perform. The representational matrix of the *Jade Register* has thus gone through a double displacement, first from purgatory to the yamen, and then from the yamen to the stage (and back again).

The extravagance of these pictures, unreliable as evidence of what anyone actually did, together with the stagy fictionality of the settings, might deny the *Jade Register* any historical value, other than as a figment of religious imagination. On the other hand, the double displacement should alert us that the world of shadow does not mime the world of light so much as idealize it. This is what opera does by acting out grand stories of tragic loss, great evil, and triumphant virtue: it imparts a sense of terror and redemption that real life rarely bestows. In so doing, it constructs what Qitao Guo in his study of the Mulian opera has termed a "popular ethico-religious discourse," bridging elite and popular culture so as to regulate social relations in relation to a moralistic vision of how the world should be. The displacement between these unimaginable tortures and Qing penal practices would have made perfect sense to operagoers as much as to this book's patrons. Operas often mimicked the doings of officials and the workings of the judicial system, just as the *Jade Register* invited viewers to imagine they were looking into a magistrate's yamen, which of course they weren't. If the state was made visible in either form, it was only by proxy. This was not the real state, for the real state was a system of power in which the people who paid for operas and morality books could usually only imagine. But what opera and purgatorial images projected was an entity that was statelike in its claims to construct order and justice in a disordered and immoral world.

In this sense the extreme afterlife torments in the *Jade Register* should be thought of as deriving from a political impulse, rather than from anything we might consider merely "cultural." When the Chu River King judges that rumormongers should be skewered by an iron rod, or the Emperor King of Song considers skinning alive a fitting punishment for interfering with a burial, the penalties reflect "Chinese" cultural anxieties about rumors and burials; but the violence of the punishments is powered from outside the purgatorial fiction by the anger of lesser elites who have no significant place in the system of rewards and punishments in the world of light. In the state apparatus that the *Jade Register* imagines, Son-of-Heaven Yama does a far more satisfying job of honoring moral effort than a real magistrate—socially superior to the mass of lesser elites and thoroughly compromised by power—would be expected to do.[56] The cosmocracy of the *Jade Register* thus does not so much confirm the authority of the Qing bureaucracy as supplement it, or perhaps—in the wilder dreams of politically marginal elites—supplant it.[57]

The *Jade Register* illustrations picture a kind of political utopia for those who could never gain a place in the structure of power and hated the powerlessness of their position: a flattened social terrain where the usual discriminations of wealth, class, education, and inherited status have been done away with. No elites, no property owners, no occupational categories, and no despised castes break up the featureless social landscape that the dead inhabit. It was not a realm inhabited by elite Confucians of Huang Zongxi's stature. The only holders of elevated status are those who administer this utopia and have the power to investigate and punish moral lapses with a severity that goes even beyond lingchi. So unrelenting is the severity of the moral policing and so thorough the security of the imagined apparatus that there can be no refuge from discipline nor any place from which to cast doubt on an order made absolute by torment. This is not a revolutionary vision of a hopeful future; it is a deeply conservative imagining of a world in which moral instruction and bodily torment are the twin tools of an unobstructed authoritarian regime.

The Chinese imagination was not the only field on which bloody executions had powerful emotional and political effects, however. We turn next to consider how such torments came to enter the European imagination and shape nineteenth-century Western ideas about China as a realm of cruelty.

CHAPTER 6

Chinese Torture in the Western Mind

Octave Mirbeau's macabre *Le Jardin des supplices* (translated into English as *Torture Garden*) hit the Parisian bookshops in 1899. With its provocative mix of Orientalist exoticism and sadistic sexual obsession, and its mordant critique of bourgeois mores, this notorious novel has excited diverse interpretations ever since. What some critics consider a lurid instance of romantic decadence or an erotic classic, others have decried as an example of fin de siècle literary misogyny.[1] Just how such readings square with Mirbeau's anguished portrayal of the West's addiction to violence and his stinging anticolonialism remains very much open to question. Whatever reading one chooses, there remains at the heart of *Le Jardin des supplices* a highly charged juxtaposition of the refined, aesthetic modes of torture the anarchist author depicted as characteristic of imperial China, and the crude, more brutal forms he ascribed to the European powers in their dealings with the non-Western world. The hellish landscape through which the protagonist is led by his sex- and violence-crazed Clara—an anti-Beatrice par excellence—play on preexisting stereotypes of extreme Chinese cruelty: an exquisite pleasure garden fictionally sited at the heart of a Canton prison and adorned with the most delightful scenery precisely in order to sharpen the suffering of the tormented captives to the maximum.

If Mirbeau set out to shock the world of literature, his imaginative creation had the desired effect on readers. His skill at turning established conventions to the service of his artistic vision only heightened the impact. The portrayal of characters taking pleasure in pain had been firmly embedded within nineteenth-century European literature from the Romantics onward.[2] More specifically, much of Mirbeau's imagery situated his work squarely in the post-Baudelairean tradition of appropriating non-European cultures as screens on which Western authors projected their sadistic fantasies. So pronounced was this trend that Martine Astier Loutfi suggests that the entire high "literature of colonial inspiration of this era reads like a list of tortures."[3] With a few minor exceptions, however, nineteenth-century exotic fiction focused far less on China than on the Middle East, South Asia, and Africa. In terms of broader literary trends, *Le Jardin des supplices* was a watershed in annexing Chinese and pseudo-Chinese imagery into the imaginative "horror" genre that had emerged from the very colonial encounter that so troubled Mirbeau. Over the following years, his "China" novel served as inspiration for other prominent writers, including Franz Kafka, whose *In der Strafkolonie* (The Penal Colony) became one of the twentieth century's literary classics, and the theorist Georges Bataille, whose ontology of sacrifice and Sadean aesthetic of ecstatic suffering reputedly grew out of his decades-long meditation on a photograph of one of the last Chinese lingchi executions.[4]

To be sure, constructing the imagery of Chinese torture at the turn of the twentieth century was by no means the work of just one novelist. The outbreak of the Boxer Rebellion in 1900 inspired a surge of sensational reports and images linking China with torture and wartime atrocities. Newspapers across the Western world were filled that summer with shocking, gruesome stories on the theme of Chinese cruelty, as the governments of the major Western powers and Japan readied their militaries for intervention and then proceeded to occupation.[5] While few journalists outside France had likely ever heard of Mirbeau at that point, several of their most disturbing stories turned out to be based almost as much on fantasy as the atrocities penned from the novelist's imagination.[6] The suicide of the reformist emperor, the frightful assassination of the Russian ambassador and brutal rape and murder of his wife, the hideous slaughter of the entire foreign diplomatic corps in Beijing—all these terrible reports turned out to be as fictitious as Mirbeau's rat torture (rodents gnawing through a convict's innards) and his excruciating bell torture (death by exposure to incessant reverberation). Already at the height of the positivist era, the line between fact and fiction was badly blurred, obscured by the emotionally and intellectually charged ideas of Chinese cruelty that then filled the air.[7] Where did these notions come from? How had they developed within Western culture? Which traditions of thought and feeling promoted them and gave them credibility?

Chinese tortures, prisons, and punishments had been standard topics of Western sinological attention for well over three centuries by the time Mirbeau's novel appeared. Unlike other Asian institutions such as the harem, which Western authors fantasized about a great deal but could not observe directly,[8] the judicial system of late imperial China was an object of immediate, sometimes intimate knowledge. Western travelers often observed its workings firsthand, either as prisoners or as onlookers. Writers then used their testimonies for diverse purposes, from the highbrow to the sensational, shaping the stereotypical images of Chinese cruelty that were broadly disseminated at times of Sino-Western tension.

The revulsion at torture that gave force to Mirbeau's novel and sparked intense Western hostility to the Boxers was more than an intellectual pose. Throughout the nineteenth century, cruel and degrading forms of treatment were regarded as characteristic of uncivilized and semicivilized societies. Bringing such practices to an end was celebrated by colonial governments as a strong historical justification for colonial rule and, more broadly, as a major argument for bringing societies under their political jurisdiction into line with Western notions of civilization.[9] Partly for these reasons, and partly because of the broad emotional and aesthetic revulsion toward torture in Western public opinion, revelations that colonial governments were engaging in cruel and degrading interrogations of their own caused scandals within metropolitan society, and colonial governments caught indulging in such practices risked facing charges that they had blatantly contravened the imperial mandate to introduce modern humanitarian governance.[10] As a result, despite a host of ideological ironies and ambiguities, the historical shift within Western cultures away from the legitimation of torture and corporal punishment eventually contributed to the discrediting of colonial rule and to the expansion of notions of common humanity that helped undermine the distinction between metropolitan citizen and colonial subject. The revulsion against what were regarded as characteristically Chinese practices at the turn of the twentieth century thus rested on, and was powered by, emotional, intellectual, political, and aesthetic commitments quite as deep as those that shaped the Chinese aesthetic of torment discussed in the preceding chapter, albeit to different ends.

In this chapter we survey the Western literature on China prior to the publication of *Le Jardin des supplices* to trace the growth of the stereotype of Chinese judicial cruelty and to gauge the nature and tone of depictions of a broad range of Chinese tortures and punishments before 1900. Our goal here is to understand the shaping power of the broader European tradition of reporting within which images and accounts of lingchi were generated for a variety of aesthetic and political purposes that often had more to do with Western interests and preoccupations than with what actually went on in China. The method we adopt for this task is that of wide-ranging genealogical reconstruction. This approach is geared to providing context to accounts of lingchi by sketching the evolving repertoire of characterizations of the Chinese legal system available to Western writers and readers. Chapter 7 will provide a more detailed examination of several of the most important nineteenth- and early twentieth-century reports of lingchi.

Early Glimpses of the Chinese Justice System

Accounts of the Chinese judicial system and the tortures and punishments used within it date back to the earliest modern contacts between China and the West. The first European ambassador dispatched to open relations with the Ming court, the Portuguese envoy Tomé Pires, arrived off Canton in 1517 and was eventually allowed to proceed to Beijing, where he and his party were promptly jailed by order of the court. Their sudden imprisonment was occasioned by the actions of an impetuous Portuguese commander who had the temerity to attack Ming coastal installations in South China and order the beating of a mandarin who fell into his hands. The influential sixteenth-century Portuguese imperial historian João da Barros depicted Pires as dying in prison due to the harsh conditions there.[11] Stories of the arrest of the ambassador and his party, and of their torture and eventual death in captivity, would remain standard parts of Western lore about Sino-Western relations until the fall of the Qing, symbolizing the arrogance and lack of normal diplomatic sensibilities of China's rulers.

Toward the end of the sixteenth century, the Spanish Augustinian Juan Gonzales de Mendoza revisited the Chinese justice system in an account of the Ming empire commissioned by Philip II shortly after the establishment of Spanish rule in the Philippines. Mendoza's widely read treatise, *Historia de las cosas mas notables, ritos y costumbres, del Gran Reyno de la China* (1585), incorporated accounts of Chinese manners by earlier missionaries and established a number of conventions regarding Chinese courts and prisons that would become commonplaces in the later sinological literature.[12]

Prominent among the practices Mendoza detailed were two forms of judicial torture described as regularly employed by Chinese magistrates to extract confessions. The first of these "cruel torments" involved squeezing the fingers in devices made of sticks and cord, which gave rise to "such great shrieks and groans that will move any man to compassion" and, according to Mendoza, almost always succeeded in forcing the accused to own up to "that which the judge pretends to know." In the rare cases when it failed, a magistrate who was certain the accused was holding something back could order another torture, "a great deal more cruel," which consisted of squeezing the feet while simultaneously striking them with a mallet.[13] An engraving depicting both these procedures, published a few years later in the De Bry brothers' grand series on transoceanic explorations, appears to have been the first Western attempt to illustrate Chinese torture apparatuses.[14]

Mendoza also listed what he took to be the standard Ming forms of execution: hanging, impaling on stakes, quartering, and burning—the last reserved, he reported, for persons convicted of treason. Though graphic, most of this account was quite misleading, for legal Ming punishments included neither hanging nor burning, nor impaling on stakes. Lesser punishments were said to include whippings and beatings with the rod, fifty strokes of which were reportedly sufficient to cause death. Chinese magistrates were reported to be just as "cruel and severe" in imprisoning people as they were in handing down other forms of punishment. As a result, according to Mendoza, China was filled with prisons, each city having thirteen, all so terrible that inmates frequently resorted to suicide rather than endure the suffering inflicted there. Mendoza nonetheless credited the general good conduct of the Chinese people to their government's system of collectively punishing families and neighborhoods. Among the peculiarities of Chinese justice, he mentioned in particular the practice of allowing high officials to be flogged for misbehavior, despite their revered status.[15]

While political and religious ambitions supplied the main motives for most early European writing on the Chinese justice system, the subject also figured in the era's imaginative literature. In particular, Fernão Mendes Pinto featured it prominently in his semifictional autobiography-cum-travelogue. At one point, describing his supposed imprisonment along with his party, he has them all languishing in foot-irons and manacles and fearful of "suffering a most cruel death" until a defense counsel kindly secures their release. More fantastic still is his description of a huge, moated prison nearly two leagues square, located in mid-Beijing, and so large that communication within it required a system of bells. (Did Mirbeau read of these?) An astounding three hundred thousand prisoners were said to be constantly held here, waiting to be sent to the Great Wall as forced labor.[16]

A less fanciful picture of Chinese prisons was sketched a few decades later in another widely translated work, Alvaro Semedo's *Gran Monarchia della Cina* (1653). Semedo was a leading figure in the second generation of Jesuits who entered China in the early seventeenth century, following Matteo Ricci's success in officially establishing his order's mission there soon after publication of Mendoza's book. The evangelization strategy pursued by Ricci and his successors targeted the educated political elite and royal family in the hope of eventually winning over the emperor, and thereby the empire as a whole, to Christianity. In accord with this strategy inspired by the ancient conversion of the Franks, seventeenth-century Jesuit reports published in Europe frequently combined descriptions of missionary success with praise for the Chinese literati as subtle intellectuals whose evangelization required sophisticated, educated—in short, Jesuit—missionaries. These accounts detailed the hardships suffered by the missionaries and their converts, which regularly included imprisonment and cruel punishments inflicted by hostile factions of mandarins cast as the enemies of God, faith, and reason. Working within this rhetorical framework, Semedo described the Chinese judicial system from direct personal knowledge: he was imprisoned for a year during the 1616 anti-Christian campaign and spent thirty days in a cage while being transported from Nanjing to Canton. The experience could hardly have been pleasant, but Semedo let the matter pass without too much bitterness. Maybe he was relieved to be spared worse, or perhaps the widespread use of cages as mechanisms of torture and punishment in contemporary Europe inured him to the practice.[17]

In comparing Chinese and European prisons (how much he knew of Europe's is unclear), Semedo judged those in China to be "more commodious and spacious than ours." In terms of layout, he depicted Chinese prisons as generally uniform in construction, with a long entrance passage that continued through four gates, the last of which issued into a large courtyard. Onto this courtyard faced the bamboo-grated cells of the ordinary prisoners, who were free to move from cell to cell mixing with one another during the day. Criminals convicted of grave offenses generally had to remain confined to their quarters even in daytime. All prisoners were marched out for roll call each evening; at night they were chained to their beds with manacles, which the warders could twist at their discretion to cause pain. An official visited each prison regularly to make sure that convicts who appeared too comfortable were "bastinadoed," i.e., beaten with a bamboo rod. "For," wrote Semedo, "they will not have their prisons to be as ours are, for the securing only of their persons, but also to punish their bodies." Chinese warders administered corporal punishment in a variety of agonizing ways: inmates were liable to be whipped, kicked, draped in chains, tormented on the rack, and bastinadoed on their bared backs and buttocks. At the same time, Semedo observed, Chinese people found the European practice of whipping naughty children too cruel to be countenanced. He also acknowledged that his own jailers had several times excused him from the usual beatings during the long periods when he was ill.[18]

All in all, Semedo provided a fairly informative account of many of the most common "correctional" instruments used in the Chinese prisons of his day. One theme he particularly dwelled on was that in China the bastinado was administered widely to people of diverse social status: masters beat their servants, teachers beat students, and magistrates even ordered the beating of mandarins who erred in their duties. Indeed, declared the missionary, the bastinado was so commonplace in China that, just as the Japanese said their country could not be ruled without the sword, so it could be said of the Chinese that "without [the] Bambu, that is, the cudgell or baston, with which they use to beat men, it is not possible they should be ruled."[19] Another Chinese device to which Semedo referred, if only briefly, was the cangue, or portable pillory, as later authors called it.

For the European reading public, the bastinado and the cangue together soon became the penal devices most emblematic of the far-off Chinese empire, and they retained that status in the Western literature over the next three centuries. Within two decades, both received pictorial representation in influential accounts of successive Dutch East India Company (VOC) embassies to the "Celestial Middle Kingdom." The cangue was thought characteristic enough of China to be featured on the title page of Joan Nieuhof's grand memorial of Pieter De Goyer and Jacob De Kaiser's 1655–1657 VOC embassy to the Kangxi emperor; the engraving portrayed a recumbent male languishing in a particularly weighty instance of the device.[20] Olfert Dapper's companion volume of the next two Dutch embassies likewise graphically illustrated the bastinado as administered to several bare-bottomed individuals, the mandarin status of one such unfortunate clearly indicated by his regalia draped nearby (Figure 15).[21] A naked woman trussed on a pole for interrogation like an animal on a spit must have sent a shiver of repugnance (or delight?) through the dour souls of Calvinist Amsterdam (Figure 16). Translations of the Nieuhof and Dapper volumes into French, English, and German brought these illustrations to a wide European audience.[22]

A new Spanish account of China, published the same year as Dapper's work, included a notable verbal description of the bastinado. The author, Domingo Navarrete, had recently headed the Dominican mission in China and was one of the Jesuits' most articulate early opponents in the Rites Controversy that raged between rival Catholic camps from the 1660s into the 1740s. Navarrete vehemently denounced the Jesuits' toleration of Confucian beliefs and ritual practices among their converts, but he formed a high opinion of China's political system. Despite spending months in jail in China, he had even kinder words than Semedo for the country's prisons, which he judged cleaner, more peaceable, and better run than Europe's. His rather glowing account describes them as providing laundry facilities, shops, a magnificent temple, and even special married quarters, all of which made for a congenial and well-mannered body of inmates.[23]

Navarrete's rosy perceptions of Chinese prisons could hardly have contrasted more with nineteenth-century reports of corrupt and sadistic hellholes, but his enthusiasm did not stop him from painting a grueling portrait of

Figure 15. Portrayal of the beating of a mandarin. From Olfert Dapper, *Gedenkwaerdig bedryf der Nederlandsche Oost-Indische Maetschappye* (1670).

Chinese corporal punishments, particularly the public bastinado. He related, for example, how bamboo rods filled with lead were used to punish offenders as the crowd of onlookers counted out the strokes. An executioner could kill a man with four or five blows if he desired, observed Navarrete, like Mendoza before him, though the Dominican also assured his readers that their obedience to the attending mandarin generally kept them from doing so. In certain cases, he reported, they even "hold up some men's testicles, and fix them on a small cane; on them they let fall the stroke, and [with] the second or third the patient infallibly fails."[24] Curiously, this sadistic measure evoked little authorial reaction; perhaps Navarrete was too aware of the anal-genital mutilations then current in Europe for punishing heretics, witches, and homosexuals.[25] Indeed, such practices may well have been his inspiration, since smashing the genitalia would have been strictly off limits for the Chinese torturer, who would have faced severe punishment if caught at it. What seems to have impressed the Dominican more about

Figure 16. Portrayal of a tortured woman trussed up naked. From Olfert Dapper, *Gedenkwaerdig bedryf der Nederlandsche Oost-Indische Maetschappye* (1670).

the Chinese system than the punishments themselves was the extent to which money talked. He was particularly struck by the ease and frequency with which wealthy convicts hired proxies to suffer punishments on their behalf.[26]

The venality of Chinese justice likewise struck Navarrete's Jesuit contemporary, Gabriel Magaillans, who reacted to it more vehemently than the Dominican. Magaillans stopped himself from describing Chinese punishments in detail, he said, lest he go on at length, but he did specify strangulation and decapitation as the two official modes of execution. Contrary to Europeans, he noted, Chinese considered decapitation worse because it involved defiling the body given by one's parents. The Chinese horror at this was such that families of the beheaded would pay any price to get back the corpse so the head could be sewn back onto the body.[27] Until this point no mention of lingchi seems to have appeared in the Western literature, though it is hard to believe that some Jesuit missionaries did not know of it.

Toward the close of the seventeenth century, however, a major new Jesuit treatise once again addressed Chinese punishments. Louis Lecomte's *Nouveaux mémoires sur l'état present de la Chine* (1696) consists of communications he sent from China to various French dignitaries. The volume quickly became one of the Chinese Rites Controversy's most controversial publications.[28] In one letter discussing the Chinese state, which he classified as an absolute monarchy (rather than a despotism),[29] he singled out for praise the system's mixture of rewards and punishments. Chinese punishments, he stressed, were strictly allocated according to the severity of the crime committed. The most common form of correction was the bastinado, a practice he reported, like Mendoza and Semedo before him, as applicable not only to commoners but to mandarins and even princes of the blood who had done wrong. The next most common form, the cangue, was considered less painful but more disgraceful than the bastinado. Finally, he examined the various modes of execution, in the process providing the first clear Western discussion we have found of lingchi, which he described as the hacking of a convict into ten thousand pieces. This fate, he stated, was reserved for rebels and others who had committed crimes against the throne. On his telling, once the executioner finished the operation, he would abandon the corpse to "the cruelty of [the dead person's] enemies" and of the population at large.[30]

Corporal Punishment in the Enlightenment Debate on Chinese Government

The most influential of the many contributions to sinological knowledge published in the first half of the eighteenth century was undoubtedly Jean-Baptiste Du Halde's *Description géographique, historique, chronologique, politique et physique de l'empire de la Chine* (1735), a grand four-volume work that quickly became the late Enlightenment's single most important source on China.[31] Written in Paris on the basis of correspondence the author maintained with his fellow Jesuits in the "mission field," the *Description* was heavily mined for information on Chinese political and social institutions by many other writers—not only churchmen, but also some of the era's leading *philosophes*. Indeed, a number of "irreligious" critical intellectuals, led by Voltaire, were inclined to believe that Chinese institutions held valuable lessons that could guide much-needed reforms within Europe. In his *Description*, Du Halde followed his confrère Lecomte in favorably reviewing the Chinese legal system for its graded system of punishments, which he judged especially effective both in deterring crime generally and in preventing the most serious crimes, due to the special horror inspired by lingchi, which he, like Lecomte, described as reserved for cases of treason and lèse majesté.[32]

In his chapter on prisons, Du Halde repeated Semedo's affirmation of the central importance of the bastinado as a mainstay of the legal system in China. He remarked that criminals in China were so routinely subjected to the rod that "it may be said that the Chinese government subsists by the Exercise of the Battoon" (in the French original, "le gouvernement de la Chine ne subsiste guere, que par l'exercise du bâton").[33]

Elsewhere, Du Halde reproduced a precept, promulgated by the Kangxi emperor for the guidance of his officials, which condemned the use of torture as contrary to Confucian ideals of good governance. His version of this precept, which he attributed to Emperor Xuandi of the Han dynasty, reads:

In less distant times [i.e., since the Shang dynasty], great changes occurred. To frighten villains, severe laws were established. Mutilations were frequent. They were abolished under the Zhou dynasty, and during the reign of Kang wang [the fourth Zhou emperor] the number of criminals grew so small that over the course of forty years the prisons became empty. The use of tortures returned under the Qin. The horrible slaughter that took place nonetheless failed to reduce the number of crimes. As a result, an infinite number of people perished. It is impossible to think of it without horror and compassion. Alas! it is in thus continually recalling and comparing what occurred under so many Emperors who preceded me that I attempt to benefit, in order to maintain the honour of the throne and secure the good of the Empire.[34]

The sentiment was one that Frederick the Great would have been proud to share when in 1754 he became the first continental European ruler to ban judicial torture in his realm. Frederick had strong personal reasons for detesting physical torments (his father had abused him physically and had had his closest friend cruelly executed), and he was presumably well advised on the long Western tradition (going back to Gratian) critical of the efficacy of judicial torture. Yet, it is tempting to speculate that, given his sinophile bent, he might have been influenced by the counsel of the celebrated Chinese emperor whose words he likely encountered in Du Halde's widely circulated volumes.[35]

Du Halde's work was used not only by eighteenth-century sinophiles, however, but also by critics of China seeking to buttress their assessments of Chinese society and of their own. One of the most notable was Montesquieu, one-time *président* of the Bordeaux *Parlement* and a major authority in legal theory. Montesquieu's distaste for the way the Chinese judicial system treated aristocrats was a major factor in his negative view of China's constitutional order.[36] His *De l'Esprit des lois* appeared in 1748, just five short years after the definitive Jesuit defeat in the Chinese Rites Controversy. The central theoretical thrust of the book was to differentiate legitimate from illegitimate forms of government. Montesquieu made a crucial distinction between monarchies and republics, both of which he considered legitimate states subject to the rule of law, and despotism—the form of government he identified as native to Asia, Africa, and the Americas—which in his view was fundamentally arbitrary and inherently illegitimate. Montesquieu famously argued that each type of government was animated by a distinctive spirit: monarchies by honor, republics by civic virtue, and despotisms by fear. The Chinese empire could not be a legitimate monarchy, he reasoned, for even the Jesuits (whom he despised as cultivators of absolutism) admitted that its foundations rested on physical punishment and the fear thereof. To support this line of reasoning, Montesquieu shrewdly but misleadingly referred his readers to Du Halde's statement, "C'est le bâton qui gouverne la Chine" [in the English translation: "It is the cudgel that governs China"].[37] This textual reference both misquoted Du Halde's words and inflated what was essentially a passing remark by the Jesuit into decisive testimony on a fundamental constitutional and political issue.

Montesquieu highlighted another piece of Jesuit intelligence that aroused his indignation at the Chinese legal-political order, the testimony of Dominique Parennin, a Jesuit head-of-mission in Beijing, that had recently appeared in the Jesuits' *Lettres edifiantes et curieuses,* a series edited at this time by Du Halde.[38] Parennin there told of several Manchu princes who had been imprisoned and severely punished for embracing Christianity. Their punishments included flogging with the bamboo, with no regard whatever for the dignity of their aristocratic status.[39] While Parennin intended his report to illustrate the suffering and steadfastness of his Chinese converts as well as the proximity of the Jesuits to the court, for Montesquieu, the champion of the French nobility as a check on Bourbon power, the humiliation of these Manchu aristocrats demonstrated the despotic nature of the Qing state. The Chinese government, he concluded, was thus shown to be based on "un plan de tyrannie constamment suivi, et des injures faites à la nature humaine avec règle, c'est à dire de sang-froid."[40] Elsewhere, in discussing what he saw as despotism in China and Tartary, he declared that "what the peoples of Asia have called punishments those of Europe have deemed the most outrageous abuse."[41]

Nonetheless, Montesquieu does follow Lecomte and Du Halde in approving the Chinese legal system's practice of graduating punishments according to the severity of the crimes committed. At the same time, he introduces a curious innovation into the Jesuits' argument: "In China," he wrote, referring to lingchi, "those who add murder to robbery are cut to pieces, but not so the others; to this difference it is owing that though they rob in that country they never murder. In Russia, where the punishment of robbery and murder is the same, they always murder."[42] Regardless of whether this judgment contradicts the Qing practice and the Jesuit literature (oral accounts may have painted another picture), Montesquieu's assessment is notable both for revealing a distinct lack of horror at lingchi and for its focus on efficiently controlling social behavior that would come to dominate legal thinking in the following century. Neither, however, was enough to sway him from his overall assessment that the Chinese state was despotic.

The unfortunate habit of imagining "the Enlightenment" as homogeneous has too often tended to obscure the intense controversies of that period, one of which was Europe's heated mid-eighteenth-century debate on Confucian government. Reflecting a growing belief in the possibility of constructing a rational social order, the economic theorist François Quesnay incorporated an enthusiastic endorsement of China's graded system of punishments into his Physiocratic philosophy in the 1760s. One of the period's leading sinophiles and, like Voltaire, a major critic of Montesquieu's thesis that Chinese government was "unnatural" and illegitimate, Quesnay argued in his *Despotisme de la Chine* (1767) that the Chinese state, as an enlightened despotism, embodied the ideal form of "natural" government. His discussion of Chinese penal law picked up where Montesquieu's had left off by focusing on the distinction between punishments for armed and unarmed robbery. Describing China's criminal laws as "generally . . . very mild," and its punishments as graded according to the principle of proportionality,[43] Quesnay maintained that the frequent beatings with the bamboo that wrongdoers had to endure were usually only lightly administered. A prominent ancien régime critic of the hereditary aristocracy, he chose to gloss the widespread Chinese use of the bastinado in egalitarian fashion and found it edifying to think that even powerful mandarins were liable to such punishment, if convicted of wrongdoing; his approbation sharply contrasted with Montesquieu's distaste.

Quesnay rightly recognized China's three modes of capital punishment, in increasing order of severity, as strangulation, decapitation, and cutting into pieces—and he knew as well that the last was reserved for traitors and rebels. Cherry-picking his way through the missionary literature, he praised Chinese prisons as "admirable" on the grounds that they were more spacious and less filthy than Europe's. The rationality of China's prison system was further demonstrated to his mind by the fact that inmates worked to procure their subsistence and that separate prisons were maintained for men and women.[44]

Quesnay's idyllic celebration of China as the embodiment of reason and natural law marked an intellectual apex of Enlightenment chinoiserie. By the 1770s, celebrating China's government as a model for Europe had run its course for most reformists. The step-by-step dissolution of the Society of Jesus then produced an increasingly monotone chorus of critics denouncing Chinese "heathenism" from within ecclesiastical circles and establishment political institutions. Thereafter, in the decades from 1770 to 1830, closely linked political and economic trends played a vital role in raising levels of wealth in Western societies above those in Asia and Africa. The spread of modern factory production, the emergence of calls for democracy in the

Americas and Europe, the growth of nationalism, and the unfolding of a new phase of European colonialism centered primarily on Asia rather than the Americas all contributed to growing global disparities in wealth and power. Accompanying these political-economic developments were powerful intellectual trends that emphasized perceptions of difference between the West and other societies: the idea that the West's scientific achievements demonstrated the rationality of Western forms of culture generally; the notion of historical progress; the view that human sympathy and individuality were crucial marks of genuine civilization and that cruelty denoted a lack thereof; increasing acceptance of the superiority of governments founded on the rule of law; the revival of Christianity as a reaction to the French Revolution; the emergence of conservative Romanticism with its celebration of medieval European institutions and the aristocracy; and, last but not least, the sharpening of attitudes of racial superiority. All of these contributed to a distinct lowering of Western assessments of Chinese society and civilization. Exactly how they did so is beyond the scope of this book, but the following discussion suggests some of the ways that perceptions of Chinese legal and penal practice played into this shift.

"Oriental Despotism" and the Imagery of Cruel Punishments

In the late eighteenth century, more and more Western authors followed the lead of Montesquieu in assimilating China to the model of Oriental despotism that earlier writers had seen as characteristic of the Islamic empires of South and West Asia. At the same time, a related philosophical view emerged to the effect that torture and gruesome punishment were typically Asian practices that contravened the "civilized" imperative to treat other human beings with sympathy and respect for their personal rights. Over the following decades, ever firmer emotional and aesthetic links were forged between a despotic form of government deemed typically "Oriental" and Chinese punishments and judicial procedures that the expansion of print media made increasingly visible in the West. For Western intellectuals, such practices evoked both a distinct sense of horror and a gruesome fascination.

One late eighteenth-century author who led the charge in sharply denouncing China's government as an undiluted despotism was Cornelius De Pauw, the prolific Dutch contrarian who had the distinction of serving as Frederick the Great's private reader and then being named a Companion of the French Revolution by the National Assembly. De Pauw's writings had a significant impact from the 1770s to the 1820s in shaping the case for the West's historical superiority over the civilizations of Asia and the Americas.[45] Following Montesquieu in thinking Chinese society was governed principally by custom rather than law, De Pauw went further by branding China an unmitigated Oriental despotism in which the entire population was essentially enslaved. Disingenuously citing Du Halde in support, De Pauw asserted that "the principal instruments of the Chinese government are the whip and the rod [bâton]," while decrying the fact that even distinguished officials were not exempt. Depicting Chinese people as generally imbued with a "servile fear" that was the logical result of their institutions, he treated even their famed industriousness as an expression of a dread of torture and penal mutilation. The Chinese practice of punishing the relatives of convicts he judged to be the worst form of punishment in all Asia, and he identified as Asia's worst torture the forcing of confessions by using needles to pull the skin and flesh off an accused person, a practice he also ascribed to the Chinese.[46] Though citing no authority, he probably derived this idea too from Du Halde, whose Jesuit correspondents apparently had it from a precursor of the Skinning by Scraper later pictured in *Jade Register*.[47] The influence of De Pauw's negative assessment of China is clearly discernible in the analyses of Chinese society later put forward by Herder and Kant, though neither of them highlighted torture and gruesome punishments as a feature of Chinese government. The negative interpretation of China they derived from De Pauw was widely appropriated later, however.

The perception of significant differences in established notions of natural justice and individual responsibility factored importantly into the formation of European negative feelings toward Asian political culture around the turn of the nineteenth century. The distinguished British travel writer John Barrow gave forceful expression to this perception in his influential account of the Earl Macartney's 1793 embassy to China.[48] Barrow reported that while embassy members had disapproved of many aspects of Chinese civilization, from the religious to the culinary, they were particularly struck by the sight of servants being flogged for the failings of the mandarins, their masters, who were being demoted in rank for allowing the embassy to receive spoiled food. This, they felt, was an egregious instance, "ill agreeing with the feelings of Englishmen," of the cruelty that attended "arbitrary power."[49] A plebeian member of Macartney's party, Aeneas Anderson, recorded the shocked reactions of the Chinese who witnessed Macartney's officers apply fifty lashes to the back of Private James Cootie, a British soldier who had purchased some Chinese liquor in contravention of the ambassador's orders. A shocked mandarin watching the flogging exclaimed, in broken English, "Englishman too much cruel, too much bad."[50] The Qing official's reaction might have suggested that, rather than being a Western peculiarity, the notion of cruel and degrading punishment was one that Asians were quite capable of applying to treatment they found shocking. Indeed, throughout the nineteenth century, British opinion would vary on whether English or Chinese law was harsher. But while Barrow and Anderson both expressed sentiments that accorded with the Scottish Enlightenment emphasis, enunciated by Adam Smith and others, on sympathy as a defining feature of civilization, it was Barrow's patrician perception that most Western writers were inclined to share in the years leading up to the first Opium War (1839–1842).

If late Enlightenment thought fed Western attitudes of superiority in a number of ways, it is a mistake to dwell exclusively on the role of reform-minded rationalists in this process. In response to optimistic celebrations of abstract reason, Romantic and other counter-Enlightenment thinkers took to exploring the "darker," "wilder" sides of human nature, including passions that transgressed established social codes. The tendency of such authors to advance their own condemnations of despotic government demonstrates that the humane ethical universalism championed by Smith and Kant was hardly the only standpoint from which "cruel and unusual" practices associated with Asia were denounced. One of the strongest champions of the "darker" passions at the century's end was the Marquis de Sade, the rebel-aristocrat who celebrated cruelty as the most natural and transformative of passions. Distinctive as his overall vision was, Sade's notion of despotism built on Montesquieu's view that that form of government rested on a spiritual and emotional foundation of fear. Contrary to his reformist contemporaries, however, the radical Sade drew the bold conclusion that revolutionary violence alone could overcome the terror that lay at despotism's heart. He moved beyond recommending cruelty as naturally pleasurable to embracing it as morally and politically desirable. One might imagine that this stance might then lead him to defend Qing tortures and punishments, perhaps as the "sadistic" impulses of the sort that later moved Mirbeau's Clara, but in fact it didn't: While Sade indeed saw China's imperial regime as massively and consciously cruel, its cruelty failed to satisfy him. As he put it: "Now and again, China's emperor and mandarins take measures to stir up a revolt amongst the people [simply] in order to derive, from these maneuvers, the right to transform them into horrible slaughters. May that soft and effeminate people rise against their tyrants; the latter will be massacred in their turn, and with much greater justice; murder, adopted always, always necessary, will have but changed its victims; it has been the delight of some, and will become the felicity of others."[51] What excited Sade was not the institutional practice of Chinese imperial rule, but the prospect of something he predicted would be vastly crueler still: a popular Chinese revolution.

China, Torture, and Imperialism in the Nineteenth Century

The great shift in the global political-economic balance of power that began toward the end of the eighteenth century took place in a structural context of increasingly firm linkages among the world's major economic regions. Not only was wealth rising faster in the European culture-area, but Europeans were increasingly extending their power across Asia, where a new wave of Western imperial expansion was under way. The turn of the nineteenth century saw Britain's East India Company (EIC) firmly established both as the governing body in Bengal and Madras and as China's largest commercial partner at Canton, the sole seaport where the Qing government permitted Westerners to trade. These developments had cultural ramifications around the globe,[52] not least in reshaping Western attitudes toward China.

We will explore the complex interplay of knowledge and various forms of power by examining depictions of Chinese punishments and tortures, with two sets of related aims in mind. The first is to document how notions of Chinese government, judicial and penal practice, and national character were bound together in nineteenth-century Western thought and to consider how such notions tied in with justifications of Western imperialism. Edward Said, for one, has noted that Europeans caught up in the new wave of imperial expansion at this time increasingly thought of non-Westerners in terms of "disturbingly familiar ideas about flogging or death or extended punishment." Such punishments were seen as "required when 'they' misbehaved" because " 'they' mainly understood force or violence best; 'they' were not like us, and for that reason deserved to be ruled."[53] Whether this insight applies to China, which was never formally subject to colonial rule, need not detain us for long, since supporting documentation is abundant. Lord Palmerston's remark that "half-civilised governments such as those in China, Portugal and Spanish America all require a Dressing every eight or ten years to keep them in order"[54] is only one of the pithiest in a long string of similar injunctions, from the 1830s bayings of British "country-traders" to Kaiser Wilhelm II's rants at the century's end. What will occupy us instead is therefore not the well-worked theme of how notions of civilization and despotism fit into the colonial mindset, but a more precise question: whether the Western literature justified Chinese punishments and tortures, despite their cruelty, as necessary for controlling a troublesome population.

Our second set of aims is to test how much the late eighteenth century's emergent trend toward treating cruelty as a distinguishing feature of Chinese civilization found resonance in nineteenth-century treatments of the Chinese justice system, and to gauge the extent to which sinological depictions of Chinese torture displayed the propensity to aestheticize suffering and eroticize pain that pervaded much of nineteenth-century Romanticism and neo-Romanticism. As Mario Praz has shown, many of the authors who contributed to these movements followed in Sade's footsteps by painting the heights of pleasure and creativity as inseparable from agonies that could push the human spirit beyond the bounds of rational thought. Numerous examples of Orientalist writing featuring Indian and Islamic materials were cast in this mold during the nineteenth century, and Praz himself placed Mirbeau's *Le Jardin des supplices* in this tradition.[55] Were there perhaps reverberations of this typically Romantic imagery in sinological scholarship as well? Or did the China hands provide elements that fed the nineteenth century's broader sadomasochistic current?

"The Pangs of Suffering Humanity" and the Growth of a Pictorial Tradition

Declining enthusiasm in Europe for Chinese institutions was matched in the years after the Macartney embassy by growing British scrutiny of Chinese society, a trend that was aided by the same print revolution that spurred the growth of nationalist sentiment during this era. An important facet of the new scrutiny of things Chinese was the increased availability of widely marketed visual representations, which lent new aesthetic and emotional force to attitudes toward the "Celestial Empire." Most notably, the British public's focus on China during the Napoleonic wars was encouraged by the publication of several important works on China, which included major new artistic representations of Chinese life.

The first of these influential pictorial depictions appeared in the last volume of George L. Staunton's lavish *Authentic Account of an Embassy from the King of Great Britain to the Emperor of China* (1797), the formal relation of the 1793 Macartney embassy to Beijing. Staunton was the mission's secretary. His book's illustrations were based on paintings by William Alexander, the mission's official artist.[56] Alexander's depiction of the cangue (Figure 17), one of several portraying judicial procedures, gives a good impression of the painter's style. If the tone seems supercilious to our eyes, public reaction at the time must have been positive, judging by the fact that two more well-appointed volumes of illustrations, both entitled *The Costumes of China*, were commissioned shortly thereafter on the London book market. Each aimed to give readers a similarly tangible feel for everyday conditions in the "Middle Kingdom." The first was published in 1801 by Major George Henry Mason; the second, which appeared in 1805, was credited to William Alexander in his own right.[57] The latter volume presents more paintings executed in Alexander's quaint style from sketches he did in China; Mason's plates were based on watercolors by the Cantonese artist Pu Qua that Mason acquired in Canton during 1789–1790 while on sick leave from his post in Madras.[58] Like the plates for Staunton's embassy volume, those which Alexander included in his own book include several of punishments such as the cangue and the bastinado.

Mason gathered his materials on Chinese torture and punishment into a bilingual thematic volume, published anonymously in 1801 as *The Punishments of China / Les Punitions des chinois*. Featuring twenty-two hand-colored plates along with the author's notes and preface,[59] this slim tome provided Western readers with their fullest visual record to date of Chinese penal and judicial practices. Evidently a commercial success, it went through five editions by 1830. In his preface, Mason balances praise for China's system of graded punishments with condemnation of a legal system that by his account not only resorted to the rack to extract information but made it a capital crime to wear particular ornaments. His illustrations naturally include the by-now de rigueur bastinado (in primmer form than Dapper's—Mason's convict at least had his trousers on), plus several procedures and devices not previously pictured in the West. Among the interrogation techniques depicted were several that would soon become staples of the cruelty motif in Western China-lore: finger torture (Figure 18) previously described by Mendoza and others, twisting of the ears and bludgeoning of the face, burning of the eyes with lime, and a suspension technique called the "punishment of the swing," which Mason describes as a procedure for extracting information. This last torture was contrary to the Qing Code but bears distinct resemblance to what the *Jade Register* pictured as going on in the Minor Hell of Inverted Suspension. Mason's reference to criminal ornamentation presumably refers to infringements on the sartorial privileges of the imperial family and the mandarinate, but the Chinese "rack" he pictures is actually an ankle crusher rather than the stretching mechanism familiar in the West. Invoking the term "the rack" to describe both conveniently allows him to denounce the pope and the Qing together for resorting to medieval barbarity at a time when a sharp debate was turning British opinion against public punishments.[60]

Mason also pictures one malefactor in a cage, others restrained by chains or in close confinement, and another wearing a weighty cangue supported by a customized chair dutifully supplied by his family. One prisoner is depicted on his way to decapitation, but the only form of capital punish-

Figure 17. William Alexander, *Punishment of the Tcha*. From George Staunton, *An Authentic Account of an Embassy from the King of Great Britain to the Emperor of China* (1797), Volume 3, Plate 28.

ment actually shown in progress is the so-called punishment of the cord, a procedure in which the victim is bound to a cross by a rope used to strangle him (this illustration appears as Figure 3 in Chapter 1), the least disgraceful mode of execution under the Qing Code.[61] In what is probably a reference to lingchi, Mason notes at the volume's outset that showing the severe modes of execution inflicted for crimes such as regicide, parricide, and rebellion would do violence to European feelings, as well as impugn what he ironically calls the "universally acclaimed" temperance and wisdom of the Chinese government. As it was, Mason justified publishing his pictures of gruesome punishments by billing them as a patriotic gift presented for the thoughtful consideration of the British people, whose "natural intrepidity" revealed itself in their "attention to the pangs of suffering humanity." The principal recommendation of the representations thus arose, as he put it, "from the sensation of security, which they produce in those bosoms that heave upon a tract of the globe, where they are protected from being torn out by lengthened agonies; . . . where tyranny, fanaticism, or anarchy, cannot

Figure 18. *Finger Torture.* From George Mason (ed.), *The Punishments of China* (1801), Plate 10. Courtesy of the University of British Columbia Library.

exercise their demoniacal propensities for cruelty."[62] As reasonable as Mason's remarks probably seemed to most Britons, his belief in a great gulf separating English and Chinese law nevertheless did not command universal assent in an age when the former was itself being strongly challenged by Utilitarians as well as revolutionaries.

Establishing a Documentary Baseline: Translating the *Ta Tsing Leu Lee*

Scholarly understanding of the Chinese legal system received a major boost in 1810 with the publication of the *Ta Tsing Leu Lee*, the West's first translation of the Qing penal code, by George T. Staunton. The son of Macartney's secretary, the younger Staunton distinguished himself for his linguistic facility while serving as the ambassador's page during a meeting with the Qianlong emperor. Now, sixteen years later, he was an EIC employee and a leading light among Europe's handful of China experts.[63] Though his translation did not include the Code's highly important commentaries or the majority of its supplementary statutes, Staunton's 570-page edition was remarkable both for the importance and complexity of its subject matter and for being the first major contribution in a Western language to the study of Chinese law. Not surprisingly for a weighty legal translation, the content could be technical and complicated, and the prose, though clear, was definitely dry.[64] Consequently, it never enjoyed more than a narrow specialist readership.[65] It did, however, provide an essential foundation for readers who wished to examine the fundamental laws that governed China. China hands across the Western world cited it regularly as an essential resource for the rest of the century and beyond.

In his preface, Staunton resolutely distances himself from the proudly anti-Chinese views of his friend John Barrow (to whom the volume is dedicated). He declares that "a considerable proportion of the opinion most generally entertained by Chinese and Europeans of each other was to be imputed to prejudice, or to misinformation; and that, upon the whole, it was not allowable to arrogate, on either side, any violent degree of moral or physical superiority." While accepting that Chinese virtues are inferior to Christian virtues in Europe, he believes that China could compete "in respect to all the essential characteristics of civilization" with the nations of Europe—or at least some of them; and despite some evident drawbacks, there were "some very considerable and positive moral and political advantages" peculiar to the Chinese social order. One was precisely its system of penal laws, which was "if not the most just, at least the most comprehensible, uniform, and suited to the genius of the people for whom it is designed, perhaps of any that ever existed." Staunton tactically grants De Pauw's point that China was ruled by the bamboo rod and the whip, but counters the charge of cruelty by maintaining that "neither these, nor any other corporal punishments are in such universal use, or administered with such undistinguishing severity, as has sometimes been imagined." In particular, he denounces George Mason's *Punishments of China* for representing cruelties and "barbarous" executions, "which it would be very erroneous to suppose have a place in the ordinary course of justice" in his own day, though he allows that past tyrants might have occasionally resorted to them.[66]

Among the many important points established in Staunton's edition of the Qing Code, one particularly relevant to our concerns was that, pace Montesquieu, the use of judicial torture was subject to legal limitations in China. These conditions appear not in the fundamental laws or *lü* (Staunton's *leu*), but in the supplementary substatutes or *li* (Staunton's *lee*), which were operational applications of the Code elaborated over the course of the dynasty. Staunton's translation would later be criticized for lacking most *li* as well as the commentaries, which were crucial to judicial interpretation, but one of the few *li* Staunton does include as an appendix is the "Description of Ordinary Punishments." This text begins by defining the principles governing the legal use of judicial torture: "In those cases where torture is allowed," it sternly runs, "the offender, whenever he contumaciously refuses to confess the truth, shall forthwith be put to the question by torture; and it shall be lawful to repeat the operation a second time, if the criminal refuses to make a confession." The same substatute goes on to declare, as previous writers had reported, that magistrates who applied torture arbitrarily would themselves be tried before their superiors; and the latter too were liable to face charges if they concealed or abetted an infraction. Subsequent clauses stipulated the only devices legally permissible as "instruments of torture" to be "used upon an investigation of a charge of robbery or homicide," namely, the officially designated instruments for squeezing the fingers and ankles. Chains and the cangue were specified as the means by which prisoners were to be legally restrained.[67]

Staunton's translation was given prominent notice in 1810 in the whiggish *Edinburgh Review*, the English language's first great general review of books. In the previous year, the *Review* had run an anonymous piece on

China by Jeremy Bentham's Scottish bulldog, James Mill, who was then writing his massive (militantly procolonial) *History of British India*. Indicating his awareness of Staunton's translation-in-progress, Mill doubted there was an "Englishman" alive equipped to interpret it properly. He himself betrayed no hesitation in asserting that Chinese civilization was still in or near its infancy, its government "a despotism of the simplest and rudest form," with "all power lodged in the hands of the monarch" and exercised through "mercenary agents," and with "no checks, no controls, no remedy for abuse." As a result, he maintained, even the least daring or satirical political statements expressed in China were "quickly rewarded with the discipline of the bamboo."[68] Similar views are to be found in the anonymous 1810 notice that the *Review*'s editor Francis Jeffrey devoted to Staunton's volume. While once again ultimately dismissing Chinese civilization as rudimentary, its political system as bereft of freedom, and its government as clearly a despotism, however, the author also tempers his judgment at certain points and praises the Qing Code for "its great reasonableness, clearness and consistency—the business-like brevity and directness of the various provisions and the plainness and moderation of the language in which they are expressed." Using Chinese law to criticize the indigenous legal systems British administrators of the "Orientalist" school were then employing in India, he describes the Qing Code, in terms that would be echoed by later sinological authors:

> There is nothing, here, of the monstrous *verbiage* of most other Asiatic productions, the miserable incoherence, the tremendous *non sequiturs* and eternal repetitions of those oracular performances; nothing even of the rigid turgid adulation, the accompanying epithets, and fatiguing self-praise of other Eastern despotisms;—but a calm, concise, and distinct series of enactments savouring throughout of practical judgment and European good sense, and, if not always conformable to our improved notions of expediency in this country, in general approaching to them more nearly than the codes of most other nations. . . . And, redundant and absurdly minute as these laws are, in many particulars, we scarcely know of any code that is at once so copious and so consistent, or that is nearly so free from intricacy, bigotry and deception."[69]

Praise of this sort resembled the criticism Mill and Bentham deployed elsewhere against English common law, which they considered hopelessly arcane. Further on, the review daringly suggests that ending the scandalous flogging of British common soldiers should be a greater priority than condemning the Chinese for flogging their defeated generals and disgraced officials, apparently a reference to the reports by Aeneas Anderson and John Barrow on Chinese and English punishments during the Macartney embassy.

The review's reference to the bamboo rod as "the great moral panacea of China" was by now pretty much a stereotype, and the news that torture was used in China to extort confessions and enhance the death penalty for parricide was likely known to many readers. More innovative was the reviewer's view that torture and corporal punishment, as well as the Code's penchant for detail, were signs of a low level of civilization and primitive government. Given this judgment, he was willing to consider Chinese law "good enough for a race to whose habits it was originally adapted," but only on the understanding that its harshness was necessary for dealing with the Chinese, the only people in the world "altogether destitute of honour" (an opinion that reflected sour Western merchant reports of "inveterate" Chinese mendacity).[70] In short, as national character went, so went the law.

Together with De Pauw's opinions previously absorbed into the German philosophical tradition, Mill's Benthamite judgments resurfaced in Hegel's influential judgment that China's use of corporal punishment proved that the Chinese had to be "regarded as in a state of nonage,"[71] an opinion that would be used later in the century to justify imposing upon China extraterritoriality and other concessions that favored the "mature" Western states. Hegel understood "a dose of cudgelling" to be "the severest punishment for a man of honor, who desires not to be esteemed physically assailable, but who is vulnerable in directions implying a more refined sensibility." In this, Qing legal scholars at the time would have entirely agreed with him! The observation led Hegel, however, following Montesquieu, to profess that "the Chinese do not recognize a subjectivity in honor; they are the subjects rather of corrective than retributive punishment, as are children among us."[72] This condition for Hegel was owing to China's embryonic stage of historical development, at which "the determining principle is only the fear of punishment, not any consciousness of wrong; for here we cannot presume any reflection upon the nature of the action itself." Therefore, he thought, "among the Chinese all crimes—those against the laws of the Family relation, as well as against the State—are punished externally." How? By bastinado, exile, strangulation, and—for the son who would raise a hand against his father—by having "his flesh torn from his body with red hot pincers," an image probably out of De Pauw, but worthy of the *Jade Register*.[73] As if

Hegel's point couldn't be made just citing lingchi! That point—that China's lack of moral conscience, the harshness of its external punishments, the lack of distinction between intentional and unintentional wrongs, and the absence of a graded scale of punishments (so here he ignored Montesquieu) all indicated a deep-seated historical backwardness, a level of development distinctly lower than that of the ancient Israelites—reflected Hegel's fundamental belief that historical progress could come only from the West. As it was, military and economic trends seemed to many people to bear out that assertion for the rest of the century and beyond.

Chinese Judicial Practice and Rising Anglo-Chinese Tensions

The quarter century leading up to the first Opium War (1839–1842) witnessed a new wave of reporting on China as the foreign trade of the Qing empire continued to expand rapidly, especially in tea and contraband opium. In this conjuncture of heady profits and expanding contacts, British private merchants critical of the East India Company's monopoly on commerce between England and China became increasingly vocal in calling for radical changes in the relations between the two countries, even as Protestant missionaries intent on converting China's millions sought backing for opening the country to their ministrations. Under these conditions, foreign attention to the Chinese judicial system inevitably generated controversy.[74] Critical new assessments of Chinese law and judicial practice, increasingly highlighting their cruelty, were enunciated by anxious Christian missionaries of various nationalities and by Western diplomats over the following decades. In 1835, for example, the American evangelical journal *The Chinese Repository* ran a long, detailed article documenting a multitude of Chinese legal cases illustrating "various means and modes" of torture and punishment said to be in official use.[75] Citing Staunton, the author informed readers: "Instruments of torture for the investigation of offences are prescribed in the code." He then argues generally that the infliction of torture as a means of interrogation "has always been cruelly abused whenever it has been permitted, and nowhere more, apparently, than in China." This proposition was buttressed with numerous case reports taken from the *Peking Gazette* and other Qing sources, as well as from foreign travel accounts, all establishing the repeated use of the "most cruel tortures." An 1818 issue of the *Gazette*, for instance, testified that local magistrates in Sichuan preferred to torture alleged culprits to death during trial, rather than follow the cumbersome procedure of applying for the imperial approval formally required for execution. Another case dated 1820 involved a magistrate in Anhui province who was officially denounced for using beds of nails, red-hot irons, boiling water, and hamstringing as his means of torture—he even had two criminals nailed to planks by their palms—but he was nonetheless praised by the emperor for his skill at getting "the truth."[76]

Turning to punishments, the *Repository*'s correspondent provided many examples of capital and noncapital penalties, including the bastinado and the cangue, whipping, branding, pillorying, exile, and the enslavement of whole families. Drawn from Qing sources at a time when foreigners were officially excluded from China (except for Macao and Canton), these descriptions did have some solid grounding in reality. Unfortunately, the author also mixed in a fair amount of dubious material, particularly some drawn from the report of the Russian envoy E. F. Timkovski, who described China as a land of cruel tortures during interrogation and of such "horribly severe" punishments as breaking on the wheel, quartering, and having opposing teams of horses tear convicts into pieces, measures more typical of ancien régime Europe than of Qing China.[77] A more authentically Chinese, and similarly harrowing, account was published earlier that year by the British opium dealer James Matheson, who was happy to take some of the shine off the East India Company's image of a civilized Chinese polity that required careful cultivation. His weekly *Canton Register* gave a graphic account of the well-attended public execution of a "most determined" beauty brutally executed by lingchi, before a crowd of hundreds, for murdering her husband.[78]

Such examples, whether genuine or not, served to buttress one *Chinese Repository* article in the Utilitarian-sounding conclusion that Qing justice showed "no apparent effort on the part of the government to reform the criminals; but only to punish." Totals of 581 deaths at the 1826 annual execution ceremony in the capital and 579 in 1829 communicated a general sense of the vast scale of capital punishment throughout the empire. Descriptions of notable specific cases of decapitation and lingchi filled in the gory detail: 170 men hacked to pieces in Xinjiang for rebellion; a Cantonese woman cut to death for poisoning her mother-in-law. An impression of unconscionable cruelty was reinforced by the declaration that the guilty woman's husband was beaten and sentenced to a month in the cangue for sobbing while compelled to watch her die in agony.

The case that received the most attention from the correspondent, however, was that of several Chinese seamen who had robbed the crew and murdered all but one of the members of the French merchantman *Naviga-teur*. While heartily approving of the execution of the perpetrators and the magistrate's order for compensation, the article's author focused on the plight of one old man who had tried to help the French and only narrowly escaped execution after being arrested with the murderers. All in all, the apparent irrationality of the Chinese judicial proceedings left the *Repository* correspondent "sadly disgusted" at the "extreme misery that inmates of a Chinese jail must endure from the unfeeling lictors and keepers" and at the attitude of the executioners, whose mood was one "approaching to exultation at the opportunity of exercising their skill." Augmenting his revulsion was the knowledge that it was not uncommon in China for convicts, even murderers, to hire a substitute to undergo their punishment.[79]

The *Navigateur* case was taken up at length by J. F. Davis in his two-volume *The Chinese: A General Description of the Empire of China and Its Inhabitants* (1836), the first of the great nineteenth-century Western compendia on China. A career EIC official who had participated in the 1815 Amherst embassy to Beijing, Davis by the 1830s was an accomplished sinologist with long experience at Canton. Shortly after the British victory in the first Opium War, he was appointed governor of the newly acquired colony of Hong Kong. His discussion of the *Navigateur* case closes his chapter on Chinese law. After recounting the treachery and the capture of the murderers, he notes that they were conveyed in cages to Canton, where they were tried in the presence of the European representatives, on the emperor's order, with the British missionary Robert Morrison acting as translator.[80] Davis's point in telling this tale was to establish that Morrison secured the old man's release not by newly introducing the principle of the assumption of innocence based on reasonable doubt, as some commentators had supposed, but rather by producing the surviving French witness in order to appeal to that very principle as already understood by the Chinese judges. The crucial distinction Davis seeks to make is that Chinese law was not too primitive for dealing with foreigners, but that foreigners were often treated inequitably by Chinese magistrates who were too xenophobic to uphold their own laws.[81] This defense reflects the standard EIC line that Chinese institutions, though flawed, were fundamentally reasonable, but Davis deploys it here as a platform for proposing that it was high time for Western governments to follow the precedent they had established with Turkey and insist on the right to constitute their own criminal courts that would try foreign nationals at Canton according to Western law codes.[82]

Davis's treatise systematically describes Chinese law, judicial process, and punishments and carefully allots both praise and blame. Contrasted with the harsh laws of Japan, Chinese law could be considered "comparative perfection," argues the British author, who thought the legitimacy of the Qing Code was demonstrated by its support among the populace and its principle that the emperor was subject to the rule of law. Davis identifies the squeezing of hands and feet as the two legal forms of torture used in interrogations. Like earlier authors, he mentions the privileged categories of people who were exempt from such torture. Swimming against the tide, he protests indignantly the popular impression that Chinese punishments were executed with "caprice and cruelty," which he says gained sway in Britain due to the circulation of certain "vulgar daubs, commonly sold at Canton, and representing the punishment of the damned in the Buddhist hells." No doubt he has the *Jade Register* or something very similar in mind. Such pictures had been "absurdly styled 'Chinese punishments' and confounded with the real ones," he complains, in certain cases rightly. To counter the misrepresentations, Davis lays out for a popular audience the official Qing punishments well established by earlier sinological authors. In the process he presents a likeness of one of Alexander's quaint pictures of the cangue, and reminds readers that bamboo strokes were always graded to the seriousness of an offense.[83]

Davis's strongest criticism of the Chinese legal system concerns its lack of protections for those accused of treason, and the "remorseless and unrelenting cruelty and injustice" of the punishment designated for that offense—namely lingchi. This penalty he considers a consequence of the despotic character of the state and the country's "patriarchal" moral order. "Lingchy, 'a disgraceful and lingering death,' which Europeans have sometimes incorrectly styled cutting into ten thousand pieces," was reserved for people convicted of treason and parricide. In convictions for treason, he reports, the family of the offender was consigned to destruction along with the guilty party because of the duty of sons to avenge their fathers' deaths.[84]

Davis's missionary colleague, W. H. Medhurst, made a similar point on the eve of war in his summary description of the Chinese judicial and penal systems. Linking the "lingering execution" to the nature of the Qing state, he explains the harshness of the punishment as the result of the rulers' fears of assassination and rebellion: "Under an absolute despotism, it is the best dictate of policy, and where people are deprived of the privilege of thinking and speaking for themselves, nothing less than the terror of such a law will

ensure the safety of the sovereign." After further noting that the Chinese allowed judicial torture on the ground that the ruler had a paternal duty to
force the accused to accept their wrongdoing, Medhurst expressed his own
view that torture was required in China because of the "utter dereliction of
truth" characteristic of the population.[85] This belief became a commonplace
of colonial Hong Kong, where Davis and later governors insisted on the
need for certain "Chinese punishments," notably flogging and whipping, to
keep their colonial subjects under control.[86]

Chinese Punishments in an Age of Liberalism

The step-by-step "opening" of China after the first Opium War resulted in a
proliferation of new sinological works, many of which discussed the Chinese judicial system. Here we focus on three prominent two-volume studies
that appeared in Britain, France, and the United States, the leading foreign
powers in China, between the 1840s and the 1880s: *The Middle Kingdom*
(1848; revised edition, 1882) by the American Protestant missionary
Samuel Wells Williams, later the first professor of Chinese at Yale; *L'Empire
chinois* (1854–1855) by the former Catholic missionary Évariste Huc; and
China: A History of the Laws, Manners, and Customs (1878) by John Henry
Gray, Anglican archdeacon of Hong Kong.

To capture the sense of Chinese national character conveyed at this time,
let us consider first how these authors treated courtroom proceedings.
While the routine use of torture and the absence of juries and defense
counsel were well-reported features of Chinese courts by 1840, sinological
works produced by Western writers able to travel more widely in China
after the Opium War provided a new wealth of concrete accounts of actual
judicial process.[87] S. W. Williams's compendium on matters Chinese was
one of the most enduringly important of these works.[88] Gone from its pages
was any hint of dignity in a Chinese magistrate's tribunal of the sort
Quesnay or even Staunton might have sought to impart. Citing the *Edinburgh Review*'s critique of Staunton's translation, Williams emphasized the
squalor of China's courts and the summary nature of Chinese judicial process, as characterized by the absence of jury, defense counsel, and bail. He
portrayed the Chinese magistracy as deeply corrupt and oppressive, the efforts of its officers being generally geared to extorting confessions to obtain
a desired verdict.[89] The sole factor in Williams's view that kept the Chinese
judges somewhat attentive to the demands of justice was the prospect that

the population might revolt—a characteristic concern of every despotic government, according to Montesquieu (and Sade). Yet, while in principle deploring torture as inherently tending to abuse, Williams reflected that in China judicial torture corresponded to an ingrained mendacity on the part of the population. Unlike many contemporaries, he noted the distinction in the Qing Code between legal and illegal tortures, the former being confined to crushing the fingers and ankles. He also observed, however, that illegal modes were "so common as to give the impression that some of them at least are sanctioned." These cruelties included twisting the ears with roughened fingers, pummeling the lips, and making the prisoner kneel on chains (all earlier illustrated by Mason), as well as suspending the body by the fingers, bending the body back double with the hands tied to a bar under the knees, etc. As a result, "the universal dread among the people of coming before courts, and having anything to do with their magistrates, is owing in great measure to the illegal sufferings they must often endure." And while "neither imprisonment nor torture are ranked among the five [official] punishments," they nevertheless caused "more deaths, probably, among arrested persons than all other means."[90]

In the decades after the Opium War, other writers often reiterated J. F. Davis's testimony on the hellishness characteristic of Chinese prisons.[91] An early letter elaborating this point was published in *The Chinese Repository* in 1843. The journal's correspondent cited Chinese-language documents to describe the tortures Chinese prisoners inflicted on one another to extort money. As he put it, "*Tiyoh*, or hell, is the name commonly given to these places; and they doubtless bear as close resemblance to that place of human torment as human device and cruelty can make them."[92] Another correspondent writing to the same journal in 1851 reported on the deplorable state of prisoners he visited in a Ningbo prison and offered dramatic confirmation that cruelty was prevalent in such institutions: "No pen is adequate to describe accurately the horrors of a Chinese prison. Suffice it to say that they would surprise and shock even those who are best acquainted with the sordid and cruel nature of this people."[93]

In his own treatment of Chinese prisons, Williams elaborated further on the often-cited Chinese usage of calling the country's prisons "hells."[94] Assessing the degree of brutality within the Chinese justice system, he declared that "probably the number of persons who suffer by the sword of the executioner is not one-half of those who die from the effects of torture and privations in prison."[95] Thus, while the imperial government was in theory supposed to be solicitous of the welfare of prisoners and provide them with a minimum of food and clothing, in practice "the jailer starves them on half this allowance if they are unable to fee him." Williams describes the physical layout of a typical Chinese prison as similar to "a large stable," around the edge of which were a series of small stalls. Each stall housed a group of prisoners "under the control of a turnkey, who with a few old offenders spends much time torturing newly arrived persons to force money from them, by which many lose their lives." Addressing a theme later developed by Gray, Williams decries the typical gross overcrowding, which was especially severe in district capitals. As a result, he reports, the Cantonese authorities had to rent twenty-two private jails, places "where every kind of cruelty is practiced." Even in the official prisons, he reports, the pressures of court business were sometimes so heavy that the magistrate would simply jail all the principals and witnesses in a case. Since the government had no responsibility to feed those held in such circumstances, Williams reported, "many of the poorer ones die." His conclusion? "Well may the people call their prisons hells, and say, when a man falls into the clutches of the jailers or police, 'the flesh is under the cleaver.'"

Williams further detailed the standard Qing punishments, referring to Lecomte for the insight that flogging with the bamboo accompanied most sentences as a supplement to other forms of punishment. The American missionary added that those convicted of robbery and assault were often whipped through the streets as public examples, sometimes with flags of shame stuck in their ears (as Mason had pictured). Strangling and beheading were presented as the legal modes of execution; Williams explained that the former was less shameful because it left the body intact. Beheading could take the form of either the simple severing of the head or the more extensive lingchi, which ended with decapitation. Prisoners sentenced to the latter, he observed, were usually so exhausted that they submitted without a groan. After death the body was given over to the convict's family, except when it was "exposed as a warning in a cage" or, in the absence of kin, thrown into a public pit. Like the earlier *Chinese Repository* correspondent, Williams gave numbers of executions based on the imperial *Gazette*'s report on the Autumn Assizes and testified that it was not unusual to hear of twenty or more felons executed in a provincial capital on a single day then.[96]

Similarly gruesome material emerged in Évariste Huc's *L'Empire chinois*. An immediate classic upon publication in 1854, this work said little about prisons, but a great deal about court proceedings and punishments. Testifying on the basis of his travels throughout the Qing empire in the late 1840s and early 1850s, when Europe and China were both immersed in revolutionary upheaval, Huc provided his readers with a series of shocking vignettes that would reverberate around the world over the following decades. One tells of a Hebei magistrate's court that the French missionary and his party entered unexpected, seeking nourishment. Finding himself suddenly in the midst of a trial, Huc was aghast at the grisly interrogation taking place before his eyes. The accused, he reported, was suspended from the roof of the hall, the form of judicial torture Mason had designated "the swing." Around him stood five or six court lackeys armed with rods and lashes, "their clothes and faces spotted with the blood of the unfortunate creature, who was uttering stifled groans, while his flesh was torn almost to tatters." Rather than being repelled, noted Huc, "the audience at this frightful spectacle appeared quite at their ease . . . Many laughed, indeed, at the horror visible on our faces." After asking the magistrate what great crime the man had committed "to be subjected to so horrible a torture," the missionary was told that he had confessed to being the leader of a gang that had murdered over fifty merchants traveling on the Yellow River: the torture was meant to make him reveal his accomplices, as Mason's bilingual book had suggested.[97] The contrast between the horror this scene inspired in Huc and the contented, even gleeful reaction Huc reported of the Chinese onlookers served vividly to illustrate the notion that China and the West occupied different levels of civilization.

Huc reported that to avoid charges of negligence in getting convictions, Chinese officials sometimes conducted themselves with "atrocious cruelty" toward prisoners. As an example he recalls an encounter on the way to Beijing, when he and his entourage met a party of soldiers who were "escorting a number of carts, in which were literally piled up a crowd of Chinese, who were uttering horrible cries." Huc continues:

As we stopped to allow these cart-loads of human beings to pass, we were seized with horror on perceiving that these unfortunate creatures were nailed by the hands to the planks of the cart. A satellite whom we interrogated, replied, with frightful coolness, "We've been routing out a nest of thieves in a neighbouring village. We got a good many of them: and as we hadn't brought chains enough, we were obliged to contrive some way to prevent their escaping. So you see we nailed them by the hand."

"But do you not think there may be some innocent among them?"

"Who can tell? They have not yet been tried. We are taking them to the tribunal; and by-and-by, if there are any innocent men among them, they will be separated from the thieves."

"Perhaps what was most hideous of all in this dreadful spectacle," the priest remarks "was the mocking hilarity of the soldiers" as they watched the agonies of their captives.[98] The ferocity of the Qing judicial apparatus in the middle decades of the century was such that Huc's accounts ring somewhat true, but who is to say whether they really were?[99] In any case, his tone in passages like this often appears geared to encourage repugnance toward Chinese society as a whole.

Huc's readers were likely to gain a similar impression of willful cruelty from what he wrote of the Chinese treatment of convicted criminals. Confirming earlier reports transmitted by Staunton and others, the abbé concisely rehearsed the usual list of Chinese punishments for sentenced convicts. After citing the routine application of the bastinado to establish the "generally penal character" of Chinese law, he described certain sentences in more detail. Among the points he found disturbing was the fact that capital punishment for high treason could be expanded, in the most serious cases, to the beheading of all of the convict's male relatives. Further on, he gave a graphic description of lingchi, claiming that the victims' families often paid the executioner to finish the job quickly and not prolong the suffering.[100]

Huc maintained that Qing law in his day no longer held the same respect it once had among the people. That plus the lack of a genuine, religiously based morality was why, in his mind, Chinese officials were so draconian in imposing punishments. To illustrate their harshness, he recounts another frightful scene he and his companions had observed while traveling in Shandong. There in a field they came across a strangely adorned group of trees. On closer examination, each of these trees was found to hold about fifty coarsely constructed bamboo cages, each containing a human head. "Almost all were in a state of putrefaction, and the features hideously distorted," reported Huc. "We could not long endure this disgusting sight." His guide's explanation that the heads were those of a notorious band of thieves recently captured by Qing forces intent on deterring crime led the missionary to observe that, since the laws had lost the people's allegiance, officialdom often simply ignored the law code, even in cases where summary justice was legally permissible: "l'arbitraire et la fantaisie sont souvent son unique règle," observed Huc in French. The wording of his English translator was blunter still: "Their own pleasure forms their only rule."[101] Either formulation would have been grist for Mirbeau's Sadean mill. Indeed, taken together, Huc's two roadside vignettes evoke a striking scene in *Le Jardin des supplices*, where the novel's protagonist and his sadistic English lover pass through an orchard where each tree houses an accused person subjected to some garish lethal torment. "But what if the accused is found innocent?" the protagonist asks. " 'Oh, well . . . ,' said Clara."[102]

Huc's anecdotes might have been more gripping than most, but he was far from the only author trading in garish representations. One of the most vivid depictions of Chinese punishments appeared during Britain's next round of warfare against China in 1856–1860 in the form of a collection of startling illustrations considerably more gruesome and sensational than Mason's. The new booklet consisted of engravings by Percy Cruikshank based on paintings by the Cantonese artist Yoeequa.[103] Cruikshank's aim in publishing these engravings was to deride the Qing legal system and with it China's general level of civilization. It was no coincidence that a work depicting atrocities presented as typical of the Chinese judicial system appeared in 1858, just when Lord Palmerston's government was championing the immunity of British subjects as a key justification for his new round of imperial warfare against the Qing. Percy Cruikshank was the nephew of Victorian Britain's most famous illustrator, George Cruikshank, whom Palmerston had approached for the job. The prime minister, whose 1857 electoral campaign had highlighted Chinese tortures as justification for Britain's going to war, apparently supplied the originals with a request for caricatures that he hoped to see displayed in picture shops throughout London.[104] The published results, which went well beyond what Mason thought appropriate to show, pictured as typically Chinese a series of ghastly procedures: the wrenching of limbs and the tearing off of ears, penal starvation, strangling, flaying alive, basting with boiling oil, disembowelment (Figure 19), chopping in two, and full dismemberment (Figure 20). Several of these seem to come straight from the *Jade Register*.[105] In his pugnacious introduction, the elder Cruikshank endorsed the drawings as truly portraying Chinese practices, which he (echoing Mason) likened to those of the Inquisition. On the basis of French reports and the observations of his brother, a navy man who had once visited Canton, George Cruikshank fervently assured his readers that "the majority of the male population" of

Canton was composed of "the most filthy, degraded, cruel, deceitful people upon the face of the earth." These qualities Cruikshank contrasted with the high moral character of his friend Sir John Bowring, British plenipotentiary to the "Far East" and Benthamite governor of Hong Kong, whose activities had played a key role in sparking hostilities with China in 1856.[106]

How widely the Cruikshank booklet circulated is unknown, but what started out as military-political propaganda thereafter took a curious twist, for the wartime depictions were appropriated a decade later in the quasi-historical, quasi-erotic Victorian classic *Flagellation and the Flagellants*. Its author, James Bertram, who happily described China as a country ruled by the rod, referred his readers to the younger Cruikshank's engravings as evidence of typical Chinese punishments.[107] Through this channel the imagery of

Strangling   Disembowelling

Figure 19. *Strangling* and *Disembowelling*. From Percy Cruikshank, *The Criminal Punishments of the Chinese* (1858). In the drawing on the right, the illustrator has hidden the grisly sight of disembowelment by having the executioner place a fan over the victim's belly. Reproduced by kind permission of the Syndics of Cambridge University Library.

Chinese atrocities reached a new audience, on which it would have emotional and aesthetic impacts that probably surpassed Palmerston's expectations, however much he liked the idea of regularly giving the Chinese a good caning.

Depicting Chinese Justice after the Anglo-French Victory

As longtime residents of China, S. W. Williams and J. H. Gray were both able to provide their readers with more thorough descriptions of the country than Huc, who had traveled through the Qing domains for only a few years. Unlike the French missionary, whose account consists of a series of striking anecdotes regarding Chinese courts, Williams and Gray both aimed to provide systematic treatments of how the Chinese justice system worked. By the time Gray's treatise appeared in 1878, the notion that tor-

Figure 20. *Legs Nailed to a Board, Cutting the Body in Two,* and *Disjointing.* From Percy Cruikshank, *The Criminal Punishments of the Chinese* (1858). Reproduced by kind permission of the Syndics of Cambridge University Library.

ture was endemic to "Oriental" culture had become part of British colonial doctrine, via the Madras Presidency's 1854–1855 Commission on Torture.[108] While many of the judicial tortures and prison conditions Gray described were undoubtedly accurate in empirical terms, his approach to these phenomena also accorded remarkably well with the imperial expectations of his British readership.

The archdeacon informed his readers bluntly: "The mode in which trials are conducted in China is startling to all who live in lands where trial by jury is adopted. Trials in Chinese courts of law are conducted by torture." Noting that Chinese courts assumed the guilt of the accused, Gray observed that during the course of a trial the prisoner was asked a great many leading questions aimed at incriminating him. If his answers were evasive, "torture is at once resorted to as the only remaining expedient."[109] Describing the forms of such torture in ascending order of severity, Gray observed that an accused was typically forced to kneel with two warders holding his arms while a third beat him with the bamboo. If he continued to give answers construed as evasive, his jaws were beaten with a leather truncheon that could break his teeth and make his mouth swell so much that he could not chew (again, as Mason had earlier illustrated). A prisoner who continued to deny his guilt would have his ankles beaten, often to the point of breaking; and, if the desired result was still not forthcoming, the next step was the rack, on which he was stretched in a standing position and subjected to "the extremity of the torture." Gray's description of the resulting "piteous moans" and "saliva oozing freely from the mouth" underlined the cruelty of the proceeding. But if a confession was still not produced, a "still crueller" torture was waiting, in which a beam was lashed across the shoulders and outstretched arms of the kneeling victim, while another beam was placed behind his knees. The warders then stood on the lower beam and pressed on the upper one, causing excruciating pain (Figure 21). Not only were these hideous practices applied to the accused in both criminal and civil cases, Gray noted, they could also be used on other principals as well as on witnesses.

Given his opinion that Chinese officials constituted "perhaps as a class the most corrupt state servants in the world," the overall picture Gray painted of Chinese justice was bleak. While he allowed that some mandarins were men of integrity, and that Chinese law possessed "many very humane traits" (like pardoning sons who supported their parents, and permitting wives to accompany their husbands into exile), the only real ray of hope Gray saw on the dark horizon of Chinese justice was the proclamation against judicial torture issued by the foreign powers during their 1871 occupation of Canton, for him an edifying example of the West's civilizing mission in Asia.[110] In the 1882 revised edition of *The Middle Kingdom*, Williams discarded his earlier uncertainty on the extent of torture in China and adopted Gray's view by bluntly summing up standard Qing interrogation practice with the declaration: "Torture is practiced upon both criminal and witnesses, in court and in prison." However, whereas the American author had earlier condemned torture outright, he now allowed that it did have "a powerful deterrent effect in preventing crime and disorder" among a population so wanting in honor as the Chinese.[111]

In response to the many sensational depictions of Chinese prisons that had been published over the previous decades by diplomats and soldiers, Gray set himself the task of providing a thorough analysis of the Chinese prison system. His discussion of the subject, complete with Chinese line drawings, gave Western readers their fullest, most accurate account to date of Chinese prisons, which he likened to their early nineteenth-century English counterparts. Like his treatment of torture, what he had to say about the operation of these Chinese "habitations of cruelty" must have alarmed readers nearly as much as the lurid anecdotal accounts then circulating. "In point of appearance," he wrote, "the unfortunate inmates of Chinese prisons are, perhaps, of all men, the most abject and miserable. The death-

JUDICIAL TORTURE.

Figure 21. *Judicial Torture.* From John Gray, *China: A History of the Laws, Manners, and Customs of the People* (1878), Volume 1, opposite page 34.

like countenances, emaciated forms, and long, coarse, black hair, which according to prisoner rules they are not allowed to shave, give them the appearance of demons rather than of men." Gray pointed out that, as Chinese prison officials purchased their positions and received no salary, they made it their business to "enrich themselves" by taking payments from the families and friends of the prisoners. Despite the fact that imperial officials were supposed to punish prison governors in charge of institutions where more than 2 percent of prisoners died per month, in practice prison conditions were abominable. Prisoners who had no influential friends languished "neglected and forgotten, or die[d] from sheer inability to obtain even the commonest necessaries of life." As a result, "the mortality of Chinese prisons is so great that a dead-house [morgue] is regarded as a very necessary adjunct." The fact that money could buy favors naturally worked to the detriment of the great majority of prisoners who, being poor, had no choice but to be huddled together, either "in a common ward, sometimes so crowded that its inmates find it difficult to lie down," or else in private houses of detention so densely packed as to resemble the infamous Black Hole of Calcutta. In one such private institution visited by Gray in 1861, all the prisoners were naked; he was convinced that Europeans packed into a similarly confined space would undoubtedly have perished.[112] Such depictions implicitly accused the Chinese government of perpetuating conditions that his Anglophone readership would have found "cruel and degrading." Whether the venality was "unusual" was perhaps another matter, given the strong complaints about Victorian prisons in that regard.

What Gray might have made of the erotic sections of James Bertram's work on flagellation is anyone's guess, but the archdeacon did include some breathtaking material in his extensive account of Chinese punishments, many of which he found "barbarous and cruel in the extreme." His discussion, illustrated with numerous colorful anecdotes, began predictably with the commonest punishments, flogging and the cangue. People convicted of petty larceny, observed Gray, were flogged through the streets with a whip or short bamboo rod, preceded by an officer with a gong who broadcast the humiliating message, "This is the punishment due to a thief." Recalling the treatment of an aged robber who was stripped of his trousers and flogged with the long bamboo, Gray observed that the poor man's "sufferings awakened no sympathy in court," but instead were "apparently a source of delight to the judge and his officers, and the face of each official was expanded by a broad grin." Contrary to some authors, Gray treated the cangue as a punishment that was "severe to a degree," on the grounds that it not only made the wearer "an object of universal scorn and contempt," but also prevented him or her from lying down for extended periods. Discussing penal cages, Gray explained that one design was of such low construction that the occupant had to remain seated or prone, but that the two other types were fitted out with a cangue that kept the prisoner upright, either in a crouching position or else on tiptoes, the latter device invariably proving fatal. The cutting off of the ears, legally prescribed for accomplices to a conspiracy, had reportedly been recently inflicted by Qing authorities on many innocent people whose villages the Taiping rebels had occupied.[113]

Having apparently witnessed a fair number of Chinese executions, Gray provided ample testimony as to the various methods. Like Huc, he graphically depicted lingchi, which he said was inflicted on murderers of husbands, uncles, brothers, and tutors as well as on traitors, patricides, and matricides. "The criminal is bound to a cross," he wrote, "and cut either into one hundred and twenty, or seventy-two, or thirty-six, or twenty-four pieces," though in cases with extenuating circumstances imperial clemency might allow the victim to be divided into "only" eight. Gray's detailed description of how a woman who had taken a lover was executed in this manner was effective in underlining the cruelty of the practice. As for other forms of capital punishment, convicts condemned to simple decapitation ("murderers, rebels, pirates, ravishers of women, etc.") were reportedly kept in ignorance of their time of execution until the preceding day. Gray was struck by the lack of concern most showed about their fate, though he attributed this in part to their being allowed to drug themselves with betel juice before execution. It was not unusual, he continued, again confirming reports by Huc and others, for the heads of those executed to be exposed "as a warning to others"[114] (Figure 22).

Williams brought several new viewpoints to the topic of Qing punishments in his 1882 revision of *The Middle Kingdom*. Having previously highlighted the large number of executions that took place in the provincial capitals, he noted that considerably more occurred during times of rebellion. The example he chose was Canton, where captives from all of Guangdong province were gathered "during the terrible insurrection" (that of the Taipings) in 1854–1855 (Gray's "Nankin malefactor" in Figure 22 was likely charged with being a Taiping rebel). "In a space of fourteen months, up to January, 1856, about eighty-three thousand malefactors suffered death in that city alone, besides those who died in confinement," observed Williams, adding by way of justification that "these men were arrested and delivered to execution by their countrymen, who had suffered untold miseries through their sedition and rapine."[115] A radical Parisian like Mirbeau, for whom the memory of twenty thousand executed Communards was still fresh, might have felt less enamored of the forces of order. Certainly the British seaman A. F. Lindley, who proudly threw in his lot with the Taiping revolutionaries, thought the "fiendish" Qing punishments—especially those for treason, such as lingchi—constituted "the blackest spot in the annals of mankind."[116]

Necessary Cruelties? Torture in "the Orient"

Notwithstanding all the horrors of the Chinese legal system highlighted in nineteenth-century sinological works, some Western authors were impelled to justify that system, or at least certain aspects of it, even as they distanced themselves from it theoretically. We have already noted this tendency in the Protestant missionary William Medhurst. The example of the Catholic Évariste Huc is similarly instructive. Huc explained the predominantly penal character of Chinese law as the result of the absence among the Chinese of "true" religious belief and genuine sense of national solidarity, a point strongly reminiscent of Hegel. Believing that the Chinese populace sub-

HEAD OF A MALEFACTOR, EXPOSED AT NANKIN.

Figure 22. *Head of a Malefactor, exposed at Nankin.* From John Gray, *China: A History of the Laws, Manners, and Customs of the People* (1878), Volume 1, opposite page 68.

scribed to a "utilitarian," "materialistic" outlook rather than to any proper religion or morality, he thought it "quite natural that the bamboo should be the necessary and indispensable accessory of every legal prescription." Likewise, thinking that "the presence of this utilitarian principle in legislation usually indicates that the social bond is artificial," he held that China's immense population "would not subsist long as a nation, but would be speedily dismembered, were a system of legislation founded on the principles of absolute justice and right, to be suddenly substituted for the strange one that now governs it."[117] In short, his conservative moral-philosophical reading of China portrayed the country's regime of disciplinary practices as necessary for social order and predicted that it would probably be needed even if the Western powers succeeded in beginning to reform the country's legislation.

Gray, in contrast, adopted an insistently reformist tone and brooked no apologies for torture or the atrocious prison conditions and punishments he described. He instead longed for a prison reform movement led by a future Chinese John Howard. Hoping that the examples of suffering and cruelty presented in his pages would fill his readers "with pain and indignation," Gray denounced Chinese conditions as similar to those of Europe's Middle Ages: "No one can read unmoved of courts of justice where iniquity and reckless cruelty prevail—of officials whose venality is a pit in which many an innocent family has perished—of gaols in which human beings are penned in dens of noisome filth and squalor, with, in too many instances, barely such necessities as suffice to keep life in their emaciated bodies—of barbarous punishments which recall the darkest ages of European history."[118]

For his part, Williams adopted an approach that was generally reformist like Gray's, yet he sided with Huc in lecturing his readers: "One who has lived in the country long, however, knows well that they [the Chinese] are not to be held in check by rope-yarn laws or whimpering justices, and unless the rulers are a terror to evil-doers, the latter will soon get the upper hand." While deploring the Chinese justice system's many cruelties and injustices, he refrained from condemning the system wholesale, instead insisting on a more discriminating view. Portraying Chinese government as exhibiting a "strange blend of cruelty to prisoners with a maudlin consideration of their condition, and a constant effort to coax the people to obedience while exercising great severity upon individuals," he gave the system a qualified endorsement by arguing, in words reminiscent of Staunton, that the "general prosperity of the Empire proves in some measure the equity of its administration." Seen in this light, the Chinese legal system might not compare well with the European present, but it did stand up decently against the European past: "Officers and people are bad almost beyond belief to one conversant with the courtesy, justice, purity, and sincerity of Christian governments and society; and yet we think they are not as bad as [the 1848 edition said: "they are equal to"] the old Greeks and Romans, and have no more injustice or torture in their courts, nor impurity and mendacity in their lives."[119]

Fin de Siècle Perspectives

As the nineteenth century drew to a close, the grand sinological surveys of earlier decades were joined on Western bookshelves by an increasing number of more specialized works. Once again, we will confine our discussion here to three influential works. Two of these, the widely circulated fourth edition of A. H. Smith's *Chinese Characteristics* (1894) and G. E. Morrison's *An Australian in China* (1895), both written for a popular audience, appeared during the Sino-Japanese War, which initiated a new phase of imperialist encroachments in East Asia. The third work, a detailed legal treatise entitled *Notes and Commentaries on Chinese Criminal Law* by the London barrister Ernest Alabaster, was published in 1899, the same year as Mirbeau's sensational *Le Jardin des supplices*. We have cited Morrison's and Alabaster's views in Chapter 3 in discussing the rationale for lingchi; here we take the occasion to provide them with more context.

What the Protestant missionary Arthur Smith thought of Chinese punishments he stated concisely in his chapter on the "absence of sympathy" among the Chinese. For all his twenty-two years of lived experience in China, his single-minded focus on cruelty as a feature typical of the Chinese national character (or rather, lack of true "Character")[120] strongly recalled the theoretical position elaborated in the 1810 *Edinburgh Review.* In a passage thick with allusions, Smith first highlighted "the enormous number of blows with the bamboo which are constantly resorted to, often ten times the number named in the law, and sometimes one hundred times as many"; he then referred readers to the treatments of the "dreadful tortures" by Williams and Huc, recalling in particular Huc's account of prisoners with their hands nailed to the cart in which they were carried. Thus Smith's book, like so many works on "the East," fed copiously on its predecessors. In light of the "routine cruelty with which all Chinese prisoners are treated who cannot pay for their exemption," he asked, "Is it strange that the Chinese adage advises the dead to keep out of hell and the living to keep out of yamêns?" At the same time, however, Smith defended Qing tortures and punishments as suited to the Chinese character. Reminiscent of Huc and Williams, he asserted that "the Chinese being what they are, . . . it would probably be wholly impracticable to introduce any essential amelioration of their punishments without a thoroughgoing reformation of the Chinese people as individuals. Physical force cannot safely be abandoned until some moral force is at hand adequate to take its place."[121] Contrasting Chinese depravity with Anglo-Saxon virtue and success, Smith left no doubt that Christianity was the sole force capable of reforming a nation whose character and conscience had been perverted by millennia of heathenism.[122]

Smugness about British penal practice was always a hard sell in Australia, and the journalist George Morrison, who hailed from there, clearly had trouble abiding it. One of the first investigative reporters with a bureau-posting in China, Morrison acidly observed that the Chinese manner of attributing an infernal character to their prisons had parallels in England, where prison ships a mere forty years earlier had been popularly called "floating hells." Allowing for the "blunted nerve sensibility of the Chinaman," he doubted that "the cruelties practiced in Chinese jails" were any less endurable than those adumbrated in Charles Reade's 1856 exposé of English prison suicides. After likening the buying of prison appointments in China to their sale in Britain before John Howard's reforms, Morrison assured his readers that there were "no cruelties practiced in Chinese gaols greater, even if there are any equal, to the awful and degraded brutality with which the England of our forefathers treated her convicts in the penal settlements of Norfolk Island, Macquarie Harbour and the prison hulks of Williamstown." The horrendous Australian convict camps of a half century earlier and the routine imposition in them of cruelties that were justified by "the brutalised character of the prisoners" left Morrison scoffing at the haughty British habit of treating the Chinese as "centuries behind us in civilisation and humanity."[123]

Morrison provided little Chinese detail to buttress the parallels he drew, but Ernest Alabaster a few years later supported his own similar position with abundant evidence in his *Notes and Commentaries on Chinese Law*. Six hundred pages long and loaded with extensive case analysis, this learned tome was compiled from materials collected by the author's father,

Chalderon Alabaster, whose career of nearly forty years in "the East" had included a term as a British consul-general in China. A barrister at London's Inner Temple, Ernest Alabaster intended his work as a much-needed update on Staunton's edition of the Qing Code and a useful summation of Chinese legal practice. Unlike Octave Mirbeau, whose agitated *faux-mémoire* appeared that same year, Alabaster adopted a measured, academic tone, carefully mixing considered criticism with acknowledgment that the Chinese system had advantages, even as compared to the British.

In Alabaster's view, the contemporary Chinese government was the same "paternal despotism" that had prevailed throughout China's history. However, while accepting that this form of government had its negative consequences and flaws, Alabaster staunchly defended China's legal system: "Although the allowance of torture is a blot which cannot be overlooked, although the punishment for treason and parricide is monstrous, and the punishment of the wooden collar or portable pillory is not to be defended, yet the Code—when its procedure is understood—is infinitely more exact and satisfactory than our own system, and very far from being the barbarous cruel abomination it is generally supposed to be."[124] In considering the Code, Alabaster saw the minuteness of its regulations as both a strength and a weakness, on the one hand making it superior in consistency to the English code, but on the other hand erecting an "impenetrable barrier" to any expansion of the authority of the magistrate or development of forensic initiative.

Like many before him, Alabaster reiterated that the only judicial tortures legally permissible in China were the squeezing of the fingers and the feet, which he admitted could be inflicted on witnesses as well as on the accused. He also accepted that other tortures, though strictly illegal, were nonetheless "often employed and justified by the authorities on the grounds of necessity":

Where, for example, a witness refuses to answer a question, or evidently perjures himself, instead of committing him for contempt, or prosecuting him for perjury, the court is authorized to punish him summarily, by slapping his face, beating him on the outside of the thighs, or what not, as the case may be. Again where there is clear evidence of guilt, and the prisoner refuses to admit the justice of his conviction, the punishment due his offence cannot be carried out until he does so, and the application of more severe forms of torture is permitted.[125]

Situating current practice historically, Alabaster rightly reminded his readers that in antiquity Chinese law had allowed execution, castration, maiming, and branding of the forehead. He then discussed the three current modes of execution (by slicing, decapitation, and strangulation). His graphic account of lingchi might well have made attention-getting copy for newsmen covering the Boxer Rebellion a year later; Alabaster himself, however, was concerned with establishing ethnographic significance rather than with creating a sensation. "The punishment, known to foreigners as 'lingering death,'" he explained, "is not inflicted so much as a torture, but to destroy the future as well as the present life of the offender—he is unworthy to exist any longer as a man or a recognizable spirit, and, as spirits to appear must assume their previous corporeal forms, he can only appear as a collection of little bits." After describing how the convict was tied to a cross and subjected in theory to a series of cuts that left the body "sliced beyond recognition," Alabaster indicated, as we have seen, that in practice death usually came after just a few seconds, the coup de grâce usually being delivered, according to him, on the third cut. Although the punishment was clearly "severe and revolting," it was "not so painful as the half-hanging, disemboweling, and final quartering, practiced in England not so long ago." He thus judged lingchi not only less painful but, as he put it, "artistically" preferable to the hideous spectacle of François Damiens's 1757 execution for his bumbling assault on Louis XV, the iconic event with which Michel Foucault opens *Discipline and Punishment*. "[T]he destruction of future comfort to the offender's ghost" was "undoubtedly a refinement," observed the English author wryly.[126] Yet, taking into account the numerous grounds for mitigating guilt and commuting sentences in China, Alabaster concluded that the Qing legal system was "less Draconian than our own, though in some cases it is more severe."[127]

A Mixed Legacy

"'The Chinese are very cruel!' we say happily enough in Europe," observed Jean-Jacques Matignon in the 1910 volume that gave the world its first published photographs of the lingchi process. Yet, while Dr. Matignon readily granted the extreme severity of the Qing Code, he felt compelled to warn his readers against taking their ideas of Chinese punishments from *Le Jardin des supplices*. The author of that work, he avowed, had used his prodigious artistic imagination to "embellish a thin screen of reality with the most extraordinary fantasies, both horrible and appealing."[128] In fact, by the time

Octave Mirbeau set about locating his proto-surrealist tale in a Chinese setting, he had at his disposal a centuries-old fabric of Western reporting on Chinese tortures and punishments. That fabric was thickly laced with internal cross-referencing, but what the interlacing held together was a patchwork of fact, fantasy, and often tendentious comment that all too easily lent itself to sensationalism. Examining this mixed heritage historically has enabled us to discern the evolution of certain of its elements.

The Western literature, as we have seen, displays a marked shift in emphasis, from highlighting the rationality and orderliness of Chinese punishments in the early modern period to stressing the cruelty involved, from the late eighteenth century onward. During the seventeenth century, it became conventional to identify the bastinado and the cangue as characteristic Chinese punishments by which officials enforced order on behalf of the state. In the mid-eighteenth century, the practice of flogging with the bamboo or the whip was transformed into a defining mark of despotic government. From early in the nineteenth century, Chinese punishments and judicial procedures generally were seen as consequences of "Oriental" despotism and were cited as signs of the perennially "backward" and "semi-barbarous" nature of a society in which cruelty prevailed. Such assessments, as conveyed in visual and discursive forms, elicited increasingly powerful emotional and aesthetic responses of horror and disgust—responses that were periodically mobilized in the service of jingoistic colonial interests, but that eventually would serve the purposes of an anticolonial novelist as well. Among the techniques evoked to elicit such horror and disgust, the most dramatic was lingchi—at least of those grounded in actual Chinese practice. It was this, or something very close to it—the skinning and dismemberment found in the *Jade Register*—that Mirbeau evoked at the culmination of his novel to demonstrate the cultivated subtlety of Chinese "justice," in contrast to the vulgar bluntness of colonial India, where captured rebels during the great 1857 uprising were tied to the mouths of cannons and blown to bits, to the gratification of British onlookers.[129]

Not all nineteenth-century China-hands were of a single mind in regard to the Chinese use of torture and harsh punishments, it is true. While some condemned these, others, as we have seen, defended them in qualified fashion, as necessary to discipline and control the Chinese population. Despite the apparent contrast, both attitudes appear to have been compatible with Western imperial designs: outright condemnation often went together with robust notions of "civilizing mission," while qualified support coincided with the broader belief that force was needed to govern non-Western peoples. This latter belief fit closely with the general colonial mind-set positing low levels of civilization outside Europe and its settler colonies as well as with the perceived needs of government in Hong Kong and the treaty ports. In addition, judicial torture and Chinese modes of punishment were used to justify legal extraterritoriality for Western nationals in China. As we have seen, Britain's second governor of Hong Kong, J. F. Davis, explicitly associated Chinese judicial procedures and punishments with the case for extraterritoriality at a crucial moment in Sino-Western relations. If later authors refrained from doing so explicitly, the frequency with which they stressed the gap between Western and Chinese legal standards suggests their tacit support for this key component of the "unequal treaty" system, which few of them ever saw fit to criticize.

At the same time, it is worth noting that certain influential nineteenth-century authors—China-hands and others—did challenge the notion of an absolute gap between "us" ("the West," "European civilization") and "them" ("the Chinese," "Asiatics," "Orientals"). Christians, Utilitarians, socialists, and positivists all invoked notions of common humanity to provide a foundation for the possibility of conversion and improvement. Writers as diverse as the missionary Robert Morrison and the barrister Ernest Alabaster were inclined to discern empirical parallels between China and the West that undermined overly smug claims of Western superiority and fundamental cultural difference. The varying evaluations within the Western literature deserve examination as clues to divergences within the broad enterprise of empire-building.[130] Likewise, the range of emotions expressed in the literature regarding some of the most repugnant facets of Chinese society raises doubts about Alain Grosrichard's contention that a generalized paranoia provided the fundamental grounding for Western imperialism.[131] The historical record displays such a wide spectrum of emotions not easily reducible to fear—including arrogance, disgust, curiosity, and even sympathy—that it becomes difficult to reduce the colonial era's complex mental and psychological makeup to any single underlying affective condition.

Nineteenth-century Western writings about China undoubtedly did contribute to making Chinese tortures and punishments an object of revulsion and horror within European traditions of verbal and pictorial representation. By increasingly focusing on cruelty as a defining Chinese (or "Oriental," or "uncivilized") trait, the "China literature" after 1800 portrayed the Chinese as manifesting a "sadistic" national or racial character. It did so, though, in a notably nonerotic sense. Depictions of Chinese onlookers taking pleasure in the suffering of others are found in the work of Huc and others, but we find no evidence in professional sinological writings for a Chinese eroticization of suffering, such as Sade or the Romantics championed, nor for an erotic celebration of death of the sort found in Baudelaire. James Bertram's quasi-pornographic work on flagellation may thus be the exception that proves the rule. As far as China was concerned, genre-crossing into the realm of erotica was rare before Mirbeau's *Le Jardin des supplices* depicted its English anti-heroine rolling her eyes back in ecstatic pleasure at the sight of suffering torture victims.[132] Thereafter, this kind of mixing became the fiction writer's stock-in-trade, most often with the pleasure projected onto "evil Chinese" onlookers. The effect was to let China float further into the realm of the imagination and to allow its penal practices to disappear into a fantasyland as potent, as perverse, and as unrealistic as the courts of the Ten Kings.

CHAPTER 7

Misreading Lingchi

An execution is more than the killing of a person who has been found guilty of a capital crime. It is a complex event involving many people: the victim, first of all, and the man who is charged with executing the death penalty, but also officials who attend to embody the power of the state, soldiers or police who control the victim and the crowd that may assemble to witness the death, and finally the witnesses themselves. How these elements combine is profoundly shaped by the cultural and political context in which an execution is carried out. We contend in this chapter that this shaping has produced profound differences between China and the West in the orchestration and meaning of executions.

It is important on the one hand not to exaggerate or essentialize differences between cultures. On the other hand, historically these differences affected more than just how executions were performed; they also shaped people's expectations about what should happen at an execution. When those expectations were overturned, as happened in the eyes of Europeans at executions in China, a deep chasm of misunderstanding opened up, into which rushed all manner of misunderstandings about what was being done and what that said about the culture or civilization of China as a whole. In the latter half of the nineteenth century and beyond, Westerners brought back to the West reports and pictures of executions that remained public in China at a time when they were becoming less and less so in the West. And in no other executions were these differences as pronounced as they were in executions that involved lingchi.

We begin by examining reports of lingchi executions by three British visitors to China between 1860 and 1910. While these amateur ethnographic accounts suggest significant details about the performance of lingchi, our purpose is equally to probe what they misrepresent and misunderstand. To do so, we focus here on accounts that presented lingchi executions respectively as methodical, casual, and dreadful affairs. The misreadings they involved rest on the broader European traditions concerning Chinese tortures and punishments examined in Chapter 6, and they have contributed much to the confusion about what "death by a thousand cuts" was all about. To these three, we then counterpose a fourth interpretation that situates lingchi within the context of the late Qing state's self-proclaimed civilizing mission.

The Methodical Execution

The first of these ethnographies is an account written by the British consular official Thomas Meadows, who attended the execution of thirty-four rebels in Canton (Guangzhou) on the morning of July 30, 1851: "I went to the ground at about half past eight with two English residents at Canton, who had not previously witnessed any execution. We found only a few of the lowest officials on the spot. A hole in the ground, near to which a rough cross leant against the wall, showed me that one man at least was going to suffer the highest legal punishment: cutting-up alive, and called ling che, a disgraceful and lingering death. A few steps in advance of the shed at the north end, under which the mandarins sit, a fire of fragrant sandal-wood billets was burning on the ground."[1]

Notice first the presence of a cross in this description. Some sort of wooden frame was needed to hold up the lingchi victim during his execution, so that the executioner was able to maneuver about the body to do his work. It might be nothing more than a single pole buried in the ground, or it might take the form of a tripod or an X-shaped St. Andrew's cross. It is hardly surprising that someone from a Christian background might be inclined to describe the frame upon which a criminal was tormented to death as "a rough cross." Nineteenth-century Westerners often made this report,[2] despite the difficulties with this reading, including the impracticality of working on a body that was tied up to a Christian-style cross. Nonetheless, crosses figure prominently in these accounts and also appear as standard pictorial elements in Chinese export watercolors of executions. Local artists painted watercolors for export on all manner of subjects in the nineteenth century, producing what one scholar has characterized as "gaudy but meaningless tableaux" concocted to appeal to Western stereotypes of China (Figure 23).[3] Some of this distortion appears to have found its way into the execution scenes that were popular with foreign buyers, in the form of hinted Christian iconography and motifs. So too a Western iconography of martyrdom may have shaped Meadows's way of making sense of what he was seeing in terms of what he already knew and expected, although we cannot be certain that he was not reporting accurately.

Be that as it may, once the officials overseeing the executions had arrived, Meadows reports that the cross was set up in the hole that had been prepared for it, and the decapitations then began. Of the thirty-four who had been brought to the execution ground, thirty-three were beheaded. The last was reserved for lingchi:

> As soon as the thirty-three were decapitated, the same executioner proceeded, with a single-edged dagger or knife, to cut up the man on the cross: whose sole clothing consisted of his wide trousers, rolled down to his hips and up to his buttocks. He was a strongly made man, above middle-size, and apparently forty years of age. The authorities got him by seizing his parents and wife; [he confessed][4] when he surrendered, as well as to save

Figure 23. *Supplice chinois,* Chinese watercolor. Bibliothèque nationale de France.

them from torture as to secure them the seven thousand dollars offered for his apprehension. The mandarins, having future cases in mind, rarely break faith on such occasions. As the man was at the distance of twenty-five yards, with his side towards us, though we observed the two cuts across the forehead, the cutting of the left breast, and slicing of the flesh from the front of the thighs, we could not see all the horrible operation. From the first stroke of the knife, till the body was cut down from the cross and decapitated, about four or five minutes elapsed. We should not have been prohibited from going up close, but as may easily be imagined, even a powerful curiosity was an insufficient inducement to jump over a number of dead bodies and literally wade through pools of blood, to place ourselves in the hearing of the groans indicated by the heaving chest and quivering limbs of the poor man. Where we stood we heard not a single cry; and I may add that of the thirty-three men decapitated, no one struggled or uttered any exclamation as the executioner approached him.[5]

Meadows is surprised by many elements of what he saw and heard: the methodical pace of the executioner, the bloody chaos of the execution ground, the relative passivity of the victims. All these elements go against the traditional Christian expectation of how an execution should be performed: as a redemptive ordeal through which the victim is prepared for judgment in the afterlife. From that perspective, lingchi belonged to a different history altogether—not a civilized history of criminal justice, but a savage history of cruelty that betrayed the fundamental inhumanity of the Chinese. In fact, as we will demonstrate, Chinese executions followed a clear legal procedure but conformed to a logic different from the conception of punishment as redemptive ordeal that had long shaped thinking about executions in the West. A "good" ancien régime executioner there was expected to perform his execution with dramatic gestures of vengeance so that the condemned might earn salvation in the afterworld. Similarly, a "good" victim had to show all the signs of suffering that would complete his assimilation with the model of the Christian martyr or the suffering God[6]—hence the curious "duel" between the executioner and the condemned. Rather than being staged in such a way that the condemned was encouraged to repent of his crimes or otherwise act out "a brave death," Chinese executions were blunt demonstrations of the power of the state in the face of crimes against the moral order that the state embodied. By that logic, the execution ground was no place for heroes or martyrs, and no stage was provided on which the condemned could be permitted to parade either their bravery or their repentance. It was a place where evil people were disposed of and where their remains were displayed in cages above the greedy glances of stray dogs as a warning to others.[7]

Meadows finishes his account of the executions with testimony to the magic power that the blood of victims was believed to have: "Immediately after the first body fell, I observed a man put himself in a sitting posture by the neck and, with a business-like air, commence dipping in the blood a bunch of rush-pith." He explains, "This so saturated rush pith is used by the Chinese as a medicine."[8] Here too Meadows is struck by what he calls the "business-like air" that pervades the execution ground. His implicitly Christian expectation was apparently that an execution should proceed as a religious, or at least ritualized, event in which the onlookers offered collective witness to the suffering of the victim. That spirit, it seemed to him, was conspicuously absent at an event during which a bystander stepped forward to collect one victim's blood, hoping to benefit from the other's loss, without paying the least attention to his suffering. The old Christian notion that an execution should inflict suffering on the condemned and inspire compassion among the spectators was completely thwarted, even denied. There were none of the signs associated with martyrdom and crucifixion that could bring this event within the Christian "penal aesthetic."[9] It was nothing but a "horrible operation."

The Casual Execution

Sixteen years later, British traveler Isabella Bird visited the same execution ground and reported on what she saw in terms that resonate with Meadows's description:

> The criminals, who have been unceremoniously pitched out of the dust baskets into the mud or gore or dust of the execution ground, kneel down in a row or rows, and the executioner with a scimitar strikes off head after head, each with a single stroke, an assistant attending to hand him a fresh sword as soon as the first becomes blunt. It is said that Chinese criminals usually meet their doom with extreme apathy, but occasionally they yield to extreme terror, and howl at the top of their voices, "Save life! Save life!" As soon as the heads have fallen, some coolies of a pariah class take up the trunks and put them into wooden shells, in which they are eventually

buried in a cemetery outside one of the city gates, called "The trench for the bones of ten thousand men."[10]

Even more than Meadows, Bird highlights the haste, crudity, and absence of ceremony at the executions. She is scandalized by the matter-of-fact way of proceeding, and she is appalled by the general "apathy" of the condemned. What she reads as meek submission is occasionally broken by raw appeals for self-preservation: "Save life!" (*jiuming*). She interprets both the apathetic muteness and the spontaneous outbursts as vivid protests against a barbarity that refuses to grant to the victims any possibility of redemption or transfiguration. Rather than "apathy," what in fact disturbs Bird, we would suggest, is the lack of "pathos" that attends the absence of the familiar elements of dramatization—staging, casting, and directing—that gave Western executions their capacity to channel a cathartic release of emotions. Deprived of such aesthetic elements, the execution appears to be nothing but an unspectacular show of pure violence.

Ever on the lookout for Western-style clues to a meaning she might attach to these executions, Bird is unable to detect their Chinese equivalents. "*Jiuming*" strikes her as an instinctive *cri de coeur*. In fact, "save life" was the password uniting the different categories of legal professionals. Their handbooks advised jurists to seize every opportunity to commute harsh sentences to gentler penalties. The influence of this directive on those who administered judicial practice was so strong that the authorities regularly felt obliged to issue orders stressing that the laws calling for capital punishment in murder cases should be strictly enforced.[11] The shout of the men about to be executed was not a cry of despair but an expected gesture appealing to this tradition of lenience, even though it had no chance of gaining the desired response on the execution ground. Chinese legal practices and procedures offered many channels of mercy *prior to* the execution, but the set procedure included no device to disguise the final act of execution, as Christian ritual did, as some act of transcendental mercy. The judgment had been made; the sentence had to be executed.

What are we to make of Bird's allegation of "extreme apathy" among the condemned? Was Chinese behavior really different from what Westerners expected to see at executions? European writers of the period made easy use of racialist clichés regarding an alleged Chinese inability to feel suffering.[12] Was some cultural attribute such as fatalism or lack of charity directing the scene, or was it the case, as European observers often averred, that the condemned had a dazed and passive attitude because they were stunned by opium or weakened by hunger? The problem with accepting these explanations is that they remain based on an interpretative framework external to the event itself, for which we have no indigenous evidence. We would instead suggest, therefore, that the figure of the "apathetic Chinese" in European accounts of Chinese punishment expresses unease over the absence of a Western procedure of execution. What Bird sees as the pervading casualness of the proceedings rests on the fact that the criminal was allotted no active role to perform and was left no prospect of redemption. No words or deeds were required of him by the process, nor would any official care what he did or said. All he could do was kneel down and suffer his punishment. He was nothing but the embodiment of what Foucault called "the real presence of the signified." Deprived of any redemptive function, the Chinese execution could appear only as illegitimate and barbaric to those who believed that redemption or salvation was what executions should be about.

To assume, as many observers have done, that the passivity of the condemned testifies to Chinese inhumanity or insensitivity is to treat what happens as an absence of something, rather than the presence of something else. The goal of the Western execution was a total "body and soul" submission of the criminal to his sentence. The criminal who resisted suffered a double penalty, the destruction of his body and the publicly proclaimed damnation of his soul. In China, the confession of a criminal was merely a procedural requirement for delivering a verdict, not a device for the uplifting of the soul. Once the confession had been obtained, the sentence that followed resulted from a consideration of the facts of the case, whether the condemned repented or not. During the execution, the enforcement of the law on the condemned's body was supposed to edify the public. Any concern about the state of his mind or his soul was misplaced. One might propose that the Western system provided a kind of "double bind" linking external performance to internal acceptance that left no room for objection or refusal. By contrast, the Chinese system of execution confined itself to external demonstration. The Western procedure might have had a firmer grip on individuals than did the Chinese, though this observation does not enable us to draw any conclusion as to which system was more humane or moral. It certainly does not allow one to claim, as Hegel did, that moral conscience was lacking in Chinese culture.

Nowhere is Bird's debt to Christian iconography more evident than in her description of the "thrilling" discovery of the physical evidence of lingchi at the Canton execution ground:

The strangest and most thrilling sight of all was the cross in this unholy spot, not a symbol of victory and hope, but of the lowest infamy and degradation, of the vilest death which the vilest men can die. Nor was it the solid, lofty structure, fifteen or twenty feet high, which art has been glorifying for a thousand years, but a rude gibbet of unplaned wood, roughly nailed together, barely eight feet high, and not too heavy for a strong man to carry on his shoulders. Most likely it was such a cross, elevated but little above the heads of the howling mob of Jerusalem, which Paul had in view when he wrote of Him who hung upon it, "But made Himself obedient unto death, *even the death of the cross.*" To these gibbets infamous criminals, whose crimes are regarded as deserving of a lingering death, are tightly bound with cords, and are then slowly hacked to pieces with sharp knives, unless the friends of the culprit are rich enough to bribe the executioner to terminate the death agony early by stabbing a vital part.

These facts do not require to be dressed out with words. They are the most effective when most baldly stated. I left the execution ground as I left the prison—with the prayer, which had gained a new significance, "For all prisoners and captives we beseech Thee to hear us, good Lord."[13]

Bird did not actually see the execution she describes; rather she intuits it through a religious and aesthetic screen. There was indeed a terrible reality behind the magnificent Baroque aesthetics at work in this account, yet what Western witnesses as sensitive as Isabella Bird discovered at Chinese execution grounds were suppressed aspects of their own tradition. The only way to react to the strangeness of Chinese executions was to refer to familiar images, raising these as religious and aesthetic talismans against the crude reality before their eyes. This is why Bird seeks release from the horror she sees by making Chinese execution by lingchi into "death on the cross," even if none of the scaffoldings used for lingchi executions had this shape. Chinese executions affronted the marvelous aesthetic that Europeans of an earlier age had erected around execution. When confronted with the unveiled obscenity of capital punishment, they fled into religious imagery.

The Dreadful Execution

From these two accounts of the execution ground in Canton we move to Beijing and the lingchi with which we opened this book: the execution in 1904 of Wang Weiqin. The British businessman Archibald Little encountered the event while on the way to register a trademark at the newly opened Department of Commerce, which was founded as part of the same reform process that would soon bring lingchi to an end. This is the only account we have of Wang's execution by someone who was actually there, although Little saw it only in passing:

> A main street through which I passed was thronged with people gathered to witness the execution of a criminal by the *ling-chi* process, and I had difficulty in making my way through the crowd. The event was more than commonly interesting owing to the fact of the criminal being a high official. This man, it appeared, had, during the disturbances in 1900, murdered two whole families and so acquired their possessions; he was recently denounced by a woman, his guilt proved, and sentence passed accordingly. I would not be diverted, however, from my quest of the Shangpu [Department of Commerce], but a European who was present at the execution told me that it was the most tragic spectacle; the prescribed process was literally carried out, the pieces of flesh, as cut away, being thrown to the crowd, who scrambled for the dreadful relics. In China, we are still in the middle ages.[14]

Little admits that he heard the details he provides secondhand, yet they purport to be from someone who actually witnessed the event. Later commentators liked to elaborate on these details, based solely on the photographs of this and other lingchi executions that circulated thereafter in Europe. Thus Robert Heindl, a German criminologist who published photographs of the same execution, affirmed: "I saw the onlookers chattering and laughing, smoking cigarettes and chomping on fruits!"[15] Such remarks, based on armchair observation, strengthened the prejudice of a cruel and barbaric Chinese people.

Careful examination of the photographs that survive, however, suggests that such comments are ill-founded. Wang's execution has been preserved in a series of photographs, one of which appears as Figure 1 in this volume.[16] These shots, which represent all phases of the execution, tend to throw doubt on Little's claims. Not one shows a "piece of flesh" being thrown to the crowd. The only people who were clearly scrambling for "dreadful relics" of Wang's death were the Europeans who were out for the photographs. As for onlookers laughing and eating fruit while watching the fun, careful scrutiny of the photographs reveals no such evidence. In fact, the impression of anxiety on the watching faces indicates quite the opposite

(Figure 24). All evince a troubled fascination as they jostle to keep the executioners' moves in sight. There is no trace of pleasure, not a grin or even an ambiguous expression of enjoyment. There is only an anxious and absorbed, even dejected, watching.

What the photographs do reveal, by way of enhancing Little's account, is that the execution was conducted at street level in the absence of a scaffold or platform typical of European executions. No perimeter is marked separating the performers from the onlookers, nor is the action in any physical way circumscribed. Onlookers appear free to place themselves in close contact with Wang, as Meadows in his account suggested people could do if they wished. The photographs suggest that there was no metaphorical plot in which the participants were given roles to play. The execution was not structured as a cohesive series of deeds or words, nor did it conform to any clear religious paradigm, as it might have in a Christian context. In the photographs, the executioners go about their task unruffled and serious, and the condemned displays no emotion, not even signs of pain that we might expect to see. Finally, while numerous onlookers are present, they do not commune with or otherwise interact with the victim. They are immersed in an unorganized crowd and catch only snatches of the procedure, despite standing almost shoulder to shoulder with the executioners' helpers. The execution is not presented to them as a spectacle in that sense, as a series of acts performed to produce a larger pattern of meaning. Those who conduct the execution do nothing to fuse the crowd into a single body

Figure 24. Executioner and onlookers at the lingchi execution of Wang Weiqin, Beijing, 1904. © Ville de Chalon sur Saône, France, Musée Nicéphore Niépce.

of witnesses invited to share in a catharsis with the victim. The onlookers show no compassion, or hatred, or dissatisfaction with the proceedings, as their European counterparts could be expected to do.[17] There is no pantomime of cruelty, simply the unruffled dispatch of the victim. It all contrasts strikingly with European practices, so much so that some sensitive commentators have interpreted the official attitude as a paradoxical posture of mercy.[18]

By the same token, the condemned was given no role to play. He was not invited to express pain, or repent, or otherwise play a spectacular role. He was simply a body on which imperial law did its work. There was nothing for him to declare, and most reports make note of the silence of the condemned. Western observers sometimes attributed the victim's silence or passivity to opium delirium, the administration of opium to the victim appearing indeed to have been a common preexecution procedure in the Qing dynasty. But this silence was also due to an absence of dramaturgy. The victim, the person who would have been the chief protagonist in a Western setting here had no context in which to act out a role and therefore no script to follow. One could in fact propose that the chief protagonist at a Chinese execution was actually the executioner, the state's most violent servant, and not his victim.

A striking difference between Chinese and European ancien régime executions is thus that the latter were palpably imbued with religious symbolism and intent. This is not because punishment in the afterlife was of no concern to Chinese religion after all (see Chapter 5). Street processions of the City God, the deity who oversaw the operations of purgatory, were followed by hundreds of worshippers in the guise of would-be executed prisoners, some fettered or chained, some with bamboo slips inserted down the backs of their necks declaring the "crimes" for which they hoped the god would forgive them.[19] This sort of public demonstration testifies to the symbolic meaning that the death penalty had within popular religion. However, according to the reports of eyewitnesses, real legal executions were devoid of religious overtones. There are no signs that the condemned or anyone around him had to behave or speak religiously, or contemplate religious images, or otherwise bring religious meaning into the execution as in the tradition of ancien régime executions in Europe. Qing executions were secular legal events; religion did not capture them. Perhaps this is why, when seen in the light of European expectations, they appeared as simple butchery.

The photographs of Wang Weiqin show none of the affects and attitudes that were part of the Christian European model of supplice. Neither do they support some of the more elaborate interpretations that have been offered in their wake. A psychoanalytical perspective has prompted some to look for signs of a universal "sadism of the crowd" attending the "sacrifice," or even signs of "ecstasy" such as Georges Bataille thought he discerned on the face of a young man being sliced.[20] Such facile interpretations must be rejected. The human body was not being tormented in public for the purpose of experiencing, or projecting the experience of, suffering; the torment was imposed to communicate the power of the law.

In this regard, Little's careless conclusion that "China is still in the middle ages" is particularly misleading, historically speaking. This cliché misinterprets Chinese practice as a throwback to a distant past of legal atrocities when European executions were closer in brutality to Chinese. In fact, little more than a century separated the last European supplices from the last Chinese lingchi executions; Wang Weiqin's lingchi was one of the last to be performed, after all.[21] Beyond the event itself lies a much larger history of legal practice and judicial administration with high Chinese standards of legal soundness and intelligibility that exceeded anything that European jurists could boast of before the middle of the eighteenth century. Only at that late date did legal reformers in Italy and France, for example, begin to call for a more secular legal system. In this new system, which sought to distance itself from religious imagery, the "ideal penalty is transparent to the crime that it punishes," such that the "apportionment of the punishment to the crime" would appear as the "triumph of justice" and not as the intervention of the sovereign, to follow Foucault's terminology. This pursuit of a "reasoned aesthetics of punishment" required that penalties illustrate the law, not just implement it. "Posters, placards, signs, symbols must be distributed, so that everyone may learn their significations. The publicity of punishment must not have the physical effect of terror; it must open up a book to be read." A penalty must be "a visible punishment, a punishment that tells all, that explains, justifies itself, convicts" by means of signs that "tirelessly repeat the code." The reformers imagined this intelligibility as a form of sociability: "Let us conceive of places of punishment as a Garden of the Laws that families would visit on Sundays," they declared.[22] And this, paradoxically, is what some local magistrates actually tried to do.

The Model Execution

If any culture came close to this Enlightenment ideal, it may have been imperial China—not the China retailed in Western tales of "Oriental depravities," but the China represented in magistrates' handbooks and official publications: the China in which the government actively promoted the welfare and best interests of the people and expected the people to respond with loyal submission.[23] Except in exceptional circumstances, that official China rarely spoke of executions before the late Qing, as noted in Chapters 2 and 5. It also avoided presenting them in visual form, in keeping with the general taboo in Chinese culture against the representation of inauspicious matters, especially anything to do with death.[24]

Toward the end of the nineteenth century, this began to change. The growing presence in China of foreign diplomats, soldiers, and missionaries was generating considerable unrest in the countryside, the Boxer outbreak in North China in 1900 being the most dramatic manifestation of popular anxiety about the foreigners' presence. County magistrates, whether they were concerned about or indifferent to the foreigners' presence, could not be indifferent to the disruption of local order that this unrest provoked. They had to take action to prevent disturbances and also to prevent people like Wang Weiqin from taking advantage of disorder to commit crimes. They made use of a centuries-old technique: printing and posting easily understood warnings to the people about the consequences of evil conduct, always in words but sometimes including pictures. The posters produced at this juncture were collected in works with titles such as *Da Qing lüli tushuo* (Annotated illustrations of the Qing Code and substatutes), *Xinglü tushuo* (Annotated illustrations of Qing penal law), *Xinglü tufu* (Penal law charts), and *Zuiming tushuo* (Annotated illustrations of the terminology of crimes), the titles intended to highlight the legal nature of what was being communicated. This time, perhaps for the first time, the posters included scenes of executions. Two posters showing the process of lingchi have survived in printed booklets (Figures 25 and 26).[25] The first woodcut is labeled "lingchi," while the second includes an inscription that gives "the names of the crimes" *(zuiming)* for which lingchi is the legally appropriate punishment, including sedition and the killing of grandparents and parents. In the first, the victim is bound to a cross; in the second, to a single post. Strangely, in both woodcuts the victims are women, their gender revealed less by their bodies than by their tiny shoes. Modesty would not permit these to be removed, even for an execution. A shocking detail in the second print is the shoed foot lying on the ground at some distance from the body, the woman's leg having been cut above the knee.

These illustrations are valuable not just because they are rare, but because they reveal how the Chinese state, at least, understood how an execution should proceed and what it was intended to achieve. An execution was an occasion on which the state displayed its power to punish within a social framework that involved not just its own officers, but the populace as well. This impact is achieved first by having a legal authority present, in the person of the magistrate, attended by his servants and soldiers, and second by having commoners in attendance, albeit in small numbers, and including representatives of all generations. The execution is represented as a pedagogical event.

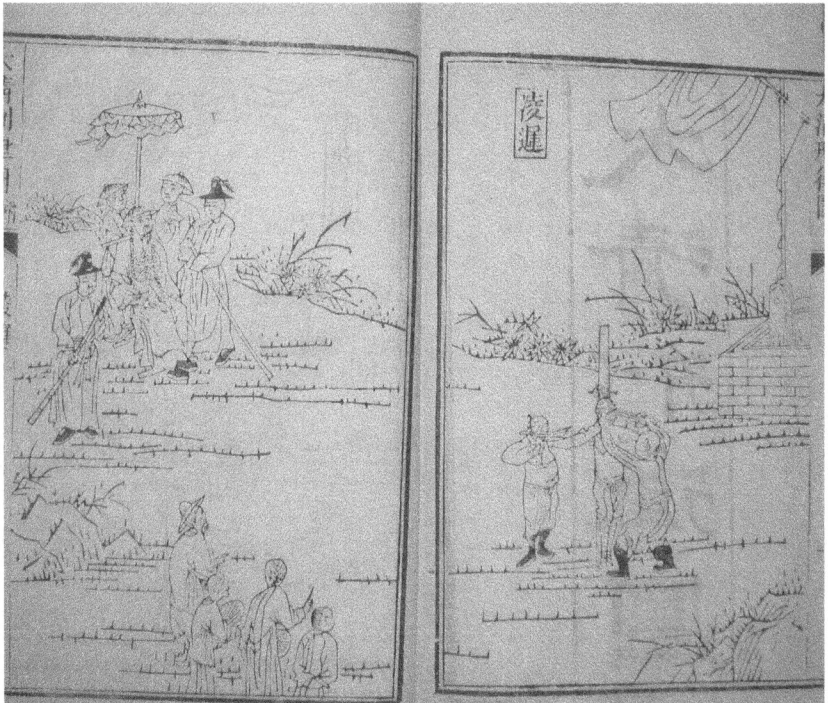

Figure 25. A woodblock illustration inscribed with the word "Lingchi." From Xu Wenda, *Da Qing lüli tushuo* (Annotated illustrations of the Qing Code and substatutes), which gives enhanced reproductions of materials from his *Da Qing xinglü tushuo* (Annotated illustrations of Qing penal law).

Commoners are shown quietly observing the execution, with elders teaching the youngsters by pointing with their fingers. In just this way, according to the prefaces to these publications, the pictures can help "the father to teach the son."

The lack of agitation among the participants is striking. Not even the victims display any agitation. Their bodies are weightless figures drawn in such a way as to de-emphasize the physicality of their suffering. They, like all the other elements in the compositions, are there to convey a transparent legal message; in their case, simple submission to the unavoidable process of the law. The focus in these woodblocks is not on the victim, after all, but on the serene figures of power. The magistrate was there to embody the Confucian principle that the good judge should not evince wrath or joy in the course of carrying out justice, and the attendants and soldiers were there to obey the

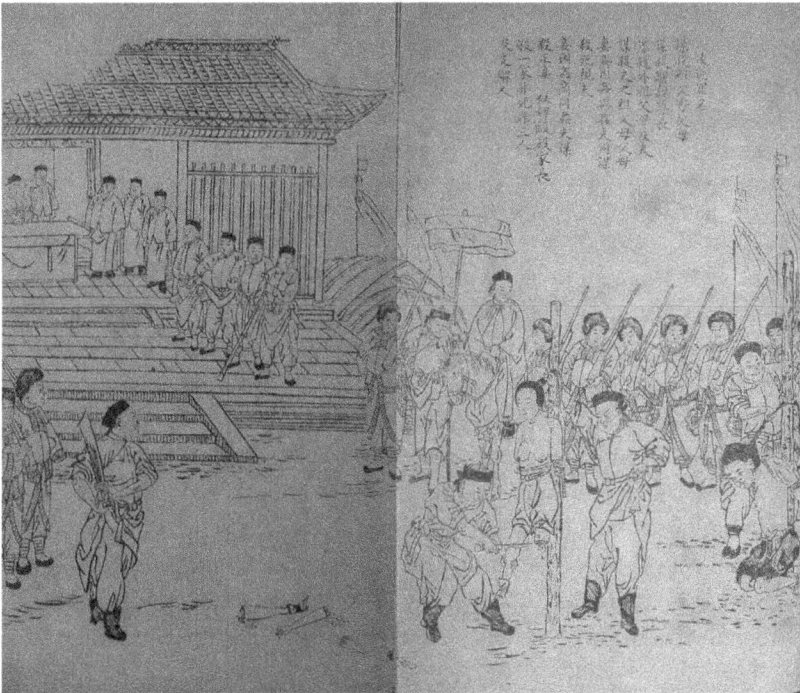

Figure 26. A woodblock illustration of lingchi, with an inscription listing the crimes for which this is the legal punishment. From *Zuiming tushuo* (Annotated illustrations of the terminology for crimes).

good official's command. By the same token, the commoners in attendance, far from succumbing to terror or experiencing other vicarious emotions, are shown quietly following the legal lesson being taught to them. "See justice being done," they are being told. "See how the punishment fits the crime."

The representations in these posters are perhaps no more "realistic" than the agitated accounts of Isabella Bird or Thomas Meadows. They are model executions, after all. Despite that, they come closer to expressing what Chinese judicial culture thought it was attempting to achieve by staging public executions. The goal was not to let execution grounds descend into bloody chaos and moral depravity. Quite the opposite: the place of punishment should be, in the language of the French penal reformers of the Enlightenment, "a Garden of the Laws that families would visit on Sundays." In practice, this ideal was probably a mirage that no official could hope to achieve. More than a few Western observers commented on what struck them as a rather different relationship between crowd and spectacle than the pedagogical setting the state sought to cultivate. Meadows, for example, noted the quick move by one enterprising individual to soak up some of a decapitated man's blood—no obvious learning going on in his case. To choose a broader example, Lewis Arlington, who spent half a century in the China Customs Service, was moved to editorialize about "the Chinese" as a result of watching the crowd's reaction to a lingchi execution in Guilin:

> The Chinese, though very inoffensive in their normal state, turn into perfect fiends when aroused; they resemble half-grown children who, when stung by an insect, will tear out its wings, legs and other convenient parts of its anatomy from pure devilment. While on the subject of the "slicing process," I am reminded of a case that also came under my personal observation when at Soochow in 1904. A woman and her son were apprehended for incest and the murder of her husband to boot. They were taken to the execution ground, where thousands of Chinese had foregathered in expectation of the treat that was to come—amongst them being many women with their children in their arms. What a training! Can we wonder at all at the callousness displayed by the Chinese to all sorts of suffering, when they at an early age have witnessed the most horrible of tortures?[26]

Arlington is so intent on using the evidence he has collected at executions to express his disdain for the Chinese that he neglects to describe what the crowd actually did to offend his sense of propriety on either occasion. Still, he may have caught some element of blood lust on the part of the onlookers that animated the proceedings as much as any ideal pedagogy represented by a Garden of the Laws.

It is no wonder that the Enlightenment reformers' schemes remained on paper in Europe. These schemes were trumped by the very different model of the modern prison almost as soon as they had been conceived, for both popular attitudes and elite values in Europe were turning against the public display of torment. What strikes the legal historian of China, though, is the resemblance between the ideals animating this Garden of the Laws and the ethical norms conjured in Chinese judicial handbooks, even if those norms failed to become practice. The similarity lies less in the punishments themselves than in the functions conferred on them. Many of the proposed new punishments had no equivalents in China. For instance, European reformers advocated forced labor as a way of turning punishment into a "living theater." Penal servitude was never construed this way in China. On the other hand, the punishment the reformers imagined for the "most terrible of crimes," parricide, approaches the Chinese lingchi in barbarity: the condemned would be suspended in an iron cage and exposed to the elements in an agony that ended only with death, as onlookers watched.[27]

The key point is that in neither system were punishments coded with redemptive symbolism intended to evoke mimetic reactions. Rather than spectacular stagings of suffering and cruelty, they were lessons in law intended to inspire a rational response from a dispassionate audience: "a school rather than a festival," in Foucault's terms.[28] The goal of Enlightenment reformers was not to soften the suffering of a supplice, but to reintroduce "the real presence of the signified—that is to say, of the penalty that, according to the terms of the code, must be infallibly associated with the offence," just as the law promised.[29] The irony of the overlap between these models is striking, and Octave Mirbeau for one seems to have noticed it, for the "Garden of the Laws" seems almost designed to serve as the very paradigm of *Le Jardin des supplices,* the Torture Garden he imagined in his Belle Époque setting as a site of new aesthetic pleasure, projected onto an imagined China. The garden would be filled not with European but Chinese executioners and their victims, though with Europeans invited in to take pleasure in watching the spectacle. The legal utopia that the two civilizations shared, of a transparent punishment regime that would encourage lawfulness to prevail over crime, became a sadistic wonderland, and the *supplice chinois* of lingchi was turned into a cross-cultural fantasy inserting fragmented information about China into a "transgressive" Western representational scheme.

The power of the supplice pattern on the Western imagination, which fused penal, religious, and aesthetic dimensions into a meaningful spectacle, shaped the responses of viewers well into the twentieth century.[30] The effect was that they had trouble comprehending the same function—punishing—when it was stripped of their familiar modes of signification. Chinese executions were not occasions for cathartic displays of emotion or mimetic identification between the public and the condemned. They were ritualized enforcements of law, in which the harshness of a penalty was justified in relation to the principle that the punishment should fit the crime, as provided in the penal code. Agitated emotions and sensations (cruelty, suffering, compassion) as well as physical consequences (bleeding, pain) were consistently occluded, lest they interfere with the legal message. Executions were supposed to teach a lesson, not lead to catharsis or redemption. Contrary to the notion that Chinese were prone to inflicting "refined cruelty" or "lingering agonies," the reality of tormented execution in late imperial China was harsher yet more straightforward, devoid of the signs and gestures through which Europeans conferred ultimate meaning on their supplices, but with its own logic nonetheless. European meanings were irrelevant in Chinese executions. Imposing them seriously impeded the readability of the penal sentence.

In short, the Western image of Chinese penal practices as grisly and disorderly atrocities reflected significant differences between the two traditions of execution. Yet the torments and exposure of bodily remains were also fascinating to Western witnesses. No doubt this had much to do with the fact that their own societies had been renouncing, and strenuously denouncing, similar punishments through the early nineteenth century. The last beheading of a corpse in Europe took place in 1820, for example, and in the 1830s a series of new regulations prohibited all the old desecrations of executed criminals such as gibbeting and hanging in chains.[31] Now Europeans were touring a country in which an unfamiliar system of judicial procedure permitted what had, in historical terms, only recently become foreign to the gaze. Bird, Little, and Meadows were adamant in insisting that the scenes of execution in China horrified them, and yet one senses beneath their explanations of how they came to visit the execution ground an ambivalent alternation between repulsion and fascination. The comments with which Jean-Jacques Matignon concluded his discussion of Chinese punishments, as accompanied by his grisly photographs of the lingchi process, perhaps throw some light on this kind of mixed reaction. His view was that a "golden mean" ought to exist between the "rather cruel" punishments of the Chinese, which at least kept people in line, and the "ridiculous, weepy humanitarianism" with which Europe treated its criminals.[32]

Nineteenth-century visitors to China were not disposed to intellectualize what they saw, and it would be fatuous of us to expect them to have been when they came across bloody punishments. What they saw disgusted them, and it seemed only natural to take the next step and declare these scenes of judicial torment to be proof that China was uncivilized, lacked all civilized law, and ignored the claims of humanity. At the same time, an irrepressible curiosity pushed them, along with the voyeurs who read their accounts, toward the Chinese execution ground to watch these gory scenes, fix them in photographs, circulate them in the mail, and offer them for moral contemplation and aesthetic pleasure—perhaps as their ancestors had done with images of crucifixion and martyrdom in the Middle Ages. Westerners could dismiss Chinese criminal law for elements that were taken to be barbaric survivals of a primitive stage in legal development, while at the same time steering what they witnessed to political uses and pleasures that often had even less to do with the realities and logic of Chinese criminal law.

CHAPTER **8**

Georges Bataille's
Interpretation

Georges Bataille (1897–1962) is famous, among other things, for his pioneering studies of visual art and culture. Scholars specializing in the history of Chinese law and punishment normally base their work on written evidence: legal texts, or court proceedings, for example. This reliance is fine for dealing with most issues that beset the field, for so much of law is enshrined in words. But what is a historian of law to do when a librarian at the Bibliothèque nationale—a position Bataille himself once held—dutifully delivers into his hands the famous lingchi photos that the philosopher published in *Les Larmes d'Éros (The Tears of Eros)?*[1] The confrontation between historian and source is enough of a shock to preclude conventional academic reflection for a while. These documents seem to exist in a register so out of the ordinary that the work of grasping what is actually going on in them proceeds slowly. To reconstruct the mode of execution they depict, as we have done in this volume, we have had to refer to other sources, including other photographs within the same genre, and to incidental details within these photographs—such as the faces of the spectators. Proceeding in this way has enabled us gradually to shed light on the execution techniques that were used, and that has taken time. But it took us even longer to look in the other direction—at the publication of these photographs rather than at what we see in them—to realize that our strongest reactions ought perhaps to be addressed less to Georges Bataille than to the editorial hand that fashioned *Les Larmes d'Éros.* The difference between the two is the focus of this chapter.

Our approach to Bataille and the Chinese lingchi victim (his *supplicié chinois*) pictured in the photographs must begin by trying to establish the facts, as far as this is possible. For this reason, we set aside most of the questions that normally preoccupy literary critics and biographers, such as those

222

about the origin and coherence of the work, the intention of the author, and the book's impact on contemporary aesthetic sensibilities. Our concern, rather, is to inquire into how appropriate Bataille thought it was to publish certain pictures and comment on them. To that end we take the liberty of submitting his book to critical examination of a sort that differs from, and goes beyond, the usual interpretations of the author's thought. Our task is to examine his sources, what he made them say, and what has been attributed to him in regard to them.

Our leitmotif in this inquiry is the notion of "mistaken identity," which we develop in three distinct but complementary iterations. First, we deal with two cases of simple misidentification based on an error in establishing the identity of the individual under torture. This might appear to be a mere detail to the story, but it is not without consequence. To address the second level of mistaken identity requires us to explore the authorship of *Les Larmes d'Éros*. Once this is done, as we shall show, serious questions emerge as to who wrote the commentaries and captions that accompany the photos of lingchi, particularly the passages that posit an erotic "ecstasy" on the part of the individual under torture. Finally, we explore a third level of mistaken identity by reflecting on the notions of "identity" and "the person" in the abstract or, more precisely, in a broadly human sense. For most commentators, including the Bataille of *Les Larmes d'Éros*, the *persona*, the visible mask of ecstatic suffering, the figure in ecstasy playing the leading role in an organized spectacle of sacrifice, burdens the tortured person, in effect concealing him. We intend to delve into this last case of mistaken identity in order to recover the *subject*, the subject of the history we seek to reconstruct.

"But It's Someone Else"

When the prominent philosopher Jean-Toussaint Desanti addresses the issue of violence in the press, he is adept at invoking certain clichés in the minds of his readers to help him make his point:

> I've never met an executioner: someone whose job it is to kill a man according to the rules in the name of the law. I have seen illustrations, though. One in particular: it was a photograph found in Georges Dumas's old *Traité de psychologie,* in the chapter on pain. It pictures the torture (Chinese, as you'd expect) "of a hundred cuts." The story is well known: A

young man had carried out an attack on the emperor's family. The law required that he be burnt alive, over a low fire. In a spirit of leniency, the emperor had declared: "The punishment by fire is too cruel; the condemned man will undergo the torture of being cut into a hundred pieces. Respect this judgment!"[2]

It was in Georges Bataille's *Les Larmes d'Éros* that Desanti read the short account that he automatically associated with the picture of an executioner and the Chinese torture victim. He cites Georges Dumas's *Le Traité de psychologie,* but that book includes no such anecdote and fails even to state that the photograph was taken in China. Not only that, but Dumas's photos are cropped in such a way as to show no executioner at all. The "well-known" story Desanti refers to was told instead in *Les Larmes d'Éros,* specifically in the note accompanying the photos of a Chinese victim of lingchi execution. Desanti adds his own details, such as that the condemned man had "carried out an attack on the emperor's family." Not true, in fact: he had killed his master, a Mongol prince with no connection to the Manchu imperial family. Nevertheless, the emperor's alleged decree that Desanti cites is indeed in Bataille's work: "The punishment by fire is too cruel; the condemned man will undergo the torture of being cut into a hundred pieces. Respect this judgment!" A typically "Chinese" form of clemency, we are meant to suppose: you get cut into a hundred pieces instead of being burned over a slow fire!

Why bring up this "well-known story"? For one thing, it gives some idea of the impact of *The Tears of Eros,* which is a kind of cult classic in certain circles. Quite apart from those who have actually read the book, there are those who remember hearing of it, and still others who "know about it" without exactly knowing its title or author. But principally we recall the story to clarify that, however "well known" and widely believed, it is false, from beginning to end.

Let us quickly review a few points that would normally be familiar only to experts in Chinese studies. The Beijing Municipal Library holds the original records of the trial of Fuzhuli, that is, Fou-tchou-li, according to the old transcription that the author of *Les Larmes d'Éros* took from Louis Carpeaux's 1913 volume, *Pékin qui s'en va* (The Beijing that was). Judged in light of the Chinese sources, Carpeaux is shown to be a false witness who embroidered a factual account with particulars of his own invention. For example, the imperial decree that so strikingly distinguishes between the punishment by fire and the dismemberment of a living convict never existed. The real case of Fuzhuli involved the murder of a Mongol prince by one of his slaves, an act that the law analogized to parricide. There never was any question of imperial clemency, any more than there was of a punishment by fire, which Chinese law deemed completely illegal. From the beginning, the only punishment under consideration was the one stipulated by the Qing Code, namely dismemberment (lingchi), a sentence that included the possibility of eventual commutation to one of the less harsh forms of execution, namely beheading or strangulation. Why this condemned man had to undergo the last lingchi in Chinese history, just two weeks before this punishment was abolished, and at a time when commutation was already the rule, is a secret of the Fuzhuli case that only Chinese archives allow us to clarify.

Our point is not to reproach the author of *Les Larmes d'Éros* or his commentators for not being sinologists. What we can fault them for, however, is a striking lack of critical spirit and an indifference to noting the most obvious mistakes, for example, by comparing the sources that were available to them. Simply opening Louis Carpeaux's book—even just glancing at the cover—is enough to realize that the person shown tortured there is not the same man as the lingchi victim in *Les Larmes d'Éros*. Carpeaux's victim was Fuzhuli, a Mongol guard dismembered for killing his master with a vegetable cleaver (Figure 27). True, both were executed at the same Vegetable Market in Beijing, by the same executioners, and in the winter of 1904–1905. (In fact, Wang Weiqin, with whose story we opened this book, was executed in the same place on October 30, 1904.) A glance at the two photographs should have revealed that the slender young man pictured in *Les Larmes d'Éros* is not Carpeaux's sturdy Fuzhuli. We shall call him pseudo-Fuzhuli (Figure 28).[3] Including the Wang Weiqin series, then, we have photographs of three separate dismemberments that happened in the same place and in the same time period. Two of the victims, Fuzhuli and Wang Weiqin, have been identified. The third, shown in Bataille's photos, has not. Far from being "well known," the story Desanti referred to was completely muddled.

How important are these names, dates, and places of execution—in short, the facts of the matter? That they were not important even to someone who paid some considerable attention to the photos we can show by adding a further fact. By the 1950s, the photography collection of the Library of Congress had acquired a curious item: a dossier of pictures said to represent a "Chinese torture." What we find in this dossier is in fact three sets of photos depicting the three lingchi executions we have just listed, but catalogued under a single heading, as if they portrayed one and the same event. Neither the cataloguers nor previous users of the collection seem to have noted the confusion. Most strikingly, their order suggests that the original collector tried to reconstruct the successive phases of the execution, without noticing that three different executions were pictured rather than one. Imagine him trying to solve his puzzle, preoccupied with concrete questions such as, did the amputation of the left arm precede that of the right, or vice versa? while completely ignoring the question of *who* was being tormented.

As historians, however, we prefer to know who we are talking about and to understand how the issue of personal identity could be so ignored. Our task is to lay bare the laws and procedures surrounding this form of tormented execution, to be sure; but it is also to explain this remarkable blindness, this incapacity to look at or truly see these images and the people in them, and further to explain what is going on precisely in order to help overcome the blindness: to see past the consumers of these images and

Figure 27. The lingchi of Fuzhuli, executed April 10, 1905. Courtesy of J. Bourgon, Turandot project collection. A cropped version was included in Carpeaux, *Pékin qui s'en va.*

uncover the actual individuals involved in the events, to restore their separate identities and thereby return them to history. Individuals that the photographic images portray as mere flesh under the butcher's knife deserve to be remembered as concrete persons bearing real identities. The facts and details we are seeking to clarify are so many steps in that direction.

Georges Bataille, for his part, did see. He recognized the difference between lingchi victims as soon as he saw the photos of the real Fuzhuli. Here is what he wrote to Joseph Marie Lo Duca while they were preparing the visuals for *Les Larmes d'Éros:*

> I've found by accident—at Fontenay—another photo of the Chinese torture of a hundred pieces. Completely the same so far as the torture, *but it's someone else* [our italics]. I've written our friend Pimpaneau who should be able, I suppose, to locate the book by a certain Dr. Matignon, which dates from the beginning of the twentieth century, from which this photo is taken.
>
> Regarding this torture, I see that the photos in my file do not include the text you have written for the caption. Can you tell me what the status of this is?[4]

It was in fact in 1910, three years before Carpeaux's volume was published, that the first photographs of the tormented execution of Fuzhuli appeared

Figure 28. The lingchi of "pseudo-Fuzhuli" (name and date unknown). Courtesy of J. Bourgon, Turandot project collection. This photograph was reproduced in Georges Bataille, *Les Larmes d'Éros.*

in a book entitled *Dix ans au pays du dragon* by Jean-Jacques Matignon.[5] Matignon was the French physician who had been among the diplomatic staff when the French legation was besieged by the Boxers in 1900. As the quoted passage shows, Bataille did not consult *Pékin qui s'en va* himself, but left that task to his collaborators—his secretary, the future sinologist Jacques Pimpaneau,[6] and Lo Duca, a well-established author who had already published several volumes with Jean-Jacques Pauvert, also the publisher of *Les Larmes d'Éros*.[7] It was Lo Duca who industriously edited *Les Larmes d'Éros* and took responsibility for its artwork. It was also he who discovered the story of Fuzhuli in Carpeaux's volume and added this information to the pictures of torture as an explanatory caption, without noting that the person depicted was indeed someone else.

Who Was the Author of *Les Larmes d'Éros?*

Les Larmes d'Éros has acquired the reputation of being the culmination of Bataille's oeuvre, a kind of intellectual testament. This is so much the case that his earlier work is often read retrospectively from the standpoint of the 1961 volume. At the time of its publication this work constituted a literary milestone for its use of innovative photographs and is still celebrated as such. It so happens that the lingchi illustrations effectively serve as the conclusion to the book as a whole. We leave it to Bataille specialists to assess the place of *Les Larmes d'Éros* in the author's overall oeuvre, but in treating the topic of Bataille and Chinese torture we cannot avoid registering our doubts as to the authenticity of the book, or at least of this part of it. "Author" and "editor" can be ambiguous terms. In writing words and choosing illustrations, an editor can end up finishing and transforming a work conceived by another. Close reading of the Bataille–Lo Duca correspondence and careful analysis of how *Les Larmes d'Éros* was composed suggest that a misadventure of this kind might well have befallen Bataille.

Frankly, we find *Les Larmes d'Éros* an obnoxious work executed in bad taste. Its tone of arid sadism infuses a decidedly uneven text, which meanders through a heterogeneous mass of pictures of similarly variable quality to produce the book's core message: that suffering intermingles with pleasure and augments it. Most of the illustrations are reproductions of drawings, engravings, and paintings of European and North American provenance. Then suddenly and without warning, in the last pages, one enters a different world—that of "bloody sacrifice," where one moves from drawings to photographs, from the world of art to the "real" world, and from the West to the non-West. The brutality inherent in the photographic medium generates a disastrous outcome: the sacrifice of a chicken during a voodoo ritual comes across as more bloody, brutal, and horrible than the execution of a man who is being sawn in two from the crotch while suspended upside down (as depicted in Lucas Cranach's famous 1539 engraving *Die Säge als Marterinstrument* (The Saw as an Instrument of Torture) reproduced in the first half of the book). The photos of the Chinese man undergoing lingchi take this appalling outcome to the point of paroxysm, both because they so plainly show a man being atrociously tormented and because these extraordinarily painful illustrations are placed next to Balthus's 1934 painting *The Guitar Lesson* [*La Leçon de guitare*], with its air of refined, even studied eroticism.[8]

Was it Bataille's intention to mix these genres? There are strong reasons to doubt that he did. A close examination of the sparse correspondence that surrounds the production of the book suggests that assembling the artwork for *Les Larmes d'Éros* was largely out of his hands and that he only discovered the result once the work was in press—that is to say, too late. Consider his letter to Lo Duca of May 22, 1961, when the book had effectively been "put to bed":

§3. Concerning the color plates, I can't work out the page numbers very well, but I am feeling confused and very tired.

§4. The most bothersome, or even truly impossible, thing is the positioning of the Capuletti painting which you've placed in the midst of horrors, of tortures that cannot be interrupted in this manner. That absolutely disrupts the logic of these illustrations. It absolutely must be changed. Beyond that, it seems to me that the Magritte, p. 216, and the Balthus, p. 218, for their part could likewise entail errors. At any rate, a way must be found to position Capuletti before the "Voodoo sacrifice—Chinese torture—final illustrations" sequence, and in any case before p. 224.

§5. It's awkward to have to demand something so categorically, I only do so because I absolutely *must*. [Bataille's italics][9]

The final word, which Bataille himself emphasized, shows that he felt he "must" fix these "errors" which he found "impossible" to let pass, errors that included the positioning of José Manuel Capuletti's *La Bouteille des danaïdes*—a fairly trite nude painting—near the photographs "of horrors, of tortures." Bataille wanted to effect a break, erect a barrier between two genres of illustration, at page 224. Did he get his way? The answer can be found in the pagination. In the 1961 published version,[10] Capuletti's painting has been moved to page 218, where Bataille had found the Balthus painting in the proofs. As a substitute, the Balthus piece is placed with the lingchi execution in the published book. In other words, having received Bataille's instructions, Lo Duca was content to swap the Capuletti and the Balthus paintings—creating an even more deplorable effect, as *La Leçon de guitare* is far more titillating than *La Bouteille des danaïdes*.

What was Bataille's reaction to the swap? We have only patchy indications. We know that a while later he angrily confronted Jean-Jacques Pauvert over something, though over what is not too clear. An embarrassed Lo Duca refers to the incident in a letter to Bataille dated September 27, 1961, three months after the book's release: "If we did have a discussion about the Capuletti painting, it took place during the printing of the plates; I could only move the Balthus piece, but binding requirements allowed only one double plate per sixteen-page signature. The options were extremely limited, and it was a toss-up. *As for the text, it was entirely from your hand.* That's why Pauvert's words amaze me."[11] What "Pauvert's words" were we do not know. However, Michel Surya, Bataille's biographer, who edited and annotated part of his correspondence, does note: "The final state of the text appears to have occasioned a difference of opinion between Bataille and Lo Duca."[12] It seems incredible that, for the final project of so prominent an author, so little material touching on the project is available—a few letters, and no manuscript or photographs at all. What has happened to the working file for *Les Larmes d'Éros?*[13]

For the time being, the text itself must remain the focus of our inquiry. Before considering what is at stake here, namely, Bataille's interpretation of lingchi, let us stick to pursuing the facts a little further and ask how this writer came to be acquainted with these pictures. The question might raise a smile in certain quarters. Isn't the answer well known to most readers of Bataille? He himself tells us in *Les Larmes d'Éros:* "Ever since 1925, I have had one of these plates in my possession (reproduced on p. 234). It was given to me by Dr. Borel, one of the first French psychoanalysts. This picture played a decisive part in my life. I have been obsessed ever since by this image of suffering, simultaneously ecstatic (?) and intolerable."[14] Setting aside for the time being the issue of "ecstatic (?)" suffering—note that the parenthetical question mark is Bataille's—let us focus on two points: (1) that Dr. Adrien Borel gave the author the plates in 1925, in the context of psychoanalytic treatment; and (2) that these photos of torment played a "decisive part" in Bataille's life and "obsessed" him from that moment on. Even taking into account the distortion that memory often involves, these two pieces of information are difficult to square with what is generally known of Bataille.

For an item that allegedly shook him so deeply, the plate of the Chinese man being tortured to death is remarkably absent from his writings until a fairly late date. Unless we are mistaken, his first mention of the Chinese torture victim is found in *L'Expérience intérieure* (Inner Experience) and the second in *Le Coupable* (Guilty), which appeared in 1943 and 1944 respectively—that is, nearly twenty years after Dr. Borel allegedly gave him the print. Add to that the fact that, apart from the well-known published letters of 1960–1961 that relate to the production of *Les Larmes d'Éros*, Bataille's correspondence in the manuscript collection of the Bibliothèque nationale makes no allusion to this executed torture victim. Then add the further fact that Dr. Borel's letters contain absolutely nothing on this subject. One has to conclude that Bataille remained remarkably discreet about his obsession.

Once these points have been established, a further curious fact emerges. Here we have a young author who in 1929–1930 published an ambitious avant-garde journal entitled *Documents*, the express purpose of which was to juxtapose iconographic items, often photographs, with literary texts. It was a method that deliberately used visual images to shock readers and disturb their usual patterns of thinking. Would this not have been an excellent vehicle to publish the lingchi image supposedly presented by Dr. Borel? Yet there is no trace or mention of it in the successive issues of *Documents*. Later, Bataille's famous 1939 article on "the sacred" was also accompanied by a set of iconographic materials. That dossier, thoroughly described by Denis Hollier, the editor of Bataille's works, includes a list of illustrations, each summarized in a one-word title. One is captioned "Torture." Is it ours? No, contrary to what Hollier thought he saw; it is the "Aztec sacrifice," not the "Chinese torture."[15] Thus, leaving aside for the moment the later association of these two images in *Les Larmes d'Éros*, we are left with the impression that throughout the first twenty years of his literary career, whenever Bataille did think of "sacrifice" or "torture," it was the Aztec drawing he had in mind, not the photo of the tortured Chinese.[16]

What about other avenues of investigation? Dr. Borel, for instance. Do we know anything of him that might throw light on our inquiries? Those unconvinced by the hagiography regarding him that has been negotiated between Bataille's disciples and French psychoanalytic circles will find themselves moving from one letdown to another. What do we know of him? Unfortunately, there are few leads to follow. We search in vain in his letters to Bataille, or in his published study of daydreamers,[17] for the least sign of the bold, anticonformist spirit one would expect of "one of France's first psychoanalysts." Instead, a reading of his letters to Bataille leaves one incredulous at the thought that it was Borel who provided the famous lingchi photos. In any case, their correspondence contains no mention of them.

Let us turn then to Michel Leiris, Bataille's closest collaborator on *Documents* and another of the patients Dr. Borel analyzed between 1929 and 1936.[18] Leiris is well known for his copious memoirs, but one is hard pressed to find in them any allusion to the Chinese lingchi victim. Indeed, reading through his works leads us to conclude that Leiris never saw the pictures. In our opinion the silence that this subtle connoisseur of Bataille's oeuvre maintained toward *Les Larmes d'Éros* is as eloquent as it was deliberate.[19] It is likewise surprising that Bataille himself left behind no vestige of a print so "decisive" in his personal development, either in his correspondence, or in his published oeuvre, or in the records we have of his conversations with people close to him.

We can approach the problem from yet another angle and ask what became of the plate Dr. Borel "provided." If this spiritual object that so "obsessed" Bataille was really so talismanic, wouldn't one expect to find it among his papers conserved in the manuscript collection of the Bibliothèque nationale? Yet all that can be found there is a photocopy of one of the published photos in *Les Larmes d'Éros*. Furthermore, all of the photographs from that publication, including the one on page 234, are reproductions of stereoscopic plates held since the 1930s at the Musée de l'Homme in Paris. The fact that the imperfections in the museum's plates are the same as those in the published photos leaves no room for doubt: the photographic reproductions in *Les Larmes d'Éros* derive from originals in the Musée de l'Homme.[20]

If we therefore remove Dr. Borel from the story, the chronology appears to be as follows. Bataille was unaware of execution by lingchi when he published the journal *Documents* in 1929–1930. He was still unaware of it, or at least had no publishable reproduction of a photograph showing it, in 1938, when he wrote his famous article on "the sacred," which pictured another human being in torment. His only reference to torture in either case was to the "Aztec sacrifice."

Bataille most probably discovered the Chinese torture photographs by accident in 1934, when he borrowed the Bibliothèque nationale's newest volume of the *Nouveau traité de psychologie* by Georges Dumas.[21] On the third of December of that year, he took out the series' third volume, published in 1933, in which the photographs of lingchi were used to illustrate the condition of "horripilation," i.e., having the hair on one's head stand on end. A passage from the text of that work eventually found its way into the commentary on the lingchi photos in *Les Larmes d'Éros,* showing that Bataille had access to Dumas's publication. (Neither the Bibliothèque nationale's borrowers list nor Bataille's later writings mention the second (1932) volume of Dumas's series, where the same photos were used to exemplify the "facial contractions" typically provoked by suffering.)[22] We therefore consider it most likely that Georges Bataille first saw a photograph of a Chinese victim of lingchi in December 1934, but at that point had no photographs of it to hand. It is unclear just when he got wind of the pictures at the Musée de l'Homme. Perhaps it was through his friend, the ethnologist Marcel Griaule. Or could he perhaps have taken them out himself? Whatever may have been the case, we find ourselves approaching the 1940s whenever we try to date the moment at which the *supplicié chinois* suddenly burst into Bataille's writings. Rather than an intimate personal talisman presented by a close confidant, the pictures appear to have been a happenstance library find. That might explain why he didn't make more of them at the time. In any case, it was not until 1943–1944 that he first turned to writing about the young Chinese man tortured to death by lingchi.[23]

Sade or Loyola?

A sampling from Bataille's works of the 1940s will suffice to show the gap, indeed the chasm, that separates them from his 1961 book. In *L'Expérience intérieure,* for example, he employs these photos after the manner of the "spiritual exercises" of Ignatius of Loyola, which Bataille carefully describes in the paragraph immediately preceding the first appearance of the Chinese lingchi victim.[24] This tormented man consequently figures as a sort of substitute for the crucified Christ during meditations that approximate the visiting of the stations of the cross, the ritual during which pious Catholics reexperience in their own flesh this or that episode of the Passion. *L'Expérience intérieure* was the first work in Bataille's *Somme athéologique* (Summa atheologica), and it shifted the suffering of Christ onto an everyman whose individual name, history, and crime the avant-garde author treated as matters of indifference. For Bataille's purpose, it sufficed that the executioner's victim was a suffering body, nothing more.

Bataille's writings of this period depict pain—unadulterated, unambiguous—without ever alluding to anything like "ecstatic joy" being present in the tortured man's experience. On the contrary, the only expression seen on his face is a grimace, as his body writhes in "hideous" pain.[25] There is indeed a passing evocation of a trance or a stepping outside oneself (though this is not an "ecstasy"), but that experience is Bataille's, not the tortured subject's.[26] Not only are these texts of the 1940s free of any conflation of joy and suffering, they explicitly reject sadism:

> The young and seductive Chinese man of whom I have spoken, left to the work of the executioner—*I love him with a love in which the sadistic instinct plays no part:* he communicated his pain to me or perhaps the excessive nature of his pain, and it is precisely that which I was seeking, *not so as to take pleasure in it,* but in order to ruin in me that which is opposed to ruin. [our italics][27]

Can this be the same author who nearly twenty years later wrote in a tone exemplified by the following extract from *Les Larmes d'Éros*?

> I have been obsessed ever since [1925] by this image of suffering, simultaneously *ecstatic (?) and intolerable.* I imagine how the Marquis de Sade, without participating in real torture—which he dreamed of, but found inaccessible—would have responded to this image if he had had it incessantly before his eyes. But Sade would have wished to view it in solitude, or at least in the relative solitude without which that *ecstatic, voluptuous effect* is inconceivable. [our italics][28]

Here, suddenly looking over the shoulder of the horrified and fraternal Bataille, is the Marquis de Sade throwing a voluptuous glance on the victim of torture.

The violent contrast between these texts has not entirely escaped Bataille's commentators. Michel Surya remarks: "One day, the Sadean perspective clarifies this scene, providing the key to it. . . . Another day, sadism is missing from it."[29] These are not two consecutive days, however. Between them twenty years have passed, not to mention several categorical declarations similar in spirit to the statement: "I don't confuse my sexual licentiousness and my mystical life. The description of tantrism in Eliade's book left me hostile. I don't like to mix my enthusiasms."[30] Between erotic desire and mystical ecstasy, Bataille constructed a gulf that he meant to be impassable, with the Chinese torture victim situated unambiguously on the mystical rather than on the erotic side of the divide. This gulf structures the oeuvre of Bataille: to suppress it is to misread him and throw his oeuvre out of joint.

Having suggested several reasons for doubting the authenticity of key parts of *Les Larmes d'Éros*, let us pause over one more issue. Consider the book's famous conclusion, to which so many have referred:

> In the face of this violence—even today I can think of no more senseless, frightful example—I was so bowled over that I gave way to ecstasy. My point here is to illustrate a fundamental linkage: that of religious ecstasy and eroticism—in particular sadism. From the most shameful to the most elevated. *This book is not based in the limited experience that is common to all men.*
>
> I cannot doubt it. . . . [our italics][31]

An empty, bombastic text, one might say, and difficult to reconcile with works written at the height of the author's powers. Still, carried along by age and fame, an author can after all change his opinions, even his style. Yet has no one noticed that this passage involves some strange French syntax? Note the sentence we have italicized, which in the original reads: "Ce livre n'est pas donné dans l'expérience limitée qu'est celle de tous les hommes." Even leaving aside the impeccable stylistic sense that Bataille himself otherwise still displayed in his other late writings, any native speaker of French would spontaneously write, "Ce livre n'est pas donné dans l'expérience limitée *qui est* celle de tous les hommes." Where might this curious elision then have come from? An Italian, perhaps, might easily allow the awkward wording, since in that language *chi* is reserved for persons, and an abstract noun like "experience" would automatically call for the use of *che*.[32] Might we thus see here an Italianism that betrays the hand of Bataille's associate, Joseph Marie Lo Duca? The slip raises a serious broader question: might the entire book have been written by Lo Duca? This might seem like a strange jump to make, but it appears less so when one considers the book that first earned Lo Duca his literary reputation. Published by Pauvert in 1948, his *Journal secret de Napoléon Bonaparte* (Secret Diary of Napoleon Bonaparte) was quickly proclaimed a literary tour de force by many writers, including Bataille. It consisted of embroiderings on passages written by Napoleon and by his biographer Antoine Henri Jomini. "Who is talking to me? Who is misleading me? . . . Is it Bonaparte? Is it Jomini? Is it Lo Duca?" Jean Cocteau asked himself in his preface. Lo Duca's introduction itself began with the conspicuous question, Does authenticity mean "from the author's own hand"? What might it have meant, practically speaking, to come to Georges Bataille's project with this kind of mindset? Could Lo Duca have presumed to write *Les Larmes d'Éros* on his own? We are more inclined to believe that he stitched together various drafts, possibly even transcripts of conversations with Bataille, while adding various "hooks" here and there to hold the whole thing together. In any case, one can now at least entertain the hope that someone will clarify the matter through archival research, for we at least know that the publication dossier for *Les Larmes d'Éros* does still exist. In 2002, two years before Lo Duca's death, Sotheby's sold it to an anonymous buyer for the sum of €27,000. Whatever that dossier contains, and whatever merited a price of that magnitude, let us hope that someday soon it will throw light onto what this clever literary trickster, who once composed a fake personal diary for Napoleon, contributed to the last great, but possibly faked, testament of Georges Bataille.[33]

Behind the Mask of Suffering: Is Anybody There?

We are finally ready to move beyond the level of concrete facts, where we have been obliged to attend to a welter of errors. We can now turn to sketching an interpretation of Bataille's treatment of Chinese torment in a few broad strokes, leaving room for more detail and nuance if others should care to fill out or revise the picture.

Our key point here centers on the distinction between "person" and "persona." In classical theater the term "persona" designated the mask that hid the face of the actor. From that derived the ideas of "role," of character, and eventually of "person." Suffering complicates this layering. To what degree can one ever succeed in getting back to the person hidden behind the mask of suffering? This issue sits at the crux of the various interpretations of Bataille. Seen in that light, each of the torture photographs we have been discussing ultimately poses a sole, haunting question: *Who is there?*

The notion of "ecstatic suffering" is precisely the kind of interpretation that traps the self inside the mask. To attribute this idea to Bataille is dubious, as we hope is now evident. Indeed, this attribution has left some of his more lucid readers feeling uncomfortable. It occasioned, for instance, a rare moment when Bataille's biographer, Michel Surya, makes a reproachful jab—which he diverts toward the unfortunate Dumas:

> However appalling the executioner's meticulous work on [his victim] might be, whatever sufferings he might have endured, there settles on his face, as his hair stands on end and his eyes roll back, an indecipherable expression. Suffering so intense as to be unrecognizable in terms of anything that we have ever before seen on a human face? Or joy—demented, ecstatic joy? Dumas, unwisely, argues for this ecstasy (unwisely because his book is that of a scientist); Bataille does not doubt he is right. He does not doubt that one needs to see the picture like this for it to have all its intolerable beauty.[34]

Surya provides Bataille with a carefully constructed defense. Yet one can hardly attribute this interpretation to Dumas, who writes as a physiologist seeking to identify the mechanism controlling facial expressions, and who set aside for another volume an analysis of emotions that might produce these expressions. When considering this man who was being tortured to death, Dumas does not ask how pain intermingles with pleasure, but rather how a pain—the unmitigated strength of which he does not doubt for a moment—can induce, mechanically, an expression that looks so deceptively like one of pleasure.[35] The same interest applies to Dumas's treatments of "horripilation," goose bumps, and other reflexive conditions studied in this third volume of his series, where the torture victim is displayed together with other subjects of observation. No notion of ecstasy is raised. It is the author of *Les Larmes d'Éros,* and he alone, who "argues for this ecstasy" by imbuing it with the scent of desire.

At the same time, the approach Dumas takes, however behavioralistic, entails a methodological error worth noting: his tendency to draw general conclusions from isolated cases without attention to context. Consider, for example, his treatment of horripilation, the condition in which the hair on the lingchi victim's head stands on end. This phenomenon impressed Dumas and Bataille alike. Caught up in the photographic record and fixed on the mask of suffering, neither author considers the possibility that there might be a different reason for this bristling than the torments endured. Simply by checking the watercolors of Chinese torture that had been in circulation for a good half century before these photographs were taken, either man would have seen that all prisoners of this era, whether they were condemned to death or to exile, displayed the same hairstyle. The reason for this was social and legal, not physiological. Every male subject of the Qing empire was required to wear his hair in the style imposed by the Manchus, with the forward part of the skull shaved clean and the hair to the rear grown out to braid into the famous "Chinese" queue. Since most convicts were unable to maintain proper grooming in prison, the hair on the front of their heads grew out into a thick brush, which became the sign by which convicts were rightly recognized throughout the Qing empire (Figure 29). "Horripilation" had far more to do with what Giorgio Agamben has called the status of *homo sacer*—the outcast who is marked by distinctive stigmata—than with physiological suffering, ecstatic or otherwise.[36]

Dumas also tangled himself in another problem of method. To have any credible explanatory value, his observations should have involved several different individuals. The same holds true for the shaky claims in *Les Larmes d'Éros* regarding a "voluptuous ecstasy" accompanying pain. In order to have any credibility whatsoever, the phenomenon would have had to be reproducible with the regularity that is possible when researchers test the hypothesis that men put to death by hanging have erections. Having viewed more than fifty photographs from at least four executions by lingchi—an experience our readers might prefer to forego—we can attest that something readable as an "ecstatic" expression is evident only in the two photos published in *Les Larmes d'Éros,* and even there only on the basis of a subjective and questionable reading of the image. It is also worth pointing out that Chinese descriptions of lingchi, written over a period of a thousand years, include no mention of anything even approaching a manifestation of "ecstasy." What is pictured in *Les Larmes d'Éros* thus constitutes a unique case, a sole instance about which it is impossible to say anything other than that it is unique, and thus devoid of explanatory significance.

The basic error of Dumas, Bataille, and their followers was to take the photographs at face value—as objective representations of reality—and therefore to focus their critical faculties not on the photographs they were looking at but on what they supposed the photographs to be evidence of. They failed to imagine, at least in this case, that a photographic process, extending from the decision to take the picture and how to shoot it to its consumption in various media, engenders a cycle of representation that is determined by a cultural, moral, and religious background so pervasive as to redetermine the real meaning of the scene.

Despite semantic cautions related to the condemned man's "decidedly undecipherable expression" and its "paradoxical aspects," his face has been deciphered and construed by Western commentators in a way that is remarkably consistent over time. The very first rendering of this execution was published six months after the fact, in an encyclopedia for the young sold in installments. Aiming at a broad and young audience, the article described the dismemberment without showing a photograph of it. A drawing was added, however, to depict the most memorable part of the execution (Figure 30).

It bears the striking caption *"la figure de joie extatique,"* "the face of ecstatic joy [of the tortured man]."[37] This picture probably best displays the interpretative pattern through which Westerners first saw these photographs. The illustrator has traced the outlines of the photograph, hence the drawing's clear similarity with the original, but that similarity soon

Figure 29. A prisoner displaying the characteristic unshaven head. One of six watercolors in the album "Watercolors illustrating modes of punishment." Art & Architecture Collection, Miriam & Ira D. Wallach Division of Art, Prints and Photographs, The New York Public Library, Astor, Lenox and Tilden Foundations.

proves purely formal when we compare the facial expression in the drawing with that in the photograph. When put beside the picture of a Christian martyr such as Andrea Mantegna's Saint Sebastian, the encyclopedia drawing reveals that the artist was in fact following a standard Christian aesthetic of suffering (Figure 31). In sum, what is represented here is the mask—the *persona*—obscuring the face of the real person. The "ecstatic joy" is the expression of the mask, not that of the real tortured Chinese, whose expression and feelings are still, and will remain, beyond our reach.

Bataille's mystical meditations during the 1940s posed the problem of the relation between the mask and the person even more explicitly. This concern is typified by the following extract: "I didn't choose God as an object [of my meditations], but, humanly, the young Chinese (a condemned felon) shown in the photos as covered with blood while the executioner tortures him (the blade's already in his knee-bone). I was connected to this unhappy being in ties of horror and friendship. But when I looked at this image to the point of harmony, the necessity of being only myself was cancelled. At the same time this object I chose disintegrated into vastness and, in a storm of pain, was destroyed."[38] Contemplation to the point of union—the final "amen" or "so be it"—resolves itself into a kind of communion, taking the form of a compulsive need to write. The text itself seals the link between the mask and the person of the torture victim by assuring the reader that the writer identifies with the dying torture victim to the point of

Figure 30. Illustration of the head of a lingchi victim, in Philippe Berthelot, "Les Supplices en Chine," in *Je sais tout, encyclopédie mondiale illustré* (October 15, 1905), p. 290.

fusion. Lost in contemplation of the image, to the question "who is there?" the author answers, "it's me."

This reply is perhaps valid in the framework of Bataille's oeuvre, but its fragility and artificiality are revealed the moment one raises one's eyes from the text. Bataille resorts to various devices in his attempts to lend substance to his identification with the torture victim, for instance, by affirming that the Chinese young man "must have been tortured to death in my lifetime," thereby establishing a claim that they were contemporaries.[39] Yet being contemporaries is a weak form of communion. More often, the author's identification with the victim takes the imagined form of physical fusion and is inspired, as already noted, by the "spiritual exercises" of Saint Ignatius. In substituting an anonymous bleeding corpse for the figure of Christ crucified, Bataille meant to substitute humanity for divinity, thereby enlarging the meaning of sacrifice. He failed to realize that by dissolving the historicity of the torture victim into his own religious abstraction, he might have sacrificed that very meaning. *Ecce homo:* the phrase is usually used in reference to the image of the suffering and humiliated Christ wearing the crown of thorns. But literally it means: "Here he is." That is, it designates the person of Jesus Christ: his identity, his history; his name, origins, and personal connections; his words, his acts, and his death—not as the tortured person, nor as pure suffering, but as event: trial, date, place, deeds, words. It is in the midst of an

Figure 31. Detail of the head of Saint Sebastian, from Andrea Mantegna, *The Martyrdom of St. Sebastian,* showing a Christian aesthetic of torment. Venice, Galleria Franchetti alla Ca' d'Oro, su concessione del Ministero per i Beni e le Attività Culturali.

entire network of information that suffering is ultimately allowed to find meaning, and agony permitted to acquire the depth of the event.

But what would one make of a Christ about whom nothing was known except Calvary, or whose image was reduced to a mask of his last moments? What would one make of a nameless saint or martyr? What does it mean to publish a photograph of an unknown torture victim whose name and personal history are unknown? Does that not amount to exhibiting a blank, empty mask, to brandishing a fake icon in which there simply is *no one* there? The paradox remained latent in Bataille's oeuvre down to the moment when the publication of the photographs of the lingchi victim abruptly brought it to light—no doubt in the lowly form of a caption: just a few lines for the public. But in agreeing to have these images published, Bataille suddenly found himself faced with insoluble questions. To reconstruct the torture victim's story would have required breaking through the confines of the Western sources and exploring the Chinese judicial archives, something that was obviously out of the question. Bataille's early texts, those concerned purely with mystic contemplation, could not have been set off by photos, because only the substitution of words for images could secure the mystic illusion, according to his thinking. Placing actual images next to the text would fatally show up the exercise as a purely literary artifice. It was this insoluble problem that left the door open to the various Sadean improvisations, the mass of empty verbiage, and the documentary misidentifications that have long afflicted *Les Larmes d'Éros*.

CHAPTER 9

Lingering On

The intellectual movement we have traced in this book—from the practice of tormented execution in Chinese history to the incorporation of images of the tormented Chinese body into Chinese and European forms of representation—has followed a course that would not have appealed to China historians of an earlier generation. What went on in the European iconosphere in particular would have been regarded as a matter at best of curiosity, and more likely of indifference—something better left to those whose study was of Europe, not of China. The concern of sinologists used to be to disengage Chinese history from the rich tangle of Western misunderstandings and mystifications that centuries of erratic contact had allowed to accumulate around the idea of China. This concern explicitly stressed separating what was considered external to China—its borrowings and its cultural influences—from what belonged to the category of culturally complete knowledge of a discrete, isolatable object labeled "China." Filtering out the more egregious effects of Eurocentrism was undoubtedly a valuable move, but it was too often carried out somewhat at the expense of recognizing the still ongoing, and usually unacknowledged, effects of the historical legacy of Western cultural perceptions on what we assume to be knowledge of China.

By including the Western appropriation of images of the lingchied body into the study of tormented execution in China, our intention has not been to reinforce the popular Orientalist misperceptions that academic knowledge has sought to challenge. Rather, we address that topic because of our convictions that certain older Orientalist assumptions about China continue to percolate through both academic discourse and popular knowledge, and that China as a historical subject cannot be studied without critical regard for the Western epistemological constructions by which it has been made known since the eighteenth century to those outside China, and since the twentieth to those inside as well.

The confusion that arises between history and stereotype is well illustrated in an article that appeared in the London *Observer* in 1928. The piece, attributed to "our own correspondent, Shanghai," reports on atrocities that Communist forces were allegedly inflicting on the residents of towns near Swatow in eastern Guangdong: "Disemboweled corpses were left for days in the streets, no one being allowed to remove them until they were torn to pieces and eaten by dogs. Babies were killed before their mother's eyes, and the mothers then executed. Men had their ears and strips of flesh cut off, fried, and eaten before their eyes before execution."[1] Real people may indeed have experienced horrendous treatment at the hands of Communist soldiers, but it is also possible that these reports emanated from a journalistic urge that was all too ready to flesh out skimpy rumors of civil war atrocities with archetypes of "Chinese" violence reminiscent of the banished penalty of lingchi ("strips of flesh cut off"), embroidered with images of being "torn to pieces and eaten by dogs" that are worthy of the overactive imagination of the compilers of the *Jade Register*.

The story did not have its day of notoriety only on the inside pages of a London newspaper and then disappear into the journalistic midden. It caught the attention of Charles Duff, an activist opponent of the death penalty, who imported the account as historical fact onto the opening page of his powerful and persuasive *A Handbook on Hanging*, where it reads as follows: "In the *Ts'in* [Qin] Dynasty in China the heads of undesirables were expeditiously removed by a stroke of the official sword, whereas in the same country in our own century men and women had their ears and strips of flesh cut off, fried, and eaten before their eyes before execution, and children were ordered to behead their parents."[2] The ancient history in this passage is hopeless, for the Qin dynasty, as we have noted earlier in this volume, was anything but content to limit the death penalty to decapitation. If the reader will recall Emperor Hongwu's demurral of 1397 (see Chapter 4), not even he—willing as he was to use the most atrocious punishments on those who offended him—would have stooped to the idea of supporting the reintroduction of the punishments of the Qin. It would perhaps be unfair to discount Duff for bad history, since he is simply drawing on a newspaper report that invoked the stock image of an evil period in the Chinese past; but it is not unfair to express our concern about the effect of the Orientalist reporting that swayed him into agreeing with this stereotype. His point in using the story is to illustrate his opening theme by citing an example from outside Europe: "The methods of dispatch are without number and of infinite variety. This history of killing is the history of the world." But the example rests on a body of misinformation and misinterpretation since the nineteenth century that still colors how China is viewed in the West.

Duff's willingness to accept the account buried one morning inside his *Observer* demonstrates why we believe that the Western obsession with Chinese torments, which has been our concern in the second half of this book, must be placed alongside the history of judicial punishment in imperial China, which is our concern in the first. The connection is historically direct; it also reflects the intellectual journey that led the three of us to write this book in this way. We did not proceed from the history of Chinese law to the history of European culture, but set to work by traveling along a more circuitous route, tacking in the face of silences and distortions on a painful theme, from several twentieth-century European images to a multiplicity of sources, Chinese and Western, related to several centuries of late imperial practice. Along the way we were impelled to genealogize the practice of lingchi in China as a way of thinking through and coming to terms with what for us was a bizarre point of entry to the subject: the promiscuous circulation of photographs of lingchi victims among Europeans a century ago.

A cross-cultural hermeneutic seemed well suited to the analysis of a practice that had its origins in the interaction between China and Inner Asia and that has been preserved most graphically in evidence collected by Western travelers. The history of lingchi as a European cultural fetish dates from the late period of European colonialism. The product of a voyeuristic impulse that imperialism appears to have released among Europeans, this fetish was intensified and distorted by the power of photography to show "real people" and "real events" without having to acknowledge the power relations shaping those events and situating those people, or even to acknowledge whose pictures were being taken. As far as we know, the French soldiers who photographed Wang Weiqin had no idea who he was or why he was being killed; it is we as historians who a century later discovered the identity of this previously anonymous *supplicié chinois*. To them he seems to have simply been a barbarous spectacle, without significant identity beyond the role this punishment assigned him.

Pointing to the Orientalist prejudices of these documents alerts the reader to the politics of their production, but does not complete the task of incorporating lingchi into our understanding of Chinese history. Historians of

China until now have managed to dodge some blunt questions that the photographs require us to ask. Who fell so atrociously afoul of the law? What was this penalty intended to punish? Was their punishment commensurate with the crimes they were found guilty of? How could a judicial system known in other ways for the sophistication of its reasoning and administration impose bodily mutilation of this character? Did this punishment not fly in the face of the humanist ideals that Confucianism was thought to promote? When questions of that sort have been answered, then what should the response of China specialists be to the knowledge that Chinese criminal law dispatched its worst capital cases in this fashion? Should we be required to incorporate these terrible images into our account of late imperial history? If so, what role should they be permitted to have? Must we endow lingchi with a central role in the maintenance of imperial rule, or was it merely incidental, even aberrational? Do the lingchi photographs in fact cancel more positive assessments of the Chinese past that we might prefer to make?

To get from Western imagery back to Chinese practice, we have offered in this volume contexts for lingchi by triangulating from the history of punishments not just in China but elsewhere in the world. When we examine the history of extreme punishments in Europe, for example, we find that the desecration and destruction of the criminalized body could be at least as elaborate and excruciating, and that distaste for punishing in this way is much more recent than many suppose. Recall, for instance, the passage from Montesquieu we quoted in Chapter 6. When Montesquieu makes a passing comment on lingchi in *The Spirit of the Laws* in 1748, it is not to deplore the practice as exceptionally disgusting, as we would expect his counterpart a century later to do. It is rather to note that the Chinese were cleverer than the Russians, who punished robbery and murder with the same penalty, thereby encouraging robbers to murder. Better to do as he thought the Chinese did, and reserve the extreme punishment of being "cut in pieces" for "those who add murder to robbery" so as to discourage robbers from murdering while robbing.[3] In fact, contrary to Montesquieu's supposition, lingchi was not the punishment the Code applied to murder in the course of robbery, though that is incidental to the point we wish to make on the basis of his comment. Our point is that lingchi did not particularly attract his moral outrage or point to China as a place in the grip of intolerable judicial aberrations. Two decades later, the great English jurist William Blackstone borrowed Montesquieu's example to make the same point in the fourth volume of his *Commentaries on the Laws of England,* observing that "in China murderers are cut to pieces, and robbers not; hence in that country they never murder on the highway, though they often rob."[4] (Curiously, though, he alleges that the French, rather than the Russians, were the fools who punished robbery and murder with equal severity.) Blackstone did not advocate adding lingchi to English punishments, but as of 1769 the penalty was not considered so atrocious as to invite the editorial comment it would routinely receive a century later.

European practice lagged behind the more humanitarian strain of European opinion. As late as 1810, the British House of Lords rejected a bill from the Commons removing pickpocketing from the capital statutes. "Terror alone could prevent the commission of that crime," thundered the lord chief justice. Pickpockets had to be hanged, in his opinion, as "no milder punishment would produce any thing like safety to the public interest."[5] We offer this observation not to deny that differences run through Chinese and Western traditions of criminal law, but to note that differences between past and present may be more profound than those between particular societies. A value that was widely accepted in one age may seem manifestly bizarre in another—and yet there is a persisting habit of allowing hugely disparate attitudes to coexist within the broad category of a particular "culture" or "civilization." It was perhaps this knowledge of the variability of convictions within a society's history—the ability to relativize not one's values so much as one's sense of standing at the end of history—that those who manipulated images of tormented Chinese executions in the nineteenth- and twentieth-century West chose not to recognize, or more pointedly were not interested in applying. They were largely uninterested in authenticating any experiences other than their own. Without some measure of recognition along these lines, lingchi could be made to stand in for Chineseness alongside any number of similarly contemptible images—opium smoking, footbinding, kowtowing, and the worship of idols, to name only a few, any of which could be invoked to show China to be a topsy-turvy and dangerous land.[6] To make this point is not to deny the existence of these practices in China; rather, it is to make us aware of the rhetoric of Western superiority that rewrote Western fantasy as Chinese reality.

The other, more direct context we have invoked to make sense of lingchi in this volume is the history of judicial administration in late imperial China. Resituating this penalty within the original judicial context in which it made sense has not been a simple matter. The sources for reconstructing the history of the death penalty in any of its forms have proved difficult to discover and problematic to interpret. Officially published regulations show how the system of imperial justice was supposed to work, but reveal almost nothing of how it did work, and what its workings meant to the people who were drawn into its procedures, or even to those who managed to steer clear of them.

Yet another way to explicate lingchi is to step back from the Chinese judicial context as well as from the Western rhetorical context and consider how it appears when placed within a global history of punishments that includes such methods of killing as burning at the stake, breaking on the wheel, keelhauling, drawing and quartering, and cannibalism. That world history contains such an extensive record of brutal punishments does nothing to justify lingchi in its specificity, but it does provide a potentially endless range of human experience within which to locate this particular technology of bodily suffering—a history in which lingchi stands as one case among many, not as a case by itself.

To gauge the manner of reasoning at work in this context, imagine a judicial system that punishes its criminals by targeting their bodies according to a gradient of milder to harsher restraints and sufferings, depending on the moral horror the crime excites. Those found guilty of a lighter offense, such as vagrancy, should be flogged in general view, a penalty entailing both physical suffering and public humiliation. Heavier offenses such as theft might also entail flogging, but the strokes should be administered more harshly and in greater numbers. Those guilty of morally repugnant offenses such as prostitution and procuring might in additional have their heads inserted into wooden frames so that they may be made to face the public that condemns their actions. More serious felons should be forced to do hard labor under penal servitude for a number of years that varies with the severity of their crimes, or else transported into exile for fixed or indefinite periods. Reserved for the very worst class of criminals would be execution, strangulation being its principal form. In extreme cases, however, other methods could be used, including the disembowelment and mutilation of the capital criminal's body and the public display of his head or corpse as a harsh warning to others of the consequences of the conduct for which the law condemned the victim.

The reader may be forgiven for assuming that the penal system just described is eighteenth-century China's. It may approximate that system, but in fact we derive it from the catalogue of punishments available to English judges in the early part of the eighteenth century, based on the research of John Beattie. The point is that the differences between the two systems are in their specifics—the stationary pillory instead of the portable cangue, transportation to the West Indies instead of exile to Xinjiang, lingchi instead of drawing and quartering, and so on—and not in the principles of whether the body should be the site of punishment, nor even in the methods employed to determine guilt and punish crime. It could even be argued in fact that Chinese law in the eighteenth century observed finer distinctions in terms of degrees of guilt and punishment than English law did. But in terms of procedures and expectations, even in terms of the rules of evidence, the two systems had far more in common than we might expect. The distance between what Chinese magistrates might mete out to their worst criminals and what English judges could impose on theirs was not as great as it would later become. The difference was more of degree than of kind.

The difference was shifting from one of degree to one of kind on the eve of the first Opium War in 1839–1842, as tormented executions were struck from the list of penalties available to European judges and came increasingly to appear barbaric in the places where they were still performed. The shift occurred in tandem with growing doubts in the West about the efficacy of cruel punishments and a growing conviction that penalties should be used to promote reform rather than to exercise revenge. As Beccaria put it in his 1765 tract against the death penalty, *On Crimes and Punishments,* more lenient and proportionate penalties would "make the most efficacious and most lasting impression on the minds of men, and the least painful of impressions on the body of the criminal."[7] As European penology increasingly aimed to touch minds rather than bodies, bodily mutilation lost its penal logic. In England by the 1830s, "a system of justice that had been intensely personal and concerned with the particular attributes of offenders and that had conceived of punishment as a means of deterring others by bloody example was giving way to a system of administration that came to emphasize equality and uniformity of treatment as ideals and that thought of punishment as reformative. Violent punishments that attacked the body, carried out in public, were replaced by incarceration and punishments that aimed to reconstruct the prisoner's mind and heart."[8] The logic of punishment had changed profoundly.

The disappearance of lingchi from China's capital statutes came about at a very specific political conjuncture, one that was thoroughly imbricated with the new relationship that China was having to construct with an imperialist

West.[9] Still, the clear distaste that Shen Jiaben and the other legal specialists who drafted the judicial reform laws in 1904–1905 felt toward the use of "violent punishments that attacked the body" was not all that different from the refusal of English judges a century earlier to apply the letter of the law in certain designated capital cases. Many Chinese jurists did not care for lingchi, even though the Code obliged them to impose it for certain cases, so there was no resistance to getting rid of the penalty when it was removed.[10] Chinese jurists then were not about to align their rejection of cruel punishments with the idea of equal treatment for all citizens, a position that had led their English counterparts in the nineteenth century to argue that punishing a teaspoon thief of any class with death was intolerable, particularly when the same penalty punished the murderer of a child. Beyond that issue lay the general argument against the death penalty, based on the conviction, famously enunciated in 1764 by Beccaria,[11] that the state should subject no one to judicial execution. This, however, was not the direction in which even reformist legal thinking in China was tending at the beginning of the twentieth century. Indeed, opposition to the death penalty remains a minority opinion in Chinese legal circles.

In the longer global history of crime and punishment, these changes belong to the recent past. Still, that recent past is long enough to have driven a substantial wedge between the criminal administrations of China and the West through the twentieth century and into the twenty-first. The thin end of that wedge was not tormented execution—officials in the Board of Punishments at the end of the Qing were able to remove lingchi from the statutes in 1905 without even a struggle, once the dynasty had committed more broadly to revise its institutions. The wedge issue was instead the death penalty itself. The overwhelming international trend since the 1950s has been to limit and then repeal the use of the death penalty, the United States being the striking anomaly within the tradition of English law. Coming from a different tradition, the East Asian region offers another major counterexample. The People's Republic of China, Taiwan, Japan, Mongolia, the Koreas, Singapore, and Vietnam, all of which operate legal systems in the shadow of Chinese traditions of justice, together execute roughly four people a day and account for over three-quarters of officially reported judicial executions worldwide.[12] The death penalty, once universal, is today primarily an East Asian punishment.

The abolition of lingchi thus has its place within a global context of legal change in which the norms and forms of punishment have altered

significantly over the past two centuries, though without producing a definitive convergence. As we have taken pains to show in this book, lingchi's
abolition also has a place within the global cultural system of European
colonial dominance, which refused to let go of images of judicial dismemberment even after 1905, when the practice was ended in China.

The penalty persisted as an aesthetic and ethical artifact capable of inspiring fear and loathing, and not only in the European imagination. Tibetans assured Flora Shelton, who traveled among them in the 1910s,
that the Chinese army that invaded and occupied Tibet between 1908
and 1910 under the command of the notorious Zhao Erfeng tormented
their captives in this way. They told her that the Chinese soldiers "would
bring slow death by slicing off a small part of the body at a time until the
heart was reached and life ended."[13] If this is indeed what Zhao's soldiers
did, they would have been acting in clear defiance of the official removal
of lingchi from the penal statutes in 1905. But this could have been justified as a military emergency, when such rules no longer applied. Soldiers
in any case have not always been bound by the rules of civilian justice, as
we know. It is also just possible, however, that the story is mistaken, and
this was a fragment of an old collective memory from Qing invasions in
the eighteenth century that had seeped into popular lore about what Chinese soldiers more recently were still doing to Tibetans who opposed
them.

The memory of lingchi also survives in the Chinese diaspora. In *The Jade
Peony* Canadian novelist Wayson Choi has the grandmother tell his alter ego
character a harrowing tale about a village girl who was executed by lingchi
for immoral behavior—with the unshakable air of believing that such a
story had to be true.[14] Never mind that the lingchi laws would never have
been extended to such a case: this was part of the lore about the Chinese
past that everyone, Chinese included, thought they knew was true.

The fantasies of Chinese grandmothers and Belle Époque aesthetes like
Octave Mirbeau lie at considerable distance from the punishments that the
Ming and Qing emperors allowed to be part of the routine work of their judicial administrations, and yet not so far that we cannot go back and retrace
the steps that got them from the past to the present. Who could have predicted that these two histories would meet at Wang Weiqin's execution at
Vegetable Market, when an amateur photographer would capture an image
that continues to lurk even now at the edge of a consciousness of evils past
and present?

Notes

1. The Execution of Wang Weiqin

1. This reconstruction is based on Li Yizhi, *Li Yizhi quanji,* pp. 780–781; *Qingmo Beijing zhi ziliao,* pp. 123–126; Little and Little, *Gleanings of Fifty Years in China;* Little, *Round about My Peking Garden;* and photographs discussed in detail in Chapter 7 below. The memorial confirming the legal judgment against Wang can be found in the records of the Henan Office of the Board of Punishments, in the thirteenth volume of memorials *(zoudi)* of the Guangxu era, China Number One Historical Archive, Beijing. See Bourgon, "Photographie et vérité historique: le lingchi de Wang Weiqin."

2. David Wang explores the powerful link between memories of the Boxers and visions of decapitation in his study of twentieth-century literature, *The Monster That Is History,* pp. 15–19.

3. To give one example of this reference to lingchi in popular literature, selected at random: in *The Family Way* (p. 302), Tony Parsons describes three sisters abandoned by their mother as having "suffered the thousand cuts of having an absent parent." The expression is now so embedded in English usage that the connection with China has largely fallen out of sight.

4. The phrase "quaint and original" is Henry Savage-Landor's, which he used to characterize Korean (not Chinese) punishments in his 1895 *Corea or Cho-sen: The Land of Morning Calm,* chap. 15. We are grateful to Neil Burton for this reference.

5. The judgment of cultural or political failure tends to stem from reliance on standards and expectations established from the European side of the China–Europe contrast. As Bin Wong observes in "Torture and Transformations of the Chinese State," this is what happens when "we operate on a general level of social theory stressing the differences between premodern states and modern ones" that is built upon distinctions "based empirically on Western cases exclusively." For the larger theoretical position from which it derives, see his *China Transformed,* chap. 4.

6. See, e.g., the United Nations' "Declaration on the Protection of All Persons from Being Subjected to Torture and Other Cruel, Inhuman or Degrading Treatment or Punishment" (1975), which defines torture as "any act by which severe pain

or suffering, whether physical or mental, is intentionally inflicted by or at the instigation of a public official on a person for such purposes as obtaining from him or a third person information or confession, punishing him for an act he has committed or is suspected of having committed, or intimidating him or other persons." Article 1, General Assembly Resolution 3452, 9 December 1975. On the distinction between torment and torture, see Foucault, *Discipline and Punish,* p. 34; Langbein, *Torture and the Law of Proof,* p. 3.

7. Douglas Hay, "Writing about the Death Penalty," p. 4.

8. This shift in logic can be detected in China as early as 1898. For later deliberations on these matters among Chinese legal experts in the 1920s, see Dikötter, *Crime, Punishment and the Prison in Modern China,* pp. 136–138; on their efforts to end the death penalty, see pp. 178–181.

9. The General Assembly addresses the issue of the death penalty annually through resolutions calling on member states to impose a moratorium on its use. The quoted passage is from the 2004 General Assembly resolution on the death penalty, which in addition called on member states "to ensure that any application of particularly cruel or inhuman means of execution, such as stoning, is stopped immediately." See United Nations Office of the High Commissioner for Human Rights, "Question of the Death Penalty" (Resolutions 2004/67), available at www.ohchr.org/documents/E/CHR/E-CN_4-RES-2004 -67.doc.

10. On the conceptual difficulty of approaching the topic of execution subsequent to its abolition—which he refers to as "post-abolitionist baggage"—see Smith, " 'I Could Hang Anything You Can Bring before Me,' " p. 304.

11. Foucault, *Discipline and Punish,* p. 34.

12. De Groot, *The Religious System of China,* vol. 1, pp. 346–347.

13. Macauley, *Social Power and Legal Culture,* p. 216. Macauley relies purely on Western sources for evidence of this notion, however.

14. *Yuli chaozhuan zhujie jingshi baofa,* 2.58b–59a.

15. Ibid., 1.80a.

16. Clarke, "The Yü-li or Precious Records," p. 366.

17. Stephen Teiser confirms our sense of the lack of Chinese sources to consult on this question. For Confucius's dictum, see Legge, *The Chinese Classics,* vol. 1, p. 191.

18. Rasmussen, *China Trader,* p. 74.

19. The standard formulation of this "socio-religious" aversion to decapitation may be found in Bodde and Morris, *Law in Imperial China,* p. 92: "strangulation is superior because it leaves the spirit of the executed man an intact body which it can continue to inhabit." See also Ch'en, *Chinese Legal Tradition under the Mongols,* p. 43. Neither cites a Chinese source for this belief.

20. Rasmussen, *China Trader,* p. 75.

21. Lu Hsun, *Selected Stories of Lu Hsun,* p. 26. On the place of decapitation in narratives of Lu Xun and other Republican writers, which David Wang has termed the "decapitation syndrome," see his *The Monster That Is History,* p. 16.

22. Paul Ch'en, "Disloyalty to the State in Late Imperial China," p. 168.

23. Guy Fawkes and the other conspirators in the Gunpowder Plot were put to death in this way in London over the last two days of January 1606.

24. Ruggiero, *Violence in Early Renaissance Venice,* pp. 47, 48.

25. Royer, "Dead Men Talking," pp. 69, 76.

26. Beattie, *Crime and the Courts in England,* p. 139.

27. Diderot, "Anatomie," p. 409. Erasistratus of Chios and the philosopher Herophilus founded a school of anatomy in Alexandria in the third century B.C. The migration of the term "anatomy" from "dissection" to "the structure of the body" posed a challenge for the joint Chinese-missionary committee that attempted to standardize Chinese translations of medical terms in August 1916: should they retain the Greek meaning via *jiepouxue,* "the study of the cutting up [of the body]," or should they shift the translation to the more generally used term *rentixue,* "the study of the human body"? They opted for the former, more literal translation. The minutes of this meeting were published that year in *Zhonghua yixue zazhi (National Medical Journal)* under the title "Yixue mingci shenchahui diyici kaihui jilu"; see pp. 30–32 for the debate on "anatomy." We are grateful to David Luesink for bringing this text to our attention. See also Pierre-Étienne Will's discussion in Furth et al., *Thinking with Cases,* pp. 85, 99 n. 70.

28. Beattie, *Crime and the Courts,* pp. 527–528. Execution victims feared not just the anatomists. It was widely believed that executioners removed and rendered human fat for sale as medicine and sold body parts for black magic; see Camporesi, *The Fear of Hell,* p. 129, quoting a 1668 Jesuit treatise advising priests how to care for those on death row.

29. Diderot, "Anatomie," pp. 409–410.

30. The association between forensic autopsy and "ritual disembowelment" is still common currency in crime fiction, as, e.g., in P. D. James, *A Taste for Death,* p. 197.

31. Blackstone, *Commentaries on the Laws of England,* vol. 4, p. 18, quoted in Beattie, *Crime and the Courts,* p. 557. Beattie notes the influence in this passage of Beccaria, whose *On Crimes and Punishments* appeared in English two years before the publication of this final volume of Blackstone's magnum opus.

32. On the connections among the notions of *supplicium,* sacrifice, and the criminal as *sacer,* see Gernet, *Recherches sur le développement de la pensée juridique et morale en Grèce,* p. 51, n. 1. On the generalization of *supplicii* to the detriment of *poenae* (penalties) in the late Roman Empire, see Callu, "Le Jardin des supplices au Bas-empire," and Grodzinski, "Tortures mortelles et catégories sociales."

33. Spence, *The Memory Palace of Matteo Ricci,* p. 246.

34. This visual tradition, which serves as a kind of iconographic literacy in the West, remains very much alive today, as Susan Sontag noted in *Regarding the Pain of Others,* p. 80.

35. When Foucault in *Discipline and Punish* (p. 11) describes the shift in European penal culture by observing, "From being an art of unbearable sensations punishment has become an economy of suspended rights," he is simply following Beccaria.

36. On the need to develop symmetrical comparison, see Wong, *China Transformed*, pp. 2–7.

37. Asad, "On Torture, or Cruel, Inhuman, and Degrading Treatment."

38. Homosexuality provides a good case for reversing norm and deviation. Ming Chinese were revolted that the Spanish colonial authorities in the Philippines condemned sodomites to be burned at the stake. They regarded the penalty as brutal, and sodomy in any case was not criminalized in Ming law. Only one case survives of criminal prosecution for sodomy in the Ming, and in that case the judgment was analogized not to heterosexual rape but to assault, for which the penalty was a beating; Sommer, *Sex, Law, and Society in Late Imperial China*, pp. 114–165, esp. 119–120. On sodomy as a capital crime in England, see Beattie, *Crime and the Courts*, pp. 434, 465–467.

39. Richard Verstegan, *Le Théâtre des cruautés des hérétiques de notre temps*.

40. A fourteenth-century version has been translated by Maria Dobozy as *The Saxon Mirror*. This handbook is one of many sources from which European scholars have worked. Foremost in the large literature on European studies of torture and torment, legal and illegal, are Edgerton, *Pictures and Punishment*, and Luppi, *Les Supplices dans l'art*.

41. For example, to illustrate punishments practiced in the thirteenth century, Brian McKnight reproduces pictures from the seventeenth (for flogging with bamboo) and the late nineteenth (for lingchi) in *Law and Order in Sung China*, pp. 450–451. These illustrations come from the plates at the beginning of Niida, *Chūgoku hōseishi kenkyū: keihō*. Sidney Shapiro recycles the same images on the cover and p. 269 of *The Law and the Lore of Chinese Criminal Justice*. In some cases the images have been "modernized," guns replacing spears.

42. Merback, *The Thief, the Cross and the Wheel*, pp. 16–19.

43. For comments on the aesthetic bridge that Chinese watercolors formed between China and the West, see Clunas, *Chinese Export Watercolours*, pp. 96–102. Clunas refers to judicial scenes only in passing (p. 92). Regarding the depiction of executions in this genre, see Bourgon, "Les Scènes de supplice dans les aquarelles chinoises d'exportation."

44. Mason, *The Punishments of China*, preface.

45. Staunton, *Ta Tsing Leu Lee*, translator's preface, p. xxvi.

46. De Quincey, *Confessions of an English Opium-Eater*, p. 241.

47. Doolittle, *Social Life of the Chinese: A Daguerreotype of Daily Life in China*, p. 272.

48. Gray, *China: A History of the Laws, Manners and Customs of the People*, vol. 1, p. 59, n. 1.

49. Pallu, *Relation de l'expédition de Chine en 1860*, p. 167.

50. The British relied on this reasoning to introduce into Hong Kong law corporal punishments that British law forbade; see Munn, *Anglo-China*, pp. 150–152, 233–238. Torture practices and police brutality in British India are usefully reviewed in Ruthven, *Torture the Grand Conspiracy*, pp. 183–215, which notes the attempts of colonial reformers from the 1840s onward to publicize such matters and the persistence of successive British governments to conceal them from the

public. On the mimetic use of corporal punishments in pre–World War I South America, see our discussion of Michael Taussig's work in Chapter 5.

51. The history of the use of torture by colonial regimes against liberation movements is still being written. For example, on the use of torture by French soldiers and intelligence agents during the 1954–1962 Algerian independence war, see Vidal-Naquet, *Torture: A Cancer of Democracy;* Pouillot, *La Villa Susini: tortures en Algérie;* Branche, "La Torture pendant la guerre d'Algérie." On British use of torture against the Mau Mau uprising in Kenya, see Elkins, *Imperial Reckoning;* Anderson, *Histories of the Hanged.*

52. For example, see Hannah Arendt in *Origins of Totalitarianism* and Sven Lindqvist in *"Exterminate All the Brutes."*

53. Woodside, *Lost Modernities,* p. 10.

54. Rasmussen, *China Trader,* pp. 75, vi.

55. For example, John Pal illustrates his 1963 memoir of old Shanghai, *Shanghai Saga,* with, among other photographs he took, a shot of decapitated heads nailed to a railing.

56. Sontag, *Regarding the Pain of Others,* p. 6.

57. The phrase "aesthetic shock" is from Merback, *The Thief, the Cross and the Wheel,* p. 16.

58. ". . . une pensée qui ne se démonte devant l'horreur"; Bataille, *L'Histoire de l'éroticisme,* in *Oeuvres Complètes,* vol. 8, p. 10. The standard English translation renders this phrase as "a thinking that does not fall apart in the face of horror"; *The Accursed Share,* vol. 2, p. 14.

59. Sontag, *Regarding the Pain of Others,* pp. 98–99. For other reflections on Bataille's use of the photograph, see Millett, *The Politics of Cruelty;* Elkins, *The Object Stares Back,* pp. 108–115.

60. As early as 1959, George Scott, who conceptualized torture as a form of "unfreedom" (*The History of Torture throughout the Ages,* p. 312), noted that the study of Chinese torture required factoring out "the description, in books of fiction, of forms of torture which have originated largely in the fertile imagination of sensational novelists" (p. 102). For a recent invocation of lingchi in poetry, see Polly Fleck's *The Chinese Execution,* a hallucinatory vision of post-Tiananmen China. For an absurd example of the nonsense lingchi has inspired at the other end of the literary spectrum, see Gary Jennings's novel *The Journeyer,* which treats the idea of a thousand cuts in a Borges-like manner by averring that the Chinese are obsessed with numbering systems, proposes that the number of cuts is triple the number of parts (333) into which Chinese anatomy allegedly divided the body, and claims that death must result from the thousandth cut.

61. Foucault, *Discipline and Punish,* p. 53.

62. See, e.g., the unfortunate characterization that Mark Costanzo offers in his novel, *Just Revenge,* p. 4.

63. Chen Chieh-jen, an artist living in Taiwan, has revived Bataille's images of lingchi in a way that reverses both roles and gaze; see Liu, "Chen Chieh-jen's

Aesthetic of Horror and His Bodily Memories of History." Lin Zhi, another contemporary artist living in the United States, weaves the Western iconography of
Chinese executions into his paintings of daily life; examples of his work are
available online at *www.koplindelrio.com/lin/lin.html* (we are grateful to Mott
Greene for introducing us to Lin's work). Others, however, turn the photographic evidence against the Europeans who collected it. See, e.g., the collection
of late Qing postcards published by Fang Ling and his associates under the title
Jiumeng chongjing (New stupor in an old dream), some 10 percent of which depict scenes of execution and torture. By including the messages foreigners wrote
on the back, they challenge readers to consider the cultural attitudes of those
who made the cards and those who sent them. Recent Chinese fiction also in-
vokes these penalties; in Yu Hua's *The Past and the Punishments*, the historian-
protagonist returns from his disappearance during the Cultural Revolution to
apply the Five Punishments on himself.

64. A comparative project on the history of torture is currently under way at
the universities of Lille and Montpellier, from which a first collection of
papers has been published: Durand and Otis-Cours (eds.), *La Torture
judiciaire*.

65. "The relationships in Confucian society" may well have been "complex," as
Daniel Kwok notes in his essay "On the Rites and Rights of Being Human,"
and the balance between "rights" and "duties" "close and dynamic," yet the capacity of the penal system to make do with purely mechanical references to
Confucian pieties to justify punishments—what Kwok terms the imperial
state's "belated appropriation of moral values"—could be startlingly simple;
pp. 88–89 and 91.

2. The Laws of Punishment in Late Imperial China

1. The point is central to Foucault's analysis of the history of punishment in Europe; *Discipline and Punish*, p. 8. Foucault somewhat controversially dates the
transition from spectacle to reticence to the period 1769–1810; a similar transition came roughly a century later in China.

2. This point is made as early as the *Shang shu* or *Book of History*; see Legge, *The Chinese Classics*, vol. 3, pp. 388, 602.

3. Ma Huan, *Yingyai shenglan: "The Overall Survey of the Ocean's Shores,"* p. 88.

4. *Xining fuzhi* (1762), 21.13a.

5. Petech, *China and Tibet in the Early Eighteenth Century*, p. 149. Petech argues that
the impact of the executions was strong: "The terrible scene made a deep impression on the populace, as indeed it was meant to do. After five years, the author of the *Mi dhan rlogs brjod* (Life of P'o-lha-nas) still feels gloomy and de-
pressed in relating it. P'o-lha-nas too was dejected at the spectacle, and in the
following days he presented offerings in the temples of Lhasa for the spiritual
good of the executed men . . . The lesson had been terrible, and Tibet was effectively cowed into submission for a long time."

6. Before the Tang dynasty, "the Five Punishments" were tattooing, cutting off of the nose, amputation of the feet, castration, and death; see Knoblock, *Xunzi*, vol. 2, p. 107.

7. Ch'en, *The Formation of the Early Meiji Legal Order*, pp. 40–41.

8. In the early Ming, these redemptions were calculated in volumes of grain, from five *shi* to commute a sentence of the light stick to sixty *shi* for a capital crime; *Ming taizong shilu*, 140.1a.

9. Jiang, *The Great Ming Code*, pp. 6, 17–18.

10. Johnson, *The T'ang Code*, pp. 55–59. According to Ch'en, *Chinese Legal Tradition under the Mongols*, p. 42, strangulation was replaced by lingchi during the Yuan dynasty In the *Yuan dianzhang* (Institutions of the Yuan dynasty); however, the Five Punishments there include only strangulation and decapitation as legal forms of the death penalty (39.1b).

11. *Yuan dianzhang*, 40.1a; Huai Xiaofeng (ed.), *Da Ming lü*, p. 446; Tian Tao and Zheng Qin (eds.), *Da Qing lüli*, p. 63.

12. For example, Zhang Yi, *Yuguang jianqi ji*, pp. 20–21, cites several instances of dying in the cangue among many cases of torment inflicted by the Tianshun emperor (r. 1457–1464) during the reign of terror following his restoration.

13. Huai Xiaofeng (ed.), *Da Ming lü*, p. 446; Tian Tao and Zheng Qin (eds.), *Da Qing lüli*, p. 63.

14. See Huang Liuhong, *Fukkei zensho*, 11.27b; differently translated in Huang Liuhung, *A Complete Book concerning Happiness and Benevolence*, p. 277.

15. This case is cited in Philip Huang, *Civil Justice in China*, p. 207.

16. Cited in Huang Zhangjian, "Ming Hongwu Yongle chao de bangwen junling," p. 282.

17. Huang, *A Complete Book*, p. 274.

18. Evelyn, *The Diary of John Evelyn*, p. 19.

19. Beattie, *Crime and the Courts*, p. 616.

20. Huai Xiaofeng (ed.), *Da Minglü*, p. 446; Tian Tao and Zheng Qin (eds.), *Da Qing lüli*, pp. 62–63.

21. Conner, "True Confessions? Chinese Confessions Then and Now," pp. 149–150.

22. *Qinding da Qing huidian shili*, 723.7b (p. 14431); Staunton, *Ta Tsing Leu Lee*, pp. 488–489.

23. Meskill (trans.), *Ch'oe Pu's Diary*, p. 157.

24. Though most European courts did not permit the torture of suspects in open court, there were exceptions to this rule, such as the flogging of juveniles in open court in the Netherlands and France; see Spierenburg, "The Body and the State."

25. The same can be said of the language of the death penalty. Europeans referred to the killing of a condemned person as "executing"—in the sense of "carrying out"—an order to put someone to death. Chinese had no such euphemisms: a criminal was either "put to death" *(chu si)* or "decapitated" *(zhan)*. Our thanks to Neil Burton for pointing this out.

26. There were mildly evasive terms, such as *yanxun*, "to interrogate minutely," and *yanjie*, "to scrutinize minutely," which did not name physical suffering yet were

understood as implying it. Both terms are used in this way by Fan Zengxiang, a judicial official active in the 1890s whose legal communications were considered a model; see his *Panshan gongdu*, 1.34a, 35b. Fan reduces ambiguity by using *yanxun* in the phrase *yanxun kaidao*, "to examine minutely in order to lead on [to the truth]" (1.34a). We are grateful to Pierre-Étienne Will for bringing this text to our attention.

27. On the role of confession in trial procedures in imperial China, contrasted with Europe, see Conner, "True Confessions?" pp. 135–140.
28. Wang Huizu, *Xuezhi yishuo*, 1.20a.
29. Xue Yunsheng, *Duli cunyi*, pp. 2–3, 1203. An unfortunate convention in the field of late imperial history has Ming historians translating Xingbu as Ministry of Justice and Qing historians as Board of Punishments. In this book we use both, according to the period to which the reference belongs.
30. See Balazs, *Le Traité juridique du "Souei-Chou,"* pp. 195–206.
31. James Low, who served as a British official in Malacca, made this comment in order to contrast Chinese and Thai practices, insisting that the punishments of the latter were not "quite so devilish"; "On the Law of Múung Thai or Siam," p. 404. The essay was published in 1840 but written in 1827.
32. Bodde and Morris, *Law in Imperial China*, p. 142, in reference to the Autumn Assizes but intended to apply to the legal system as a whole. For an analysis of Chinese "due process" and the role of confession, see Conner, "Confucianism and Due Process."
33. Huang Liuhong, *Fukkei zensho*, 11.30b (differently translated in *A Complete Book*, p. 277).
34. Huang Yu, *Bixue lu*, 30b–31a.
35. *Qinding da Qing huidian shili*, 723.7b.
36. Huang Liuhong, *Fukkei zensho*, 11.31b (rephrased in *A Complete Book*, p. 278, to read: "Such practices are not proper conduct in the administration of public affairs"). For a very different account of the role of punishment in state formation in Confucius's own era, see Lewis, *Sanctioned Violence in Early China*, chap. 2.
37. Huang Liuhong, *Fukkei zensho*, 17.21a (*A Complete Book*, pp. 399–400).
38. The locus classicus for this view is Confucius's statement in the *Analects* (20:2), "To put the people to death without having instructed them;—this is called cruelty"; translated by James Legge in *The Chinese Classics*, vol. 1, p. 353.
39. *Jiading xianzhi* (1684), 2.19a. On Lu's reputation as an upright magistrate and conservative Confucian, see Brook, *The Chinese State in Ming Society*, pp. 169–170. The wisdom of avoiding torture was a common theme in popular court case fiction; see Sanders, "The Good Magistrate Never Tortures."
40. Quoted in Huang Zongxi, *Huang Zongxi quanji*, vol. 1, p. 216. Liu in the same passage argues similarly that the most powerful army is the one that does not go into battle. The emperor derided Liu's views as "perverse" and declined to respond to his suggestions.
41. See the cases quoted in Harrison, "Wrongful Treatment of Prisoners."
42. Huai Xiaofeng (ed.), *Da Ming lü*, p. 445; Tian Tao and Zheng Qin (eds.), *Da Qing lüli*, p. 62.

43. "If the punishment shall be increased to strangulation, then it shall not be increased to decapitation"; Jiang (trans.), *The Great Ming Code*, p. 45. See also Johnson (trans.), *The T'ang Code*, p. 270; Jones (trans.), *The Great Qing Code*, p. 70.

44. Johnson (trans.), *The T'ang Code*, p. 60.

45. Ibid., p. 39.

46. Wyatt, *The Recluse of Loyang*, p. 175.

47. *Ming taizong shilu*, 30.5b.

48. Ch'en, *Chinese Legal Tradition under the Mongols*, pp. 46, 153.

49. The seasonal practice of hearings and executions is laid out in Bodde and Morris, *Law in Imperial China*, pp. 561–562. On the Autumn Assizes, see pp. 46–48, 134–143.

50. The role of amnesties is explored in McKnight, *The Quality of Mercy*.

51. For example, late in 1391, the Hongwu emperor ordered that all punishments for first-time offenses by soldiers in the capital garrison, other than for capital crimes, be excused; *Ming taizu shilu*, 214.1a.

52. The Yongle emperor began in 1404 to review the cases of those awaiting sentences in the hottest period of the summer at what were called the Hot Weather Assizes *(reshen)*; see *Ming taizong shilu*, 30.5b; McKnight, *The Quality of Mercy*, p. 101. Yongle also instituted Cold Weather Assizes for parallel reasons; see *Ming taizong shilu*, 61.2b, 121.5a, 158.1a.

53. *Ming xiaozong shilu*, 198.10b–198.11a.

54. Ibid., 132.4a.

55. *Qing shizu zhang huangdi shilu*, 116.13a–116.14a.

56. Jones usefully correlates the crimes in the Ten Abominations with the actual articles in the Qing Code dealing with these crimes; *The Great Qing Code*, pp. 35–36.

57. These tallies were made by the Qing legal scholar Shen Jiaben; Ch'en, *Chinese Legal Tradition under the Mongols*, p. 43.

58. Foucault, *Discipline and Punish*, p. 14; Beattie, *Crime and the Courts*, pp. 590–592.

59. These numbers are taken from the revised list of 1585, reprinted in Huai Xiaofeng (ed.), *Da Ming lü*, pp. 273–291.

60. Bodde and Morris, *Law in Imperial China*, pp. 103–104.

61. According to Niida Noboru, the number of cuts could vary from 8 to 24 to 26 to 120; *Chūgoku hōseishi kenkyū: keihō*, pp. 153–165.

62. Ch'en, *Chinese Legal Tradition under the Mongols*, pp. 46–47.

63. Jiang (trans.), *The Great Ming Code*, pp. 154, 170–172, 183, 185, 187–188; Jones (trans.), *The Great Qing Code*, pp. 237, 270–271, 273–274, 297, 299, 303–304.

64. The application of lingchi to the slave who murders his master was introduced under the Yuan dynasty; see Ratchnevsky, *Un Code des Yuan*, vol. 4, p. 34.

65. Huai Xiaofeng (ed.), *Da Ming lü*, pp. 273–274. This provision is incorporated into the Qing Code under this article (307 in the Ming Code, 284 in the Qing Code) as subarticle 3. The 1497 list boosts the number of lingchi crimes to twelve by doubling several of the laws to refer specifically to crimes against affinal as well as agnatic relatives.

66. Huai Xiaofeng, *Da Ming lü*, pp. 293–294.
67. These articles are not translated in their entirety; only the sections related to lingchi appear here. We are grateful to Luca Gabbiani for assistance in translating these statutes.
68. Promulgated in 1811.
69. Promulgated in 1729; revised in 1740, 1788, 1801, and 1809.
70. Promulgated in 1801; revised in 1810. De Groot, *The Religious System of China*, vol. 3, p. 887, dates this article to 1845, possibly on the basis of a minor alteration made at that time.
71. Promulgated in 1811 on the basis of an imperial edict.
72. Promulgated in 1805 on the proposal of the governor of Shandong in the case of Liang Wangtai and Yu Fengjia, who in the course of poisoning Liang's uncle also killed his uncle's wife and her younger sister.
73. Promulgated in 1787 following a sentence of lingchi proposed by the governor of Shandong in the case of Woman Kong née Hu, concubine of Kong Erniu, who plotted to kill Kong's wife.
74. Promulgated in 1734.
75. Revised in 1740.
76. This provision originates in the *Wenxing tiaoli* of 1500, though the punishment was there phrased not as "put to death by lingchi" but as "break up the corpse and expose the head" (p. 417).
77. Codified in 1804 following an 1801 memorial from the governor-general of Sichuan and an 1802 memorial from the governor of Shandong; revised in 1852.
78. This article was promulgated in 1756 from three provisions, one that came into force in the Kangxi era, one from a memorial submitted by the governor of Hubei in 1748, and another from a memorial submitted by a grand secretary in 1754; revised in 1801 and 1807.
79. This article was promulgated in response to a memorial of 1783 concerning a case of matricide; the command to break up the corpse *(cuoshi)*, an archaic punishment, may be unique in the Qing Code.
80. Wang Yongkuan has minutely listed these acts of exceptional cruelty in his *Zhongguo gudai kuxing* (Cruel punishments in ancient China). The Japanese edition of 1997 bears the eye-catching but unfaithful title of *Kokkei: chi to senritsu no Chūgoku keibatsu shi* (Cruel punishments: China's penal history of gore and horror), unfaithful in the sense that much of what the book catalogues is illegal punishments imposed *outside* the law, not within it.
81. Twentieth-century sources are little better. The one exception is an article Niida Noboru wrote about the execution ground in Beijing, excerpts of which appear in his masterwork, *Chūgoku hōseishi kenkyū: keihō*. It recounts a visit he made in 1941 with Dong Kang, a jurist of the late Qing and early Republic who later died in jail on the charge of collaborating with Japan. But even these qualified observers produced an account that is short, anecdotal, and impressionistic, not scholarly or systematic. The article was first published in 1941 as "Shindai no Pekin no keijō keihō gakusha Dō Kō shi o tō."

82. Huang Liuhong, *Fukkei zensho,* 11.26b–11.32a; *A Complete Book,* pp. 274–279; see also pp. 458–460. The same is true of Wang Huizu, whose best-selling administrative handbook, *Zuozhi yaoyan* (Precepts for private secretaries), alludes to the death penalty but records nothing about executions.

83. Ch'ü T'ung-tsu's systematic study of Qing local administration is typical in this respect. The word "execution" appears only in one endnote distinguishing immediate and delayed executions; *Local Government in China under the Ch'ing,* p. 206, n. 36.

84. In an ambitious presentation of an alternative model to the Western conception of law, Thomas Stephens has put forward "principles of disciplinary theory" for China, but even he subsumes executions within general patterns in a way irresistibly reminiscent of Karl Wittfogel's absolutizing notion of "total power"; Stephens, *Order and Discipline in China,* pp. 23–26. His intellectual debt to Wittfogel is acknowledged by the title of his fifth chapter: "Total Terror, Total Submission, and Total Solitude."

85. This problem can be detected even in such useful studies as Dutton, *Policing and Punishing in China,* and McKnight, *Law and Order in Sung China.* Dutton furnishes sound textual evidence on the function of executions in the repressive apparatus, yet he relies on the abstract schemata in the writings and charts of Ming and Qing officials, not on real performances. McKnight's conclusions, that "penalties are messages" informing "both the powerful and the weak" to "tell the victim of his powerlessness" (p. 351), are true as far as they go, but there is no direct exemplification of these principles in practice.

86. There is one killing in *Water Margin* that is conducted something like a lingchi: Yang Xiong's murder of his wife in Chapter 45. This, however, is an act of private revenge rather than a legal punishment, and it is not phrased as a lingchi in the text. Shih Nai-an, *Water Margin,* p. 645.

87. For examples from the Liao dynastic history, see Tuotuo (ed.), *Liao shi,* pp. 9, 946.

88. In one brief exception to the lack of such accounts in Ming prefectural gazetteers, we read of a prefectural judge who in 1539 executed a gang of bandits, whose victims included a county registrar, in the marketplace of the prefectural capital; *Yunyang fuzhi* (1578), 2.22b.

89. The one historian who has included the execution ground in her work is Susan Naquin, who locates and describes the site in her *Peking: Temples and City Life,* pp. 271, 359, 419, n. 116; see also Bodde's "Prison Life in Eighteenth-Century Peking."

90. Nothing has been written for a Chinese city to match what Alain Corbin has done in "Le Sang de Paris," where the execution ground serves as the touchstone of a new urban sensibility in nineteenth-century Paris.

91. A glance at standard reference works indicates how little we know. Charles Hucker's *Dictionary of Official Titles in Imperial China* gives two terms for "executioner" (*zhanglu* in §157 and *sici* in §5805), neither of which dates from later than the first half of the first millennium B.C. (pp. 111, 458). Brunnert and Hagelstrom's *Present Day Political Organization of China* lists no term for executioner not even the standard word *kuaizi* (chopping hand).

92. The equipment includes an iron chain for restraining convicts, finger presses (costing a hundredth of an ounce of silver), a pair of ankle presses (costing a tenth of an ounce), a chopping block, half a dozen boards of various sorts, and some writing brushes; Shen Bang, *Wanshu zaji*, p. 147.

93. *Dan-Xin dang'an xuanlu: xinzheng bian chuji*, p. 342.

94. And even about the men who applied for the post when it fell vacant; see Smith, " 'I Could Hang Anything You Can Bring before Me.' "

95. For instance, no executioner appears among the many specialized subofficials Reed notes in *Talons and Teeth*, pp. 132–133, 150. He refers to torture and flogging in the subchapter devoted to the "use of punishments in the yamen," yet these references are to disciplinary sanctions imposed on yamen agents, not to the punishments they imposed.

96. Reasoning from Buddhist studies, Hannson assimilates executioners to professions like barber, butcher, skinner, and coroner, all of whom shared exposure to "permanent forms of pollution," yet he relies entirely on Korean *paekchong* and Japanese *burakumin* to corroborate this supposition; *Chinese Outcasts*, pp. 48–50, 135–136. In fact, the status of executioners in Tokugawa Japan is far from clear. Historians disagree about whether they belonged to the *burakumin*. The occupations to which the *burakumin* were restricted included "the meting out of punishments" *(keiri no shitabataraki)*, though the source—the *Buraku mondai jiten (Encyclopedia of Buraku Issues)*—that gives this information does not specify the nature of these punishments. *Hinin* (literally, "nonhumans," another outcast category) were designated as "executioners' helpers" but never said to act as executioners or *shikkei shikkōnin* themselves. According to Shiomi Senichirō, *Danzaemon to sono jidai*, pp. 14–16, the "execution of punishment" *(shioki)*, a term likely to signify the death penalty, was a prerogative of the *danzaemon*, the chief of an *eta* community, but there is no unambiguous evidence that Japanese executioners were outcasts. We are indebted to Dorothée Cibla for these observations.

97. Freeman-Mitford, *The Attaché at Peking*, pp. 195–198. For a more condescending eyewitness account of an execution in Guangzhou in 1894, see Norman, *The Peoples and Politics of the Far East*, pp. 229–230. One of the more interesting "facts" Norman learns from the executioner regards the fee for decapitation: "Formerly he used to get two dollars a head for all he cut off; now he only gets fifty cents." As Norman liked to portray East Asia as "the last Wonderland of the World" (p. vii), it is difficult to trust the veracity of this account. Norman bought the man's sword and took it back to England to hang on his wall as a cynical conversation piece, "a valuable antidote to much that I read about the advancing civilisation of China."

3. The Origins of Lingchi and Problems of Its Legitimacy

1. Norman, *The Peoples and Politics of the Far East*, p. 226. The chapter in which this statement appears displays the same tone. To offer another example: "But how

is the Western world to know what the Celestial Empire really is unless people are willing to see and hear of its innumerable horrors? The utterly mistaken notion of China which is so wide-spread at home is due in great part to this very unwillingness to look straight in the face what a French writer has so well called the 'rotten East' " (p. 223).

2. See, e.g., Wang Yongkuan, *Zhongguo gudai kuxing.* The curious reader may also refer to Des Rotours's fascinating articles on anthropophagy in Chinese history, most cases of which might be more insightfully discussed as slicing or dismembering than as cannibalism; "Quelques mots sur l'anthropophagie en Chine" and "Encore quelques mots sur l'anthropophagie en Chine."

3. A striking example of misinterpretation caused by lack of awareness of the basic characteristics of Chinese history is the chapter on China in Courtois et al., *The Black Book of Communism.* While other authors go back no further than the nineteenth century in their search for the roots of totalitarianism, the China specialist in this chapter wanders about picking up events recorded in the official histories across two thousand years, naively presenting them as evidence of an immemorial tendency to cruelty.

4. Quoted by Xue Yunsheng, *Tang Ming lü hebian,* 6a. Elman, *From Philosophy to Philology,* examines the *kaozheng* movement and situates Qian Daxin within it.

5. On Shen Jiaben's role in reforming China's prison system, see Dikötter, *Crime, Punishment and the Prison in Modern China,* pp. 46–49.

6. Even Shen Jiaben ("Xingfa fenkao," 2.19a) adopts the reading "delayed death" in referring to Xunzi's passage quoted below, in which the meaning is clearly "institutional decay."

7. The radical for "ice" is no. 15, while that for "hillock" is no. 170.

8. See particularly Yan Shigu's comments in Ban Gu, *Han shu, juan* 10, p. 317; *juan* 52, p. 2406.

9. Knoblock, *Xunzi,* vol. 3, book 28 ("Youzuo"), p. 247, with slight revisions. For other early passages in which *lingchi* connotes "institutional decay," see Ban Gu, *Han shu* ("Xingfa zhi," *juan* 3), p. 1109: "The *Book* [*of Documents*] says: 'Bo Yi bestowed ritual codes upon the populace so as to make them wiser instead of punishing them.' This means that the rites were settled as an embankment is raised against flooding waters. Now the embankments have collapsed [*lingchi*], the rites are no longer settled, death penalties are too harsh, and the corporal punishments are too lenient." In Sima Qian's biography of Zhang Shizhi in the *Shiji,* p. 2751, *lingchi* is used to refer to the "ruin of the Qin dynasty sealed in two generations."

10. Shen Jiaben, "Xingfa fenkao," 2.19a.

11. The character *chi* also underwent some variation, though of no great significance. A homophone, meaning "to hold" or "to compel," is attested in the *Liao shi;* see Qian Daxin, "Lingchi," 7a.

12. We agree with McKnight, *Law and Order in Sung China,* p. 451 n. 7—"The term *ling-ch'ih* is probably of foreign origin. The attempts to find Chinese roots for it

are unconvincing"—with the reservation that the characters are still worth scrutinizing for clues to the word's history.

13. Our thanks to Juha Janhunen for answering questions about Khitan origins of the term *lingchi.*

14. Franke notes the increasing harshness of Liao and Jin laws in "The Legal System of the Chin Dynasty," p. 403.

15. Franke, "The 'Treatise on Punishments' in the *Liao History:* An Annotated Translation," p. 12. This statement ironically anticipates the comments of nineteenth-century Westerners on the lawlessness and barbarism of the Chinese.

16. Shen Jiaben used the argument of the non-Chinese origin of lingchi in his memorial asking for its abolition. His more scholarly writings show, however, that he was not content with so simple an argument.

17. This construct dovetailed with a Chinese myth that the Yellow Emperor borrowed cruel punishments in antiquity from the barbarian Miao before the latter were "civilized" by Chinese laws. Playing with etymology, imperial scholars established many connections between "barbarian" peoples and the most fearsome legal atrocities. For instance, *luange* or "slicing" could be easily changed into *mange* or "barbarian cuts." The terrifying Extermination of the Three Clans *(yi sanzu),* treated later in this chapter, was in the same way connected to the Yi, non-Chinese who supposedly initiated this practice of annihilating all relatives of a criminal.

18. See Tachikawa and Shimada, *Ryōritsu no kenkyū,* pp. 1–3. On the Liao Code, see Shiga, *Chūgoku hōseishi ronshū,* pp. 155–58.

19. Tuotuo (ed.), *Liao shi,* p. 936.

20. Ibid., p. 937; translated with minor emendations in Wittfogel and Fêng, *History of Chinese Society: Liao,* p. 496. On "devil arrows," so called because shooting them was deemed to influence the outcome of a battle, see Wittfogel and Fêng, p. 268. For an example of pulling apart by carts in 913, see Wittfogel and Fêng, p. 412 *(Liao shi,* p. 8).

21. See McKnight, *Law and Order in Sung China,* p. 415.

22. For an instance of burial alive in 918, see Wittfogel and Fêng, *History of Chinese Society: Liao,* p. 413; for a shooting by devil arrows in 923, p. 414; for hacking to pieces *(zhe)* in 1100, p. 594; for dismemberment *(zhijie)* in 1115, p. 423.

23. Tachigawa and Shimada (*Ryōritsu no kenkyū,* p. 89) accept Shen Jiaben's affirmation that "this was the beginning of the punishment of lingchi, which did not exist previously." The definition is attributed to the later Song scholar Lu You, whose memorial is translated in the second part of this chapter.

24. The phrases "to die by lingchi" *(lingchi si)* and "to kill by lingchi" *(lingchi shasi)* are also attested. "To put to death" *(chusi)* was the standard term for execution, then as now (e.g., *Liao shi,* p. 939). It is worth noting, however, that similar extended phrases were used for other forms of execution; e.g., "to die by throwing oneself from a cliff" *(zi touya er si);* "to kill by being shot with devil arrows" *(yi guijian shesha zhi);* and "to be killed by strangling" *(jiaosha zhi, yisha zhi),* for which see *Liao shi,* pp. 8, 9, 1498.

25. See Niida, *Chūgoku hōseishi kenkyū: keihō,* pp. 392–393, where he connects the term *qishi* with lingchi.
26. Ibid., p. 542. The expression was used for Liu Jin's execution by lingchi in 1510 (see Chapter 4).
27. Takikawa and Shimada, *Ryōritsu no kenkyū,* p. 190.
28. See Hulsewé, *Remnants of Han Law,* pp. 112–122. For a principled objection to collective family punishments, see *Mencius* (1.2), "zuiren bu nu," translated by Legge in *The Chinese Classics,* vol. 2, p. 162, as "the wives and children of criminals were not involved in their guilt."
29. Niida, *Chūgoku hōseishi kenkyū: keihō,* pp. 183–185.
30. For conditions allowing a magistrate to excuse relatives of someone convicted of high treason from punishment, see Huang Liuhong, *Fukkei zensho,* 20.15b–16a; Huang Liu-hung, *A Complete Book concerning Happiness and Benevolence,* pp. 457–458.
31. See Ban Gu, *Han shu,* p. 317: "I can only abide by the Way, unless the imperial institution day by day enter into decay *(diwang zhi dao ri yi lingyi),*" which Yan Shigu glosses there (note 5) as follows: "*Ling* is a hill; *yi* means 'to level'; this expression means 'to decay like a hill is gradually eroded.' In other words, this is similar to the expression *qiuling zhi weichi* [the second and fifth characters make *lingchi*] which means 'to gradually lower.'"
32. Ban Gu, *Han shu,* p. 3494.
33. Tuotuo (ed.), *Song shi,* p. 4973.
34. Qian Daxin, "Lingchi," 7.7a–b.
35. Ma Duanlin, *Wenxian tongkao,* p. 1449, quoted in Shen Jiaben, "Xingfa fenkao," 17b.
36. See the collections of anthropophagous deeds in Chinese historical sources by des Rotours in "Quelques mots sur l'anthropophagie en Chine" and "Encore quelques mots sur l'anthropophagie en Chine." For some eloquent examples of slicing vendettas, see Shek, "Sectarian Eschatology and Violence," p. 104.
37. See the translation of "Order the circuit to ban human sacrifices to demons," in McKnight and Liu, *The Enlightened Judgments,* pp. 481–482.
38. See Wei Tai, *Dongxuan bilu,* 5.54; Shao Bowen, *Shaoshi wenjian lu,* pp. 92, 714. We are indebted to Christian Lamouroux for explaining this difficult case and mentioning private sources that question the verdict proclaimed in official histories.
39. Ma Duanlin, *Wenxian tongkao,* p. 1449.
40. See Lu You, "Tiaodui zhuang," in his *Weinan wenji,* 5.5a–6b. Praising Han Wendi for doing away with harsh penalties became a conventional trope for arguing for mitigation of punishments by not just officials but emperors as well. For example, the Ming emperor Hongzhi (r. 1488–1505) declared his admiration for Wendi on this point and wondered aloud to his officials how he managed to do it; *Ming xiaozong shilu,* 73.3b.
41. Remonstrating officials—"reminders" is a more exact translation of the Chinese term *shiyi*—were responsible for catching and correcting errors of substance and style in state documents; see Hucker, *A Dictionary of Official Titles in*

Imperial China, §5256, p. 425. Dou Yan's biography is in Tuotuo (ed.), *Song shi, juan* 263.

42. Xue Juzheng (ed.), *Jiu wudai shi,* p. 1971; quoted also in the biography of Dou Yan (see preceding note). This memorial is mentioned in McKnight, *Law and Order in Sung China,* p. 451, n. 9: "In the Treatise on Punishments of the Old History of the Five Dynasties, there is a description of an execution using a short knife. Although the term *ling-ch'ih* is not used, it seems clear that it was the punishment used."

43. Hulsewé, *Remnants of Han Law,* pp. 55–61; most of the long list of legislative changes are ameliorations of harsh punishments obtained by memorials of this kind.

44. Ibid., p. 333.

45. Ibid., pp. 42, 60.

46. Ouyang Xiu (ed.), *Xin Tang shu,* p. 221. Beccaria made his case in his *On Crimes and Punishments,* first published in Italian in 1764.

47. From the report in the dynastic history, the Taihe Code adopted the punishment system of the Tang Code; Tuotuo (ed.), *Jin shi,* p. 1024. The highest codified punishment in the Jin, as in the Tang, was decapitation; see Franke, "The Legal System of the Chin Dynasty," p. 400.

48. Song Lian (ed.), *Yuan shi,* p. 2605; Ratchnevsky, *Un Code des Yuan,* vol. 1, p. 8.

49. See Qiu Jun, *Daxue yanyi bu,* 104.12a–b (p. 1002 in the modern edition).

50. See Umehara, *Chūgoku kinsei keihō shi,* p. 6, n. 14; p. 8.

51. Ratchnevsky, *Un Code des Yuan,* vol. 4, pp. 41–42.

52. Song Lian (ed.), *Yuan shi,* p. 103 ("Xingfa zhi," *juan* 2); Umehara, *Chūgoku kinsei keihō shi,* pp. 170, 174, 185.

53. See Xue Yunsheng (ed.), *Tang Ming lü hebian,* 17.5a–b [p. 171], 17.1a [p. 169]; Xue Yunsheng, *Duli cunyi,* pp. 255, 556.

54. See, for instance, the Western Mountain trial studied by Pierre-Henri Durand, *Lettrés et pouvoirs: un procès littéraire dans la Chine impériale.*

55. This can be found in cases in the *Xing'an huilan* (Conspectus of criminal cases), one of which is translated in Bodde and Morris, *Law in Imperial China,* pp. 321–323; also Lauwaert, *Le Meurtre en famille,* pp. 95ff.

56. Wang Mingde, *Dulü peixi, juan* 4, "Wuxing," 8b–9a.

57. The term *run* in Wang Mingde's expression *runxing* refers to the intercalary days or years that were periodically added to make lunar months square with the solar year; the term also connoted "illegitimacy" of a sovereign or dynasty. In the influential *Daxue yanyi bu,* 104.7–8, Qiu Jun uses the more explicit term *fawai,* literally "outside the law." On the notion of *run* and *zheng* in assessing legitimacy of the dynasties in Chinese history, see Hok-lam Chan, "Chinese Official Historiography at the Yüan Court," pp. 70–71.

58. Shen Jiaben, "Xingfa fenkao," 19a.

59. The idea that Chinese law aimed at restoring cosmic order has been much repeated in Western sinology. Hsu Dau-lin, "Crime and Cosmic Order," pp. 111–115, argues that this is a misinterpretation of Chinese law and ethics.

60. Hulsewé, *Remnants of Han Law*, p. 42.

61. Tuotuo (ed.), *Liao shi*, p. 943, quoted from a memorial of the following year.

62. Bo Yikao, the eldest son of future King Wen of the Zhou dynasty, was cut up and cooked by cruel King Zhou of the Shang dynasty, to be offered to his father in a banquet.

63. Wang Mingde, "Wuxing," in his *Dulü peixi*, 4.9b–4.10a.

64. See the description of lingchi and decapitations in Meadows, "Description of an Execution at Canton ," written in 1851 a month after the author attended the executions. "Callousness" is the expression used by Norman, *The Peoples and Politics of the Far East*, p. 227.

65. Morrison, *An Australian in China*, pp. 231, 232.

66. Ibid., p. 232.

67. Alabaster, *Notes and Commentaries on Chinese Criminal Law and Cognate Topics*, pp. 57–58.

68. De Groot, *The Religious System of China*, vol. 1, pp. 342, 344.

69. Ibid., vol. 3, pp. 1068–1069 (emphasis added).

70. For example, Lauwaert translates *can* as "suffering" *(souffrance)*, which in our view pushes this view to its logical, absurd conclusion: "The coffin is a part of the corpse, which unambiguously resents the same sufferings as the living body"; *Le Meurtre en famille*, p. 92.

71. On the concept of *peine réfléchissante*, translating the German *spiegelstrafe*, see Carbasse, *Introduction historique au droit pénal*, pp. 210–211.

72. On the widespread repugnance toward corporal punishments in general at the end of the Qing, see Dikötter, *Crime, Punishment and the Prison*, pp. 39–46.

73. Bourgon, " 'Sauver la vie': de la fraude judiciaire en Chine à la fin de l'empire," pp. 32–39.

74. The last lingchi in Chinese history—the execution of Fuzhuli on 9 April 1905—was prosecuted by commissioners selected from the specialized service of the Board of Punishments that was at the same moment preparing the documents for abolition. This dilemma is echoed sixty years later in Xu Shiying's memoirs, *Xu Shiying huiyi lu*.

75. Meijer, *The Introduction of Modern Criminal Law in China*, p. 32.

76. Bourgon, "Abolishing 'Cruel Punishments, pp. 853–856.' "

4. Lingchi in the Ming Dynasty

1. On Hongwu's reign and vision, see Edward Farmer, *Zhu Yuanzhang and Early Ming Legislation*; he briefly introduces the *Grand Pronouncements* (see below) on pp. 52–58. The entries in the *Grand Pronouncements* are numbered. Parenthetical citations are to this text and designate first, second, or third compilation followed by the entry number.

2. Yu Jideng, *Diangu jiwen*, p. 73.

3. Ratchnevsky, *Un Code des Yuan*, vol. 4, pp. 41–42. Hongwu's role in the compilation of the Ming Code is outlined in Dardess, "The Code and *ad hoc* Legislation in Ming Law," pp. 86–87.

4. *Imperially Compiled Grand Pronouncements (Yuzhi dagao)* was completed at the end of 1385 (tenth month), *Further Collection of Grand Pronouncements (Dagao xubian)* in the late spring of 1386 (third month), and *Third Collection of Grand Pronouncements (Dagao sanbian)* early in 1387 (twelfth month). *Grand Pronouncements to Military Officials (Dagao wuchen)* was issued in 1388, but since neither its preface nor its case summaries contain any references to lingchi, we exclude it from consideration in this book. The history and significance of the text are examined in Anita Andrew, "Zhu Yuanzhang and the 'Great Warnings,'" and Yang Yifan, *Ming dagao yanjiu*. We are grateful to Tim Sedo for sharing these materials with us. On the harsh punishments in the *Grand Pronouncements*, see Huang Zhangjian, "Ming Hongwu Yongle chao de bangwen junling," pp. 241–243.

5. *Gong'an* (*kōan* in Japanese) is the term used for problems Chan / Zen teachers set for their students. The genre is explored in Furth et al., *Thinking with Cases*; see in particular the chapter by Jiang Yonglin and Wu Yanhong on Ming courts.

6. This statement assumes that he was indeed the writer of the stories. The books appeared too quickly for Hongwu to have authored them single-handedly, yet they have a colloquial style that suggests someone other than a scholarly ghost-writer was authoring them. The strongly oral tone could indicate that Hongwu dictated them to his secretaries.

7. Andrew, "Zhu Yuanzhang and the 'Great Warnings,'" pp. 208–209.

8. Dardess, "The Code and *ad hoc* Legislation in Ming Law," p. 88, citing the *Huang Ming zuxun* (Ancestral instructions of the Ming dynasty).

9. Zhu Yuanzhang, "Wen xingshang" (Soliciting opinions on penalties and rewards), *Ming taizu ji*, p. 200. Emperor Wen's suspension of corporal punishments is mentioned in Ban Gu, *Han shu*, pp. 125, 1099. On the Five Punishments in the Han, which were different from those in the Ming, see *Han shu*, p. 1079.

10. The same shift can be detected in Zhu Yuanzhang's treatment of religion; see Brook, *The Chinese State in Ming Society*, pp. 139–146.

11. *Ming taizu shilu, juan* 253, fifth month, jiayin day.

12. Zhu Yuanzhang, "Yuzhi dagao sanbian xu" (Preface to the third compilation of imperially authored Grand Pronouncements), in Yang Yifan, *Ming dagao yanjiu*, p. 342.

13. The punishments in the *Grand Pronouncements* attracted the attention of Shen Jiaben at the end of the Qing dynasty. His notes on the text were published as "*Ming dagao* junling."

14. Shen Jiaben, "*Ming dagao* junling," 3b; Lei Menglin, *Dulü suoyan*, p. 436.

15. In pre-Ming texts, the term jixing ("extreme punishment") is used for such penalties as strangulation, decapitation, and beating to death, as it is for all three in the standard history of the Five Dynasties: Xue Juzheng, *Jiu wudai shi*, pp. 1966, 1977. Shen Jiaben too suspected that the *jixing* cases were lingchi cases, this being the most extreme penalty, but did not provide proof; "*Ming dagao* junling," 9b. Shen chose to read the case that follows as a lingchi case.

16. Shen Jiaben makes this point (ibid., 9b); see also his comment on 5b concerning the untouchability of banner soldiers.
17. According to the Suzhou gazetteer of 1506, Zhang Heng, a northerner, took up his post in 1380 (*Gusu zhi*, 3.39a). No magistrate by the name of Yao Xu appears in the list of county officials, though the entries for Wu and Changzhou magistrates are entirely blank for the period 1373–1388 (ibid., 4.37b–4.38b). Possibly the blank is a telltale sign that Yao and others were removed on suspicion of involvement in plots against the dynasty.
18. Shen Jiaben, "*Ming dagao* junling," 4a.
19. A contributor to the Ming dynastic history (Zhang Tingyu, *Ming shi*, p. 2318) declares the third collection more lenient than the first and second—a curious judgment that glosses over the striking increase in the number of lingchi cases in the third collection.
20. Shen Jiaben, "*Ming dagao* junling," 5b, notes that many commentators subsequently criticized this sentence as excessively harsh.
21. Ibid., 6a–6b.
22. The corresponding Code punishments for the crimes for which Hongwu imposed lingchi are given in Yang Yifan, *Ming dagao yanjiu*, pp. 65–67. He is not quite correct in every case, however, and particularly in his assessment of Pan Xing's actions as amounting to abetting high treason.
23. The severity of Hongwu's response can help us understand the continuing use of the death penalty for such crimes in China today. Whereas jurists outside China regard execution for economic crime simply as a failure to adopt international norms, the case of the soaked beans suggests that Chinese courts today are working within a tradition that goes back at least to the late fourteenth century.
24. As we noted in Chapter 2, an official on a maritime expedition Java to was dismayed to discover that the Malays did not flog criminals but put them to death without differentiating the severity of the crimes; Mills, *Yingyai shenglan*, p. 88. Indiscriminate punishments were offensive to the Chinese legal sensibility because they failed to acknowledge the specific moral weights of different offenses.
25. Zhu Yuanzhang, "Yuanxing lun" (On the nature of punishments), in *Ming taizu ji*, p. 233.
26. Ibid., p. 232.
27. "Yuzhi dagao xu" (Preface to the imperially authored Grand Pronouncements), in Yang Yifan, *Ming dagao yanjiu*, p. 197.
28. *Ming taizu shilu*, 214.1a.
29. *Da Ming huidian*, 20.22a–20.22b; regarding the tribute student exam, see 77.14a, 78.7b. The notion of families as the unit within which knowledge of and respect for penal law would be passed down through the generations was one of the hopes in the 1760s of French penal reformer Jean-Jacques Servan, who sought to change punishments not to mitigate them as much as turn them to pedagogical uses; see Foucault, *Discipline and Punish*, p. 112. The defeat of this reform ideal by the disciplinary prison model is discussed briefly in Chapter 7.

30. Yang Yifan, *Ming dagao yanjiu,* p. 65.
31. *Ming taizu shilu,* 251.3a.
32. Ibid., 253.1a.
33. Zhang Tingyu (ed.), *Ming shi,* p. 2284.
34. These lists are reproduced in Huang Zhangjian's study of the lost book; see his "*Da Ming lügao* kao," pp. 157–166. On the use of cash redemption in Ming law, see Dardess, "The Code and *ad hoc* Legislation in Ming Law," pp. 102–110.
35. Anita Andrew states that Hongwu's combination of the Ming Code and the Grand Pronouncements "ceased to be a viable code even before the end of the fifteenth century"; see her "Zhu Yuanzhang and the 'Great Warnings,'" p. 214.
36. These proclamations were published in the ministry's Jiajing-era gazetteer, *Nanjing xingbu zhi,* and have been transcribed in Huang Zhangjian, "Ming Hongwu Yongle chao de bangwen junling," pp. 263–286. This material rather undercuts Yonglin Jiang's suggestion (*The Great Ming Code,* p. lxxxiii) that Hongwu came to realize the limited value of cruel punishments toward the end of his reign.
37. The case of lingchi being used to punish a minor official for hiding his father's death so as to not have to observe mourning is mentioned by Zhang Yi, *Yuguang jianqi ji,* p. 9, who cites the case from a set of Hongwu-era legal precedents in the Ministry of Justice.
38. On Jianwen's view, see Zhang Tingyu (ed.), *Ming shi,* p. 2285.
39. Yongle's statement confirming the authority of the Hongwu judicial system at the end of 1402 is quoted in Huang Zhangjian, "Ming Hongwu Yongle chao de bangwen junling," p. 244.
40. *Ming taizong shilu,* 27.4a.
41. Zhang Tingyu (ed.), *Ming shi,* p. 4019. Fang's death is described in Elman, "The Formation of the 'Dao Learning' as Imperial Ideology," pp. 58–59.
42. Zhang Yi, *Yuguang jianqi ji,* p. 11. See pp. 234–235 for two cases of lingchi during the Yongle reign that involved feeding the sliced flesh to either the victim or his kinsman.
43. *Ming taizong shilu,* 17.2a; Huang Zhangjian, "Ming Hongwu Yongle chao de bangwen junling," pp. 285–286; *Da Ming huidian,* 20.23a.
44. Huang Zhangjian, "Ming Hongwu Yongle chao de bangwen junling," pp. 259–262.
45. Lu Rong, *Shuyuan zaji,* p. 123; Lu does not refer to lingchi in these comments.
46. Ye Chunji, *Huian zhengshu,* 9.21a.
47. Chen Zizhuang, preface to Yan Junyan, *Mengshui zhai cundu,* p. 3.
48. According to Zhang Wenlin, *Duanyan gong nianpu,* 20b–21b, Liu Jin was scheduled to be cut an unprecedented 3,357 times. The tormentors got through 357 cuts the first day, leaving Liu well enough to eat gruel that evening—his ability to digest being taken as further evidence of his criminality. Liu expired after several dozen cuts the following morning. The families of those whom he had harmed got pieces of his flesh to present as sacrificial offerings before their ancestors' spirit tablets.
49. Robinson, *Bandits, Eunuchs, and the Son of Heaven,* p. 154; Zhang Yi, *Yuguang jianqi ji,* p. 25.

50. For some prominent cases of lingchi execution from the Jiajing, Wanli, and Chongzhen eras, see Wang Yongkuan, *Zhongguo gudai kuxing*, pp. 4–6.
51. Zhang Yi, *Yuguang jianqi ji*, p. 25.
52. Gui Youguang, *Zhenchuan xiansheng ji*, p. 923. Gui compared his own era unfavorably with the Kaiyuan era of the high Tang (713–741), when it was said that there were only twenty-four capital cases in the entire country. To give context to Gui's numbers, Changxing county in 1488 had a registered population of 30,184 households, based on the census figures produced when county boundaries were redrawn that year; *Changxing xianzhi* (1805), 7.3a.
53. Yan Junyan, *Mengshui zhai cundu*, pp. 21, 41, 556, 670.

5. Tormenting the Dead

1. Le Goff, *The Birth of Purgatory*, p. 4. Isabel Moreira argues that hell begins to take clear form in the European imagination only in the sixth century; *Dreams, Visions, and Spiritual Authority in Merovingian Gaul*, p. 143, n. 30. On the vivid imaginings of the torment awaiting sinners in the Christian hell, see Camporesi, *The Fear of Hell*, pt. 1.
2. Étiemble discusses how medieval European iconography drew on East Asian precedents for images of hell and the devil; *L'Europe chinoise*, vol. 1, pp. 165–175.
3. The pioneering prison reformer Cesare di Beccaria alludes to the Christian theology of purgation through pain—and scoffs at the idea that anyone could still believe such a thing in the eighteenth century; *On Crimes and Punishments*, p. 36.
4. Richard von Glahn endorses this methodology in the closing sentences of *The Sinister Way*, where he notes that "by examining the ever-changing world of vernacular religion we can catch a glimpse of how the lives and thoughts of ordinary Chinese were conditioned by the time they lived in" (p. 265).
5. Le Goff, *The Birth of Purgatory*, p. 359.
6. The following observations, based on nineteenth-century sources, are not unique to this period, though the thinness of visual materials depicting popular conceptions of the afterlife before the nineteenth century makes it difficult to reconstruct the earlier history of these images. What Stephen Teiser reconstructs of views of the afterlife in the Tang dynasty in *The Scripture on the Ten Kings and the Making of Purgatory in Medieval Chinese Buddhism* suggests continuity over the millennium separating the Tang and the Qing, yet the visual representations he reproduces from Tang documents depict a realm much less terrifying and tortured than what nineteenth-century sources show. Studies of Chinese conceptions of purgatory, including an essay by Sawada Mizuho on the *Jade Register*, have been published in Sakamoto Kaname (ed.), *Jigoku no sekai*.
7. In *Chinese Ritual and Politics*, Emily Ahern lends the homology critical meaning by observing that people were capable of manipulating this relationship in their own interests. By acting out bureaucratic experience, "the Chinese religious and ritual system served a teaching function in which peasants learned about their government" (p. 96). She suggests that "religion and ritual in the hands of those

outside officialdom could have threatened the authority of officials" and as well "could have served the interests of those subject to imperial power" (p. 78).

8. Edgerton, *Pictures and Punishment*, p. 66.

9. Niida Noboru, *Chūgoku hōseishi kenkyū: keihō*, p. 612.

10. The torture of being bound front-first to a heated pillar, one of the penalties shown in the *Jade Register*, is attested in the Liao dynastic history; see Wittfogel and Fêng, *History of Chinese Society: Liao*, p. 414. The possibility of Central Asian origins for some of the tortures is suggested by a measure of correspondence to Islamic (notably Ottoman) traditions; see Peters, *Crime and Punishment in Islamic Law*, p. 101.

11. Taussig, *Mimesis and Alterity*, pp. 2, 86.

12. *Yuli chaozhuan zhujie jingshi baofa* (1892), 2.60a.

13. This text attracted the attention of missionary scholars a century ago. The more optimistic proselytizers read its colorful depiction of hell as a realm from which one could be redeemed only through faith as "a sort of preparation for Christianity, in the way of familiarizing the minds of the people with phraseology which may be used in describing the Christian redemption in several particulars," as Joseph Edkins put it (*Chinese Buddhism*, p. 365). For a quick survey of early studies of this text by Giles, Doré, and Wieger, see Goodrich, *Chinese Hells*, p. 79.

14. Although the *Jade Register* was the most widely circulated morality book at the end of the imperial era, its textual history has never been reconstructed; see Sawada Mizuho, *Jigoku hen: Chūgoku no meikai setsu*, pp. 30–36. A nineteenth-century version was translated into English and published in 1898 in the *Journal of the China Branch of the Royal Asiatic Society*. The translator, George Clarke, provided no bibliographic data, not even a Chinese title, but the style of illustration suggests that it is *Yuli zhibao bian* (1873). Clarke worked as a missionary in Yunnan and Guizhou in the 1880s and likely acquired his copy in the southwest.

15. The price was modest but not negligible. By way of comparison, a peck *(dou)* of rice in the Guangxu era in Guan county, Sichuan, cost several hundred cash; *Guanxian zhi*, p. 325.

16. The copy used here was discarded by the East Asian Library of the University of Toronto as a duplicate about 1973. It had probably been donated by the family of one of the many Canadian missionaries who worked in Sichuan. The copy of *Yuli chaozhuan jingshi* (1883) in the United Church of Canada archives at Victoria College, University of Toronto, was donated by Canadian missionary D. S. Korn, who acquired it in Sichuan in 1917.

17. *Ming Taizu shilu*, 203.2b.

18. A preface and phonetic glossary of difficult characters were added in 1809, by which time the book may have been in wide circulation. No editions we have been able to see predate the 1860s. An undated postface by Liu Pinghai from Xuzhou prefecture, Sichuan, says that the book languished unprinted in Weiyuan county (70 miles to the north) until he raised the funds to have the blocks recut; the testimonial of another patron in the book notes that he received his copy from Liu in 1871 after being away for two years. Liu's dating is

corroborated by a sample prayer to the Stove God that directs the petitioner to fill in the blanks for name and date, using the reign era of Tongzhi (1862–1874).

19. For a late Ming example of a purgatorial scene from a popular novel employing similar visual rhetoric, see Zhou Xinhui (ed.), *Mingdai banke tushi*, p. 584.

20. Dai Dayi, "Longhua si xinjian Mituo dian bei" (Stele commemorating the newly built Amida Hall in Longhua Monastery, 1572), in Chai Zhiguang and Pan Mingquan (eds.), *Shanghai fojiao beike wenxian ji*, p. 137.

21. On "imperial cosmocracy," see Feuchtwang, *Popular Religion in China*, p. 211.

22. The original text is translated in Teiser, *The Scripture on the Ten Kings*, pp. 197–216; see also Niida Noboru, *Chūgoku hōseishi kenkyū*, pp. 597–614. Another religious text that employs this motif is the apocryphal *Shiwang baojuan* (Precious scroll of the Ten Kings), reprinted in vol. 14 of the Baojuan chuji (Precious scrolls, first series) collection edited by Zhang Xishun.

23. The relationship between transformation texts and the Mulian drama is briefly explored in Qitao Guo, *Ritual Opera and Mercantile Lineage*, pp. 94–95; we return to the Mulian story below.

24. Von Glahn, *The Sinister Way*, pp. 136, 142.

25. The Ten Kings are (1) King Guang of Qin (Qin guang wang), (2) Chu River King (Chujiang wang), (3) Emperor King of Song (Songdi wang), (4) King of the Five Offices (Wuguan wang), (5) Son-of-Heaven Yama (Yanluo tianzi), (6) King of Kaifeng City (Biancheng wang), (7) King of Mount Tai (Taishan wang), (8) King of the Capital (Shoudu wang), (9) King of the Common Denominator (Pingdeng wang), and (10) King Who Turns the Wheel of Rebirth (Zhuanlun wang).

26. The Chaozhou edition is also distinctive in including medical lore. Its second chapter prints 200 medical prescriptions, and there are several more in the appendix. One modern edition, the 1979 Taiwan edition of *Yuli baochao jingshi wen*, also includes medical information, giving 106 prescriptions.

27. The predominance of Sichuan editions may also reflect the history of foreign collection since these texts were of particular interest to missionaries and Sichuan was an active mission field at the turn of the twentieth century, particularly for Canadian missionaries, who were responsible for preserving three of the editions examined in this chapter.

28. The Baodingshan complex is studied in Kucera, "Lessons in Stone: Baodingshan and its Hell Imagery"; see also von Glahn, *The Sinister Way*, pp. 135–139.

29. Harrison, *The Man Awakened from Dreams*, p. 51.

30. See the reproductions in Teiser, *The Scripture of the Ten Kings*, pp. 180–195; plates 6a, 6b, 7b, 8b, and 11b show what the text calls "annoyances" (pp. 212, 215).

31. Stevenson, "Text, Image, and Transformation in the History of the *Shuilu fahui*," p. 39, notes that the Ten Kings were among the deities represented at these masses. For a woodblock illustration from the Chongzhen era (1628–1644) very much in the style of the nineteenth-century images reproduced in this chapter, see Zhou Xinhui, *Zhongguo gudai xiqu banhua ji*, p. 584, which reproduces the illustration from the Yuming tang edition of *Tanhua ji* included in *Zhongguo banhua congshu*.

32. On the Stove God, see Chard, "Rituals and Scriptures of the Stove God."

33. On the fit between hell punishments and crimes, see Goodrich, *Chinese Hells*, pp. 108–110.

34. Zhenjizi, "*Yuli chaozhuan zhu* bianxu" (Compiler's preface), 1.6a, in *Yuli chaozhuan zhujie jingshi baofa*.

35. Huang shi, "Guan shengdi jun jiangxu" (Preface of invocation to Emperor Guan), 1.2b–1.3a, in *Yuli chaozhuan zhujie jingshi baofa*.

36. In the tenth century, the *chu* in the title meant "first," indicating that this river is where the dead crossed into purgatory; see Teiser, *The Scripture on the Ten Kings*, pp. 33, 185. By the nineteenth century, it had been replaced by the place name Chu, the literary toponym for Hunan province; the original name had lost its meaning, allowing *chu* to signal a location on the familiar administrative map of China. Nineteenth-century texts also alter the title of Biancheng wang, who oversees the sixth court. The *bian* of Biancheng, originally "transformation," was substituted for by a rare homophone that, with a water radical added to the right, would be the literary toponym for the city of Kaifeng. *Cheng* is here altered accordingly, from "completion" to "city." A process of semiliterate re-rendering may have been at work.

37. On the literal signs of punishment for sexual misconduct in tenth-century accounts of hell torture, see Alan Cole, *Mothers and Sons in Chinese Buddhism*, chap. 5, esp. pp. 178–179.

38. The punishment of being cut in two was associated popularly with Yama, according to the tale told to Sister Xianglin in Lu Xun's story "New Year's Sacrifice," published in 1924; see *Selected Stories of Lu Hsun*, p. 141.

39. Zhu Yuanzhang, *Dagao xubian*, in Yang Yifan, *Ming dagao yanjiu*, p. 293.

40. On the displeasure of viewing, see Elkins, *The Object Stares Back*, pp. 29, 33, 95, 115.

41. *Yuli chaozhuan zhujie jingshi baofa* (1892), 1.6b–8b.

42. *Wujiang zhi* (Gazetteer of Wujiang county, 1488), 5.22b–5.23a.

43. *Yuli chaozhuan zhujie jingshi baofa* (1892), 2.26b.

44. Dunch, *Fuzhou Protestants and the Making of a Modern China*, p. 8.

45. *Wanguo gongbao*, no. 480 (16 March 1878), quoted in Edkins, *Chinese Buddhism*, p. 367.

46. Missionary George Clarke, who translated one version of the *Jade Register*, found the similarity between Christian and Chinese hells troubling, when he had to explain to his Chinese flock how they were different. He had similar difficulty explaining that the Jade Emperor and the Christian God were not the same; see Clarke, "The Yü-li or Precious Records," p. 241.

47. Baudrillard, *Symbolic Exchange and Death*, pp. 144–145.

48. *Yuli chaozhuan zhujie jingshi baofa* (1892), 2.21b (Pang Yangzhi); 26b (Qui Fuchu); 61b (Li Hengfa and Fan); 62b (Li Shuyu).

49. *Yuli chaozhuan jingshi* (1883), 2.54a, 55b.

50. Huang Zongxi, "Diyu" (Purgatory/hell), in *Huang Zongxi quanji*, pp. 198–199.

51. Taussig, "Culture of Terror—Space of Death," pp. 164–165.

52. Feng Yaoyan's preface to *Yuli zhibao bian* (1873), 1a–1b.

53. Taussig, "Culture of Terror—Space of Death," p. 138.

54. A photograph taken by a missionary in a Sichuan (Chengdu?) monastery about 1910, now in the Foreign Missions Photograph Collection of the United Church of Canada / Victoria University Archives (ACC 2000.017, Item 1193), shows figurines in various states of torment at the bridge the dead must take to cross the River Nai (the Chinese counterpart to the River Styx in Roman mythology, which may explain the photographer's interest in this scene). The bridge was under the supervision of the Chu River King. Statues of this sort were on display in at least one Beijing monastery at the end of the nineteenth century, as Anne Goodrich shows in *Chinese Hells*.

55. Qitao Guo has reproduced some of these images in his study of the Mulian epic in *Ritual Opera and Mercantile Lineage*, pp. 118–127.

56. Liu Dapeng, the village literatus featured in Henrietta Harrison's *The Man Awakened from Dreams*, may be typical of this sort of marginalized figure: tied to the old order as it was collapsing, morally conservative for want of any other foundation for his ethics, and supportive of purgatory temples to show people the consequences they must suffer later for their evil conduct. Significantly, he recalls playing a childhood game that involved catching another boy and interrogating him as though young Liu himself were King Yama (p. 24).

57. Jonathan Spence suggests that the dreadful images in the *Jade Register* may have shaped the religious imagination of Hong Xiuquan, the messianic leader of the Taiping Rebellion, although Hong later came to regard the book's theology as blasphemous; see *God's Chinese Son*, pp. 38–46, 92.

6. Chinese Torture in the Western Mind

1. For interpretations of *Le Jardin des supplices* as decadent Sadean romanticism, see Praz, *The Romantic Agony*, pp. 278–279, and Hsieh, *From Occupation to Revolution*, p. 158 n. 13; as literary misogyny, see Carr, *Anarchism in France*, p. 19, and Dijkstra, *Idols of Perversity*. For the novel's denunciations of colonial violence in India and Algeria, see *Le Jardin des supplices*, pp. 159–164, 179–180; *Torture Garden*, pp. 171–175, 188–189.

2. See Praz, *The Romantic Agony*.

3. Astier Loufti, *Littérature et colonialisme*, p. 31.

4. The influence of *Le Jardin des supplices* on Kafka's novel is explored in Burns, *"In the Penal Colony."* The importance of Bataille's lingchi photographs to his overall philosophy is asserted in his last book, *Les Larmes d'Éros* (p. 627); we contest that assertion in Chapter 8 below.

5. Cohen, *History in Three Keys*.

6. Schau, *The Carnival of Blood and Fire*.

7. J. J. Matignon, the French embassy's medical attaché in Beijing, testified to the sense of terror that gripped the besieged Western diplomatic legations in the summer of 1900, when their members contemplated the prospect that they might all be "tortured, roasted, impaled, [or] flayed alive" by the Boxers; *Dix ans aux pays du dragon*, e.g. pp. 32, 52, 59.

278 **Notes to Pages 154–158**

8. Stereotypical Orientalist fantasies of the harem are examined in Grosrichard, *The Sultan's Court*, and Kabbani, *Europe's Myths of Orient*, though neither pays much attention to China. Ballaster, *Fabulous Orients*, examines British treatments of Confucian morality as well as seraglio tales pertaining to Persia and Turkey, but does not consider accounts of the Chinese emperor's household.

9. Asad, "On Torture, or Cruel, Inhuman, and Degrading Treatment," pp. 1091–1094.

10. Torture practices and police brutality under the British Raj are reviewed in Ruthven, *Torture: The Grand Conspiracy*, pp. 183–215, which notes the attempts of reformers from the 1840s to publicize such matters, and the persistent efforts of successive governments to conceal official reports on the grounds that the British public would react negatively.

11. Armando Cortesao's introduction to Pires's *Suma Oriental* analyzes the different versions of the ambassador's personal fate.

12. Mendoza's work went through multiple editions in Spanish as well as in Italian, Latin, French, English, Dutch, and German translations. Citations here are from the 1588 English translation, revised to modern spelling conventions. On prisons and punishments, as on diverse other topics, Mendoza drew on materials prepared earlier by the missionaries Martin de Rada and Gaspar da Cruz, who had worked underground in China; see Boxer (ed.), *South China in the Sixteenth Century*, pp. 18–20, 178–179, 298–299; also Spence, *The Chan's Great Continent: China in Western Minds*, chap. 2.

13. Mendoza, *History of the Great and Mighty Kingdom*, pp. 83–85.

14. De Bry and De Bry, *Orientalisch Indien*, vol. 2 (1598); the plate showing these tortures is reproduced as Abbildung-Nr. 13 in Sun, *Wandlungen des europäischer Chinabildes*, p. 163.

15. Ibid., pp. 41–42, 82, 84, 86, 89.

16. Mendes Pinto, *The Voyages and Adventures of Fernand Mendes Pinto*, pp. 126, 138.

17. Semedo, *The History of the Great and Renowned Monarchy of China*, pp. 219–220. Cantini, *Torture Instruments*, illustrates several cages used as penal devices in central Europe from the sixteenth to the eighteenth centuries (pp. 40–41, Plates 18–20 and 22).

18. Semedo, *History*, pp. 133–137, 140–143, 215, 219.

19. Ibid., p. 142. The Spanish Jesuit Adriano de las Cortes expressed a similar idea in a text he composed in the mid-1620s, in which he states that no people in the world show greater obedience to their judges and ministers than the Chinese, though their compliance is won by fear of the rod (Las Cortes, *Le Voyage en Chine*, p. 139). Las Cortes's manuscript, long buried in the archives, has recently been published in the original Spanish and in French translation. Several pages are devoted to the bastinado and the cangue as well as to Chinese prisons, from which, the author reported, few prisoners emerged alive (pp. 137–145).

20. Nieuhof, *Het Gesandtschap der Neêrlandtsche Oost-Indische Compagnie*, p. 182.

21. Dapper, *Gedenkwaerdig bedryf der Nederlandsche Oost-Indische Maetschappye*. The plates appear to derive from ink drawings in a manuscript by Adriano de las Cortes (see n. 19 above). These drawings too include a woman trussed on a

pole and two trouserless men being bastinadoed, with the note that officials had to remove their insignia of office before their beatings (Las Cortes, *Le Voyage en Chine,* pp. 453–455). How Dapper gained access to these images is a question for further research.

22. See Montanus, *Atlas sinensis,* for the English translation.

23. Navarrete, *The Travels and Controversies of Friar Domingo Navarrete,* vol. 1, pp. 199–202; discussed in Cummins, "Fray Domingo Navarrete," p. 43.

24. Navarrete, *The Travels and Controversies of Friar Domingo Navarrete,* vol. 1, p. 194.

25. Cantini, *Torture Instruments,* pp. 46–51, Plates 32–38.

26. Navarrete, *Travels and Controversies,* vol. 1, pp. 194–195.

27. Magaillans, *Nouvelle relation de la Chine,* pp. 206–207.

28. Unless otherwise noted, materials in this paragraph come from the 1990 critical edition of Lecomte, *Nouveaux mémoires sur l'état present de la Chine,* pp. 335–337. This edition is based on the 1697 version of Lecomte's text.

29. On the emperor's absolute power, see, e.g., Lecomte, *Nouveaux mémoires,* p. 305.

30. Noting that some convicts were put to death cruelly and slowly under the whip, the Jesuit added almost as an afterthought that the Chinese regularly applied torture during interrogation—most commonly the squeezing of the fingers and hands—and that sometimes this could be worse than the cruelest death.

31. Isabelle Landry's *La Preuve par la Chine* provides an excellent analysis of Du Halde's study and its significance.

32. Du Halde, *Description de la Chine,* vol. 1, p. 6.

33. Du Halde, *The General History of China,* vol. 2, p. 229; *Description de la Chine,* vol. 2, p. 134.

34. Du Halde, *Description de la Chine,* vol. 2, pp. 399–400.

35. Frederick was an admirer of both Voltaire and Christian Wolff, the two most avid philosophical sinophiles of the day; the Sans Souci Palace he constructed near Potsdam was a notable example of Enlightenment chinoiserie.

36. Étiemble takes a contrary view in his magisterial work on Sino-Western relations, but though his readings always command respect, his interpretation of Montesquieu as a cryptosinophile (*L'Europe chinoise,* vol. 2, chap. 3) is not especially convincing. Montesquieu's contemporaries certainly read him differently, as we show in what follows. He did consider Chinese despotism to be moderated in significant ways, however.

37. Montesquieu, *De l'Esprit des lois,* vol. 1, pt. 8, pp. 123, 354, n. 372; *The Spirit of the Laws,* p. 123.

38. Parennin's four long letters to Du Halde on this subject were written between July 1726 and September 1728 and first published in the 1730s in the Jesuits' *Lettres édifiantes et curieuses.* They are collected together in vols. 19 and 20 of the 1810–1811 Toulouse re-edition of that work.

39. The exemption of officials from corporal punishment that characterized Confucian government until the twelfth century was abolished thereafter, as a result of innovations by the Jin, which were taken over by the Yuan and later dynasties. There are different ways of reading these changes. As Herbert Franke notes, "The privileges accorded to gentry-officials in China proper were therefore not

observed by the Jurchen. This led on the one hand to a certain brutalization within the bureaucracy, and on the other it may be seen as an egalitarian tendency because not even a high dignitary was formally exempted from the punishments which were regarded as normal for the population at large." Franke, "The Legal System of the Chin Dynasty," p. 402. See also Franke, "Jurchen Customary Law and the Chinese Law of the Chin Dynasty," pp. 231–232.

40. For Montesquieu's discussion of the trial of the "princes du sang néophytes," see the 1922 French edition of *De l'Esprit des lois*, vol. 1, pt. 8, p. 123. Nugent's English translation—"settled plan of tyranny, and barbarities committed by rule, that is, in cold blood" (*The Spirit of the Laws*, p. 123)—loses some of the sense of ethical transgression against "la nature humaine" expressed in the French.

41. Montesquieu, *The Spirit of the Laws*, p. 268.

42. Ibid., p. 90.

43. Quesnay, *Despotisme de la Chine*, p. 614.

44. Ibid., pp. 714–716.

45. On De Pauw, see Gerbi, *La Disputa del nuovo mondo*, esp. pp. 76–116; Cañizares-Esguerra, *How to Write the History of the New World*, pp. 13, 29–36.

46. De Pauw, *Recherches philosophiques sur les Egyptiens et les Chinois*, vol. 2, pp. 292, 296–299.

47. Du Halde, *Description de la Chine*, vol. 2, p. 137. On the *Jade Register*'s Minor Hell of Skinning by Scraper, see p. 138 above.

48. For a shrewd assessment of what was at stake in the Macartney embassy, see Hevia, *Cherishing Men from Afar*.

49. Barrow, *Travels in China*, p. 85; discussed in Hibbert, *The Dragon Wakes*, pp. 15–16.

50. Anderson, *A Narrative of the British Embassy to China*, p. 164. Macartney was intent on enforcing strict discipline to counter the British reputation for loutishness.

51. Sade, *Philosophy in the Bedroom* (French original, 1795), p. 334. The two-volume French original, entitled *La Philosophie dans le boudoir*, was published privately in London in 1795.

52. Bayly, *Imperial Meridian: The British Empire and the World*.

53. Said, *Culture and Imperialism*, p. xi.

54. Palmerston, autograph note, 29 September 1850 (F.O. 17/173); cited in Costin, *Great Britain and China*, pp. 149–150.

55. Praz, *The Romantic Agony*, p. 278.

56. On Alexander, see Susan Legouix, *Image of China: William Alexander*.

57. Both volumes were originally published in W. Miller's "Costumes of China" series. Studio Editions (London) has recently reissued the illustrations and accompanying notes from both, together with the original introduction to Mason's book, in a single integrated volume: William Alexander and George Henry Mason, *Views of 18th Century China: Costumes, History, Customs* (1988), of which there have been several translations.

58. Mason's introduction to his *Costumes of China* (reproduced in Alexander and Mason, *Views of 18th Century China*, pp. 5–7) provides glimpses of his time in

Canton. Both he and the engraver, J. Dadney, acknowledge Pu Qua's paintings as the source of their illustrations. On Pu Qua, see Crossman, *Decorative Arts of the China Trade*, esp. pp. 185–189.

59. In the absence of contrary evidence, we assume Mason acquired the Pu Qua originals for his "punishments" plates at the same time as he obtained the tints used in his *Costumes of China.*

60. Mason, *The Punishments of China*, note to Plate XI. On the British debate about public punishments at this time, see McGowan, "The Well Ordered Prison," p. 84.

61. The botanist E. H. Wilson, a major photographer of Chinese scenes during the last decade or so of the Qing dynasty, captured the sight of two convicts bound to crosses in this manner in a grim photo from 1899 or 1900 that is reproduced in *The Face of China*, p. 38. The caption indicates that they are awaiting execution by strangulation.

62. Mason, *The Punishments of China*, preface.

63. Staunton's edition of the *Ta Tsing Leu Lee* included translations of the fundamental laws and a very restricted selection of the Code's supplementary statutes. W. C. Jones's *The Great Qing Code* gives a full translation of the fundamental laws alone. An English translation of cases from the legal compendium *Xing'an huilan* is found in Bodde and Morris, *Law in Imperial China.*

64. Nineteenth-century commentators hailed Staunton's work as path-breaking, but later legal scholarship has not always been so appreciative. In the preface to his own highly technical translation of the Qing Code, Jones complains that Staunton's "was so free as to be inaccurate"; *The Great Qing Code*, p. v. Its historic importance is nonetheless indisputable.

65. Renouard de Sainte Croix's French translation of Staunton's version was published in 1812. Staunton's English original was reissued in 1884. The bulk of the Qing Code, including the commentaries, was independently translated into French at about the same time in Philastre, *Le Code Annamite.* Boulais's *Manuel du code chinois,* a full French translation, appeared in 1924.

66. Staunton, *Ta Tsing Leu Lee*, pp. ix–xii, xxi–xxvii.

67. Ibid., pp. 488–489.

68. Anon. [J. Mill], Review of *Voyage à Peking*, by J. de Guignes, *Edinburgh Review* (1809), pp. 412–414, 428. The attribution to James Mill comes from Bain's *James Mill, a Biography*, pp. 97–98.

69. Anon. [F. Jeffrey], Review of *Ta Tsing Leu Lee*, by George Staunton, *Edinburgh Review* (1810), pp. 481–482. We wish to express our gratitude to Mr. Li Chen of Columbia University for identifying Jeffrey as the author of this piece.

70. Ibid., pp. 489, 496, 499.

71. Hegel, *The Philosophy of History*, p. 127.

72. Ibid., p. 128. The passage continues: "corrective punishment aims at improvement, that which is retributive implies veritable imputation of guilt."

73. Ibid., pp. 128–129.

74. It did not do so straightaway, however. For example, Henry Ellis's official account of the 1815 Amherst embassy to Beijing made remarkably little of the issue of Chinese justice. His description of the now famous cangue was anodyne.

He declared himself surprised by the comparative leniency of the bastinado, discomfort from which, he thought, "did not certainly exceed that of a tolerably severe flogging at school." At least as remarkable to him was the sight of the beaten man thanking the mandarin who had ordered the punishment, an attitude that, however "absurd in appearance, and unnatural in reality," Ellis felt was a logical result of China's "patriarchal theory of government, which supposes that judicial punishments are the corrections of natural affections"; *Journal of the Proceedings of the Late Embassy to China*, pp. 190, 230–231. Still more philosophical was the attitude of the Spanish-American reformer José Joaquín Fernández de Lizardi, whose 1816 novel *El Periquillo Sarniento* posited an Enlightenment-style Chinese utopia based on a regime of punishments and prisons so terrifying that they deterred crime and reformed criminals, in effective Utilitarian fashion. Lizardi drew his materials on Chinese justice from Mendoza's sixteenth-century account discussed above; see De Alba-Koch, " 'Enlightened Absolutism' and Utopian Thought: Fernández de Lizardi and Reform in New Spain," pp. 297–300. Such emotionally detached approaches to the Chinese judicial system were on the wane, however.

75. Anon., "Notices of Modern China," pp. 361–386.
76. Ibid., p. 364.
77. Ibid., p. 366. The *Liao shi* (ed. Tuotuo, p. 8) mentions the execution of twenty-nine people who were torn apart by carts. While it is not inconceivable that Timkovski might have heard of this eight-hundred-year-old incident from a member of the Russian ecclesiastical mission in Beijing, it seems more likely he was projecting.
78. Anon., "Canton," *Canton Register*, August 25, 1835, p. 1.
79. Anon., "Notices of Modern China," pp. 379, 384–385, 370–377.
80. A contemporary painting of this or a very similar trial scene is reproduced on the front-paper of Crossman, *The China Trade*.
81. Davis, *The Chinese*, vol. 1, pp. 373–377.
82. Ibid., pp. 378–383. Thereafter, in the 1840 British parliamentary debate on war with China, the Tory opposition supported Palmerston's military action with the argument that no British subject should ever be abandoned to the indignity of submitting to non-European laws. See the interventions by Wellington and Colchester in *Hansard's Parliamentary Debates*, 1840, vol. 3, cols. 39, 44. Judicial extraterritoriality was imposed in the five newly opened "treaty ports" in 1842, after China's defeat.
83. Davis, *The Chinese*, vol. 1, pp. 223–224, 236, 238–239, 227–231.
84. Ibid., pp. 224–225, 228.
85. Medhurst, *China: Its State and Prospects*, pp. 136–137, 139.
86. Munn, *Anglo-China*, esp. pp. 150–152, 233–238, 402 n. 134.
87. Older sources continued to be treated as authorities for some time. For instance, the widely read German cultural historian Gustav Klemm, a significant source for later anthropologists, derived most of his 1847 account of Chinese courts and punishments from Du Halde and the French version of Staunton's

rendering of the Qing Code; see Klemm, *Allgemeine Cultur-Geschichte*, vol. 6, pp. 213–218. He cited a recent informant, though, for the mistaken view that torturing plaintiffs in court cases was no longer practiced (p. 216).

88. Williams's *Middle Kingdom* originally appeared in 1848. The second edition keeps many parts unchanged, but its revised and expanded discussion of the judicial system was considerably more sympathetic to the "forces of order." Our examination of this work distinguishes between the two editions for that reason.

89. Williams, *The Middle Kingdom* (1848), vol. 1, pp. 404–407.

90. Ibid., pp. 408–409.

91. The twentieth-century terminological distinction between jails as holding facilities for persons awaiting trial and prisons as institutions for incarcerating convicts was not adhered to in nineteenth-century works, which often used the terms interchangeably.

92. Anon., "Notices of the Prisons in the City of Canton," p. 608.

93. Anon., "Protestant Missionaries to the Chinese," vol. 20, p. 536.

94. J. F. Davis might have introduced this convention into the English-language literature when he noted, "Nothing tends more effectually to deter from crime than the prospect of incarceration in those miserable abodes which the Chinese emphatically style 'Ty-yŏ', or hell." *The Chinese*, vol. 1, p. 227.

95. Quotations throughout this paragraph are from Williams, *The Middle Kingdom* (1848), vol. 1, pp. 416–417 (in the 1882 edition, vol. 1, pp. 514–515).

96. Williams, *Middle Kingdom* (1848), vol. 1, pp. 410–415, and revised edition (1882), vol. 1, pp. 508–513.

97. Huc, *The Chinese Empire*, pp. 428–429; *L'Empire chinois*, vol. 2, pp. 236–237.

98. Huc, *The Chinese Empire*, pp. 443–444; *L'Empire chinois*, vol. 2, pp. 254–256.

99. T. T. Meadows, who had extensive experience of Chinese official proceedings, sharply rebuked Huc for sowing sensational stories despite a marked paucity of such experience. *The Chinese and Their Rebellions*, p. 55.

100. Huc, *The Chinese Empire*, pp. 433–434, 437, 441–42; *L'Empire chinois*, vol. 2, pp. 242–243, 247–248, 253. Huc's comment that such payments paralleled Sicilian practice in the age of Cicero indicates the broader ideological inclination, shared by many of his contemporaries, to equate Chinese culture with antiquity. For instance, Léopold Pallu, whose official report was sponsored by the French Minister of the Navy, commented poignantly on the deaths of two French captives during the 1859–1860 Anglo-French campaign in China: "Nos moeurs répugnent jusqu'au récit même de ces crimes d'un autre âge"; Pallu, *Relation de l'expédition de Chine en 1860*, p. 167.

101. Huc, *The Chinese Empire*, p. 448; *L'Empire chinois*, vol. 2, pp. 260–261.

102. Mirbeau, *Torture Garden*, pp. 226–227; *Le Jardin des supplices*, pp. 226–227.

103. Cruikshank, *The Criminal Punishments of the Chinese* (unpaginated).

104. Wong, *Deadly Dreams*, pp. 216–217; Southgate, *"The Most English Minister,"* pp. 424–425.

105. In particular, the chopping in two and the disembowelment to which Yama devoted himself in the netherworld.

106. G. Cruikshank, "Preface" to P. Cruikshank, *The Criminal Punishments of the Chinese.*
107. Bertram, *Flagellation and the Flagellants,* pp. 224–225, 229.
108. On the commission, see Dirks, *Castes of Mind,* pp. 190–192.
109. Gray, *China,* vol. 1, pp. 32–33.
110. Ibid., pp. 33–35, 38–39, 44, 73.
111. Williams, *The Middle Kingdom* (1848), vol. 1, p. 409; revised edition (1882), vol. 1, p. 507.
112. Gray, *China,* vol. 1, pp. 46, 48, 50, 52, 53.
113. Ibid., pp. 46, 55, 57–59.
114. Ibid., pp. 59–63.
115. Williams, *Middle Kingdom* (1882 ed.), vol. 1, pp. 512–513.
116. Lindley, *Ti-Ping Tien-Kwoh,* p. 105.
117. Huc, *The Chinese Empire,* pp. 435–436; *L'Empire chinois,* vol. 2, pp. 245–246.
118. Gray, *China,* vol. 1, p. 74.
119. Williams, *The Middle Kingdom* (1882 ed.), vol. 1, pp. 510, 517–518.
120. Smith, *Chinese Characteristics,* p. 320.
121. Ibid., p. 214.
122. Ibid., pp. 329–330.
123. Morrison, *An Australian in China,* pp. 209–211.
124. Alabaster, *Notes and Commentaries on Chinese Criminal Law,* pp. lxii–lxiii.
125. Ibid., pp. 17–18.
126. Ibid., pp. 57–59.
127. Ibid., pp. lxviii–lxix.
128. Matignon, *Dix au pays du dragon,* p. 248.
129. *Le Jardin des supplices,* pp. 172, 175; *Torture Garden,* pp. 182, 185. Compare Hibbert, *The Great Mutiny,* pp. 124–125.
130. Two recent valuable contributions to our understanding of Western colonial strategies toward China are James Hevia's *English Lessons* and Lydia Liu's *The Clash of Empires.*
131. Grosrichard, *The Sultan's Court.*
132. *Le Jardin des supplices,* pp. 130, 248; *Torture Garden,* pp. 147, 244. We resist speculating much on the inspiration for Mirbeau's "exquisite" torture garden, which far surpasses anything in the sinological literature. If the novelist did have a real-life source for the sexual dimension of his tale, a likely candidate might be the Yoshiwara pleasure quarter in Tokagawa-era Edo, which he would have known from the wave of japonaiserie that swept French artistic circles from the 1870s. Then again, he might have taken inspiration partly from another work of China-ward imagination, Samuel Taylor Coleridge's dreamy homage to the "stately pleasure-dome" of Khubilai Khan, one of China's most fearsome conquerors.

7. Misreading Lingchi

This chapter includes material, now heavily revised, that was first published by Jérôme Bourgon as "Chinese Executions: Visualizing Their Differences with European Supplices," *European Journal of East-Asian Studies* 2, no. 1 (2003): 151–182.

1. Meadows, *The Chinese and Their Rebellions*, p. 653. "Ling che, a disgraceful and lingering death" was a phrase that Meadows picked up from J. F. Davis, cited in Chapter 6.
2. See, e.g., Mayers, Dennys, and King, *The Treaty Ports of China and Japan*, p. 503; Norman, *The Peoples and Politics of the Far East*, p. 225.
3. Clunas, *Chinese Export Watercolours*, p. 69.
4. We assume that these words were omitted in the original.
5. Meadows, *The Chinese and Their Rebellions*, pp. 655–656.
6. Foucault has argued that "the slowness of the process of torture and execution, its sudden dramatic moments, the cries and sufferings of the condemned man" play a necessary role in the ordeal, for "the torture of the execution anticipates the punishments of the beyond." In that "theatre of hell, . . . the pains here below may also be counted as penitence and so alleviate the punishments of the beyond. . . . The cruelty of the earthly punishment will be deducted from the punishment to come: in it is glimpsed the promise of forgiveness"; *Discipline and Punish*, pp. 45–46.
7. Alphonse Favier provides this highly colored description of the Vegetable Market execution ground in Beijing in the 1890s: "The convicts, on their knees, are executed one after the other, their bodies carried to the dump, their heads hung in little cages on a tripod frame made of poles. Passersby can view the bloodless heads, their huge, terrified eyes half eaten by magpies and crows that peck through the rungs; each queue trails down to the ground; dogs look on and stand on their hind legs trying to get to them; it is a sickening sight." Favier, *Péking: histoire et description*, pp. 394–395.
8. Meadows, *The Chinese and Their Rebellions*, p. 656.
9. Edgerton, *Pictures and Punishment*, p. 13.
10. Bird, *The Golden Chersonese and the Way Thither*, p. 104. The book is mostly an anodyne and genteel account of Malaysia, from which this description of Chinese punishments was a harsh departure. Bird's publisher wanted her to remove the passage so as not to offend her readers' sensibilities but could not prevail; see Harper, *Solitary Travelers*, p. 162.
11. See Bourgon, " 'Sauver la vie': de la fraude judiciaire en Chine à la fin de l'empire."
12. The cliché of Chinese impassiveness was stated with a bluntness typical of the period by the French naval officer Léopold Pallu: "The impassivity of executioners and their victims is a collective trait in these societies, and pity, which resides in the nerves, does not exist in China; one cuts a man into pieces, but show him no anger"; *Relation de l'expédition de Chine en 1860*, p. 167. For comments in a more scientistic vein alleging a Chinese "absence of nerves" and lack of mercy, see Jean-Jacques Matignon's discussion of lingchi in *Dix ans au pays du dragon*, pp. 263, 269. Interestingly, missionaries inverted this native "apathy" into a Christian fortitude when narrating the martyrdom of Chinese converts.
13. Bird, *The Golden Chersonese*, pp. 106–107.
14. Little and Little, *Gleanings of Fifty Years in China*, p. 106.
15. Heindl, *Der Berufsverbrecher*, pp. 85–86. Although connected to the lingchi photographs in an ambiguous way, these comments have been taken at face

value and reproduced in books intended for the general public, e.g., Monestier, *Peines de mort,* p. 71.

16. The photographs are on stereoscopic glass plates and preserved in the Musée Nicéphore Niépce at Chalon sur Saône. Whoever labeled them "Exécution chinoise, Kouantcheou wan [Guan gzhouwan, near Canton], 1908" got both place and date entirely wrong. See the critical commentary on this set at http://turandot.ish-lyon.cnrs.fr/Event.php?ID=8.

17. Public outbursts against the condemned or the executioner, sometimes turning to riots, were common at European executions and were one reason for the abolition of public executions. No similar crowd reaction has been reported for Chinese executions, though the sources are scarce. The European crowd reacted as a "public," something the Chinese onlookers were not allowed to constitute.

18. Desanti, "La Violence."

19. Ho, "Butchering Fishes and Executing Criminals." Such processions are again being performed in rural China. One of us [TB] had the opportunity to observe such an event, albeit on a smaller scale, in May 2007, in a town southwest of Shanghai.

20. See Jean-Luc Nancy's critical remarks on Bataille's reading of lingchi as a "sacrifice" in his essay, "L'Insacrifiable."

21. In France, breaking on the wheel was practiced until the 1780s; in England, the punishment of quartering for bandits was abolished only in 1814.

22. Foucault, *Discipline and Punish,* pp. 111, 113.

23. On interpreting imperial China as a failed modernity, see Woodside, *Lost Modernities.*

24. See Cahill, *The Painter's Practice,* pp. 115–117: "The cultivated artist, always apprehensive of being mistakenly classed with the artisan-painters who were willing to depict stimulating and entertaining subjects assigned by others, limited his repertory generally to themes that were harmonious and charged with auspicious meanings, and that could be understood as reflective of his own rich but stable inner-life." As a consequence, "the decline of such themes of actual or suggested violence I see as merely the most conspicuous aspect of a process that ended by depriving all figure painting in China of any serious hold on the emotions."

25. Xu Wenda, *Da Qing lüli tushuo* and *Da Qing xinglü tushuo; Xinglü tufu; Zuiming tushuo.* A detail from the latter is reproduced out of context in Antony, *Like Froth Floating on the Sea,* p. 117, where it is mistakenly attributed to the Shanghai pictorial magazine *Dianshizhai huabao.*

26. Arlington, *Through the Dragon's Eyes,* p. 214. Our thanks to Alison Bailey for this reference.

27. Foucault, *Discipline and Punish,* pp. 113–114.

28. Ibid., p. 111.

29. Ibid., p. 128.

30. See Potter, *Hanging in Judgment: Religion and the Death Penalty in England;* our thanks to Simon Devereaux for this reference.

31. Pratt, *Punishment and Civilization*, p. 16.
32. Matignon. *Dix ans au pays du dragon*, p. 271.

8. Georges Bataille's Interpretation

An earlier version of this chapter was published in French by Jérôme Bourgon as "Bataille et le 'supplicié chinois': erreurs sur la personne" in Antonio Dominguez Leiva and Muriel Détrie, eds., *Le Supplice oriental dans la littérature et les arts* (Dijon: Les Éditions du Murmure, 2005), pp. 93–115.

1. Bataille's *Les Larmes d'Éros* was originally published in Paris in 1961 by J.-J. Pauvert in the series Bibliothèque internationale d'érotologie. An expanded edition appeared in 1971 with an introduction by Joseph Marie Lo Duca; references in this chapter are to that edition unless otherwise noted. The text was reproduced with a selection of the original visual materials, but without the lingchi photographs, in volume 10 of Bataille's *Oeuvres complètes*. An English translation is available under the title *The Tears of Eros*. References in this chapter are to the French editions of Bataille's work in addition to the English translations, as much of our argument revolves around issues of textual interpretation and publishing history.
2. Desanti, "La Violence."
3. See Bourgon, *Supplice chinois*.
4. Lo Duca published this passage in his foreword to the 1971 expanded edition of *Les Larmes d'Éros*, p. xix; it was the third paragraph of a letter now available in full in the volume of Bataille's correspondence edited by Michel Surya; Bataille, *Choix de letters 1917–1962*, p. 559. Surya retold the "well-known story" there, but again without acknowledging that the torture victim in Louis Carpeaux's work was not the same as that of Lo Duca / Bataille.
5. Matignon's lingchi photographs appear on pp. 265–269 of *Dix ans au pays du dragon*.
6. Jérôme Bourgon consulted Jacques Pimpaneau about these matters in a series of letters and telephone conversations in 2001, but Dr. Pimpaneau unfortunately could recall little about the events in question.
7. Born Giuseppe Maria Lo Duca in 1910, Lo Duca lived and worked in France for many decades, using the French "Joseph Marie" as the international form of his name, though usually publishing simply under his surname. He also worked as a journalist and filmmaker in addition to his literary writing.
8. Balthus is the moniker of Balthazar Klossowski de Rola (1908–2001). *La Leçon de guitare* [*The Guitar Lesson*], which pictures lesbian activity between a music teacher and her student, caused a scandal even in 1977, when Pierre Matisse displayed it in a retrospective of Balthus's career at the Museum of Modern Art in New York.
9. Bataille, *Choix de lettres 1917–1962*, p. 571. The paragraph numbering was added by the French editors.
10. Reproduced in 2001 in a facsimile edition.

11. Bataille, *Choix de lettres 1917–1962*, p. 571.
12. Ibid., note 1. Surya, the editor of the letters, observes further that Lo Duca addressed this difference of opinion in his letter of 27 September in the clause, "Quant au texte même, il est entièrement de votre main" ("As for the text, it was entirely from your hand"), which suggests that Bataille must have had doubts on the matter.
13. The fact that the French Interior Ministry placed the book on the Index of banned books explains nothing, for no book burning was involved. It was the struggle between sexual liberation and moral indignation that obscured the problems of the book's authenticity.
14. Bataille, *Les Larmes d'Éros*, p. 234.
15. Bataille, "Notes sur 'Le Sacré.'" The three pages joined to the manuscript include a note on the theme, an outline of the article, and a brief sketch of illustration strategies. Four of the seven iconographic items are reproduced as Plates 27–30; the seventh and last is, as noted, an "Aztec sacrifice" rather than Chinese torture, despite what Hollier claims in Bataille, *Oeuvres complètes*, vol. 1, p. 559.
16. Though he expressed himself with a caution bordering on euphemism, Georges Didi-Huberman recognized this when he observed, "Bataille was obsessed at least as much by Aztec sacrifice as by the Chinese torture victim"; *La Ressemblance informe*, p. 162.
17. Borel and Robin, *Les Rêveurs éveillés*.
18. Leiris, *Journal 1922–1989*, p. 859 n. 66, briefly sketches Borel's relations with Bataille and Leiris.
19. The entries for 1959–1960 in Leiris's *Journal 1922–1989* include multiple allusions to China, but no mention of torture or lingchi. The issue of torture crops up on many occasions elsewhere without Leiris making the least allusion to photos of Chinese lingchi victims. The lingchi victim is similarly absent from Leiris's discussions of Bataille in *À Propos de Georges Bataille* and his *Journal de Chine*, published posthumously from travel diaries he kept on his 1955 visit to the People's Republic.
20. Our thanks to Christine Barthe, the photograph librarian at the Musée de l'Homme, for her patience and perspicacious comments on the origins of the photos in *Les Larmes d'Éros*.
21. *Nouveau traité de psychologie* was a collective work written under the direction of Georges Dumas. Its first four volumes were published by Félix Alcan between 1930 and 1935. *Les Larmes d'Éros*, p. 234, confuses it with *Traité de psychologie*, published in 1923–1924, which includes no photographs of lingchi whatsoever. This misidentification has been conscientiously repeated by Bataille enthusiasts for over forty years.
22. Our analysis here is based on the article "Emprunts de Georges Bataille à la B.N. (1922–1950)," included in Bataille, *Oeuvres complètes*, vol. 12, pp. 584–585.
23. Compare two passages: Bataille states in *L'Expérience intérieure* (p. 153), first published in 1943: "In particular, I would gaze at the photographic *image*—or sometimes the memory which I have of it—of a Chinese man who must have been tortured in my lifetime" (*Inner Experience*, p. 119. In *Le Coupable* (p. 57),

published in 1944, he writes of "the young Chinese (a condemned felon) shown in the photos as covered with blood while the executioner tortures him" (*Guilty*, p. 46). In the first passage, he mentions only one photo and phrases his looking in the past tense, whereas in the second, later extract he refers to several photos and writes of looking at them at the moment in which he writes, suggesting a closer familiarity with these images.

24. Bataille, *Inner Experience*, p. 119: "Saint Ignatius' discipline creates for himself a theatrical representation. He is in a peaceful room: one asks him to have the feelings he would have on Calvary" (*L'Expérience intérieure*, p. 152).

25. Bataille, *Guilty*, pp. 38–39: "The victim bound to a stake, eyes turned up, head thrown back, and through a grimacing mouth you see his teeth" (*Le Coupable*, p. 48). Compare *Inner Experience*, p. 119: "In the end, the patient writhed, his chest flayed, arms and legs cut off at the elbows and at the knees. His hair standing on end, hideous, haggard, striped with blood, beautiful as a wasp" (*L'Expérience intérieure*, p. 153).

26. Bataille, *Guilty*, p. 35: "Chancing on an image of torture, I can turn away in fright. But if I look I'm *beside myself*" (*Le Coupable*, p. 37).

27. Bataille, *Inner Experience*, p. 120 (*L'Expérience intérieure*, p. 154). This idea is echoed in *Guilty*, p. 46: "I was connected to this unhappy being in ties of horror and friendship" (*Le Coupable*, p. 57).

28. Bataille, *Les Larmes d'Éros*, p. 234.

29. Surya, *Georges Bataille: la mort à l'oeuvre*, p. 104.

30. *Guilty*, p. 20; Bataille, *Le Coupable, in Oeuvres complètes*, vol. 5, p. 255. The French original reads: "Je ne confonds pas mes désbauches et ma vie mystique. La description du tantrisme dans l'ouvrage d'Éliade a laissé dans moi un sentiment d'aversion. Je m'en tiens de part et d'autre à des emportements sans mélange."

31. Bataille, *Les Larmes d'Éros*, p. 239.

32. Rendered into Italian ("Questo libro non é dato nell'esperienza limitata *che é* quella di tutti gli uomini"), the sentence admittedly makes no more sense, but it does not sound as odd as in French.

33. *Journal secret de Napoléon Bonaparte*, pp. 13, 20.

34. Surya, *Georges Bataille*, p. 104.

35. Dumas, *Nouveau traité de psychologie*, vol. 2, pp. 284–285: "Extreme suffering thus leads to unclassifiable expressions such as expression 3, or to paradoxical expressions like expression 2 which seems to defy explanation. How, in this unheard of suffering, can one account for these half-closed eyes and drawn-in cheeks, this thrusting up and back of the head, this mouth that seems to smile?"

36. If we apply the theses of Agamben's *Homo Sacer* to this example, the convict's uncut hair is the sign that he exists beyond society's norms, outside the civilized world: that he is *sacer*, i.e. set apart, separated, condemned to death, by analogy with werewolf-bandits and wild forest-people, whose status lay ambiguously between nature and culture, between savagery and the order of the state. In imperial China, the convict with uncut hair was reduced to the condition of barbarism the moment his sentence was imposed.

37. Berthelot, "Les Supplices en Chine," p. 290. The author explains the "ecstatic joy" as the effect of being stunned with opium.
38. Bataille, *Guilty*, p. 46; *Le Coupable*, p. 57.
39. Bataille, *Inner Experience*, p. 119. Assuming this lingchi occurred in 1904–1905, Bataille would have been about seven years old, traditionally considered the "age of reason," the point when moral responsibility begins.

9. Lingering On

1. "Chinese War Horrors: Children Ordered to Behead Parents," *The Observer* (12 Feb. 1928), p. 17.
2. Duff, *A Handbook on Hanging*, p. 3.
3. Montesquieu, *The Spirit of the Laws*, bk. 6, chap. 16 ("Of the Just Proportion between Punishments and Crimes"), p. 90.
4. Blackstone, *Commentaries on the Laws of England*, vol. 4, p. 18.
5. *Parliamentary Debates* 17 (1810), col. 197, quoted in Beattie, *Crimes and the Courts*, pp. 633–634.
6. On the construction of opium as an arbitrary symbol of Chinese degradation and weakness, see Dikötter et al., *Narcotic Culture: A History of Drugs in China;* for a similar challenge to the symbolic place of foot-binding in Western views of Chinese culture, see Ko, *Cinderella's Sisters: A Revisionist History of Footbinding*.
7. Beccaria, *On Crimes and Punishments*, p. 42.
8. Beattie, *Crime and the Courts*, p. 636.
9. Bourgon, "Shen Jiaben et le droit chinois à la fin des Qing."
10. See Bourgon, "Abolishing 'Cruel Punishments.' "
11. *On Crimes and Punishments*.
12. Of the 1,526 people legally executed in 2002 worldwide, 1,060 were put to death in China alone. On the status of the death penalty in China, see Zhang Ning, "The Debate over the Death Penalty in Today's China," p. 2. Hood, *The Death Penalty: A Worldwide Perspective*, pp. 51–55, places China's recent record in a global perspective.
13. Shelton, *Shelton of Tibet*, p. 173.
14. Choi, *The Jade Peony*, p. 316.

Bibliography

Agamben, Giorgio. *Homo Sacer: Sovereign Power and Bare Life*, trans. Daniel Heller-Roazen. Stanford: Stanford University Press, 1998.

Ahern, Emily. *Chinese Ritual and Politics*. Cambridge: Cambridge University Press, 1981.

Alabaster, Ernest. *Notes and Commentaries on Chinese Criminal Law and Cognate Topics*. London: Luzac, 1899. Reprint, Taipei: Chengwen, 1968.

Alexander, William. *Costumes of China*. London: W. Miller, 1805.

Alexander, William, and George Henry Mason. *Views of 18th Century China: Costumes, History, Customs*. London: Studio Editions, 1988.

Anderson, Aeneas. *A Narrative of the British Embassy to China, in the Years 1792, 1793 and 1794; containing the various circumstances of the embassy, with accounts of the customs and manners of the Chinese, and a description of the counties, towns, cities, etc. etc.* London: Debrett, 1795.

Anderson, David. *Histories of the Hanged: The Dirty War in Kenya and the End of Empire.* New York: Norton, 2005.

Andrew, Anita. "Zhu Yuanzhang and the 'Great Warnings' *(Yuzhi Da Gao):* Autocracy and Rural Reform in the Early Ming." Ph.D. diss., University of Michigan, 1991.

L'Année religieuse des théophilanthropes. 2 vols. Paris, 1797–1798.

Anon. "Canton." *Canton Register,* August 25, 1835, p. 1.

Anon. "Notices of Modern China: Various Means and Modes of Punishment; Torture, Imprisonment, Flogging, Branding, Pillory, Banishment, and Death." *Chinese Repository* 4 (December 1835): 361–386.

Anon. "Notices of the Prisons of the City of Canton, their number and extent, character and condition of their inmates," *Chinese Repository* 12 (November 1843): 604–608.

Anon. "Protestant Missionaries to the Chinese, with the present position of those now among them." *Chinese Repository* 20 (August 1851): 513–545.

Anon. [Francis Jeffrey]. Review of *Ta Tsing Leu Lee,* by George Staunton. *Edinburgh Review* (1810): 481–499.

Anon. [James Mill]. Review of *Voyage à Peking,* by J. de Guignes. *Edinburgh Review* (1809): 412–428.

Anon. "Yixue mingci shenchahui diyici kaihui jilu" (Minutes of the first meeting of the medical terms examination committee). *Zhonghua yixue zazhi (National Medical Journal)* 3, no. 2 (1916): 30ff.

Antony, Robert J. *Like Froth Floating on the Sea: The World of Pirates and Seafarers in Late Imperial South China.* Berkeley: Center for Chinese Studies, Institute of East Asian Studies, University of California, 2003.

Arendt, Hannah. *The Origins of Totalitarianism.* New York: Harcourt, Brace and World, 1966.

Arlington, Lewis Charles. *Through the Dragon's Eyes: Fifty Years of Experiences of a Foreigner in the Chinese Government Service.* Foreword by E. Alabaster. London: Constable, 1934.

Asad, Talal. "On Torture, or Cruel, Inhuman, and Degrading Treatment." *Social Research* 63, no. 4 (1996): 1081–1109.

Astier Loutfi, Martine. *Littérature et colonialisme: l'expansion coloniale vue dans la littérature romanesque française, 1871–1914.* Paris: Mouton, 1971.

Bain, Alexander. *James Mill, a Biography.* London: Longmans, Green, 1882.

Balazs, Étienne. *Le Traité juridique du "Souei-Chou."* Vol. 2 of *Études sur la société etl'économie de la Chine médiévale.* Leiden: Brill, 1954.

Ballaster, Ros. *Fabulous Orients: Fictions of the East in England, 1662–1785.* Oxford: Oxford University Press, 2005.

Ban Gu. *Han shu* (Standard history of the Han dynasty). Beijing: Zhonghua shuju, 1975.

Bataille, Georges. *The Accursed Share: An Essay on General Economy,* trans. Robert Hurley. 3 vols. New York: Zone, 1991.

———. *Choix de lettres 1917–1962,* ed. Michel Surya. Paris: Gallimard, 1997.

———. *Le Coupable.* Paris: Gallimard, 1944.

———. *L'Expérience intérieure.* Paris: Gallimard, 1943.

———. *Guilty,* trans. Bruce Boone. Venice, Calif.: Lapis Press, 1988.

———. *Inner Experience,* trans. Leslie Anne Boldt. Albany: SUNY Press, 1988.

———. *Les Larmes d'Éros,* ed. J. M. Lo Duca. Bibliothèque internationale d'érotologie, no. 6. Paris: Jean-Jacques Pauvert, 1961. Reprint, 2001. Also included in *Oeuvres complètes,* vol. 10.

———. "Notes sur 'Le Sacré.'" *Cahiers d'art* 14, no. 1–4 (1939): 47–50. Also included in *Oeuvres complètes,* vol. 1, pp. 559–563.

———. *Oeuvres complètes,* ed. Denis Hollier. 12 vols. Paris: Gallimard, 1970–1988.

———. "The Sacred." In *Visions of Excess: Selected Writings, 1927–1939,* ed. Allan Stoekl, trans. Allan Stoekl with C. R. Lovitt and D. M. Leslie Jr., pp. 240–245. Theory and History of Literature, vol. 14. Minneapolis: University of Minnesota Press, 1985.

———. *La Somme athéologique.* Paris: Gallimard, 1954.

———. *The Tears of Eros,* trans. Peter Connor. San Francisco: City Lights Books, 1989.

Baudrillard, Jean. *Symbolic Exchange and Death,* trans. Iain Hamilton Grant. London: Sage, 1993.

Bayly, Christopher A. *Imperial Meridian: The British Empire and the World.* London: Longman, 1989.

Beattie, J. M. *Crime and the Courts in England, 1660–1800*. Princeton: Princeton University Press, 1986.

Beccaria, Cesare di. *On Crimes and Punishments, and Other Writings*, ed. R. Bellamy, trans. R. Davis, with V. Cox and R. Bellamy. Cambridge: Cambridge University Press, 1995.

Berthelot, Philippe. "Les Supplices en Chine." In *Je sais tout, encyclopédie mondiale illustrée*, 15 October 1905, pp. 289–296.

Bertram, James Glass. *Flagellation and the Flagellants: A History of the Rod in All Countries*. London: Hotten, 1870.

Bird [Bishop], Isabella. *The Golden Chersonese and the Way Thither: Travels in Malaya in 1879*. London: John Murray, 1883.

Blackstone, William. *Commentaries on the Laws of England*. 4 vols., 1765–1769. Reprint, ed. Wayne Morrison. London: Cavendish, 2001.

Blue, Gregory. "China and Western Social Thought in the Modern Period." In *China and Historical Capitalism: Genealogies of Sinological Knowledge*, ed. Timothy Brook and Gregory Blue, pp. 57–109. Cambridge: Cambridge University Press, 1999.

Bodde, Derk. "Prison Life in Eighteenth-Century Peking." *Journal of the American Oriental Society* 89 (1969): 311–369.

Bodde, Derk, and Clarence Morris. *Law in Imperial China: Exemplified by 190 Ch'ing Dynasty Cases*. Cambridge, Mass.: Harvard University Press, 1967.

Borel, Adrien, and Gil Robin. *Les Rêveurs éveillés*. Paris: Gallimard, 1925.

Boulais, G., ed. *Manuel du code chinois*. Shanghai, 1924. Reprint, Taipei: Chengwen, 1966.

Bourgon, Jérôme. "Abolishing 'Cruel Punishments': A Reappraisal of the Chinese Roots and Long Term Efficiency of the *Xinzheng* Legal Reforms." *Modern Asian Studies* 37, no. 4 (2003): 851–862.

———. "Bataille et le 'supplicié chinois': erreurs sur la personne." In *Le Supplice oriental dans la littérature et les arts*, ed. Antonio Dominguez Leiva and Muriel Détrie, pp. 93–115. Dijon: Éditions du murmure, 2005.

———. "Chinese Executions: Visualizing Their Differences with European Supplices." *European Journal of East-Asian Studies* 2, no. 1 (2003): 151–182.

———. "Photographie et vérité historique: le lingchi de Wang Weiqin." Unpublished essay available at http://turandot.ish-lyon.cnrs.fr/Essay.php?ID=11.

———. " 'Sauver la vie': de la fraude judiciaire en Chine à la fin de l'empire." *Actes de la recherche en sciences sociale* 133 (June 2000): 32–39.

———. "Les Scènes de supplice dans les aquarelles chinoises d'exportation." Unpublished essay, available at http://turandot.ish-lyon.cnrs.fr/Essay.php?ID=33.

———. "Shen Jiaben et le droit chinois à la fin des Qing." Ph.D. diss., École des Hautes Études en Sciences Sociales, Paris, 1994.

———. *Supplices chinois*. Brussels: La Maison d'à côté, 2007.

Boxer, Charles R., ed. *South China in the Sixteenth Century*. London: Hakluyt Society, 1957.

Branche, Raphaëlle. "La Torture pendant la guerre d'Algérie." In *La Guerre d'Algérie, 1954–2004*, ed. Mohammed Harbi and Benjamin Stora, pp. 383–401. Paris: Robert Lafont, 2004.

Brook, Timothy. *The Chinese State in Ming Society.* London: RoutledgeCurzon, 2005.

Brook, Timothy, and Gregory Blue, eds. *China and Historical Capitalism: Genealogies of Sinological Knowledge.* Cambridge: Cambridge University Press, 1999.

Brunnert, H. S., and V. V. Hagelstrom. *Present Day Political Organization of China.* 1911. Reprint, Taipei: Chengwen, 1978.

Buraku kaihō kenkyūjo. *Buraku mondai jiten* (Encyclopedia of Buraku Issues). Osaka: Buraku kaihō kenkyūjo / Hakutsubai kaihō shuppansha, 1986.

Burns, W. "*In the Penal Colony:* Variations on a Theme by Octave Mirbeau." *Accent* 17 (Winter 1957): 45–51.

Cahill, James. *The Painter's Practice: How Artists Lived and Worked in Traditional China.* New York: Columbia University Press, 1995.

Callu, J.-P. "Le Jardin des supplices au Bas-empire." In *Du châtiment dans la cité,* pp. 313–359. Rome: École Française de Rome, 1984.

Camporesi, Piero. *The Fear of Hell: Images of Damnation and Salvation in Early Modern Europe,* trans. Lucinda Byatt. Cambridge: Polity, 1981.

Cañizares-Esguerra, Jorge. *How to Write the History of the New World: Histories, Epistemologies, and Identities in the Eighteenth-Century Atlantic World.* Stanford: Stanford University Press, 2001.

Cantini, Lorenzo. *Torture Instruments / Instrumentos de Tortura: A Bilingual Guide to the Exhibit "Torture Instruments from the Middle Ages to the Industrial Era,"* trans. Donatella Montina. Florence: published by the author, 2001.

Carbasse, Jean-Marie. *Introduction historique au droit pénal.* Paris: Presses Universitaires de France, 1990.

Carpeaux, Louis. *Pékin qui s'en va.* Paris: A. Maloine, 1913.

Carr, Reg. *Anarchism in France: The Case of Octave Mirbeau.* Montreal: McGill-Queen's University Press, 1977.

Chai Zhiguang and Pan Mingquan, eds. *Shanghai fojiao beike wenxian ji* (Buddhist epigraphic documents from Shanghai). Shanghai: Shanghai guji chubanshe, 2004.

Chan, Hok-lam. "Chinese Official Historiography at the Yüan Court: The Composition of the Liao, Chin, and Sung Histories." In *China under the Mongol Rule,* ed. John D. Langlois, pp. 56–106. Princeton: Princeton University Press, 1981.

Changxing xianzhi (Gazetteer of Changxing county). 1805.

Chard, Robert. "Rituals and Scriptures of the Stove God." In *Ritual and Scripture in Chinese Popular Religion: Five Studies,* ed. David Johnson, pp. 3–54. Berkeley: Chinese Popular Culture Project, 1995.

Ch'en, Paul Heng-chao. *Chinese Legal Tradition under the Mongols: The Code of 1291 as Reconstructed.* Princeton: Princeton University Press, 1979.

———. "Disloyalty to the State in Late Imperial China." In *State and Law in East Asia: Festschrift Karl Bünger,* ed. Dieter Eikemeier and Herbert Franke, pp. 159–183. Wiesbaden: Otto Harrassowitz, 1981.

———. *The Formation of the Early Meiji Legal Order: The Japanese Code of 1871 and Its Chinese Foundation.* Oxford: Oxford University Press, 1981.

Choi, Wayson. *The Jade Peony.* Vancouver: Douglas & McIntyre, 1995.

Ch'ü, T'ung-tsu. *Law and Society in Traditional China.* Paris: Mouton, 1965.

———. *Local Government in China under the Ch'ing.* Cambridge, Mass.: Harvard University Press, 1962.

Clarke, George. "The Yü-li or Precious Records." *Journal of the Royal Asiatic Society,* new series, 28 (1893–94): 233–400.

Clunas, Craig. *Chinese Export Watercolours.* London: Victoria and Albert Museum, 1984.

Cobbe, Frances Power. "Wife Torture in England." 1878.

Cohen, Paul A. *History in Three Keys: The Boxers as Event, Experience, and Myth.* New York: Columbia University Press, 1997.

Cole, Alan. *Mothers and Sons in Chinese Buddhism.* Stanford: Stanford University Press, 1998.

Confucius. *The Analects. See* Legge, James.

Conner, Alison W. "Chinese Confessions and the Use of Torture." In *La Torture judiciare,* ed. Bernard Durand and Leah Otis-Cours, vol. 1, pp. 63–91. Lille: Centre de Histoire Judiciare, Université de Lille, 2002.

———. "Confucianism and Due Process." In *Confucianism and Human Rights,* ed. Wm. Theodore de Bary and Tu Weiming, pp. 179–192. New York: Columbia University Press, 1998.

———. "True Confessions? Chinese Confessions Then and Now." In *The Limits of the Rule of Law in China,* ed. Karen Turner, James Feinerman, and R. Kent Guy, pp. 132–162. Seattle: University of Washington Press, 2000.

Corbin, Alain. "Le Sang de Paris: réflections sur la généaologie de l'image de la capitale." In *Le Temps, le désir, l'horreur. Essais sur le dix-neuvième siècle,* pp. 215–225. Paris: Aubier, 1991.

Costanzo, Mark. *Just Revenge: Costs and Consequences of the Death Penalty.* New York: St. Martin's, 1997.

Costin, W. C. *Great Britain and China, 1833–1860.* London: Oxford University Press, 1937.

Courtois, Stéphane, et al. *The Black Book of Communism,* ed. Mark Kramer, trans. Jonathan Murphy. Cambridge, Mass.: Harvard University Press, 1999.

Crossman, Carl L. *The China Trade: Export Paintings, Furniture, Silver and Other Objects.* Princeton: Pyne Press, 1972.

———. *The Decorative Arts of the China Trade: Paintings, Furnishings, and Exotic Curiosities.* Woodbridge, Suffolk, England: Antique Collectors' Club, 1991.

Cruikshank, Percy. *The Criminal Punishments of the Chinese, Drawn on Stone by Percy Cruikshank from Original Drawings by Yoeequa, a Chinese Artist.* Preface by George Cruikshank. London: Darton and Co., 1858.

Cummins, J. S. "Fray Domingo Navarrete: A Source for Quesnay." *Bulletin of Hispanic Studies* 36 (1959): 37–50.

Da Ming huidian (Collected administrative precedents of the Ming dynasty). 1587.

Dan-Xin dang'an xuanlu: xinzheng bian chuji (Selected records from the archives of Danshui and Xinzhuang: first collection from the New Policies period). Taiwan wenxian ziliao ku (Collection of Taiwan documentary materials), vol. 1.

Dapper, Olfert. *Gedenkwaerdig bedryf der Nederlandsche Oost-Indische Maetschappye, op de kuste en in het keizerrijk van Taising of Sina*. Amsterdam: J. van Meurs, 1670. For an English translation, see Montanus, Arnoldus.

Dardess, John. "The Code and *ad hoc* Legislation in Ming Law." *Asia Major*, 3rd ser., 6, no. 2 (1993): 85–112.

Davis, John Frances. *The Chinese: A General Description of the Empire of China and Its Inhabitants*. 2 vols. London, 1836.

De Alba-Koch, Beatriz. " 'Enlightened Absolutism' and Utopian Thought: Fernández de Lizardi and Reform in New Spain." *Revista canadiense de estudios hispanicos* 24, no. 2 (Winter 2000): 296–306.

de Bary, Wm. Theodore, and Tu Weiming, eds. *Confucianism and Human Rights*. New York: Columbia University Press, 1998.

De Bry, Hans Theodor [Dietrich], and Hans Israel De Bry. *Orientalisch Indien*. 3 vols. Frankfurt a.M., 1597–1599.

de Groot, Jan Jakob Maria. *The Religious System of China*. 6 vols. Leyden: E. J. Brill, 1892–1910.

De Pauw, Cornelius. *Recherches philosophiques sur les Egyptiens et les Chinois*. 2 vols. Amsterdam: B. Vlam, 1773.

De Quincey, Thomas. *Confessions of an English Opium-Eater*. London: Dent, 1960.

Dershowitz, Alan. "Tortured Reasoning." In *Torture: A Collection*, ed. Sanford Levinson, pp. 257–280. New York: Oxford University Press, 2004.

Des Rotours, Robert. "Encore quelques mots sur l'anthropophagie en Chine." *T'oung-pao* 54, no. 1–3 (1968): 1–3.

———. "Quelques mots sur l'anthropophagie en Chine." *T'oung-pao* 53, no. 4–5 (1967): 386–427.

Desanti, Jean-Toussaint. "La Violence." In "Douze leçons de philosophie." *Le Monde dimanche*, Summer 1982, 17.

Devereaux, Simon, and Paul Griffiths, eds. *Penal Practice and Culture, 1500–1900: Punishing the English*. Basingstoke: Palgrave, 2004.

Di Bella, Maria Pia. "Performances of Repentance in Sicilian Public Executions." Paper presented at the conference "The Ethics and Aesthetics of Torture," Toronto, March 2001.

Dianshi zhai huabao (Lithograph Studio pictorial). Shanghai, 1884–1908.

Diderot, Denis. "Anatomie." In *Encyclopédie, ou, Dictionnaire raisonné des sciences, des arts et des métiers*, ed. Denis Diderot and Jean Le Rond d'Alembert. 17 vols.; vol. 1, pp. 409–437. Paris: Briasson, 1751–1765. Reprint, New York: Pergamon, 1969.

Didi-Huberman, Georges. *La Ressemblance informe, ou le Gai-Savoir visuel selon Georges Bataille*. Paris: Macula, 1995.

Dijkstra, Bram. *Idols of Perversity: Fantasies of Feminine Evil in Fin-de-Siècle Culture*. Oxford: Oxford University Press, 1986.

Dikötter, Frank. *Crime, Punishment and the Prison in Modern China*. New York: Columbia University Press, 2002.

Dikötter, Frank, Lars Laaman, and Zhou Xun. *Narcotic Culture: A History of Drugs in China*. London: Hurst, 2005.

Dirks, Nicholas B. *Castes of Mind: Colonialism and the Making of Modern India.* Princeton: Princeton University Press, 2001.

Dobozy, Maria, trans. *The Saxon Mirror: A Sachsenspiegel of the Fourteenth Century.* Philadelphia: University of Pennsylvania Press, 1999.

Doolittle, Justus. *Social Life of the Chinese: A Daguerreotype of Daily Life in China,* ed. Edwin Paxton. London: Sampson Low, Son, and Marston, 1868.

Dorfman, Ariel. "The Tyranny of Terror: Is Torture Inevitable in Our Century and Beyond?" In *Torture: A Collection,* ed. Sanford Levinson, pp. 3–19. New York: Oxford University Press, 2004.

Du Halde, Jean-Baptiste. *Description géographique, historique, chronologique, politique et physique de l'empire de la Chine et de la Tartarie chinoise.* Paris, 1735.

———. *The General History of China, Containing a Geographical, Historical, Chronological, Political and Physical Description of the Empire of China, Chinese-Tartary, Corea and Thibet; Including an Exact and Particular Account of Their Customs, Manners, Cere- monies, Religion, Arts and Sciences,* trans. R. Brookes. London: Watts, 1736.

Duff, Charles. *A Handbook on Hanging.* [1929]. New York: New York Review of Books, 2001.

Dumas, Georges. *Nouveau traité de psychologie.* 8 vols. Paris: Presses universitaires de France, 1930–1943.

Dunch, Ryan. *Fuzhou Protestants and the Making of a Modern China, 1857–1927.* New Haven: Yale University Press, 2001.

Durand, Bernard, and Leah Otis-Cours, eds. *La Torture judiciare: approches historiques et juridiques.* 2 vols. Lille: Centre d'Histoire Judiciaire, Université de Lille, 2002.

Durand, Pierre-Henri. *Lettrés et pouvoirs: un procès littéraire dans la Chine impériale.* Paris: Éditions de l'École des Hautes Études en Sciences Sociales, 1992.

Dutton, Michael. *Policing and Punishing in China: From Patriarchy to the People.* Cam- bridge: Cambridge University Press, 1992.

Edgerton, Samuel Y., Jr. *Pictures and Punishment: Art and Criminal Prosecution during the Florentine Renaissance.* Ithaca: Cornell University Press, 1985.

Edkins, Joseph. *Chinese Buddhism: A Volume of Sketches, Historical, Descriptive, and Crit- ical.* 2nd rev. ed. London: Kegan Paul, Trench, Trübner, 1893.

Elkins, Caroline. *Imperial Reckoning: The Untold Story of Britain's Gulag in Kenya.* New York: Henry Holt, 2004.

Elkins, James. *The Object Stares Back: On the Nature of Seeing.* New York: Simon and Schuster, 1996.

———. "The Ten Most Intolerable Photographs Ever Taken." Paper presented at the conference "The Ethics and Aesthetics of Torture," Toronto, March 2001.

Ellis, Henry. *Journal of the Proceedings of the Late Embassy to China.* London: J. Murray, 1817.

Elman, Benjamin A. "The Formation of the 'Dao Learning' as Imperial Ideology during the Early Ming Dynasty." In *Culture and State in Chinese History: Conven- tions, Accommodations, and Critiques,* ed. Theodore Huters, R. Bin Wong, and Pauline Yu, pp. 58–82. Stanford: Stanford University Press, 1997.

———. *From Philosophy to Philology: Intellectual and Social Aspects of Change in Late Imperial China*. Cambridge, Mass.: Council on East Asian Studies, Harvard University, 1984.

Étiemble [Réné]. *L'Europe chinoise*. 2 vols. Paris: Gallimard, 1988–1989.

Evelyn, John. *The Diary of John Evelyn*, ed. John Bowle. Oxford: Oxford University Press, 1983.

The Face of China as Seen by Photographers and Travelers, 1860–1912. Preface by L. Carrington Goodrich; historical commentary by Nigel Cameron. Millerton, N.Y.: Aperture, 1972.

Fang Ling, Chen Shouxiang, and Bei Ning, eds. *Jiumeng chongjing: Qingdai mingxinpian xuanji* (New stupor in an old dream: selected postcards from the Qing dynasty), vol. 1. Nanning: Guangxi meishu chubanshe, 1998.

Farmer, Edward. *Zhu Yuanzhang and Early Ming Legislation: The Reordering of Chinese Society following the Era of Mongol Rule*. Leiden: Brill, 1995.

Favier, Alphonse. *Péking: histoire et description*. Beijing: Imprimerie des Lazaristes au Pé-t'ang, 1897.

Feuchtwang, Stephan. *Popular Religion in China: The Imperial Metaphor*. London: Curzon, 2001.

Fleck, Polly. *The Chinese Execution*. Toronto: Wolsak and Wynn, 1993.

Foucault, Michel. *Discipline and Punish: The Birth of the Prison*, trans. Alan Sheridan. New York: Pantheon, 1977.

———. *Surveiller et punir*. Paris: Gallimard, 1975.

Franke, Herbert. "Jurchen Customary Law and the Chinese Law of the Chin Dynasty." In *State and Law in East Asia: Festschrift Karl Bünger*, ed. Dieter Eikemeier and Herbert Franke, pp. 212–233. Wiesbaden: Otto Harrassowitz, 1981.

———. "The Legal System of the Chin Dynasty." In *Ryū Shiken hakushi shōju kinen Sōshi kenkyū ronshū* (Collected essays on Song history in honor of Dr. James T. C. Liu on his seventieth birthday), pp. 387–409. Kyoto: Dōhōsha, 1989.

———. "The 'Treatise on Punishments' in the *Liao History*: An Annotated Translation." *Central Asiatic Journal* 27, nos. 1–2 (1983): 9–38.

Frederick of Prussia. *The Refutation of Machiavelli's Prince or Anti-Machiavel*, trans. Paul Sonino. Athens: Ohio University Press, 1981.

Freeman-Mitford, Algernon B. *The Attaché in Peking*. London: Macmillan, 1900.

Furth, Charlotte, Judith T. Zeitlin, and Ping-chen Hsiung, eds. *Thinking with Cases: Specialist Knowledge in Chinese Cultural History*. Honolulu: University of Hawai'i Press, 2007.

Gatrell, V. A. C. *The Hanging Tree: Execution and the English People, 1773–1868*. Oxford: Oxford University Press, 1992.

Gerbi, Antonello. *La Disputa del nuovo mondo: storia di una polemica*. 2nd ed. Milan: Ricciardi, 1983.

Gernet, Louis. *Recherches sur le développement de la pensée juridique et morale en Grèce*. Paris: Albin Michel, 2001.

Goodrich, Anne Swann. *Chinese Hells: The Peking Temple of Eighteen Hells and Chinese Conceptions of Hell*. St. Augustin, Germany: Monumenta Serica, 1981.

Gotlieb, Marc. "Beheadings: The Depiction of Blood in Orientalist Paintings of the Nineteenth Century." Paper presented at the conference "The Ethics and Aesthetics of Torture," Toronto, March 2001.

Gray, John H. *China: A History of the Laws, Manners, and Customs of the People.* 2 vols. London: Macmillan, 1878.

Grodzinski, Danièle. "Tortures mortelles et catégories sociales: les *summa supplicia* dans le droit romain aux IIIe et IVe siècle." In *Du Châtiment dans la cité,* pp. 361–403. Rome: École Française de Rome, 1984.

Grosrichard, Alain. *The Sultan's Court: European Fantasies of the East,* trans. L. Heron; introduction by M. Dolar. London: Verso, 1998. French original, Paris: Seuil, 1979.

Guanxian zhi (Gazetteer of Guan county). Chengdu: Sichuan renmin chubanshe, 1991.

Gui Youguang. *Zhenchuan xiansheng ji* (The collected writings of Master Zhenchuan). Shanghai: Shanghai guji chubanshe, 1981.

Gundry, R. S. "Judicial Torture in China." *Fortnightly Review* 279 (new series), 1 March 1890, 404–420.

Guo, Qitao. *Ritual Opera and Mercantile Lineage: The Confucian Transformation of Popular Culture in Late Imperial Huizhou.* Stanford: Stanford University Press, 2005.

Gusu zhi (Gazetteer of Suzhou prefecture). 1506.

Hamilton, Susan. "Making History with Frances Power Cobbe: Victorian Feminism, Domestic Violence, and the Language of Imperialism." *Victorian Studies* 43, no. 3 (2001): 437–460.

Hansard's Parliamentary Debates. 3rd ser. 356 vols. London: T. C. Hansard et al., 1831–1891.

Hansson, Anders. *Chinese Outcasts: Discrimination and Emancipation in Late Imperial China.* Leiden: Brill, 1996.

Harbi, Mohammed, and Benjamin Stora, eds. *La Guerre d'Algérie, 1954–2004: la fin de l'amnéstie.* Paris: Robert Lafont, 2004.

Harfeld [Commandant]. *Opinions chinoises sur les barbares d'Occident.* Paris: Plon-Nourrit, 1909.

Harper, Lila Marz. *Solitary Travelers: Nineteenth-Century Women's Travel Narratives and the Scientific Vocation.* Madison: Fairleigh Dickinson University Press, 2001.

Harrison, Henrietta. *The Man Awakened from Dreams: One Man's Life in a North China Village, 1857–1942.* Stanford: Stanford University Press, 2005.

Harrison, Judy Feldman. "Wrongful Treatment of Prisoners: A Case Study of Ch'ing Legal Practice." *Journal of Asian Studies* 23 (1964): 227–244.

Hay, Douglas. "Writing about the Death Penalty." *Legal History* 10 (2006): 1–18.

Hegel, G. W. F. *The Philosophy of History.* New York: Dover, 1956.

Heindl, Robert. *Der Berufsverbrecher: Ein Beitrag zur Strafrechtreform.* Berlin: Pan-Verlag R. Heise, 1926.

Hevia, James. *Cherishing Men from Afar: Qing Guest Ritual and the Macartney Embassy of 1793.* Durham, N.C.: Duke University Press.

———. *English Lessons: The Pedagogy of Imperialism in Nineteenth-Century China.* Durham, N.C.: Duke University Press, and Hong Kong: Hong Kong University Press, 2003.

Hibbert, Christopher. *The Dragon Wakes: China and the West, 1793–1911*. Harmondsworth: Penguin, 1984.

———. *The Great Mutiny: India, 1857*. London: Allen Lane, 1978.

Ho, Virgil Kit-yiu. "Butchering Fishes and Executing Criminals: Public Executions and the Meanings of Violence in Late-Imperial and Modern China." In *Meanings of Violence: A Cross Cultural Perspective*, ed. Göran Aijmer and Jon Abbink, pp. 141–160. Oxford: Berg, 2000.

Hochschild, Adam. *King Leopold's Ghost: A Story of Greed, Terror, and Heroism in Colonial Africa*. Boston: Houghton Mifflin, 1998.

Hood, Roger. *The Death Penalty: A Worldwide Perspective*, 3rd ed. Oxford: Oxford University Press, 2002.

Hsieh, Yvonne Y. *From Occupation to Revolution: China through the Eyes of Loti, Claudel, Segalen, and Malraux (1895–1933)*. Birmingham, Ala.: Summa, 1996.

Hsu Dau-lin. "Crime and Cosmic Order." *Harvard Journal of Asiatic Studies* 30 (1970): 111–125.

Huai Xiaofeng, ed. *Da Ming lü* (The great Ming Code). Beijing: Falü chubanshe, 1999.

Huang Liuhong. *Fukkei zensho* (The complete book concerning happiness and benevolence), ed. Obata Shizan, with an introduction by Yamane Yukio [1850]. Tokyo: Kyūko shoin, 1973.

Huang Liu-hung. *A Complete Book Concerning Happiness and Benevolence: A Manual for Local Magistrates in Seventeenth-Century China*, trans. Djang Chu. Tucson: University of Arizona Press, 1984.

Huang Ming zuxun (The ancestral instructions of the Ming dynasty). In *Huang Ming zhishu* (Regulations of the Ming dynasty), ed. Zhang Lu. 1579. Reprint, Tokyo: Koten kenkyūkai, 1967.

Huang, Philip C. C. *Civil Justice in China: Representation and Practice in the Qing*. Stanford: Stanford University Press, 1996.

Huang Yu. *Bixue lu* (A record of the man whose blood turned to jade). In *Tianren hezheng jishi* (A record of true facts for the verification of heaven and mankind), ed. Yanke. Baibu congshu jicheng reprint, Taibei: Yiwen chubanshe, 1966.

Huang Zhangjian. "*Da Ming lügao* kao" (Study of the *Code and Pronouncements of the Ming Dynasty*). Reprinted in Huang Zhangjian, *Ming-Qing shi yanjiu conggao* (Draft research essays on Ming-Qing history), pp. 155–207. Taibei: Shangwu yinshuguan, 1977.

———. "Ming Hongwu Yongle chao de bangwen junling" (Harsh laws in the proclamations of the Hongwu and Yongle reigns of the Ming dynasty). Reprinted in Huang Zhangjian, *Ming-Qing shi yanjiu conggao* (Draft research essays on Ming-Qing history), pp. 237–326. Taibei: Shangwu yinshuguan, 1977.

Huang Zongxi. *Huang Zongxi quanji* (Complete works of Huang Zongxi). 2 vols. Hangzhou: Zhejiang guji chubanshe, 1985.

Huc, Régis-Évariste. *The Chinese Empire: A Sequel to Recollections of a Journey through Tartary and Thibet*. Rev. ed. London: Longman, Brown, Green, Longman & Roberts, 1859.

———. *L'Empire chinois*. 3rd ed. 2 vols. Paris: Librairie de Gaume Frères, 1857. [First ed., 1854] Reprinted with annotations, a foreword, and new illustrations added, by J. M. Planchet, 1926. Reprinted from the 1926 edition with a preface by M. Cartier and an introductory note by J. Thevenet, Paris: Kimé, 1992.

Hucker, Charles. *A Dictionary of Official Titles in Imperial China.* Stanford: Stanford University Press, 1985.

Huidian shili. See *Qinding da Qing huidian shili.*

Hulsewé, A. F. P. *Remnants of Han Law: Introductory Studies and an Annotated Translation of Chapters 22 and 23 of the History of the Former Han Dynasty.* Leiden: Brill, 1955.

James, P. D. *A Taste for Death.* Toronto: Vintage, 1999.

Jennings, Gary. *The Journeyer.* New York: Atheneum, 1984.

Jeffrey, Francis. *See* Anon. [Francis Jeffrey].

Jiading xianzhi (Gazetteer of Jiading county). 1684.

Jiang Xun, ed. *Zhongguo gujiu shukan paimai mulu* (Index of rare and used books offered at auction in China). Beijing: Beijing chubanshe, 2002.

Jiang Yonglin, trans. *The Great Ming Code / Da Ming lü.* Seattle: University of Washington Press, 2006.

Johansen, Baber. "The Legitimation of Judicial Torture under Islamic Law in the Fourteenth Century." Paper presented at the conference "The Ethics and Aesthetics of Torture," Toronto, March 2001.

Johnson, Wallace, trans. *The T'ang Code.* Vol. 1, *General Principles.* Princeton: Princeton University Press, 1979.

Jones, William C., trans. *The Great Qing Code.* Oxford: Clarendon Press, 1994.

Kabbani, Rana. *Europe's Myths of Orient: Devise and Rule.* London: Pandora, 1986.

Kellberg, Love. "Torture: International Rules and Procedures." In *An End to Torture: Strategies for Its Eradication,* ed. Bertil Dunér, pp. 3–38. London: Zed Books, 1998.

Klemm, Gustav. *Allgemeine Cultur-Geschichte der Menschheit.* Vol. 6, *China und Japan.* Leipzig: Teubner, 1847.

Knoblock, John. *Xunzi: A Translation and Study of the Complete Works.* 3 vols. Stanford: Stanford University Press, 1994.

Knoblock, John, and Jeffrey Riegel, trans. *The Annals of Lü Buwei: A Complete Translation and Study.* Stanford: Stanford University Press, 2000.

Ko, Dorothy. *Cinderella's Sisters: A Revisionist History of Footbinding.* Berkeley: University of California Press, 2006.

Kucera, Karil J. "Lessons in Stone: Baodingshan and Its Hell Imagery." *Bulletin of the Museum of Far Eastern Antiquities* 67 (1995): 81–157.

Kwok, D. W. Y. "On the Rites and Rights of Being Human." In *Confucianism and Human Rights,* ed. Wm. Theodore de Bary and Tu Weiming, pp. 83–93. New York: Columbia University Press, 1998.

Landry, Isabelle. *La Preuve par la Chine. La "Description" de J.B. Du Halde, jésuite.* Paris: l'École des Hautes Études en Sciences Sociales, 2002.

Langbein, John H. *Torture and the Law of Proof: Europe and England in the Ancien Régime.* Chicago: University of Chicago Press, 1977.

Las Cortes, Adriano de. *Viaje de la China*, ed. Monco Rebollo. Madrid: Allianza universdad, 1991.

———. *Le Voyage en Chine d'Adriano de las Cortes s.j. (1625)*, trans. Pascale Girard and Juliette Monbeig. Paris: Chandeigne, 2001.

Lauwaert, Françoise. *Le Meurtre en famille: parricide et infanticide en Chine (XVIIIe siècle)*. Paris: Éditions Odile Jacob, 1999.

Le Goff, Jacques. *The Birth of Purgatory*, trans. Arthur Goldhammer. Chicago: University of Chicago Press, 1984.

Lea, Henry C. *Superstition and Force: Essays on the Law of Wager, the Wager of Battle, the Ordeal, Torture*. 2nd rev. ed. Philadelphia: published by the author, 1870. Reprint, New York: Haskell House, 1971.

Lecomte, Louis. *Nouveaux mémoires sur l'état present de la Chine*, ed. F. Touboul-Bouyeure. Paris: Éditions Phébus, 1990.

Legge, James. *The Chinese Classics*. 5 vols. Oxford: Clarendon Press, 1893.

Legouix, Susan. *Image of China: William Alexander*. London: Jupiter, 1980.

Lei Menglin. *Dulü suoyan* (Desultory reading notes on the Ming code). 1557. Reprint, Beijing: Falü chubanshe, 2000.

Leiris, Michel. *À Propos de Georges Bataille*. Paris: Forubis, 1988.

———. *Journal de Chine*. Paris: Gallimard, 1992.

———. *Journal 1922–1989*. Paris: Gallimard, 1992.

Leiva, Antonio Dominguez, and Muriel Détrie, eds. *Le Supplice oriental dans la littérature et les arts*. Dijon: Éditions du murmure, 2005.

Lettres édifiantes et curieuses écrites des missionaires étrangères, ed. Charles Le Gobien and Yves Mathurin Marie Tréaudet de Querbeuf. Nouvelle édition. 26 vols. Toulouse: Noel-Etienne Sens, 1810–1811.

Levinson, Sanford, ed. *Torture: A Collection*. New York: Oxford University Press, 2004.

Lewis, Mark Edward. *Sanctioned Violence in Early China*. Albany: State University of New York Press, 1990.

Li Yizhi. *Li Yizhi quanji* (Complete works of Li Yizhi). Taibei: Zhonghua congshu weiyuanhui, 1956.

Lindley, A. F. [Lin-Le]. *Ti-Ping Tien-Kwoh; the History of the Ti-Ping Revolution, Including a Narrative of the Author's Personal Adventures*. London: Day, 1866.

Lindqvist, Sven. *"Exterminate All the Brutes."* New York: New Press, 1996.

Little, Archibald, and Mrs. Archibald [Alicia] Little. *Gleanings of Fifty Years in China*. London: Sampson Low, Marston, 1910.

Little, Mrs. Archibald [Alicia]. *Round about My Peking Garden*. London: T. Fisher Unwin, 1905.

Liu, Joyce. "Chen Chieh-jen's Aesthetic of Horror and His Bodily Memories of History." Paper presented at the conference "The Ethics and Aesthetics of Torture," Toronto, March 2001.

Liu, Lydia H. *The Clash of Empires: The Invention of China in Modern World Making*. Cambridge, Mass.: Harvard University Press, 2004.

Lo Duca, Joseph Marie (Giuseppe). *Journal secret de Napoléon Bonaparte*. Paris: Pauvert, 1948. Reprint, Paris: Phébus, 1997.

Loutfi. *See* Astier Loutfi, Martine.

Low, James. "On the Law of Múung Thai or Siam." *Journal of the Indian Archipelago* 1 (1840).

Lu Hsun [Lu Xun]. *Selected Stories of Lu Hsun*, trans. Yang Hsien-yi and Gladys Yang. Peking: Foreign Languages Press, 1972.

Lu Rong. *Shuyuan zaji* (Miscellaneous writings from Bean Garden). 1494. Reprint, Beijing: Zhonghua shuju, 1985.

Lu You. *Weinan wenji* (Collected works of Master Weinan). Sibu congkan facsimile.

Luo Guanzhong. *Sanguo zhi yanyi* (Romance of the Three Kingdoms). 1630s edition.

Luppi, Lionello. *Les Supplices dans l'art: cérémonial des exécutions et iconographie du martyre dans l'art européen du XIIe au XIXe siècle.* Paris: Éditions Larousse, 1991.

Ma Duanlin. *Wenxian tongkao* (General examination of official documents). Taibei: Xinxing shuju, 1960.

Ma Huan. *Yingyai shenglan: "The Overall Survey of the Ocean's Shores,"* trans. Feng Ch'eng-chün, ed. J. V. G. Mills. Cambridge: Cambridge University Press, 1970.

Macauley, Melissa. *Social Power and Legal Culture: Litigation Masters in Late Imperial China.* Stanford: Stanford University Press, 1998.

Magaillans, Gabriel. *Nouvelle relation de la Chine contenant le description des particularitez les plus considerables de ce grand empire, composée en l'année 1668,* trans. Claude Bernout. Paris: Barbin, 1688.

Majumdar, R. C., H. C. Raychauduri, and Kalikinkar Datta. *An Advanced History of India,* 4th ed., with an appendix on Bangladesh. Madras: Macmillan, 1978.

Mason, George Henry, ed. *The Punishments of China / Les Punitions des chinois.* Engravings by J. Dadney. London: William Miller, 1801.

Matignon, Jean-Jacques. *Dix ans au pays du dragon.* Paris: A. Maloine, 1910.

Maverick, Lewis Adams. *China, a Model for Europe.* San Antonio, Tex.: P. Anderson, 1946.

Mayers, Fred, N. B. Dennys, and Charles King. *The Treaty Ports of China and Japan.* London: Trübner, 1967.

McGowan, Randall. "The Well Ordered Prison: England, 1780–1865." In *The Oxford History of the Prison: The Practice of Punishment in Western Society,* ed. Norval Morris and David J. Rothman, pp. 71–99. Oxford: Oxford University Press, 1998.

McKnight, Brian E. *Law and Order in Sung China.* Cambridge: Cambridge University Press, 1992.

———. *The Quality of Mercy: Amnesties and Traditional Chinese Justice.* Honolulu: University of Hawaii Press, 1981.

———. "Sung Justice: Death by Slicing." *Journal of the American Oriental Society* 93, no. 3 (1973): 359–360.

McKnight, Brian E., and James T. C. Liu. *The Enlightened Judgments: Ch'ing-ming Chi, the Sung-Dynasty Collection.* Albany: State University of New York Press, 1999.

Meadows, Thomas Taylor. *The Chinese and Their Rebellions Viewed in Connection with Their National Philosophy, Ethics, Legislation, and Administration.* London: Smith, Elder & Co., 1856. Reprint, Stanford: Academic Reprints, 1953.

———. "Description of an Execution at Canton." *Journal of the Royal Asiatic Society* 16 (1856): 54–58.

Medhurst, W. H. *China: Its State and Prospects, with Special Reference to the Spread of the Gospel.* London: J. Snow, 1838.

Meijer, Martinus J. *The Introduction of Modern Criminal Law in China.* Batavia: De Unie, 1950.

Mencius. See Legge, James.

Mendes Pinto, Fernão. *The Voyages and Adventures of Fernand Mendes Pinto.* London: Cripps, 1653.

Mendoza, Juan Gonzales de. *The History of the Great and Mighty Kingdom of China and the Situation Thereof,* trans. R. Parke. London, 1588. Reprint, ed. George T. Staunton. London: Hakluyt Society, 1853. [Translation of *Historia de las cosas mas notables, ritos y costumbres del gran reyno de la China* (1585).]

Merback, Mitchell. *The Thief, the Cross and the Wheel: Pain and the Spectacle of Punishment in Mediaeval and Renaissance Europe.* London: Reaktion Books, 2000.

Meskill, John, trans. *Ch'oe Pu's Diary: A Record of Drifting across the Sea.* Tucson: University of Arizona Press, 1965.

Mill, James. *See* Anon. [James Mill].

Millett, Kate. *The Politics of Cruelty.* New York: Norton, 1984.

Mills, J. V. G. *See* Ma Huan.

Ming taizong shilu (Veritable records of Emperor Taizong [Yongle] of the Ming). Reprint, Taibei: Zhongyang yanjiuyuan lishi yanjiusuo, 1962.

Ming taizu shilu (Veritable records of Emperor Taizu [Hongwu] of the Ming). Reprint, Taibei: Zhongyang yanjiuyuan lishi yanjiusuo, 1962.

Ming xiaozong shilu (Veritable records of Emperor Xiaozong [Hongzhi] of the Ming). Reprint, Taibei: Zhongyang yanjiuyuan lishi yanjiusuo, 1962.

Mirbeau, Octave. *Le Jardin des supplices.* Reprint, Paris: Folio-Gallimard, 1991.

———. *Torture Garden,* trans. Michael Richardson. Sawtry, Cambs., England: Dedalus, 1995.

Monestier, Martin. *Peines de mort: histoire et techniques des exécutions capitales.* Paris: Cherche midi, 1994.

Montanus, Arnoldus. *Atlas sinensis,* trans. John Ogilby. London: Thomas Johnson, 1671. [Translation of Dapper's *Gedenkwaerdig bedryf.*]

Montesquieu, Baron de (Charles de Secondat). *De l'Esprit des lois, avec des notes de Voltaire.* 2 vols. Paris: Garnier, 1922.

———. *The Spirit of the Laws,* trans. Thomas Nugent. New York: Colonial Press, 1900.

Moreira, Isabel. *Dreams, Visions, and Spiritual Authority in Merovingian Gaul.* Ithaca: Cornell University Press, 2000.

Morohashi Tetsuji. *Dai Kan-Wa jiten* (Comprehensive Sino-Japanese dictionary). Tokyo: Taishūkan shoten, 1966–1968.

Morris, Norval, and David J. Rothman, eds. *The Oxford History of the Prison: The Practice of Punishment in Western Society.* Oxford: Oxford University Press, 1998.

Morrison, George Ernest. *An Australian in China, Being a Narrative of a Quiet Journey across China to British Burma.* London: H. Cox, 1895. Reprint, Sydney: Angus & Robertson, 1972.

Munn, Christopher. *Anglo-China: Chinese People and British Rule in Hong Kong, 1841–1880*. Richmond: Curzon, 2001.

Nancy, Jean-Luc. "L'Insacrifiable." In his *Une Pensée finie*, pp. 83–90. Paris: Galilée, 1990.

Naquin, Susan. *Peking: Temples and City Life, 1400–1900*. Berkeley: University of California Press, 2000.

Navarrete, Domingo Fernandez. *The Travels and Controversies of Friar Domingo Navarrete, 1616–1686*, ed. J. S. Cummins. 2. vols. Cambridge: Cambridge University Press, 1962.

Nietzsche, Friedrich. *The Birth of Tragedy and The Genealogy of Morals*, trans. Francis Golffing. New York: Doubleday, 1956.

Nieuhof, Joan. *Het Gesandtschap der Neêrlandtsche Oost-Indische Compagnie, aan den Grooten Tartartischen Cham, den Tegenwoordigen Keizer van China*. Amsterdam: Jacob van Meurs, 1665.

Niida Noboru. *Chūgoku hōseishi kenkyū: keihō* (Studies on the history of Chinese law: criminal law). 2nd ed. Tokyo: Tōkyō daigaku shuppankai, 1981.

———. "Shindai no Pekin no keijō: keihō gakusha Dō Kō shi o tō" (The execution ground of modern Beijing: my visit with Mr. Dong Kang, a Chinese scholar of criminal law). *Bungei shunjū* 19 (1941): 4.

Norman, Henry. *The Peoples and Politics of the Far East: Travels and Studies in the British, French, Spanish and Portuguese Colonies, Siberia, China, Japan, Korea, Siam and Malaya*. London: T. F. Unwin, 1895.

Ouyang Xiu, ed. *Xin Tang shu* (New standard history of the Tang dynasty). Beijing: Zhonghua shuju, 1975.

Pal, John. *Shanghai Saga*. London: Jarrolds, 1963.

Pallu de la Barrière, Léopold Augustin Charles. *Relation de l'expédition de Chine en 1860*. Paris: Imprimerie impériale, 1863.

Pan Zengxiang. *Panshan gongdu* (The official letters of Master Panshan). First published 1894, undated reprint.

Park, Nancy. "Imperial Chinese Justice and the Law of Torture." Paper presented at the conference "The Ethics and Aesthetics of Torture," Toronto, March 2001.

———. "Torture and Its Limits in Late Imperial China." In *La Torture judiciare*, ed. Bernard Durand and Leah Otis-Cours, vol. 1, pp. 92–106. Lille: Centre d'Histoire Judiciaire, Université de Lille, 2002.

Parsons, Tony. *The Family Way*. London: Harper Collins, 2004.

Petech, Luciano. *China and Tibet in the Early 18th Century. History of the Establishment of Chinese Protectorate in Tibet*. 2nd rev. ed. Leiden: Brill, 1972.

Peters, Rudolph. *Crime and Punishment in Islamic Law: Theory and Practice from the Sixteenth to the Twenty-first Century*. Cambridge: Cambridge University Press, 2005.

Philastre, P.-L.-F., ed. *Le Code Annamite*. 2 vols. Paris, 1909. Reprint, Taipei: Chengwen, 1967.

Pires, Tomé. *The Suma Oriental of Tomé Pires*, ed. Armando Cortesao. London: Hakluyt Society, 1944.

Potter, Harry. *Hanging in Judgment: Religion and the Death Penalty in England*. New York: Continuum, 1993.

Pouillot, Henri. *La Villa Susini: tortures en Algérie: un appelé parle, juin 1961–mars 1962.* Paris: Tirésias, 2001.

Pratt, John. *Punishment and Civilization: Penal Tolerance and Intolerance in Modern Society.* London: Sage, 2002.

Praz, Mario. *The Romantic Agony*, trans. A. Davidson, foreword by F. Kermode. 3rd ed. Oxford: Oxford University Press, 1970.

Qian Daxin. "Ba *Weinan wenji*" (Postface to *Weinan wenji*), *Qianyan tang wenji* (Collected writings from Qianyan Hall), *juan* 31. Reprinted in *Jiading Qian Daxin quanji* (The complete works of Qian Daxin of Jiading), ed. Chen Wenhe, pp. 527–528. Nanjing: Jiangsu guji chubanshe, 1997.

———. "Lingchi." In *Shijia zhai yangxin lu* (Records of New Things from Shijia Studio). 7.7a–b. Reprint, Shanghai: Shangwu yinshu guan, 1937.

Qinding da Qing huidian shili (Imperially endorsed collection of administrative precedents and substatutes of the Qing dynasty). Promulgated 1886, printed 1899. Reprint, Taibei: Qiwen chubanshe / Zhongwen shuju, 1963.

Qing shizu zhang huangdi shilu (Veritable records of the founding Qing emperor [Shunzhi reign]).

Qingmo Beijing zhi ziliao (Historical materials on Beijing at the end of the Qing). Beijing: Yanshan chubanshe, 1994. [Translation of *Pekin shi* (A history of Beijing), 1908.]

Qiu Jun. *Daxue yanyi bu* (Supplement to *Expositions on the Great Learning*). *Qiu Wenzhuang gong congshu* (Complete writings of Master Qiu Wenchuang), vol. 1. Taibei: Qiu Wenzhuang gong congshu jiyin weiyuanhui, 1972.

Quach, Gianna. "Mirbeau et la Chine." *Cahiers Octave Mirbeau* 2 (1995): 87–101.

Quesnay, François. *Despotisme de la Chine* [1767]. Reproduced in Auguste Oncken, ed., *Ouevres économiques et philosophiques de F. Quesnay, fondatur du système physiocratique.* Frankfurt a.M.: Baer, 1888.

Rasmussen, A. H. *China Trader.* New York: Thomas Y. Cromwell, 1954.

Ratchnevsky, Paul. *Un Code des Yuan.* 4 vols. Paris: Institut des Hautes Études Chinoises, Collège de France, 1937–1985.

Reed, Bradly. *Talons and Teeth: County Clerks and Runners in the Qing Dynasty.* Stanford: Stanford University Press, 2000.

Renouard de Sainte Croix, Félix, trans. *Ta-tsing-leu-lée, ou les Lois Fondamentales du Code pénal de la Chine.* 2 vols. Paris, 1812.

Robinson, David. *Bandits, Eunuchs, and the Son of Heaven: Rebellion and the Economy of Violence in Mid-Ming China.* Honolulu: University of Hawaii Press, 2001.

Royer, Katherine. "Dead Men Talking." In *Penal Practice and Culture, 1500–1900: Punishing the English*, ed. Simon Devereaux and Paul Griffiths, pp. 63–84. Basingstoke: Palgrave, 2004.

Ruggiero, Guido. *Violence in Early Renaissance Venice.* New Brunswick, N.J.: Rutgers University Press, 1980.

Rusche, Georg. *Punishment and Social Structure.* New York: Columbia University Press, 1939.

Ruthven, Malise. *Torture: The Grand Conspiracy.* London: Weidenfeld & Nicolson, 1978.

Sade, Donatien Alphonse François de. *The Complete Justine, Philosophy in the Bedroom, and Other Writings*, trans. R. Seaver and Austryn Wainhouse, introductions by Jean Paulhan and Maurice Blanchot. New York: Grove Press, 1965.

Said, Edward W. *Culture and Imperialism*. New York: Knopf, 1993.

———. *Orientalism*. New York: Random House, 1978.

Sakamoto Kaname, ed. *Jigoku no sekai* (The world of hell). Tokyo: Keisuisha, 1990.

Sanders, Graham. "The Good Magistrate Never Tortures: Chinese Court Case Fiction." Paper presented at the conference "The Ethics and Aesthetics of Torture," Toronto, March 2001.

Sanguo shuihu quanzhuan yingxiong pu (Album of the heroes in the complete editions of *Three Kingdoms* and *Water Margin*). Chongzhen era (1628–1644).

Savage-Landor, A. Henry. *Corea or Cho-sen: The Land of Morning Calm*. New York: Macmillan, 1895.

Sawada Mizuho. *Jigoku hen: Chūgoku no meikaisetsu* (The transformations of hell: Chinese doctrines of the netherworld). Kyoto: Hōzōkan, 1968.

———. "Jigoku no keiden" (The classics of hell). In *Jigoku no sekai* (The world of hell), ed. Sakamoto Kaname, pp. 357ff. Tokyo: Keisuisha, 1990.

Scarry, Elaine. *The Body in Pain: The Making and Unmaking of the World*. New York: Oxford University Press, 1987.

Schau, Torben. *The Carnival of Blood and Fire: Responses to the Boxer Rebellion, a Canadian Case Study*. M.A. thesis, University of Victoria, Victoria, B.C., Canada, 2002.

Scott, George Riley. *The History of Torture throughout the Ages*. London: Luxor, 1959.

Semedo, Alvaro. *The History of the Great and Renowned Monarchy of China*. London: Crook, 1655.

Shao Bowen. *Shaoshi wenjian lu* (Master Shao's record of things heard and seen). Posthumously published after 1134. Beijing: Zhonghua shuju, 1983.

Shapiro, Sidney. *The Law and the Lore of Chinese Criminal Justice*. Beijing: New World Press, 1990.

Shek, Richard. "Sectarian Eschatology and Violence." In *Violence in China: Essays in Culture and Counterculture*, ed. Jonathan N. Lipman and Stevan Harrell, pp. 87–114. Albany: State University of New York Press, 1990.

Shelton, Flora. *Shelton of Tibet*. New York: George A. Doran, 1923.

Shen Bang. *Wanshu zaji* (Miscellaneous notes from the Wanping county office). 1596. Reprint, Beijing: Zhonghua shuju, 1980.

Shen Jiaben. "*Ming dagao* junling" (The harsh laws in the *Grand Pronouncements of the Ming*). In Shen Jiaben, *Shen Jiyi xiansheng yishu, jiabian* (The surviving writings of Master Shen Jiyi, first collection), vol. 2. Taibei: Wenhai chubanshe, 1964.

———. "Xingfa fenkao" (Analytical study of penal law). In Shen Jiaben, *Shen Jiyi xiansheng yishu, jiabian* (The surviving writings of Master Shen Jiyi, first collection), vol. 1. Taibei: Wenhai chubanshe, 1964.

Shi Naian. *Shuihu zhuan* (Water margin), engraved by Liu Qixian and Huang Cheng. 1614.

———. *Zhongyi shuihu quanzhuan* (Complete account of the loyal and righteous of the water margin). Chongzhen era (1628–1644).

Shiga Shūzō. *Chūgoku hōseishi ronshū* (Collected essays on the history of the Chinese legal system). Tokyo: Sōbunsha, 2003.

Shih Nai-an. *Water Margin*, trans. J. H. Jackson. 2 vols. Hong Kong: Commercial Press, 1963.

Shiomi Senichirō. *Danzaemon to sono jidai: senmin bunka no doramatsurugi* (*Eta* chiefs in their time: The dramaturgy of outcaste culture). Tokyo: Hiyōsha, 1991.

Shiwang baojuan (Precious scroll of the Ten Kings). Reprinted in the *Baojuan chuji* (Precious scrolls, first series), ed. Zhang Xishun, vol. 14, pp. 413–480. Taiyuan: Shanxi renmin chubanshe, 1992.

Silverman, Lisa. *Tortured Subjects: Pain, Truth, and the Body in Early Modern France.* Chicago: University of Chicago Press, 2001.

Sima Qian. *Shi ji* (Records of the Grand Historian). Beijing: Zhonghua shuju, 1973.

Smith, Arthur H. *Chinese Characteristics.* New York: Fleming H. Revell, 1894.

Smith, Greg T. " 'I Could Hang Anything You Can Bring before Me': England's Willing Executioners in 1883." In *Penal Practice and Culture, 1500–1900: Punishing the English*, ed. Simon Devereaux and Paul Griffiths, pp. 285–308. Basingstoke: Palgrave, 2004.

Sommer, Matthew. *Sex, Law, and Society in Late Imperial China.* Stanford: Stanford University Press, 2000.

Song Lian, ed. *Yuan shi* (Standard history of the Yuan dynasty). Beijing: Zhonghua shuju, 1974.

Sonino, Paul. "Introduction" to Frederick of Prussia, *The Refutation of Machiavelli's Prince or Anti-Machiavel*, trans. Paul Sonino. Athens: Ohio University Press, 1980.

Sontag, Susan. *Regarding the Pain of Others.* New York: Farrar, Straus & Giroux, 2003.

Southgate, Donald. *"The Most English Minister": The Policies and Politics of Palmerston.* London: Macmillan, 1966.

Spence, Jonathan D. *The Chan's Great Continent: China in Western Minds.* New York: Norton, 1998.

———. *God's Chinese Son: The Taiping Heavenly Kingdom of Hong Xiuchuan.* New York: Norton, 1996.

———. *The Memory Palace of Matteo Ricci.* New York: Penguin, 1984.

Spierenburg, Pieter. "The Body and the State." In *The Oxford History of the Prison: The Practice of Punishment in Western Society*, ed. Norval Morris and David J. Rothman, pp. 41–70. Oxford: Oxford University Press, 1998.

———. *The Spectacle of Suffering: Executions and the Evolution of Repression; from a Preindustrial Metropolis to the European Experience.* Cambridge: Cambridge University Press, 1984.

Staunton, George [Leonard]. *An Authentic Account of an Embassy from the King of Great Britain to the Emperor of China.* 3 vols. London: G. Nicol, 1797.

Staunton, George Thomas. *Ta Tsing Leu Lee; Being the Fundamental Laws and a Selection of the Supplementary Statutes of the Penal Code of China.* London: Cadell, 1810. Reprint, Taipei: Chengwen, 1966.

Stephens, Thomas B. *Order and Discipline in China: The Shanghai Mixed Court 1911–1927.* Seattle: University of Washington Press, 1992.

Stevenson, Daniel. "Text, Image, and Transformation in the History of the *Shuilu fahui*, the Buddhist Rite for Deliverance of Creatures of Water and Land." In

Cultural Intersections in Later Chinese Buddhism, ed. Marsha Weidner, pp. 30–70. Honolulu: University of Hawaii Press, 2001.

Sun, Ying. *Wandlungen des europäischer Chinabildes in illustrietrten Reiseberichten des 17. und 18. Jahrhunderts.* Frankfurt a.M.: Peter Lang, 1996.

Sung Tz'u. *The Washing Away of Wrongs: Forensic Medicine in Thirteenth-Century China,* trans. Brian McKnight. Ann Arbor: Center for Chinese Studies, University of Michigan, 1981.

Surya, Michel. *Georges Bataille: la mort à l'oeuvre.* Paris: Librairie Séguier, 1987.

Takikawa Masajirō and Shimada Masao. *Ryōritsu no kenkyū* (Study of the Liao Code). Tokyo: Nippon shuppan haikyū, 1943.

Tan Jiaqi. "Ming taizu dui xingfa qingzhong de taidu" (Ming Taizu's attitudes toward judicial penalties), pt. 1. *Zhongguo wenhua yanjiusuo xuebao* (Journal of Chinese studies), no. 41 (2001): 87–108.

Taussig, Michael. "Culture of Terror—Space of Death: Roger Casement's Putumayo Report and the Explanation of Torture." In *Colonialism and Culture,* ed. Nicholas Dirks, pp. 135–173. Ann Arbor: University of Michigan Press, 1992.

———. *Mimesis and Alterity: A Particular History of the Senses.* New York: Routledge, 1993.

Teiser, Stephen. *The Scripture on the Ten Kings and the Making of Purgatory in Medieval Chinese Buddhism.* Honolulu: University of Hawaii Press, 1994.

Thomson, John. *China and Its People in Early Photographs* [1873–1874]. Reprint, New York: Dover, 1982.

Tian Tao and Zheng Qin, eds. *Da Qing lüli* (The great Qing Code with precedents). Beijing: Falü chubanshe, 1999.

Tuotuo, ed. *Jin shi* (Standard history of the Jin dynasty). Beijing: Zhonghua shuju, 1975.

———, ed. *Liao shi* (Standard history of the Liao dynasty). Beijing: Zhonghua shuju, 1974.

———, ed. *Song shi* (Standard history of the Song dynasty). Beijing: Zhonghua shuju, 1985.

Turner, Karen, James Feinerman, and R. Kent Guy, eds. *The Limits of the Rule of Law in China.* Seattle: University of Washington Press, 2000.

Umehara Kaoru. *Chūgoku kinsei keihō shi* (The history of judicial punishments in early-modern China). Tokyo: Sōbunsha, 2002.

United Nations. "Declaration on the Protection of All Persons from Being Subjected to Torture and Other Cruel, Inhuman or Degrading Treatment or Punishment." In *Human Rights: A Compilation of International Instruments.* 2 vols. New York and Geneva: United Nations, 2002; vol. 1, pp. 313–314. Also available at www.ohchr.org/english/law/declarationcat.htm.

Verstegan, Richard. *Le Théâtre des cruautés des hérétiques de notre temps.* 1587. Reprint, Paris: Éditions Chandeigne, 1995.

Vidal-Naquet, Pierre. *Torture: A Cancer of Democracy, France and Algeria 1954–62.* Harmondsworth: Penguin, 1963. Translated into French as *La Torture dans la République.* Paris: Éditions de Minuit, 1972.

Von Glahn, Richard. *The Sinister Way: The Divine and the Demonic in Chinese Religious Culture*. Berkeley: University of California Press, 2004.

Wang, David Der-wei. *The Monster That Is History: History, Violence, and Fictional Writing in Twentieth-Century China*. Berkeley: University of California Press, 2004.

Wang Huizu. *Xuezhi yishuo* (Personal views on learning governance). 1793. Duhua zhai congshu (Collectanea from the Studio for Reading Paintings) edition. Baibu congshu jicheng reprint, Taibei: Yiwen chubanshe, 1968.

———. *Zuozhi yaoyan* (Precepts for private secretaries). Shenjian tang, 1871. Baibu congshu jicheng reprint, Taibei: Yiwen chubanshe, 1966.

Wang Mingde. *Dulü peixi* (Portable guide to the penal code). 1678–1682. Siku quanshu cunmu congshu (Collectanea of the indexed complete library of the four treasuries) reprint: zibu, vol. 37. Beijing: Beijing daxue chubanshe, 1994.

Wang Qi, ed. *Sancai tuhui* (Illustrated compendium of the three powers [heaven, earth, humanity]). Nanjing: Wuyun xuan, 1609.

Wang Yongkuan. *Kokkei: chi to senritsu no Chūgoku keibatsu shi* (Cruel punishments in ancient China). Translation of *Zhongguo gudai kuxing*. Tokyo: Tokuma shoten, 1997.

———. *Zhongguo gudai kuxing* (Cruel punishments in ancient China). 1991. 2nd ed., Taibei: Yunlong chubanshe, 1998.

Wei Tai. *Dongxuan bilu* (Jottings from the Eastern Pavillion). Baibu congshu jicheng reprint, Taibei: Yiwen chubanshe, 1965.

Wenxing tiaoli (Itemized substatutes for pronouncing judgments). Composed 1500; last revised edition 1585. Reprinted in Huai Xiaofeng, ed., *Da Ming lü*, pp. 332–444.

Williams, Samuel Wells. *The Middle Kingdom*, rev. ed. 2 vols. New York: Scribner's Sons, 1882.

———. *The Middle Kingdom: A Survey of the Geography, Government, Education, Social Life, Arts, Religion, &c . . . of the Chinese Empire and Its Inhabitants*. 2 vols. New York: Putnam, 1848.

Wittfogel, Karl A., and Fêng Chia-shêng. *History of Chinese Society: Liao (907–1125)*. Philadelphia: American Philosophical Society, 1949.

Wong, John Y. *Deadly Dreams: Opium and the Arrow War (1856–1860) in China*. Cambridge: Cambridge University Press, 1998.

Wong, R. Bin. *China Transformed: Historical Change and the Limits of European Experience*. Ithaca: Cornell University Press, 1997.

———. "Torture and Transformations of the Chinese State." Paper presented at the conference "The Ethics and Aesthetics of Torture," Toronto, March 2001.

Woodside, Alexander. *Lost Modernities: China, Vietnam, Korea, and the Hazards of World History*. Cambridge, Mass.: Harvard University Press, 2006.

Wujiang zhi (Gazetteer of Wujiang county). 1488.

Wyatt, Don J. *The Recluse of Loyang: Shao Yung and the Moral Evolution of Early Sung Thought*. Honolulu: University of Hawaii Press, 1996.

Xinglü tufu (Penal law charts). In *Shengyu guangxun zhijie* (Expanded instructions on the Sacred Edict, with righteous commentary). Late nineteenth century.

Xining fuzhi (Gazetteer of Xining prefecture). 1762.

Xu Shiying. *Xu Shiying huiyi lu* (Memoirs of Xu Shiying). Taibei: Renjian shi congshu, 1966.

Xu Wenda. *Da Qing lüli tushuo* (Annotated illustrations of the Qing Code and sub-statutes). Late nineteenth century.

———. *Da Qing xinglü tushuo* (Annotated illustrations of Qing penal law), ed. Huang Renji. Author's preface to the first edition, 1887; editor's preface to the reprint edition, 1894.

Xue Juzheng, ed. *Jiu wudai shi* (Former standard history of the Five Dynasties). Beijing: Zhonghua shuju, 1975.

Xue Yunsheng. *Duli cunyi* (Concentrating on doubtful matters while reading the substatutes), ed. Huang Jingjia. Taibei: Chinese Materials and Research Aids Service Center, 1970.

———, ed. *Tang Ming lü hebian* (Joint edition of the Ming and Tang codes). Tianjin: Tuigeng tang, 1922. Facsimile reprint, Beijing: Zhongguo shudian, 1980.

Yan Junyan. *Mengshui zhai cundu* (Case summaries from Mengshui Studio). 1632. Reprint, Beijing: Zhongguo zhengfa daxue chubanshe, 2002.

Yang Yifan. *Ming dagao yanjiu* (Studies on the *Grand Pronouncements* of the Ming). Nanjing: Jiangsu renmin chubanshe, 1988.

Ye Chunji. *Huian zhengshu* (Administrative handbook of Huian county). 1573. Reprinted in Ye Chunji, *Shidong wenji* (Collected writings from Stone Grotto), 1672.

Yu Hua. *The Past and the Punishments*, trans. Andrew F. Jones. Honolulu: University of Hawaii Press, 1996.

Yu Jideng. *Diangu jiwen* (Notes on statutory precedents). Beijing: Zhonghua shuju, 1981.

Yuan dianzhang (Institutions). 1303. Reprint, Taibei: Guoli gugong bowuyuan, 1976.

Yuli baochao jingshi wen (Precious currency of the Jade Register as a text to warn the age). Taiwan, 1979.

Yuli chaozhuan jingshi (Precious account of the Jade Register to warn the age). Wanxian, 1883.

Yuli chaozhuan zhujie jingshi baofa (Precious account of the Jade Register, annotated and explicated, as a precious raft to warn the age), ed. Zhenjizi. Chengdu: Chengwen zhai, 1890. Reprint, 1892.

Yuli zhibao bian (The most precious edition of the Jade Register). Sanyi: Baihao tang, 1873.

Yunyang fuzhi (Yunyang prefectural gazetteer). 1578.

Zhang Ning. " 'Banditisme' et peine de mort en Chine: catégories judiciares et pratiques d'exception." Unpublished manuscript.

———. "The Debate over the Death Penalty in Today's China." *China Perspectives* 62 (November–December 2005): 2–10.

Zhang Tingyu, ed. *Ming shi* (Standard history of the Ming dynasty). Reprint, Beijing: Zhonghua shuju, 1974.

Zhang Wenlin. *Duanyan gong nianpu* (Chronological biography of Master Duanyan), ed. Zhang Haipeng. Reprinted as *Ming Zhang Duanyan gong (Wenlin) nianpu* (Chronological biography of Master Duanyan, Zhang [Wenlin] of the Ming). Taibei: Shangwu yinshuguan, 1978.

Zhang Yi. *Yuguang jianqi ji* (Collected notes in the spirit of the jade sword), ed. Wei Lianke. Beijing: Zhonghua shuju, 2006.

Zhongguo gudai xiaoshuo banhua jicheng (Collection of woodcut illustrations from old Chinese novels). 8 vols. Shanghai: Hanyu dacidian chubanshe, 2002.

Zhou Xinhui, ed. *Zhongguo gudai xiqu banhua ji* (Woodcut illustrations from old Chinese play scripts). Beijing: Xueyuan chubanshe, 1998.

Zhongyi shuihu quanzhuan (Complete account of the loyal and the righteous of the water margin). 1630s edition.

Zhu Yuanzhang. *Ming taizu ji* (Collected writings of the founding Ming emperor [1582]), ed. Hu Shi'e. Hefei: Huangshan shushe, 1991.

Zuiming tushuo (Annotated illustrations of the terminology for crimes). Appended to *Jinshan xian baojia zhangcheng* (*Baojia* regulations for Jinshan county). [ca. 1901].

Index

www.ingramcontent.com/pod-product-compliance
Lightning Source LLC
Chambersburg PA
CBHW051727260326
41914CB00031B/1778/J

.